Essential Macroeconomics
Principles, Cases, Problems

Essential Macroeconomics

Principles, Cases, Problems

EDWIN MANSFIELD

University of Pennsylvania

W. W. Norton & Company

NEW YORK ■ LONDON

Photo for Part One courtesy of UPI/Corbis-Bettmann.
Photo for Part Two courtesy of Neil Hoos.
Photos for Parts Three and Five courtesy AP/Wide World Photos.
Photo for Part Four courtesy of Corbis-Bettmann.

The text of this book is composed in Meridien
with the display set in various weights of Eras
Composition by New England Typographic Service
Manufactured by Courier
Book design by Martin Lubin Graphic Design

Library of Congress Cataloging-in-Publication Data

Mansfield, Edwin.
    Essential macroeconomics : principles, cases,
problems / Edwin Mansfield.
        p. cm.
    Includes index.
    ISBN 0-393-97041-8 (pbk.)
    1. Macroeconomics. I. Title.
  HB 172.5.M359 1998
  339–dc21   97-46627

W. W. Norton & Company, Inc., 500 Fifth Avenue, New York, N.Y. 10110 http://www.wwnorton.com
W. W. Norton & Company Ltd., 10 Coptic Street, London WC1A 1PU

1 2 3 4 5 6 7 8 9 0

CONTENTS

PART TWO
Fiscal Policy and Budget Deficits

▪ CHAPTER 6

Fiscal Policy 72

▪ CHAPTER 7

Budget Deficits and the National Debt 84

▪ CHAPTER 8

What Should Be Done about the Federal Deficit? 98

PART THREE
Monetary Policy

▪ CHAPTER 9

Money and the Economy 114

▪ CHAPTER 10

The Federal Reserve and the Banking System 130

PREFACE

The importance of the elementary course in the principles of macroeconomics is widely recognized. In such a course, students gain a knowledge of a variety of subjects and techniques that are essential for further training in business and economics, as well as for competent decision making as a citizen.

The purpose of this volume is to provide a brief treatment of basic macroeconomic principles, as well as a variety of case studies describing how these principles have been utilized in actual situations, and many types of self-tests and questions to enable the student to determine his or her progress and problems.

This book is designed so that it can be used either as a supplement to a standard textbook or as a stand-alone text. For those who use it as a stand-alone text, it is worth noting that the standard topics are taken up. The emphasis is on brevity, but the coverage of basic theory is quite sufficient for many principles courses.

Finally, Ed Parsons and W. Drake McFeely of Norton did a fine job with the editorial and publishing work. Also, special thanks go to my wife, who helped in countless ways.

E.M.
Philadelphia, 1997

PART ONE

National Output, Unemployment, and Inflation

▪ CHAPTER 1

National Output

Essentials of **National Output**

▪ Gross domestic product (GDP) measures national output; it tells you how much the economy produces in a particular period of time.

▪ GDP is expressed either in current dollars or in constant dollars; figures expressed in current dollars are actual dollar amounts, whereas those expressed in constant dollars are corrected for changes in the price level.

▪ GDP is not an ideal measure of economic well-being. It is not very meaningful unless you know the size of the population of the country in question, and it does not take adequate account of leisure, quality changes, or environmental damage.

▪ There are two approaches to measure GDP: the expenditures approach and the income approach.

1 ▪ Gross Domestic Product

Gross domestic product (GDP) is a measure of national output, or of how much the economy produces in a particular period of time. But the U.S. economy produces millions of types of goods and services. How can we add up the output of everything from lemon meringue pies to helicopters, from books to houses? The only feasible answer is to use money as a common denominator and to make the price of a good or service—the amount the buyer is willing to pay—the measure of value. In other words, we add up the value in money terms of the total output of goods and services in the economy during a certain period, normally a year, and the result is the gross domestic product during that period.

Although the measurement of gross domestic product may seem straightforward ("just add up the value in money terms of the total output of the economy"), this is by no means the case. Some of the more important pitfalls that must be avoided and problems that must be confronted are the following:

DOUBLE COUNTING Gross domestic product does not include the value of *all* goods and services. It includes only the value of *final* goods and services produced. **Final goods and services** are those destined for the ultimate user. For example, flour purchased for family consumption is a final good, but flour to be used in manufacturing bread is an **intermediate good,** not a final good. We would be double counting if we counted both the bread and the flour used to make the bread as output. Thus the output of intermediate goods—goods that are not destined for the ultimate user, but are used as inputs in producing final goods and services—must not be included in gross domestic product.

NONMARKETED GOODS Some final goods and services that must be included in gross domestic product are not bought and sold in the marketplace, so they are valued at what they cost. Consider the services performed by government—police protection, fire protection, the use of the courts, defense, and so forth. Such services are not bought and sold in any market (despite the old saying about the New Jersey judge who was "the best that money could buy"). Yet they are an important part of our economy's final output.

Economists and statisticians have decided to value them at what they cost the taxpayers. This is by no means ideal, but it is the best practical solution advanced to date.

OMITTED FINAL OUTPUT It is necessary for practical reasons to omit certain types of final output from gross domestic product. In particular, some non-marketed goods and services, such as the services performed by homemakers, are excluded from the gross domestic product. This is not because economists fail to appreciate these services, but because it would be extremely difficult to get reasonably reliable estimates of the money value of a homemaker's services. At first glance, this may seem to be a very important weakness in our measure of total output, but so long as the value of these services does not change much (in relation to total output), the variation in gross domestic product will provide a reasonably accurate picture of the variation in total output—and, for many purposes, this is all that is required.

NONPRODUCTIVE TRANSACTIONS Purely financial transactions are excluded from gross domestic product because they do not reflect current production. Such financial transactions include government transfer payments, private transfer payments, and the sale and purchase of securities. **Government transfer payments** are payments made by the government to individuals who do not contribute to production in exchange for them. Payments to welfare recipients are a good example of government transfer payments. Since these payments are not for production, it would be incorrect to include them in GDP. **Private transfer payments** are gifts or other transfers of wealth from one person or private organization to another. Again, these are not payments for production, so there is no reason to include them in GDP. The sale and purchase of securities are not payments for production, so they too are excluded from GDP.

SECONDHAND GOODS Sales of secondhand goods are also excluded from gross domestic product. The reason for this is clear. When a good is produced, its value is included in GDP. If its value is also included when it is sold on the secondhand market, it would be counted twice, and thus lead to an overstatement of the true GDP. Suppose that you buy a new bicycle and resell it a year later. The value of the new bicycle is included in GDP when the bicycle is produced. But the resale value of the bicycle is not included in GDP; to do so would be double counting.

 TEST YOUR UNDERSTANDING

True or false?

_____ **1** Private transfer payments are included in GDP.

_____ **2** When you sell 100 shares of stock, the amount you receive is included in GDP.

_____ **3** If you buy a used car, this is included in GDP.

_____ **4** If you buy a new car and do not use it for business purposes, it is a final good.

_____ **5** One of the major limitations of GDP is that services like health care are not included.

Exercises

1 If Bill Clinton wins $100,000 from Al Gore in a poker game, will this increase, decrease, or have no effect on GDP? Explain.

2 Which of the following are included in calculating GDP this year?
  a. Interest on a government bond
  b. Payment by the government to a naval officer
  c. Wages paid by the University of Michigan to a professor
  d. Payment for a secondhand car by a Florida student

e. The amount a person would be willing to pay for his or her spouse's homemaking services

f. The amount John Jones pays for 30 shares of IBM stock

g. The allowance a parent gives a 12-year-old child

2 ▪ Adjusting GDP for Price Changes

Since gross domestic product values all goods and services at their current prices, it is bound to be affected by changes in the price level as well as by changes in total output. If all prices doubled tomorrow, this would produce a doubling of gross domestic product. Clearly, if gross domestic product is to be a reliable measure of changes in total output, we must correct it somehow to eliminate the effects of such changes in the price level.

To correct for price changes, economists choose some base year and express the value of all goods and services in terms of their prices during the **base year.** For example, suppose we want to compare beef output in 1989 with that in subsequent years. If 1989 is taken as the base year and if the price of beef was $3 per pound in 1989, beef is valued at $3 per pound in all other years. Thus, if 100 million pounds of beef were produced in 1997, this total output is valued at $300 million even though the price of beef in 1997 was actually higher than $3 per pound. In this way, distortions caused by changes in the price level are eliminated.

Gross domestic product is expressed in either current dollars or in constant dollars. Figures expressed in **current dollars** are actual dollar amounts, whereas those expressed in **constant dollars** are corrected for changes in the price level. Expressed in current dollars, gross domestic product is affected by changes in the price level. Expressed in constant dollars, gross domestic product is not affected by the price level because the prices of all goods are maintained at their base-year level. GDP, after being corrected for changes in the price level, is called **real gross domestic product.**

Figure 1.1 shows the behavior of both real GDP and GDP expressed in current dollars. GDP expressed in current dollars has increased more rapidly (due to inflation) than GDP in constant dollars.

PRICE INDEXES

It is often useful to have some measure of how much prices have changed over a certain period of time. One way to obtain such a measure is to

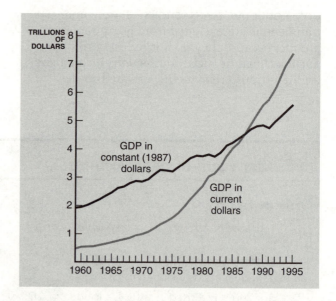

▪ **FIGURE 1.1**

Gross Domestic Product, Expressed in Current Dollars and 1987 Dollars, United States, 1959–1995

Because of inflation, GDP expressed in current dollars has increased more rapidly in recent years than GDP in constant (1987) dollars. This was particularly true in the 1970s and 1980s, reflecting the price surge then.

divide the value of a set of goods and services expressed in current dollars by the value of the same set of goods and services expressed in constant (or base-year) dollars. Suppose that a set of goods and services costs $100 when valued at 1997 prices, but $70 when valued at 1994 prices. Apparently, prices have risen an average of 43 percent for this set of goods between 1994 and 1997. How do we get 43 percent? The ratio of the cost in 1997 prices to the cost in 1994 prices is $100 \div 70 = 1.43$: thus prices must have risen on the average by 43 percent for this set of goods.

The ratio of the value of a set of goods and services in current dollars to the value of the same set of goods and services in constant (base-year) dollars is a **price index.** Thus 1.43 is a price index in the example above. An important function of a price index is to convert values expressed in current dollars into values expressed in constant dollars. This conversion, known as **deflating,** can be achieved simply by dividing values expressed in current dollars by the price index. In the illustration above, values expressed in 1997 dollars can be converted into constant (that is, 1994) dollars by dividing by 1.43. This procedure is an important one, with applications in many fields other than the measurement of gross domestic product. For example, firms use it to compare their output in various years. To correct for price changes, they deflate their sales by a price index for their products.

In many cases, price indexes are multiplied by 100; that is, they are expressed as percentage changes. Thus, in the case described in the previous paragraph, the price index might be expressed as 1.43×100, or 143, which would indicate that 1997 prices on the average were 143 percent of their 1994 level. In the next chapter, we shall say more about price indexes that are expressed in this way. For now, we assume that the price index is not multiplied by 100.

☑ TEST YOUR UNDERSTANDING

True or false?

_____ **1** GDP in constant dollars has been adjusted for changes in the price level.

_____ **2** If a price index (which has been multiplied by 100) equals 130, this means that the price level is 30 percent higher than in the base period.

Exercise

1 The following table shows the value of GDP in the nation of Puritania. The figures shown are in millions of 1970 dollars and current dollars. Fill in the blanks.

YEAR	GDP (in millions of 1970 dollars)	GDP (in millions of current dollars)	PRICE INDEX (current price level / 1970 price level)
1974	1,000	_____	1.00
1976	_____	1,440	1.20
1978	1,300	_____	1.40
1980	1,500	_____	1.60
1997	_____	2,720	1.70

---

3 ▪ Using Value-Added to Calculate GDP

You have seen that gross domestic product includes the value of only the final goods and services produced. Obviously, however, the output of final goods and services is not due solely to the efforts of the producers of the final goods and services. The total value of an automobile when it leaves the plant, for example, represents the work of many industries besides the automobile manufacturers. The steel, tires, glass, and many other components of the automobile were not produced by the automobile manufacturers. In reality, the automobile manufacturers only added a certain amount of value to the value of the intermediate goods—steel, tires, glass, and so forth—they purchased. This point is basic to an understanding of how the gross domestic product is calculated.

To measure the contribution of a firm or industry to final output, you use the concept of value-added. **Value-added** means just what it says: *the amount of value added by a firm or industry to the total worth of the product*. It is a measure in money terms of the extent of production taking place in a particular firm or industry. Suppose that $160 million of bread was produced in the United States in 1997. To produce it, farmers harvested $50 million of wheat, which was used as an intermediate product by flour mills, which turned out $80 million of flour. This flour was used as an intermediate product by the bakers who produced the $160 million of bread. What is the value-added at each stage of the process? For simplicity, assume that the farmers did not have to purchase any materials from other firms in order to produce the wheat. Then the value-added by the wheat farmers is $50 million; the value-added by the flour mills is $30 million ($80 million − $50 million); and the value-added by the bakers is $80 million ($160 million − $80 million). The total of the value-added at all stages of the process ($50 million + $30 million + $80 million) must equal the value of the output of final product ($160 million), because each stage's value-added is its contribution to this value. Since the total of the value-added by all industries must equal the value of all final goods and services, which, of course, is gross domestic product, it follows that you can calculate GDP by adding up the value-added by all industrial groups in the economy.

 TEST YOUR UNDERSTANDING

True or false?

_____ **1** If the Miller Company's sales in 1997 are $160 million and if it purchases $60 million worth of intermediate goods from other firms in 1997, its value-added in 1997 equals $100 million.

_____ **2** All flour produced in the United States is an intermediate good.

Exercise

1 A (small) country contains only ten firms. William Moran, the country's top statistician, calculates the country's GDP by totaling the sales of these ten firms. Do you agree with this procedure? Why, or why not?

---

4 ▪ Limitations of GDP

You should understand the limitations of gross domestic product, as it is by no means an ideal measure of economic well-being. Five limitations of GDP should always be borne in mind.

POPULATION GDP is not very meaningful unless you know the size of the population of the country in question. For example, the fact that a particular country's GDP equals $50 billion means one thing if the country has 10 million inhabitants, and quite another thing if it has 500 million inhabitants. To correct for the size of the population, GDP per capita—GDP divided by the population—is often used as a rough measure of output per person in a particular country.

LEISURE   GDP does not take into account one of humankind's most prized activities, leisure. During the past century, the average work week in the United States has decreased substantially. It has gone from almost 70 hours in 1850 to about 40 hours today. As people have become more affluent, they have chosen to substitute leisure for increased production. Yet this increase in leisure time, which surely contributes to our well-being, does not show up in GDP. Neither does the personal satisfaction (or displeasure and alienation) people get from their jobs.

QUALITY CHANGES   GDP does not take adequate account of changes in the quality of goods. An improvement in a product is not reflected accurately in GDP unless its price reflects the improvement. For example, if a new type of drug is put on the market at the same price as an old drug, and if the output and cost of the new drug are the same as the old drug, GDP will not increase, even though the new drug is twice as effective as the old one. Because GDP does not reflect such increases in product quality, it is sometimes argued that the commonly used price

indexes overestimate the amount of inflation, since although prices may have gone up, quality may have gone up too.

VALUE AND DISTRIBUTION   GDP says nothing about the social desirability of the composition and distribution of the country's output. Each good and service produced is valued at its price. If the price of a Bible is $10 and the price of a pornographic novel is $10, both are valued at $10, whatever you or I may think about their respective worth. Moreover, GDP measures only the total quantity of goods and services produced. It tells you nothing about how this output is distributed among the people. If a country's GDP is $500 billion, this is its GDP whether 90 percent of the output is consumed by a relatively few rich families or the output is distributed relatively equally among the citizens.

SOCIAL COSTS   GDP does not reflect some of the social costs arising from the production of goods and services. In particular, it does not reflect the environmental damage resulting from the operation of a country's factories, offices, and farms. It is common knowledge that the atmosphere and water supplies are being polluted in various ways by firms, consumers, and governments. Yet these costs are not deducted from GDP, even though the failure to do so results in an overestimate of the country's true economic welfare.

 TEST YOUR UNDERSTANDING

True or false?

_____ **1** The gross domestic product of Switzerland is much smaller than that of the United States; thus, U.S. citizens are much better off than Swiss.

_____ **2** GDP could be increased tomorrow if we all agreed to work 80 hours a week.

Exercise

1 If a paper mill produces $1 million worth of paper this year, but adds considerably to the pollutants in a nearby river, are the social costs arising from this pollution reflected in the gross domestic product? If so, how? Should these costs be reflected in the GDP? If so, why?

5 ▪ The Expenditures Approach to GDP

To use the **expenditures approach** to determine GDP, one must add up all the spending on final goods and services. Economists distinguish among four broad categories of spending, each of which is taken up below.

PERSONAL CONSUMPTION EXPENDITURES

Personal consumption expenditures include the spending by households on durable goods, nondurable goods, and services. This category of spending includes your expenditures on items like food and drink, which are **nondurable goods.** It also includes your family's expenditures on a car or on an electric washer or dryer, which are **durable goods.** Further, it includes your payments to a dentist, who is providing a **service** (painful though it sometimes may be). Table 1.1 shows that in 1995 personal consumption accounted for about two-thirds of the total

▪ **TABLE 1.1**

Expenditures on Final Goods and Services, United States, 1995

TYPE OF EXPENDITURE		AMOUNT (billions of dollars)
Personal consumption		4,925
Durable goods	606	
Nondurable goods	1,486	
Services	2,833	
Gross private domestic investment		1,066
Expenditures on plant and equipment	739	
Residential structures	290	
Increase in inventories	37	
Net exports		−95
Exports	807	
Imports	902	
Government purchases of goods and services		1,358
Federal	517	
State and local	842	
Gross domestic product		7,254

SOURCE: U.S. Department of Commerce.

amount spent on final goods and services in the United States. Expenditures on consumer durable goods are clearly much less than on consumer nondurable goods, whereas expenditures on services are now larger than expenditures on either durable or nondurable goods.

GROSS PRIVATE DOMESTIC INVESTMENT

Gross private domestic investment consists of all investment spending by U.S. firms. As shown in Table 1.1, three broad types of expenditures are included in this category. First, all *final purchases of tools, equipment, and machinery* are included. Second, all *construction expenditures*, including expenditures on residential housing, are included. (One reason houses are treated as investment goods is that they can be rented out.) Third, the *change in total inventories* is included. An increase in inventories is a positive investment; a decrease in inventories is a negative investment. The change in inventories must be included, because GDP measures the value of all final goods and services produced, *even if they are not sold this year.* Thus GDP must include the value of any increases in inventories that occur during the year. On the other hand if a decrease occurs during the year in the value of inventories, the value of this decrease in inventories must be subtracted in calculating GDP because these goods and services were produced prior to the beginning of this year. In other words, a decline in inventories means that society has purchased more than it has produced during the year.

Gross private domestic investment is "gross" in the sense that it includes all additions to the country's stock of investment goods, whether or not they are replacements for equipment or plant that are used up in producing the current year's output. *Net private domestic investment* includes only the addition to the country's stock of investment goods after allowing for the replacement of used-up plant and equipment.

Net private domestic investment indicates the change in the country's stock of capital goods. If it is positive, the nation's productive capacity, as gauged by its capital stock, is growing. If it is negative, the country's productive capacity, as gauged by its capital stock, is declining.

GOVERNMENT PURCHASES OF GOODS AND SERVICES

This category of spending includes the expenditures of the federal, state, and local governments for the multitude of functions they perform: defense, education, police protection, and so forth. It does not include transfer payments, since they are not payments for current production. Table 1.1 shows that government spending in 1995 accounted for about one-fifth of the total amount spent on final goods and services in the United States. State and local expenditures are bigger than federal expenditures. Many of the expenditures of the federal government are on items like national defense, health, and education, while at the state and local levels the biggest expenditure is for items like education and highways.

NET EXPORTS

Net exports equal the amount spent by other countries on our goods and services less the amount we spent on other countries' goods and

services. This factor must be included since some of our national output is destined for foreign markets and since we import some of the goods and services we consume. There is no reason why this component of spending cannot be negative; indeed in 1995 it was negative, since imports exceeded exports. The quantity of net exports tends to be quite small. Table 1.1 shows that net exports in 1995 were equal (in absolute terms) to about 1 percent of the total amount spent on final goods and services in the United States.

PUTTING TOGETHER THE SPENDING COMPONENTS

Finally, because the four categories of expenditure described above include all possible types of spending on final goods and services, their sum equals the gross domestic product. In other words,

GDP = personal consumption expenditures
      + gross private domestic investment
      + government purchases of goods and services
      + net exports.

As shown in Table 1.1, the gross domestic product in 1995 equaled $4,925 + $1,066 + $1,358 − $95, or $7,254 billion.

 TEST YOUR UNDERSTANDING

True or false?

_____ **1** Expenditures by General Motors on paper, typewriters, and fuel oil are all included in consumption expenditure.

_____ **2** Net exports can be positive or negative.

_____ **3** Consumption includes your expenditures on meals and clothing, and your parents' expenditures on the family car or on an electric washer and dryer.

_____ **4** If the Malone family buys a 15-year-old house from Mr. D. Blair, a (hypothetical) real estate speculator, this purchase would be included in gross private domestic investment.

Exercises

1 Given the following data (in millions of dollars) concerning the Puritanian economy in 1996, compute its gross domestic product.

Gross private domestic investment	400
Personal consumption expenditure	1,000
Exports	300
Imports	100
Government purchases	300
Increase in inventories	50
Depreciation	100

2 What is the difference between gross private domestic investment and net private domestic investment? If net private domestic investment is negative, does this mean that the country's capital stock is increasing or decreasing?

3 In 1989, there was a $28.3 billion increase in business inventories. Why should this be regarded as a form of investment? Explain why GDP would be calculated incorrectly if this increase in inventories were ignored?

6 ■ The Income Approach to GDP

Another, equally valid way to measure GDP is to use the **income approach.** To do so, you must add up all the income stemming from the production of this year's output. This income is of various types: compensation of employees, rents, interest, proprietors' income, and corporate profits. In addition, you must include a capital consumption allowance and indirect business taxes. Each of these items is defined and discussed below.

COMPENSATION OF EMPLOYEES

This is the largest of the income categories (see Table 1.2). It includes the wages and salaries that are paid by firms and government agencies to suppliers of labor. In addition, it contains a variety of supplementary payments by employers for the benefit of their employees, such as payments into public and private pension and welfare funds. These supplementary payments are part of the employers' costs and are included in the total compensation of employees.

RENT

In the present context, **rent** is defined as a payment to households for the supply of property resources. For example, it includes house rents received by landlords. Quite different definitions of rent are used by economists in other contexts.

INTEREST

Interest includes payments of money by private businesses to suppliers of money capital. If you buy a bond issued by General Motors, the interest payments you receive are included. Interest payments made by the government on Treasury bills, savings bonds, and other securities are excluded on the grounds that they are not payments for current goods and services. They are regarded as transfer payments.

PROPRIETORS' INCOME

Profits are split into two parts in the national income accounts: proprietors' income and corporate profits. **Proprietors' income** consists of the

■ TABLE 1.2

Claims on Output, United States, 1995

TYPE OF CLAIM ON OUTPUT	AMOUNT OF CLAIM (billions of dollars)
Employee compensation	4,223
Rental income	122
Interest	404
Income of proprietors and professionals	478
Corporate profits	587
Indirect business taxes	596
Depreciation	826
Statistical discrepancy[a]	18
Gross domestic product	7,254

[a]This also includes some minor items that need not be of concern here. See the source.
SOURCE: U.S. Department of Commerce.

net income of unincorporated businesses—businesses that are not corporations.

CORPORATE PROFITS

Corporate profits consist of the net income of corporations. (A corporation is a fictitious legal person separate and distinct from the stockholders who own it.) This item is equal to corporate profits before the payment of corporate income taxes.

DEPRECIATION

All the items discussed above—compensation of employees, rents, interest, proprietors' income, and corporate profits—are forms of income. In addition, there are two nonincome items, depreciation and indirect business taxes, that must be added to the sum of the income items to obtain GDP. **Depreciation** is the value of the country's plant, equipment, and structures that are worn out this year. In the national income accounts, depreciation is often called a *capital consumption allowance*, because it measures the value of the capital consumed during the year.

INDIRECT BUSINESS TAXES

The government imposes certain taxes, such as general sales taxes, excise taxes, and customs duties, which firms treat as costs of production. These taxes are called **indirect business taxes** because they are not imposed directly on the business itself, but on its products or services instead. A good example of an indirect business tax is the tax on cigarettes; another is the general sales tax. Before a firm can pay out incomes to its workers, suppliers, or owners, it must pay these indirect business taxes to the government. These indirect business taxes, like depreciation, must be added to the total of the income items to get GDP.

PUTTING TOGETHER THE INCOME COMPONENTS

The sum of the five types of income described above (plus depreciation and indirect business taxes) equals gross domestic product. In other words,

GDP = compensation of employees + rent + interest
+ proprietors' income + corporate profits
+ depreciation + indirect business taxes.

☑ TEST YOUR UNDERSTANDING

True or false?

_____ **1** The Guiliani Restaurant is not a corporation; thus, its profits are included in proprietors' income.

_____ **2** If your employer contributes to a pension fund for you, this contribution is included in compensation of employees.

_____ **3** Interest payments by the U.S. government are included in interest in calculating GDP.

Exercise

1 Based on the data to the right (in millions of dollars), use the income approach to determine GDP.

Compensation of employees	50
Interest	10
Rents	5
Indirect business taxes	8
Corporate profits	10
Transfer payments	22
Proprietors' income	6
Depreciation	4

7 ▪ The Two Approaches Yield the Same Result

Suppose that you want to measure the market value of an automobile. One way to do this is to look at how much the consumer pays for the automobile. Although this is the most straightforward way to measure the automobile's market value, it is not the only way it can be done. Another, equally valid way is to add all the wage, interest, rental, and profit incomes generated in the production of the automobile. The amount that the automobile producer receives for this car is equal to its profit (or loss) on the car plus the amount it pays the workers and other resource owners who contributed their resources to its production. Thus, if you add all the wage, interest, rental, and profit incomes resulting from the production of the automobile, the result is the same as if you determine how much the consumer pays for the automobile.

By the same token, there are two ways to measure the market value of the output of the economy as a whole. Or, put differently, there are two ways of looking at GDP. One is the *expenditures approach,* which regards GDP as the sum of

all the expenditures on the final goods and services produced this year. The other is the *income approach,* which regards GDP as the sum of incomes derived from the production of this year's total output.

Since both these approaches are valid, it follows that GDP can be viewed as either the total expenditure on this year's total output or as the total income stemming from the production of this year's total output. In other words,

$$
\begin{array}{c}
\text{total} \\
\text{expenditure} \\
\text{on this year's} \\
\text{total output}
\end{array}
\;=\; \text{GDP} \;=\;
\begin{array}{c}
\text{total income} \\
\text{stemming from} \\
\text{the production} \\
\text{of this year's} \\
\text{total output.}
\end{array}
$$

This is an identity; the left-hand side of this equation must equal the right-hand side. Or to be more precise, this is true if the right-hand side also includes depreciation and indirect business taxes, as you saw in Section 6.

 TEST YOUR UNDERSTANDING

True or false?

_____ **1** For the income approach to yield the same result as the expenditures approach, depreciation and indirect business taxes must be added to the sum of incomes.

_____ **2** Depreciation is the value of the country's plant, equipment, and structures that are worn out during the period.

Exercise

1 Using Tables 1.1 and 1.2, demonstrate that the income and expenditures approaches yield the same result.

▪ CHAPTER REVIEW

KEY TERMS

gross domestic product

final goods and services

intermediate good

government transfer payments

private transfer payments

base year

current dollars

constant dollars

real gross domestic product

price index

deflating

expenditures approach

personal consumption
expenditures

nondurable goods

durable goods

service

gross private domestic
investment

net exports

income approach

interest

proprietors' income

corporate profits

depreciation

indirect business taxes

COMPLETION QUESTIONS

1 The four parts of the total amount spent on final goods and services are _____, _____, _____, and _____.

2 Bread purchased by a consumer is a(n) (final, intermediate) _____ good, but flour to be used in manufacturing bread is a(n) (final, intermediate) _____ good. Clearly, you would be double counting if you counted both the bread and the flour used to make the bread as _____. To avoid this, include only the value of (final, intermediate) _____ goods and services in gross domestic product.

3 Government transfer payments are payments made by the government to individuals who (do, do not) _____ contribute to production in exchange for them. Since these payments are not for _____, it would be (correct, incorrect) _____ to include them in GDP.

4 Private transfer payments are gifts or other transfers of wealth from one _____ or _____ to another. These are not payments for _____, so they are not included in GDP.

5 Expressed in (current, constant) _____ dollars, gross domestic product is affected by changes in the price level. Expressed in (current, constant) _____ dollars, gross domestic product is not affected by the price level because the prices of all goods are maintained at their _____ level. In recent decades, inflation has caused gross domestic product expressed in (current, constant) _____ dollars to increase more rapidly than gross domestic product in (current, constant) _____ dollars.

6 An important function of a price index is to convert values expressed in (current, constant) _____ dollars into values expressed in (current, constant) _____ dollars. This conversion, known as _____, can be achieved simply by dividing values expressed in (current, constant) _____ dollars by the price index.

ANSWERS TO COMPLETION QUESTIONS

consumption expenditure, investment, government purchases of goods and services, net exports

final

intermediate

output
final

do not
production
incorrect

person, private organization
production

current

constant

base-year

current

constant

current

constant
deflating
current

7 The contribution of a firm or industry to the final output is measured by the concept of _____. Wheat and the _____ of flour mills and bakers are utilized in the process of making bread. GDP figures indicate that the U.S. economy is turning more toward producing _____, rather than _____.

value-added
services

services, goods

8 Gross domestic product equals the income paid out (or owed) as _____, _____, _____, and _____, plus two other items: indirect business taxes and depreciation. Indirect business taxes are _____ taxes, _____ taxes, and other taxes that firms consider as part of their costs. In other words, gross domestic product exactly equals the total _____ on output.

wages, rent, interest
profits

sales, excise

claims

NUMERICAL PROBLEMS

1a Gopherland is a country where the price level has been rising at a rate of 5 percent per year. Gross domestic product in current dollars was 10 percent higher in 1997 than in 1996, and 3 percent higher in 1996 than in 1995. In terms of constant dollars, how much greater was Gopherland's GDP in 1997 than in 1995?

b Gopherland's largest firm, the Gopherland Iron Company, sold $3 million worth of iron in 1991. It purchased $1.2 million worth of goods and services from other firms, paid $.5 million in interest, and paid $.3 million in excise and property taxes. Since its depreciation allowance was $.3 million, its profit was $.7 million. How much was its value-added in 1991?

c In 1987, Gopherland's exports equaled its imports, and its gross private domestic investment equaled its government expenditures. Its personal consumption expenditure was double its government expenditure, and equaled $400 million. What was its GDP in 1987?

2 Close to Gopherland is the smaller country of Badger. In Badger, the GDP is $400 million, and personal consumption expenditure is $300 million. Are the inhabitants of Badger better or worse off than those of Gopherland? Can you tell? Why or why not?

3 Suppose that, in a third country called Hanover, there are only two firms, a tomato producer and a catsup producer. Suppose that all tomatoes are intermediate goods used to produce catsup. The sales and expenses of the two firms are shown at the right:

TOMATO PRODUCER		**CATSUP PRODUCER**	
(thousands of dollars)			
Sales of tomatoes	200	Sales of catsup	500
Wages	100	Wages	150
Interest	20	Interest	30
Rent	25	Rent	40
Depreciation	10	Depreciation	10
Indirect business taxes	5	Indirect business taxes	10
Profit	____	Tomatoes	200
		Profit	____

a Fill in the level of profit for each firm.

b What is the value of GDP in Hanover?

c What is value-added in the tomato firm?

d What is value-added in the catsup firm?

e Complete the following table:

GROSS DOMESTIC PRODUCT, HANOVER
(thousands of dollars)

Wages	____
Rent	____
Interest	____
Profits	____
Indirect business taxes	____
Depreciation	____
Total: Gross domestic product	____

4 The CIA has collected the following data concerning a fourth country which shall remain nameless (for security reasons, of course):

	(millions of dollars)
Personal consumption expenditures	240
Corporate profits (before taxes)	20
Rental income of persons	10
Proprietors' income	30
Net investment	30
Compensation of employees	200
Indirect business taxes	20
Imports	5
Exports	6
Net interest	60
Depreciation	40

The CIA would like to know what GDP is in this country. Can you tell them?

5a The country of Erewhon reports that personal saving in 1995 is −$3 billion. Is this possible? Why or why not?

b It also reports that gross private domestic investment is negative. Is this possible? Why or why not?

6 Suppose that you could add up all of the money transactions in the United States during this year. Would this total amount equal, exceed, or be less than this year's GDP? Why?

7 Erewhon reports that its capital consumption allowance in 1996 is negative. What would this mean? Is it possible or not?

8 The country of Zanadu reports that its personal consumption expenditure is 85 percent of its GDP, that government purchases of goods and services equal $10 million, and that gross private domestic investment is double the amount of government purchases of goods and services.

a If exports equal imports, what is Zanadu's GDP?

b If exports equal imports, what are personal consumption expenditures in Zanadu?

c If exports are $5 million more than imports, what is Zanadu's GDP?

d If exports are double imports, can one figure out Zanadu's GDP from the information given? Why or why not?

 ANSWERS TO
TEST YOUR UNDERSTANDING

SECTION 1

TRUE OR FALSE: 1. False   2. False   3. False   4. True
5. False

EXERCISES

1. It will have no effect on GDP.

2. Items a, b, and c.

SECTION 2

TRUE OR FALSE: 1. True   2. True

EXERCISE

1. From top to bottom, the numbers are: 1,000, 1,200, 1,820, 2,400, and 1,600.

SECTION 3

TRUE OR FALSE: 1. True   2. False

EXERCISE

1. No. He should total value-added.

SECTION 4

TRUE OR FALSE: 1. False   2. True

EXERCISE

1. No. If GDP is used to gauge the net social value of economic output, pollution's costs should be subtracted from the market value of the goods produced.

SECTION 5

TRUE OR FALSE: 1. False   2. True   3. True   4. False

EXERCISES

1. GDP = $1,900 million.

2. Depreciation. Decreasing.

3. Inventories represent goods that can be sold without drawing on the economy's current productive capacity. Ignoring inventory increase excludes the value of these goods from the GDP calculation, even though they were produced during the year.

SECTION 6

TRUE OR FALSE: 1. True   2. True   3. False

EXERCISE

1. $93 million.

SECTION 7

TRUE OR FALSE: 1. True   2. True

EXERCISE

1. The totals are the same.

■ CHAPTER 2

Unemployment and Inflation

Essentials of **Unemployment and Inflation**

■ To obtain the unemployment rate, the Bureau of Labor Statistics divides the estimated number of people who are unemployed by the estimated number of people in the labor force.

■ Unemployment can result in substantial economic costs because it reduces the amount of goods and services produced by society.

■ Contrary to the classical economists, John Maynard Keynes concluded that no automatic mechanism in a capitalistic society could be counted on to generate a high level of employment. His views have been challenged and modified by new classical and new Keynesian economists.

■ Inflation is a general upward movement of prices; runaway inflation wipes out the value of money quickly and thoroughly, while creeping inflation erodes its value gradually and slowly.

■ Inflation tends to hurt lenders and to benefit borrowers, since it results in the depreciation of money; it can have a devastating and inequitable effect on savers.

1 ■ Measuring Unemployment

Each month, the federal government conducts a scientific survey of the U.S. people, asking a carefully selected sample of the population whether they have a job, and, if not, whether they are looking for one. To obtain the unemployment rate, the Bureau of Labor Statistics (the government agency responsible for producing the unemployment data) divides the estimated number of people who are unemployed by the estimated number of people in the *labor force.* To be in the labor force, a person must either be employed or unemployed. Note that the unemployment rate can rise either because people who formerly were employed are thrown out of work or because people who formerly were not in the labor force decide to look for jobs. For example, an increasing number of married women who decide to enter the labor force tends to raise the unemploy-

ment rate. Table 2.1 shows the unemployment rates in the United States for various segments of the population in 1996.

Why should you be concerned about the unemployed? Because some of them become demoralized, suffer loss of prestige and status, and their families tend to break apart. Sometimes they are pushed toward crime and drugs; often they feel despair. Their children may be innocent victims, too. Indeed, perhaps the most devastating effects of unemployment are on children, whose education, health, and security may be ruined.

Of course, this does not mean that all unemployment, whatever its cause or nature, should be eliminated. (For example, some unemployment may be voluntary.) It is important that you distinguish among three different kinds of unemployment.

▪ **TABLE 2.1**

Unemployment Rate, Selected Segments of the Population, United States, 1996

POPULATION SEGMENT	UNEMPLOYMENT RATE
Whites	
Males	
16–19 years	15.5
20 years and over	4.1
Females	
16–19 years	12.9
20 years and over	4.1
Blacks	
Males	
16–19 years	36.9
20 years and over	9.4
Females	
16–19 years	30.3
20 years and over	8.7

SOURCE: *Economic Report of the President* (Washington, D.C.: Government Printing Office, 1997).

FRICTIONAL UNEMPLOYMENT

Some people quit their jobs and look for something better. They may get angry at their bosses, or they may feel that they can get more money elsewhere. Others, particularly ex-students, are looking for their first job. Still others are temporarily laid off because their work is seasonal, as in the construction industry. Unemployment of this sort is called **frictional unemployment.** Frictional unemployment is inevitable, since people find it desirable to change jobs, and such job changes often involve a period of temporary unemployment.

STRUCTURAL UNEMPLOYMENT

Changes continually occur in the nature of consumer demand and in technology. For example, consumers grow tired of one good and become infatuated with another. And new technologies supplant old ones. Thus some workers are thrown out of work, and because the new goods and the new technologies call for different skills than the old ones did, they cannot use their skills elsewhere. Unemployment of this sort is called **structural unemployment.** It exists when jobs are available for qualified workers, but the unemployed do not have the necessary qualifications. This sort of unemployment results from a mismatch between job requirements and the skills of the unemployed. Consider the case of Mary Jones, a 58-year-old bookkeeper who was thrown out of work by the introduction of a new technology and who lacks the skills needed to get a job in another field. Ms. Jones is one of the structurally unemployed.

CYCLICAL UNEMPLOYMENT

Cyclical unemployment occurs when, because of an insufficiency of aggregate demand, there are more workers looking for work than there are jobs. Cyclical unemployment is associated with business fluctuations, or the so-called business cycle. Industrialized capitalistic economies have been subject to fluctuations, with booms often succeeding busts and vice versa. One feature of these fluctuations has been that the U.S. economy has periodically gone through depressions, during which unemployment has been high. The Great Depression of the 1930s was particularly long and severe, and when World War II ended, many Americans worried that the gigantic social costs of the enormous unemployment of the 1930s might be repeated in the postwar period. In response, Congress passed the Employment Act of 1946, which says,

> It is the continuing policy and responsibility of the Federal Government to use all practicable means . . . [to create and maintain] conditions under which there will be afforded useful employment opportunities, including self-employment, for those able, willing, and seeking to work and to promote maximum employment, production, and purchasing power.

TEST YOUR UNDERSTANDING

True or false?

_____ **1** Martin Moriarty has been thrown out of work by new technology and does not have the skills to get new employment; he is structurally unemployed.

_____ **2** Joan Jeffrey is unemployed but not actively seeking employment; she is not included in the government's unemployment figures.

Exercises

1 The unemployment rate shows the percentage of the labor force out of work, but not how long these people have been out of work. Does the average duration of unemployment matter too?

2 Explain the differences among frictional unemployment, structural unemployment, and cyclical unemployment. Should the government attempt to reduce all types of unemployment to zero? Why, or why not?

3 The following data came from the 1997 _Economic Report of the President._ Fill in the blanks.

	1995	1996
Percent of civilian labor force unemployed	5.6	5.4
Percent of civilian labor force employed	_____	_____
Civilian labor force	132.3 million	133.9 million
Total employment	_____	_____
Total unemployment	_____	_____

2 ▪ Economic Costs of Unemployment

According to most economists, _unemployment can result in substantial economic costs, since it reduces the amount of goods and services produced by society._ To determine how much society loses in this way by tolerating an unemployment rate above the minimum level resulting from frictional (and some structural) unemployment, economists estimate the **potential GDP,** which is the level of gross domestic product that could be achieved if there had been full employment. Thus, if full employment is defined as a 5 percent unemployment rate, potential GDP can be estimated by multiplying 95 percent of the labor force by the normal hours of work per year times the average output per hour of work at the relevant time.

If actual GDP is less than potential GDP, the estimated gap between actual and potential GDP is a measure of what society loses by tolerating less than full employment. One important problem in estimating this gap stems from the difficulty of defining "full employment." For many years, a common definition of **full employment** was a 4 percent unemployment rate, since it was felt that frictional and structural unemployment could not be reduced below this level. During the 1970s, there was criticism of this definition on the grounds that an unemployment rate of about 5 percent was a more realistic measure because there were more young people, women, and minority workers in the labor force. All these groups find it relatively difficult to find jobs. In the 1980s and early 1990s, many economists felt that 6 percent was closer to the mark; in 1997, some lowered the figure to about 5 percent.

TEST YOUR UNDERSTANDING

True or false?

_____ **1** Unemployment is a private, not a social, problem which has an effect only on the unemployed.

_____ **2** The concept of full employment can be defined and measured without difficulty.

Exercise

1 "Unemployed workers make about as much as when they were employed because of unemployment insurance, so the nation need not worry about the unemployed." Specify at least two fundamental errors in this statement.

3 ▪ The Classical View of Unemployment

Until the 1930s, most economists were convinced that the price system, left to its own devices, would hold unemployment to a reasonable minimum. Thus most of the great names of economics in the nineteenth and early twentieth centuries— including John Stuart Mill, Alfred Marshall, and A. C. Pigou—felt that there was no need for government intervention to promote a high level of employment. To be sure, they recognized that unemployment was sometimes large, but they regarded these lapses from high employment as temporary aberrations that the price system would cure automatically.

The classical economists recognized the fact that the level of total spending determines the unemployment rate. They believed that total spending was unlikely to be too small to purchase the full-employment level of output, because of **Say's Law** (named after the nineteenth-century French economist, J. B. Say). According to this law, the production of a certain amount of goods and services results in the generation of an amount of income that, if spent, is precisely sufficient to buy that output. In other words, _supply creates its own demand, since the total amount paid out by the producers of the goods and services to resource owners must equal the value of the goods and services. Thus, if this amount is spent, it must be sufficient to purchase all the goods and services that are produced._

But what if resource owners do not spend all their income, but save some of it instead? How, then, will the necessary spending arise to take all the output off the market? The answer the classical economists offered is that each dollar saved will be invested. Therefore, investment (made largely by business firms) will restore to the spending stream what resource owners take out through the saving process. Recall that the economist's definition of investment is different from the one often used in common parlance. To the economist, investment means expenditure on plant, equipment, and other productive assets. The classical economists believed that the amount invested would automatically equal the amount saved because the interest rate—the price paid for borrowing money—would fluctuate in such a way as to maintain equality between them. In other words, there is a market for loanable funds, and the interest rate will vary so that the quantity of funds supplied equals the quantity demanded. Thus, since funds are demanded to be used—that is, invested—the amount saved will be invested.

Further, the classical economists said that the amount of goods and services firms can sell depends on the prices they charge, as well as on total spending. For example, $1 million in spending will take 100 cars off the market if the price is $10,000 per car, and 200 cars off the market if the price is $5,000 per car. Recognizing this, the classical economists argued that firms would cut prices to sell their output. Competition among firms would prod them to reduce their prices in this way, with the result that the high-employment level of output would be taken off the market.

Looking at this process more closely, it is obvious that the prices of resources must also be reduced under such circumstances. Otherwise firms would incur losses because they would be getting less for their product, but paying no less for resources. The classical economists believed that it was realistic to expect the prices of resources to decline in such a situation. Indeed they were quite willing to assume that the wage rate—the price of labor—would be flexible in this way. Through the processes of competition for jobs, they felt that wage rates would be bid down to the level where everyone who really wanted to work could get a job.

 TEST YOUR UNDERSTANDING

True or false?

_____ **1** According to Say's Law, the production of a certain amount of goods and services results in the generation of an amount of income precisely sufficient to buy that output.

_____ **2** The classical economists believed that the amount invested would automatically equal the amount saved because the interest rate—the price paid for the use of money—would fluctuate in such a way as to maintain equality between them.

_____ **3** The classical economists believed that it was realistic to expect the wage rate to be inflexible.

4 ■ The Keynesian View of Unemployment

In 1936, while the world was still in the throes of the Great Depression, John Maynard Keynes (1883–1946) published his *General Theory of Employment, Interest, and Money.*[1] His purpose in this book was to explain how the capitalist economic system could get stalled in the sort of depressed state of equilibrium that existed in the 1930s. He also tried to indicate how governments might help to solve the problem. Contrary to the classical economists, Keynes concluded that no automatic mechanism in a capitalistic society would generate a high level of employment or at least would generate it quickly enough to be relied on in practice. Instead, the equilibrium level of national output might for a long time be below the level required to achieve high employment.

There were at least two basic flaws in the classical model, as Keynes and his followers saw it. First, in their view, *there is no assurance that intended saving will equal intended investment at a level ensuring high employment.* The people and firms who save are often not the same as the people and firms who invest, and they often have quite different motivations. In particular, a considerable amount of saving is done by families who want to put something aside for a rainy day or for a car or appliance. On the other hand, a considerable amount of investment is done by

[1] John Maynard Keynes, *The General Theory of Employment, Interest, and Money* (New York: Harcourt, Brace, 1936).

firms that are interested in increasing their profits by expanding their plants or by installing new equipment. According to Keynes, you cannot be sure that changes in the interest rate will bring about the equality of saving and investment visualized by the classical economists. In his view, intended saving may not equal intended investment at a level ensuring high employment. Instead, they may be equal at a level corresponding to considerable unemployment (or to considerable inflation). Thus a purely capitalist economic system, in the absence of appropriate government policies, has no dependable rudder to keep it clear of the shoals of serious unemployment or of serious inflation.

Second, *Keynes and his followers objected to the classical economists' assumption that prices and wages are flexible*. They contended that, contrary to the classical economists' view, the modern economy contains many departures from perfect competition that are barriers to downward flexibility of prices and wages. In particular, many important industries are dominated by a few producers who try hard to avoid cutting prices. Even in the face of a considerable drop in demand, such industries have sometimes maintained extraordinarily stable prices. Moreover, the labor unions fight hard to avoid wage cuts. In view of these facts of life, Keynes believed that the classical assumption of wage and price flexibility was unrealistic, and he questioned whether price and wage reductions can be depended on to maintain full employment.

 TEST YOUR UNDERSTANDING

True or false?

_____ **1** Keynes stated that there was no automatic mechanism in a capitalist society that would quickly generate a high level of employment.

_____ **2** Keynes insisted that intended saving must equal intended investment at a level ensuring high employment.

_____ **3** Keynes and his followers built their theory on the assumption of complete flexibility of wages and prices.

5 ■ The New Classical and New Keynesian Views of Unemployment

Over fifty years have elapsed since Keynes's death, and theories of unemployment have continued to develop and change. Even during the 1950s and 1960s, Keynes's views were challenged by an influential minority of economists known as the *monetarists*. This group, discussed in Chapter 9, stresses the influence of changes in the money supply on the economy. During the 1970s and 1980s, other groups—such as the supply-side economists, discussed in Chapter 6, and the *new classical macroeconomists* discussed in Chapter 12—mounted an attack on Keynesian views. In many respects, the new classical macroeconomists harked back to the classical view of unemployment; in particular, they rejected Keynes's argument that prices and wages are inflexible.

Keynes's own ideas have been extended and modified. Just as there is a new classical macroeconomics, so there is a new Keynesianism. Like the original Keynesians, the new Keynesians do not believe that markets clear continuously; that is, they do not believe that the quantity demanded of a product or input always equals the quantity supplied. In their view, the economy can stay in a state of disequilibrium for years if prices adjust slowly enough. But whereas old Keynesians merely assumed that wages tend to be rigid and that prices are sticky, new Keynesians have developed theories (described in Chapter 12) to help explain why such wage and price stability can be expected, given the rational behavior of individuals and firms.

 TEST YOUR UNDERSTANDING

True or false?

_____ **1** The new classical macroeconomists attacked Keynes for exaggerating the extent to which wages and prices are flexible.

_____ **2** New Keynesians argue that new classical macroeconomists underestimate the flexibility of wages and prices.

_____ **3** The new Keynesians believe that markets clear continuously.

6 ■ Measuring Inflation

Economic problems as well as economic theories have changed in the fifty years since Keynes's death. The Great Depression of the 1930s is a distant memory, while double-digit inflation is fresh in the minds of everyone over 35 years of age. The unemployment problem is still of concern to the United States, but the electorate has learned to fear inflation as well as unemployment.

It is hard to find anyone these days who does not know the meaning of inflation firsthand. Try to think of commodities you regularly purchase that cost less now than they did several years ago. Chances are that you can come up with precious few, if any. **Inflation** is a general upward movement of prices. In other words, inflation means that goods and services that currently cost $10 may soon be priced at $11 or even $12, and wages and other input prices increase as well. It is essential to distinguish between the movements of individual prices and the movement of the entire price level. If the price of a particular good—corn, say—goes up, this need not be inflation, since the prices of other goods may be going down at the same time, so that the overall price level—the general average level of prices—remains much the same. Inflation occurs only if most prices for goods and services in the society move upward—that is, if the average level of prices increases.

The most widely quoted measure of inflation in the United States is the Consumer Price Index, published monthly by the Bureau of Labor Statistics. Until 1978, the purpose of this index was to measure changes in prices of goods and services purchased by urban wage earners and clerical workers and their families. In 1978, the index was expanded to include all urban consumers (although the narrower index was not discontinued). The first step in calculating the index is to find out how much it costs in a particular month to buy a market basket of goods and services that is representative of the buying patterns of these consumers. Then this amount is expressed as a ratio of what it would have cost to buy the same market basket of goods and services in the base period (1982–84),[2] and this ratio is multiplied by 100. In contrast to the price indexes in the previous chapter, this (like most commonly used indexes) shows the *percentage,* not the proportional, change in the price level. For example, the Consumer Price Index equaled 158.6 in December 1996; this meant that it cost 58.6 percent more to buy this market basket in December 1996 than in 1982–84. (To obtain results based on Chapter 1's definition of a price index, all you have to do is divide this index by 100.) Figure 2.1 shows the behavior of the Consumer Price Index in recent decades.

[2] Other base periods, such as 1967, have been used in the past.

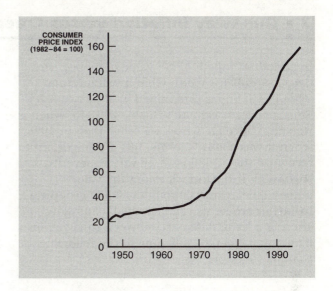

▪ **FIGURE 2.1**

Consumer Price Index, 1946–1995

Inflation has been a continual problem in the United States, particularly in the late 1970s and early 1980s.

 TEST YOUR UNDERSTANDING

Exercise

1 In many situations, ranging from discussions of government economic policy to a particular labor negotiation between a management and a union, it is important to distinguish between *money* and *real* wages. Money wages are wages expressed in current dollars, whereas real wages are adjusted for changes in the price level. The average weekly earnings in U.S. manufacturing are shown below for 1947 to 1990, together with the Consumer Price Index for the same years.

YEAR	AVERAGE WEEKLY EARNINGS (current dollars)	CONSUMER PRICE INDEX (1982–84 = 100)
1947	49.13	22.3
1957	81.59	28.1
1967	114.49	33.4
1977	228.50	60.6
1990	442.27	130.7

a. Convert the above money wages into real wages expressed in 1982–84 dollars.

b. In percentage terms, did real money wages in U.S. manufacturing increase as much during 1967 to 1977 as during 1947 to 1957?

c. John Murphy, a vegetarian who spends the bulk of his income on spinach, cauliflower, and books, received the average wage (shown in the table at the left) during 1947 to 1990. Are you confident that the changes in real wages you calculated in (a) are a good indication of the changes in Mr. Murphy's standard of living during this period?

d. If the Consumer Price Index had been calculated so that 1977 = 100, would the value of this index for 1967 have been higher or lower than that shown above?

7 ▪ Runaway Inflation versus Creeping Inflation

In periods of inflation, the value of money is reduced. A dollar is worth what it will buy, and what it will buy is determined by the price level. Thus a dollar was more valuable in 1940, when a Hershey chocolate bar was 5 cents, than in 1996, when it was about 50 cents. But it is important to recognize that inflations may vary in severity. **Runaway inflation** wipes out the value of money quickly and thoroughly, while **creeping inflation** erodes its value gradually and slowly. There is a lot of difference between runaway inflation and creeping inflation, as the following examples indicate.

(the unit of German currency) to buy what one mark would buy before the war.

The effect of this runaway inflation was to disrupt the economy. Prices had to be adjusted from day to day. People rushed to the stores to spend the money they received as soon as possible, since very soon it would buy much less. Speculation was rampant. This inflation was a terrible blow to Germany. The middle class was wiped out; its savings became completely worthless. It is no wonder that Germany has in recent years been more sensitive than many other countries to the evils of inflation.

RUNAWAY INFLATION

The case of Germany after World War I is a good example of runaway inflation. Germany was required to pay large reparations to the victorious Allies after the war. Rather than attempting to tax its people to pay these amounts, the German government merely printed additional quantities of paper money. This new money increased total spending in Germany, and the increased spending resulted in higher prices because the war-devastated economy could not increase output substantially. As more and more money was printed, prices rose higher and higher, reaching utterly fantastic levels. By 1923, it took a *trillion* marks

CREEPING INFLATION

For the past fifty years, the price level in the United States has tended to go one way only—up. In practically all years during this period, prices have risen. Since 1955, there hasn't been a single year when the price level has fallen. Certainly, this has not been a runaway inflation, but it has resulted in a very substantial erosion in the value of the dollar. Like a beach slowly worn away by the ocean, the dollar has gradually lost a considerable portion of its value. Specifically, prices now tend to be about 5 times what they were forty years ago. Thus the dollar now is worth about a fifth of what it was worth then.

 TEST YOUR UNDERSTANDING

True or false?

____ **1** No matter whether an inflation is severe or not, it will bankrupt the middle class in a few years.

____ **2** Creeping inflation inevitably leads to runaway inflation, so it is essential that the price level be constant.

8 ▪ Major Effects of Inflation

To see why people fear inflation so much, you must understand its effects, described below.

REDISTRIBUTIVE EFFECTS

Because all money incomes do not go up at the same rate as prices, inflation results in an arbitrary redistribution of income. People with relatively fixed incomes, lenders, and savers tend to be hurt by it, and major inflations tend to cripple total output as well. To understand the redistributive effects of inflation, it is necessary to distinguish between **money income** and **real income.** A family's money income is its income measured in current dollars, whereas its real income is adjusted for changes in the price level. During periods of inflation, a family with a relatively fixed money income will experience a declining real income.

Suppose that the Murphy family earns $41,000 this year and $40,000 last year, and that the price level is 10 percent higher this year than last year. Under these circumstances, the Murphy family's money income has increased by $1,000, but its real income has fallen (because its money income has risen by a smaller percentage than the price level). This is the sort of effect that inflation has on people with relatively fixed incomes, lenders, and savers—three groups that tend to be hit hard by inflation.

FIXED MONEY INCOMES Inflation may seem no more than a petty annoyance; after all, most people care about relative, not absolute, prices. For example, if the Howe family's money income increases at the same rate as the price level, the Howe family may be no better or worse off under inflation than if its money income remained constant and no inflation occurred. But not all people are as fortunate as the Howes. Some people cannot increase their wages to compensate for price increases, for example, because they work under long-term contracts, among other reasons. These people take a considerable beating from inflation. One group that sometimes is particularly hard hit by inflation is the elderly, since old people often must live on pensions and other relatively fixed forms of income. Thus inflation sometimes has a substantial, inequitable, and unwelcome impact on older citizens.

LENDERS Inflation hurts lenders and benefits borrowers, since it results in the depreciation of money. A dollar is worth what it will buy, and what it will buy is determined by the price level. If the price level increases, a dollar is worth less than it was before. Consequently, if you lend Bill Dvorak $100 in 1996 and he pays you $100 in 1999—when a dollar will buy much less than in 1996—you are losing on the deal. In terms of what the money will buy, he is paying you less than what he borrowed. Of course, if you anticipate considerable inflation, you may be able to recoup by charging him a high enough interest rate to offset the depreciation of the dollar, but it is not so easy to forecast the rate of inflation and protect yourself.

SAVERS Inflation can have a devastating and inequitable effect on savers. The family that works hard and saves for retirement (and a rainy day) finds that its savings are worth far less, when it finally spends them, than the amount it saved. Consider the well-meaning souls who invested $1,000 of their savings in U.S. savings bonds in 1939. By 1949, these bonds were worth only about 800 1939 dollars, including the interest received in the ten-year period. Thus these people had $200 taken away from them, in just as real a sense as if their pockets had been picked.

EFFECTS OF ANTICIPATED AND UNANTICIPATED INFLATION

Economists are fond of pointing out that the effects of anticipated inflation tend to be less severe than those of unanticipated inflation. To see why this is the case, suppose that everyone anticipates (correctly) that the price level will be 6 percent higher next year than this year. In such a situation, everyone will build this amount of inflation into his or her decisions. Workers will realize that their money wage rates must be 6 percent higher next year just to avoid a cut in their real wage rates. The Murphy family, which earns $41,000 this year, will realize that it must earn 1.06 × $41,000, or $43,460, next year if it is to avoid a reduction in its real earnings. And people who are thinking of lending money for a year will recognize that they must charge 6 percent interest just to break even. Why? Because when the money is repaid next year, $1.06 will be worth no more in real terms than $1.00 is now.

Because people build the anticipated rate of inflation into their calculations, the effects of anticipated inflation are likely to be less pronounced than those of unanticipated inflation. However, in the real world in which we all live, this frequently is of small comfort, since it is very difficult to anticipate the rate of inflation correctly. Even the most sophisticated econometric models have not had a very distinguished record in forecasting the rate of inflation. Thus it seems foolish to believe that the typical citizen (like those who invested in United States savings bonds in 1939) can anticipate inflation well enough to protect himself or herself against its consequences.

AN ARBITRARY "TAX"

While inflation hurts some people, it benefits others. Those who are lucky enough to invest in goods, land, equipment, and other items that experience particularly rapid increases in price may make a killing. For this reason, speculation tends to be rampant during severe inflations. However, it is important to recognize that the rewards and penalties resulting from inflation are meted out with little or no regard for society's values or goals. As the late Arthur Okun, a former chairman of the Council of Economic Advisers, put it, "'sharpies' . . . make sophisticated choices and often reap gains from inflation which do not seem to reflect any real contribution to economic growth. On the other hand, the unsophisticated saver who is merely preparing for the proverbial rainy day becomes a sucker." This is one of the most undesirable features of inflation, and it helps to account for inflation's sometimes being called an arbitrary "tax."

EFFECTS ON OUTPUT

Creeping inflation, unlike unemployment, does not seem to reduce national output; in the short run, output may increase, for reasons taken up in subsequent chapters. But, although a mild upward creep of prices at the rate of a few percent per year is not likely to reduce output, a major inflation can have adverse effects on production. For one thing, it encourages speculation rather than productive use of savings. People find it more profitable to invest in gold, diamonds, real estate, and art (all of which tend to rise in monetary value during inflations) than in many kinds of productive activity. Also, managers of firms tend to be discouraged from carrying out long-range projects because of the difficulty of forecasting what future prices will be. If the rate of inflation reaches the catastrophic heights that prevailed in Germany after World War I, the monetary system may break down. People may be unwilling to accept money. They may insist on trading goods or services directly for other goods and services. The result is likely to be considerable inefficiency and substantially reduced output.

 TEST YOUR UNDERSTANDING

Exercises

1 "The Employment Act of 1946 should be amended to include the goal of stabilizing the purchasing power of the dollar as well as the goal of maintaining high-level employment." Comment and evaluate.

2 "Inflation is a necessary cost of economic progress." Comment and evaluate.

3 Suppose that a family's money income remains constant at $40,000, and that the price level increases 10 percent per year. How many years will it take for the family's real income to be cut in half?

4 If you believe that the United States is about to suffer severe inflation, would you be better off to invest money in land or in government bonds? Explain your answer.

5 According to a 1976 statement by the Research and Policy Committee of the Committee for Economic Development, "The inflation rate has receded substantially from its double-digit levels of 1974, but it still remains unacceptably high, particularly for a period in which the economy is operating far below its potential." Why does it say this is particularly true for a period when output is far less than its potential? Explain.

▪ CHAPTER REVIEW

KEY TERMS

frictional unemployment
structural unemployment
cyclical unemployment

potential GDP
full employment
Say's Law
inflation

runaway inflation
creeping inflation
money income
real income

COMPLETION QUESTIONS

1 If a recession occurs, with the result that automobile sales decline and John Martin (an auto salesperson) is laid off, this is a case of _____ unemployment. If a skilled worker in the printing industry is laid off because of the adoption of a new technology, and if his skills do not enable him to find employment elsewhere, this is a case of _____ unemployment.

2 If 1 million people who formerly were not in the labor force decide to look for jobs, and if it takes time for them to find jobs, the initial result is likely to be (a decrease, an increase, no change) _____ in the unemployment rate.

3 Potential GDP is the level of GDP that could be achieved if there were _____. In the past, full employment was defined as _____ percent unemployed; recently, many economists have believed that it should be defined as about _____ percent unemployed (but in 1996, some economists felt that the figure should be lower).

4 If the Murphy family's money income is increasing by 10 percent per year, and its real income is increasing by 8 percent per year, the price level must be rising by

ANSWERS TO COMPLETION QUESTIONS

cyclical

structural

an increase

full employment
4

5 or 6

_____ percent per year. If the price level continues to rise at this rate and if you invest in a bond yielding 6 percent interest per year, you will receive _____ percent interest in real terms.

5 If lenders foresee an inflation rate of 10 percent per year, they are unlikely to lend money at 10 percent or less because it would mean they would receive an interest rate of _____ percent or less in real terms. If lenders anticipate increased inflation, they will tend to (increase, decrease) _____ interest rates.

6 If the U.S. Treasury offsets the effects of inflation on both the principal and interest on a particular type of U.S. Treasury bond, and if you bought such a bond in 1996 for $1,000, you would receive _____ in principal when it falls due in 2000 if the price level were 30 percent higher in 2000 than in 1996. If the bond yields interest of $60 (in 1996 dollars) per year, you would receive interest (in current dollars) of _____ in 2000 if the price level were 16 percent higher in 2000 than in 1996.

7 The classical economists maintained that the amount of _____ businesses can sell depends on the _____ charged, as well as on total spending. Recognizing this, they further argued that firms would cut prices to sell their _____. _____ among firms would prod them to reduce their prices in this way, with the result that the _____ level of output would be taken off the market.

8 _____ and his followers attacked the classical economists' assumption that _____ and _____ are flexible. Contrary to the classical economists' argument, they said that the modern economy contains many departures from _____ that are barriers to _____ flexibility of prices and wages.

2

4

zero

increase

$1,300

$69.60

goods and services
prices

output, Competition

high-employment

Keynes
prices
wages

perfect competition
downward

NUMERICAL PROBLEMS

1 The data below pertain to country *A* in 1996 and 1997. Fill in the blanks.

	1996	1997
Percent of civilian labor force unemployed	7.0	6.0
Percent of civilian labor force employed	____	____
Civilian labor force	97.4 million	100.4 million
Total employment	____	____
Total unemployment	____	____

2 In Israel the annual inflation rate was about 50 percent in 1978, and nearly 100 percent during the summer of 1979, according to William C. Freund of the New York Stock Exchange. In the *New York Times* on June 24, 1979, Freund concluded that: "The solution lies in marshalling the necessary political courage and consensus. . . . It is political fortitude, above all else, which is needed now—to cut back on excess claims against resources, to promote production and productivity, and to relieve intense demand pressures." Indicate how this advice is related to the discussion presented in this chapter. What specific measures would you suggest to accomplish these results?

3 Commenting on the inflation during the 1970s in

Israel, the *Jerusalem Post* observed that "75 percent of Israeli families live in flats they own. Most of these were bought with government assistance and low interest mortgages. The payments on these mortgages are peanuts in light of our current inflation spiral. Someone who received a loan of 200,000 Israeli pounds at the beginning of the year—even at 32 percent interest—will have earned about 65,000 Israeli pounds by the end of it, clear and nontaxable. This sum is possibly more than his annual wages, so why complain?"[3] Does this prove that inflation is of no consequence? Why or why not? Explain in detail.

4 Mr. Rich has $1 million in cash, bank accounts, and savings and loan accounts. They are his only assets.

a If the inflation rate is 8 percent, how much must Mr. Rich save per year to maintain the real value of his assets?

b Mr. Rich must pay 70 percent of his income in taxes. If all Mr. Rich's income is taxable, what is the minimum amount that Mr. Rich must make per year if he wants to maintain the real value of his assets?

 ANSWERS TO
TEST YOUR UNDERSTANDING

SECTION 1

TRUE OR FALSE: 1. True   2. True

EXERCISES

1. Yes. Long bouts of unemployment are more serious and painful than short ones.

2. Frictionally unemployed people have left one job (often voluntarily) and have not as yet begun a new one. Structural unemployment occurs when jobs are available for qualified workers, but the unemployed do not have the necessary qualifications. Cyclical unemployment occurs when, because of an insufficiency of aggregate demand, there are more people looking for work than there are jobs. The government should not attempt to reduce all types of unemployment to zero because severe inflation would be likely to result.

3.

Percent of civilian labor		
force employed	94.4	94.6
Total employment	124.9	126.7
Total unemployment	7.4	7.2

SECTION 2

TRUE OR FALSE: 1. False   2. False

EXERCISES

1. (1) Unemployment benefits are temporary, and average less than what unemployed workers made when employed. (2) Unemployed workers result in an opportunity cost to the country in the form of the goods and services that these workers could produce.

SECTION 3

TRUE OR FALSE: 1. True   2. True   3. False

[3] *New York Times,* June 24, 1979.

SECTION 4

TRUE OR FALSE: 1. True   2. False   3. False

SECTION 5

TRUE OR FALSE: 1. False   2. False   3. False

SECTION 6

EXERCISE

1. a. 1947: $49.13 ÷ 0.223 = $220.31
   1957: $81.59 ÷ 0.281 = $290.36
   1967: $114.49 ÷ 0.334 = $342.78
   1977: $228.50 ÷ 0.606 = $377.06
   1990: $442.27 ÷ 1.307 = $338.39

   b. During 1967 to 1977, real wages increased by 10.0 percent (from $342.78 to $377.06). During 1947 to 1957, they increased by 31.8 percent (from $220.31 to $290.36). Thus, percentagewise, they rose less during 1967 to 1977 than during 1947 to 1957.

   c. No, because the prices of the goods on which he spends most of his income may have behaved quite differently from the Consumer Price Index (since the goods he buys are quite different from the market basket of goods and services bought by all urban consumers). Also, his standard of living may depend on the extent of his assets as well as the size of his earnings.

   d. It would have been higher. If the 1977 price level were set equal to 100, the 1967 price level would have to be more than 33.4.

SECTION 7

TRUE OR FALSE: 1. False   2. False

SECTION 8

EXERCISES

1. The point is that there may be trade-offs between inflation and unemployment, and a full-employment

policy should take inflation into consideration as well. Much more will be said on this score in subsequent chapters.

2. Economic progress has been achieved without serious inflation.

3. About 7 years.

4. Land, because its price is likely to go up more than that of government bonds.

5. When the economy is producing less than it can, inflation tends to be reduced. There are lots of excess capacity and unemployed resources, which put a damper on price increases.

CHAPTER 3

Aggregate Demand

Essentials of **Aggregate Demand**

- The consumption function is the relationship between consumption spending and disposable income.

- The saving function is the relationship between total saving and disposable income.

- For GDP to be at its equilibrium value, total intended spending on final goods and services must equal GDP.

- A $1 billion increase in intended investment often results in more than a $1 billion increase in GDP.

1 ■ The Consumption Function

Reductions in national output tend to trigger increases in the unemployment rate. Thus, to understand why unemployment sometimes rises substantially, you must study the forces determining national output. Basically, the simple model you will learn in this chapter is the one put forth in the 1930s by John Maynard Keynes. Given that recent decades have seen persistent inflation, not a constant price level, this model is obviously incomplete, but it throws useful light on the factors influencing aggregate demand.

An important part of our theory is the **consumption function,** *which is the relationship between consumption spending and disposable income.* **Disposable income** is the total amount of income that people get to keep after paying personal taxes. It seems clear that *consumption expenditures— whether those of a single household or the total consumption expenditures in the entire economy—are influenced heavily by income.* Families with higher incomes spend more on consumption than families with lower incomes. Of course, individual families vary a good deal in their behavior; some spend more than others even if their incomes are the same. But, on the average, a family's consumption expenditure is tied very closely to its income. What is true for individual families also holds for the entire economy: total personal consumption expenditures are closely related to disposable income.

Suppose that you know what the consumption function for a given society looks like at a particular period in time. For example, suppose that it is given by the figures for disposable income and personal consumption expenditure in the first two columns of Table 3.1. On the basis of your

■ TABLE 3.1

The Consumption Function

DISPOSABLE INCOME	PERSONAL CONSUMPTION EXPENDITURE	MARGINAL PROPENSITY TO CONSUME
(billions of dollars)		
1,000	950	
		$\frac{30}{50} = 0.60$
1,050	980	
		$\frac{30}{50} = 0.60$
1,100	1,010	
		$\frac{30}{50} = 0.60$
1,150	1,040	
		$\frac{30}{50} = 0.60$
1,200	1,070	
		$\frac{30}{50} = 0.60$
1,250	1,100	
		$\frac{30}{50} = 0.60$
1,300	1,130	

knowledge of the consumption function, you can determine the *extra* amount families will spend on consumption if they receive an *extra* dollar of

disposable income. *This amount—the fraction of an extra dollar of income that is spent on consumption—is called the* **marginal propensity to consume.**

 TEST YOUR UNDERSTANDING

True or false?

_____ **1** If the marginal propensity to consume is .8 and disposable income is $200 billion, personal consumption expenditure equals $160 billion.

_____ **2** The proportion of total income consumed

must always equal the marginal propensity to consume.

_____ **3** Families with high incomes tend to spend more on consumption than families with low incomes.

2 ▪ The Saving Function

If people don't devote their disposable income to personal consumption expenditure, what else can they do with it? Of course, they can save it. When families refrain from spending their income on consumption goods and services—that is, when they forgo present consumption to provide for larger consumption in the future—they save. Thus you can derive from the consumption function the total amount people will save at each level of disposable income. All you have to do is subtract the total personal consumption expenditure at each level of disposable income from disposable income. The difference is the total amount of saving at each level of disposable income. This difference is shown in the next to last column of Table 3.2. The resulting relationship between total saving and disposable income is the **saving function.** Like the consumption function, it plays a major role in our theory.

If you know the saving function, you can calculate the marginal propensity to save at any level of disposable income. The **marginal propensity to save** *is the proportion of an extra dollar of disposable income that is saved.* To see how to calculate it, consult Table 3.2 again. The third column shows that, when income rises from $1,000 billion to $1,050 billion, saving rises from

$50 billion to $70 billion. Consequently, the fraction of the extra $50 billion of income that is saved is $20 billion ÷ $50 billion, or 0.40. Thus the marginal propensity to save is 0.40. Similar

▪ **TABLE 3.2**

The Saving Function

DISPOSABLE INCOME	PERSONAL CONSUMPTION EXPENDITURE	SAVING	MARGINAL PROPENSITY TO SAVE
	(billions of dollars)		
1,000	950	50	
			$\frac{20}{50} = 0.40$
1,050	980	70	
			$\frac{20}{50} = 0.40$
1,100	1,010	90	
			$\frac{20}{50} = 0.40$
1,150	1,040	110	
			$\frac{20}{50} = 0.40$
1,200	1,070	130	
			$\frac{20}{50} = 0.40$
1,250	1,100	150	
			$\frac{20}{50} = 0.40$
1,300	1,130	170	

calculations show that the marginal propensity to save when disposable income is between $1,050 billion and $1,100 billion is 0.40; the marginal propensity to save when disposable income is between $1,100 billion and $1,150 billion is 0.40; and so forth.

 TEST YOUR UNDERSTANDING

True or false?

_____ **1** The marginal propensity to save is equal to the slope of the consumption function.

_____ **2** The relationship between total saving and disposable income is the saving function.

_____ **3** If people don't devote their disposable income to personal consumption expenditure, they can save it.

Exercises

1 Suppose that only three families inhabit a country and that (regardless of the level of its income) each family spends 90 percent of its income on consumption goods. For the country as a whole, what is the marginal propensity to save? To what extent does the country's marginal propensity to consume depend on the distribution of income? Is this realistic?

2 Assume that the consumption function is as follows:

DISPOSABLE INCOME	PERSONAL CONSUMPTION EXPENDITURE
(billions of dollars)	
900	750
1,000	800
1,100	850
1,200	900
1,300	950
1,400	1,000

a. How much will be saved if disposable income is $1,000 billion?

b. What is the marginal propensity to consume if disposable income is between $1,000 billion and $1,100 billion?

c. What is the marginal propensity to save if disposable income is between $1,000 billion and $1,100 billion?

3 Suppose that the relationship between personal consumption expenditure and disposable income in the United States were as follows:

CONSUMPTION	DISPOSABLE INCOME
(billions of dollars)	
750	700
830	800
910	900
970	1,000
1,030	1,100
1,100	1,200

Would the marginal propensity to consume remain constant, or would it vary with the level of disposable income?

3 ▪ Determinants of Investment

In Chapter 1, it was stressed that investment consists largely of the amount firms spend on new buildings and factories, new equipment, and increases in inventory. Investment plays a central role in the theory of output and employment. To understand this theory, it is essential that you understand the factors determining the level of gross private domestic investment. Basically, there are two broad determinants of the level of gross private domestic investment—the expected rate of return from capital, and the interest rate.

RATE OF RETURN

The **expected rate of return from capital** is the perceived rate of return that managers of firms believe they can obtain if they put up new buildings or factories, add new equipment, or increase their inventories. Each of these forms of investment requires the expenditure of money. The rate of return measures the profitability of such an expenditure; it shows the annual profits to be obtained per dollar invested. Thus a rate of return of 10 percent means that, for every dollar invested, an annual profit of 10 cents is obtained. Clearly, the higher the expected rate of return

from a particular investment, the more profitable the investment is expected to be.

INTEREST RATE

The **interest rate** is the cost of borrowing money. More specifically, it is the annual amount that a borrower must pay for the use of a dollar for a year. Thus, if the interest rate is 8 percent, a borrower must pay 8 cents per year for the use of a dollar. And if the interest rate is 12 percent, a borrower must pay 12 cents per year for the use of a dollar. Anyone with a savings account knows what it is to earn interest; anyone who has borrowed money from a bank knows what it is to pay interest. Clearly, the higher the interest rate that a firm has to pay to finance an investment, the less profitable the investment is.

 TEST YOUR UNDERSTANDING

True or false?

_____ **1** A firm pays a higher interest rate to finance investment *A* than investment *B*; thus investment *B* must be more profitable than investment *A*.

Exercises

1 "Unless firms make profits, they cannot invest in plant and equipment. Profits set an upper limit on how much they can invest." Comment and evaluate.

2 What effect would each of the following have on the amount of investment? That is, would each increase it, decrease it, or have no effect on it?

a. Expectations of greater likelihood of impending recession by firms

b. A decrease in interest rates

c. An increased rate of invention of important new synthetic materials

d. A marked reduction in the percent of existing plant that is utilized

e. An increase in the perceived profitability of building up inventories

---

4 ▪ The Equilibrium Level of Gross Domestic Product: A Closed Economy with No Government

At this point, you can show how the equilibrium level of GDP is determined if the price level is held constant. Three simplifying assumptions, all of which are relaxed subsequently in this or later chapters, are made:

1 Assume that there are no government expenditures and that the economy is closed (no exports or imports). Thus *total spending on final output— that is, on gross domestic product—in this simple case equals consumption expenditure plus gross investment.*

(Why? Because the other two components of total spending—government expenditures and net exports—are zero.) These assumptions will be relaxed in the latter part of this chapter.

2 Assume that there are no taxes, no transfer payments, and no undistributed corporate profits. Indeed, assume that GDP *equals disposable income in this simple case.* Later chapters relax this assumption.

3 Assume that the total amount of intended investment is *independent* of the level of gross domestic product. This, of course, is only a rough simplification, since, as noted in a previous section, the amount firms invest will be affected by the level of national output. But this simplification is very convenient and it can easily be relaxed.

An equilibrium is a situation where there is no tendency for change; in other words, it is a situation that can persist. GDP is at its equilibrium value when the flow of income (generated by this value of GDP) results in a level of spending that is just sufficient (not too high, not too low) to take this level of output off the market. To understand this equilibrium condition, it is essential to keep the circular flow of the macroeconomy in mind:

1 Output determines income: The production of goods and services results in a flow of income to the workers, resource owners, and managers who help to produce them. Each level of GDP results in a certain flow of income. More specifically, under the assumptions made here, GDP equals disposable income. Thus, whatever the level of GDP may be, you can be sure that the level of disposable income will be equivalent to it.

2 Income determines spending: The level of spending on final goods and services is dependent on the level of disposable income. As you saw earlier in this chapter, consumption expenditure depends on the level of disposable income. (For the moment, assume that investment is independent of the level of output in the economy.) Thus, if you know the level of disposable income, you can predict what level of spending will be forthcoming.

3 Spending affects output: If producers find that they are selling goods faster than they are producing them, their inventories will decline. If they find that they are selling goods slower than they are producing them, their inventories will rise. *If GDP is at its equilibrium value, the intended level of spending must be just equal to GDP.* Why? Because otherwise there will be an unintended increase or decrease in producers' inventories—a situation which cannot persist.

AGGREGATE FLOWS OF INCOME AND EXPENDITURE

Consider in more detail the process whereby national output (that is, GDP) determines the level of income, which in turn determines the level of spending. Suppose that the first column of Table 3.3 shows the various possible output levels—that is, the various possible values of GDP—that the economy might produce this year. This column shows the various output levels that might be produced *if producers expected that there would be enough spending to take this much output off the market at the existing price level.* And, as stressed above, disposable income equals GDP.

Since disposable income equals GDP (under the current assumptions), the first column of Table 3.3 also shows the level of disposable income corresponding to each possible level of GDP. From this, it should be possible to determine the level of spending corresponding to each level of GDP. Specifically, suppose that the consumption function is as shown in Table 3.1. In this case, intended consumption expenditure at each level of GDP will be shown in column 2 of Table 3.3. For example, if GDP equals $1,000 billion, intended consumption expenditure equals $950 billion.

But consumption expenditure is not the only type of spending. What about investment? Suppose that firms want to invest $90 billion regardless of the level of GDP. Under these circumstances, total spending at each level of GDP will be as shown in column 5 of Table 3.3. (Since total intended spending equals intended consumption expenditure plus intended investment, column 5 equals column 2 plus column 4.)

For GDP to be at its equilibrium value, total in-

▪ **TABLE 3.3**

Determination of Equilibrium Level of Gross Domestic Product (Billions of Dollars)

(1) GROSS DOMESTIC PRODUCT (= disposable income)	(2) INTENDED CONSUMPTION EXPENDITURE	(3) INTENDED SAVING	(4) INTENDED INVESTMENT	(5) TOTAL INTENDED SPENDING (2) + (4)	(6) TENDENCY OF NATIONAL OUTPUT
1,000	950	50	90	1,040	Upward
1,050	980	70	90	1,070	Upward
1,100	1,010	90	90	1,100	No change
1,150	1,040	110	90	1,130	Downward
1,200	1,070	130	90	1,160	Downward
1,250	1,100	150	90	1,190	Downward

tended spending on final goods and services must equal GDP. Consider Table 3.3. Column 5 of this table shows the level of total intended spending at each level of national output (and income). The equilibrium value of GDP is $1,100 billion, where total intended spending equals GDP. In this and the following section, we prove this is the case.

The easiest way to prove this is to show that, if intended spending is not equal to GDP, GDP is *not* at its equilibrium value. The following discussion provides such a proof. First we show that, if intended spending is greater than GDP, GDP is not at its equilibrium level. Then we show that, if intended spending is less than GDP, GDP is not at its equilibrium level.

If intended spending is *greater* than GDP, what will happen? Since the total amount that will be spent on final goods and services exceeds the total amount of final goods and services produced (which is, by definition, GDP) firms' inventories will be reduced. Consequently, firms will increase their output rate to avoid continued depletion of

their inventories and to bring their output into balance with the rate of aggregate demand. Since an increase in the output rate means an increase in GDP, it follows that GDP will tend to increase if intended spending is greater than GDP. GDP therefore is not at its equilibrium level.

On the other hand, what will happen if intended spending is *less* than GDP? Since the total amount that will be spent on final goods and services falls short of the total amount of final goods and services produced (which is, by definition, GDP), firms' inventories will increase. As inventories pile up unexpectedly, firms will cut back their output to bring it into better balance with aggregate demand. Since a reduction in output means a reduction in GDP, it follows that GDP will tend to fall if intended spending is less than GDP. Once again, GDP is not at its equilibrium level.

Since GDP is not at its equilibrium value when it exceeds or falls short of intended spending, it must be at its equilibrium value only when it equals intended spending.

TEST YOUR UNDERSTANDING

True or false?

_____ **1** If GDP is at its equilibrium value, the intended level of spending must be just equal to GDP.

_____ **2** If intended spending is below GDP, firms will increase their output.

_____ **3** If intended spending is above GDP, firms will reduce their output.

Exercise

1 Economists find it useful to ask "what if" questions. For example, what if GDP in a particular country assumed various alternative values? What would be the results? Suppose that you know four things about the country in question. First, in this country, personal consumption expenditure = $100 million + 0.75D, where D is disposable income. Second, intended investment in this country equals $150 million. Third, this country has a primitive economy with neither a government nor foreign trade. Fourth, the price level in this country is fixed.

a. Suppose that GDP in this country assumes the alternative values shown in the table at the right. What are the corresponding values of intended consumption expenditure, intended investment, and total intended spending? Fill in the blanks in the table.

GROSS DOMESTIC PRODUCT	INTENDED CONSUMPTION EXPENDITURE	INTENDED INVESTMENT	TOTAL INTENDED SPENDING
(millions of dollars)			
800	____	____	____
900	____	____	____
1,000	____	____	____
1,100	____	____	____

b. What is the equilibrium level of gross domestic product?
c. If GDP equals $900 million, what is the intended value of saving?
d. At what value of GDP does intended saving equal intended investment?

5 ▪ Using a Graph to Determine Equilibrium GDP

For the sake of absolute clarity, you can represent the same argument in a diagrammatic, rather than tabular, analysis. Since disposable income equals gross domestic product in this simple case, you can plot consumption expenditure (on the vertical axis) versus gross domestic product (on the horizontal axis), as shown in Figure 3.1. This is the consumption function. Also, we can plot the sum of consumption expenditure C and investment expenditure I against GDP, as shown in Figure 3.1. This relationship, shown by the C + I line, indicates the level of total intended spending on final goods and services for various amounts of GDP. Finally, plot a **45-degree line,** as shown in Figure 3.1. This line contains all points where total intended spending equals gross domestic product.

You are concerned with one of these points in particular, the one that also lies on the C + I line. The *equilibrium level of GDP will be at the point on the horizontal axis where the C + I line intersects the 45-degree line.* In Figure 3.1, this occurs at $1,100 billion. Under the conditions assumed here, no other level of GDP can be maintained for any considerable period of time.

Why can you be sure that the point where the

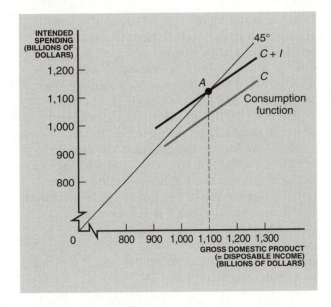

▪ **FIGURE 3.1**

Determination of Equilibrium Value of Gross Domestic Product

The consumption function is C, and the sum of consumption and investment expenditure is C + I. The equilibrium value of GDP is at the point where the C + I line intersects the 45-degree line, here $1,100 billion.

C + *I* line intersects the 45-degree line is the point where intended spending equals GDP? Because a 45-degree line is, by construction, a line that includes all points where the amount on the horizontal axis equals the amount on the vertical axis. In this case, as noted above,

intended spending is on the vertical axis and GDP is on the horizontal axis. Thus at point *A*, the point where the *C* + *I* line intersects the 45-degree line, intended spending must equal GDP, because point *A* is on the 45-degree line.

 TEST YOUR UNDERSTANDING

True or false?

_____ **1** The 45 degree line contains all points where total intended spending equals GDP.

_____ **2** The equilibrium level of GDP will be at the

point on the horizontal axis where the *C* + *I* line intersects the vertical axis.

_____ **3** The equilibrium level of GDP is at the point where the *C* + *I* line intersects the 45-degree line.

6 ▪ Effects of Changes in Intended Investment

Looking at the highly simplified model constructed in previous sections to explain the level of national output, what is the effect of a change in the amount of intended investment? Specifically, if firms increase their intended investment by $1 billion, what effect will this increase have on the equilibrium value of gross domestic product, according to this model?

This is an interesting question, the answer to which sheds light on the reasons for changes in national output. The following sections are devoted to answering it. For simplicity, assume that the change in investment is autonomous, not induced. An *autonomous* change in spending is one that *is not* due to a change in income or GDP. An *induced* change in spending is one that *is* due to a change in income or GDP.

THE SPENDING CHAIN: ONE STAGE AFTER ANOTHER

If there is a $1 billion increase in intended investment, the effects can be divided into a number of stages. In the first stage, firms spend an additional $1 billion on plant, equipment, or inventories. This extra $1 billion is received by workers and

suppliers as extra income, which results in a second stage of extra spending on final goods and services. How much of their extra $1 billion in income will the workers and suppliers spend? If the marginal propensity to consume is 0.6, they will spend 0.6 times $1 billion, or $.6 billion. This extra expenditure of $.6 billion is received by firms and disbursed to workers, suppliers, and owners as extra income, and so brings about a third stage of extra spending on final goods and services. How much of this extra income of $.6 billion will be spent? Since the marginal propensity to consume is 0.6, they will spend 60 percent of this $.6 billion, or $.36 billion. This extra expenditure of $.36 billion is received by firms and disbursed to workers, suppliers, and owners as extra income; this results in a fourth stage of spending, then a fifth stage, a sixth stage, and so on.

TOTALING UP THE STAGES

Table 3.4 shows the total increase in expenditure on final goods and services arising from the original $1 billion increase in intended investment. The total increase in expenditures is the increase in the first stage, plus the increase in the second

▪ TABLE 3.4

The Multiplier Process

STAGE	AMOUNT OF EXTRA SPENDING (billions of dollars)
1	1.00
2	.60
3	.36
4	.22
5	.13
6	.08
7	.05
8	.03
9 and beyond	.03
Total	2.50

stage, plus the increase in the third stage, and so on. Since there is an endless chain of stages, you cannot list all the increases. But because the successive increases in spending get smaller and smaller, you can determine their sum, which in this case is $2.5 billion. Thus the $1 billion increase in intended investment results—after all stages of the spending and responding process have worked themselves out—in a $2.5 billion increase in total expenditures on final goods and services. In other words, it results in a $2.5 billion increase in GDP.

WHY $2.5 BILLION? Why does the $1 billion increase in intended investment result in a $2.5 billion increase in GDP? Because 0.6 is the marginal propensity to consume, a $1 billion increase in intended investment will result in increased total spending of $(1 + .6 + .6^2 + .6^3 + \cdots)$ billions of dollars. This is evident from Table 3.4, which shows that the increased spending in the

first stage is $1 billion, the increased spending in the second stage is $.6 billion, the increased spending in the third stage is $.6^2$ billion, and so on. But it can be shown that $(1 + .6 + .6^2 + .6^3 + \cdots) = 1/(1 - .6)$. Consequently, since $1/(1 - .6) = 2.5$, the total increase in GDP must be $2.5 billion.

Since the marginal propensity to save equals $(1 - .6)$, another way to state the finding of the previous paragraph is: *a $1 billion increase in intended investment results in an increase in equilibrium GDP of 1/MPS billions of dollars, where MPS is the marginal propensity to save.*

THE MULTIPLIER

Since the marginal propensity to save is less than 1, it follows from the previous paragraph that a $1 billion increase in intended investment results in a more than $1 billion increase in GDP. In the simple model considered here, it results in an increase in equilibrium GDP of 1/MPS billions of dollars. The term 1/MPS is called the **multiplier** for its role in translating the spending change into the corresponding change in the level of output. If you want to estimate the effect of a given increase in intended investment on GDP, multiply the increase in intended investment by 1/MPS. The result will be the increase in GDP. This means that GDP is relatively sensitive to changes in intended investment.

The same multiplier holds for decreases in intended investment as well as for increases. That is, a dollar less of intended investment results in 1/MPS dollars less of GDP. Consequently, if you want to estimate the effect of a given change in intended investment (positive or negative) on GDP, multiply the change in intended investment by 1/MPS.

☑ **TEST YOUR UNDERSTANDING**

True or false?

_____ **1** The multiplier equals 1/MPS.

_____ **2** An autonomous increase in spending is due to a change in income or GDP.

_____ **3** An induced change in spending is not due to a change in income or GDP.

7 ▪ The Equilibrium Level of Gross Domestic Product: An Open Economy with Government Spending

Having taken up the determinants of GDP in the highly simplified case where the economy is closed (no exports, no imports) and where no government exists, you can now extend your analysis to include exports and imports as well as government spending. As pointed out in Chapter 1, gross domestic product equals consumption expenditure plus gross investment plus government expenditure plus net exports. Thus, if government expenditures and net exports are no longer assumed to be zero, total intended spending on final goods and services equals

$$C + I + G + (X - M_I),$$

where C is intended consumption expenditure, I is intended gross investment expenditure, G is intended government expenditure on final goods and services, X is intended exports, and M_I is intended imports.

For simplicity, take the values of G and $(X - M_I)$

as given. In Chapter 7, a discussion of the determinants and effects of government expenditure (and taxes) is provided. In Chapter 16, there is a treatment of the determinants and effects of net exports. For now, it is convenient to assume that both intended government expenditure and intended net exports are given (and the same, regardless of GDP). In other words, treat G and $(X - M_I)$ in the same way that you have treated I throughout this chapter.

For GDP to be at its equilibrium value, total intended spending on final goods and services must equal GDP. This is one of the central points stressed in this chapter. Thus, if the consumption function and intended investment are as shown in Table 3.3, and if intended government spending equals $30 billion, and intended net exports equal $10 billion, the equilibrium value of GDP equals $1,200 billion. To see why, look carefully at Table 3.5, which shows all the relevant infor-

▪ **TABLE 3.5**

Determination of Equilibrium Level of Gross Domestic Product (Billions of Dollars)

(1) GROSS DOMESTIC PRODUCT (= disposable income)[a]	(2) INTENDED CONSUMPTION EXPENDITURE	(3) INTENDED INVESTMENT	(4) INTENDED NET EXPORTS	(5) INTENDED GOVERNMENT EXPENDITURE	(6) TOTAL INTENDED SPENDING (2) + (3) + (4) + (5)	(7) TENDENCY OF NATIONAL OUTPUT
1,000	950	90	10	30	1,080	Upward
1,050	980	90	10	30	1,110	Upward
1,100	1,010	90	10	30	1,140	Upward
1,150	1,040	90	10	30	1,170	Upward
1,200	1,070	90	10	30	1,200	No change
1,250	1,100	90	10	30	1,230	Downward

[a] For simplicity, assume here, as in Table 3.3, that GDP equals disposable income.

mation. As you can see, if GDP is *less* than $1,200 billion, total intended spending is *more* than GDP; this means that there is a tendency for GDP to *rise,* since firms' inventories are going down. On the other hand, if GDP is *greater* than $1,200 billion, total intended spending is *less* than GDP; this means that there is a tendency for GDP to *fall,* since firms' inventories are going up. Thus, as shown in Table 3.5, total intended spending equals GDP only when GDP equals $1,200 billion; this means that this is the equilibrium value of GDP.

Figure 3.2 shows the same thing graphically. The $C + I + G + (X - M_l)$ line shows the level of total intended spending—that is, $C + I + G + (X - M_l)$ at each level of GDP. *The equilibrium level of GDP will be at the point on the horizontal axis where the $C + I + G + (X - M_l)$ line intersects the 45-degree line.* As shown in Figure 3.2, you get the same result as in Table 3.5: the equilibrium level of GDP is $1,200 billion. Of course, it will always be true that a tabular analysis and a graph of this sort will produce the same answer. (The $C + I$ line in Figure 3.1 is a special case of the $C + I + G + (X - M_l)$ line in Figure 3.2; it is valid when G and $(X - M_l)$ are zero, as assumed in Figure 3.1.)

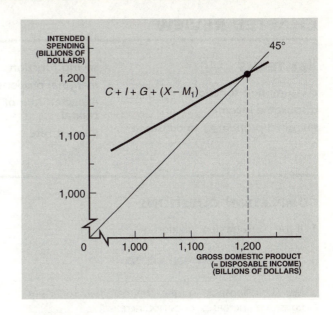

▪ **FIGURE 3.2**

Determination of Equilibrium Value of Gross Domestic Product, Open Economy with Government Spending

The $C + I + G + (X - M_l)$ line shows total intended spending—the sum of consumption, investment, and government expenditure plus net exports—at each level of GDP. The equilibrium value of GDP is at the point where the $C + I + G + (X - M_l)$ line intersects the 45-degree line, here $1,200 billion.

 TEST YOUR UNDERSTANDING

True or false?

____ **1** For GDP to be at its equilibrium value, total intended spending on final goods and services must equal GDP.

____ **2** The equilibrium level of GDP will be at the point on the horizontal axis where the $C + I + G + (X - M_l)$ line intersects the vertical axis.

Exercise

1 Suppose that the consumption function in a particular economy is given by the table to the right. Suppose that the sum of intended investment, government spending, and net exports increases from

DISPOSABLE INCOME	CONSUMPTION EXPENDITURE
(billions of dollars)	
400	300
500	360
600	410
700	440
800	470

$140 billion to $141 billion. Using a graph showing the old and new $C + I + G + (X - M_l)$ line, indicate what effect this will have on the equilibrium value of GDP. (Assume the price level is fixed.)

CHAPTER REVIEW

KEY TERMS

consumption function
disposable income
marginal propensity to consume

saving function
marginal propensity to save
expected rate of return from capital
interest rate

intended spending
45-degree line
multiplier

COMPLETION QUESTIONS

1 If the consumption function is

$$C = 400 + 0.7D,$$

where D is disposable income, the marginal propensity to consume (increases, does not increase) _____ as income rises. When $D = 1,000$, the marginal propensity to save is (positive, negative) _____. The marginal propensity to consume equals _____.

2 In general, a (more, less) _____ rapid rate of technological change is likely to result in more investment. Also, if a firm's sales go (up, down) _____, its need for plant, equipment, and inventories goes up. And the more (optimistic, pessimistic) _____ business expectations are, the greater the amount of investment.

3 If the consumption function is

$$C = 0.8D^2,$$

the marginal propensity to consume (increases, decreases, does not change) _____ as disposable income increases. This (is, is not) _____ a typical situation.

4 If the marginal propensity to consume is 2/3, the multiplier equals _____.

5 Holding disposable income constant, total consumption expenditure will tend to be higher if the public has few _____ on hand.

6 Holding disposable income constant, total consumption expenditure would be expected to be higher if a country's income became (more, less) _____ equally distributed.

7 The equilibrium value of GDP will be at the point on the horizontal axis where the _____ line intersects the _____ line. If GDP is below this point,

ANSWERS TO COMPLETION QUESTIONS

does not increase

positive
0.7

more

up

optimistic

increases
is not

3

durable goods

more

$C + I + G + (X - M_i)$
45 degree

intended spending (exceeds, is less than) _____
GDP. If GDP is above this point, intended spending
(exceeds, is less than) _____ GDP.

exceeds

is less than

NUMERICAL PROBLEMS

1 In the country of Chaos-on-the-Styx, there is the
following relationship between consumption expenditure and disposable income:

CONSUMPTION EXPENDITURE	DISPOSABLE INCOME
(billions of dollars)	
120	100
200	200
270	300
330	400
380	500
420	600

a Plot the consumption function for this country
below:

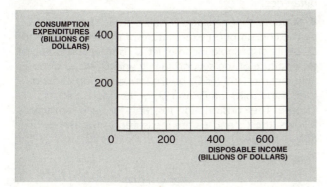

b What is the marginal propensity to consume when
disposable income is between $100 billion and $200
billion? When disposable income is between $300
billion and $400 billion? When disposable income is
between $500 billion and $600 billion?

c If Chaos-on-the-Styx consumes $5 billion more at
each level of disposable income than shown above, is
this a shift in the consumption function or a movement
along the consumption function?

d On the basis of the data shown above, plot the
saving function for Chaos-on-the-Styx on the following
grid:

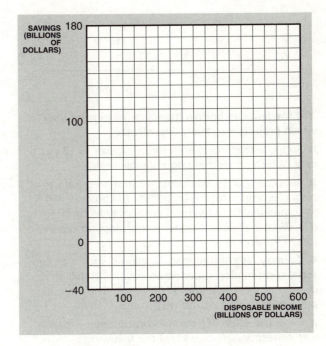

e What is the marginal propensity to save when disposable income is between $100 billion and $200
billion? When disposable income is between $300
billion and $400 billion? When disposable income is
between $500 billion and $600 billion?

f Combining your answers to parts b and e, what is
the sum of the marginal propensity to consume and
the marginal propensity to save under the three situations covered there?

g If, as described in part c, the country consumes $5
billion more at each level of disposable income than
shown above, draw the new consumption function (in
the graph provided in part a) and the new saving
function (in the graph provided in part d). If no
change occurs in either function, write "no change" as
your answer.

2 Suppose that the Bugsbane Music Box Company is considering investing in 7 projects, identified as *A* to *G* below. The expected rate of return from each project is given below.

PROJECT	EXPECTED RATE OF RETURN (percent)
A	12
B	8
C	7
D	15
E	25
F	11
G	9

a If the firm can borrow money at 10 percent interest, which projects are clearly unprofitable?

b Suppose that the interest rate increases to 13 percent. Which projects are unprofitable now?

3 Suppose that $1 of income is transferred from a person whose marginal propensity to consume is 0.9 to someone whose marginal propensity to consume is 0.8. What is the effect on total consumption expenditure? On saving?

4 Country *X*'s consumption function is such that personal consumption expenditure equals $90 billion if disposable income equals $100 billion. The marginal propensity to save equals 1/3.

a Fill in the value of personal consumption expenditure corresponding to each of the following values of disposable income:

DISPOSABLE INCOME	PERSONAL CONSUMPTION EXPENDITURE
(billions of dollars)	
150	_____
200	_____
250	_____
300	_____

b In 1998 Country *X*'s economists believe that the consumption function described above is no longer valid. In that year disposable income is $200 billion and personal consumption expenditure is $175 billion. Is there evidence of a shift in the consumption function?

c Can you tell what the new marginal propensity to consume is? If so, how? If not, why not?

5 Suppose that each of the following events occurred in 1998. Taken by itself, would it increase the amount that firms want to invest?

a A major invention occurs which makes it possible to convert coal into gasoline cheaply.

b A major recession occurs.

c One-fifth of California's capital stock is obliterated because of an earthquake.

d Interest rates fall by about 2 percentage points.

e Because of decreases in productivity, costs rise rapidly in the construction industry.

6 Jan Davis is given the job of forecasting the demand for railway passenger cars. She concludes that whenever the number of passenger-miles increases, the number of railway passenger cars purchased by the railroads goes up. Does this seem reasonable? In what way would you amend this proposition?

7 After World War II Japan devoted a much higher proportion of its GDP to investment than did the United States. What reasons can you give for this difference?

8 Suppose that a village contains three families. Let C_1 be the consumption expenditure of the first family and D_1 be its disposable income; let C_2 be the consumption expenditure of the second family and D_2 be its disposable income; and let C_3 be the consumption expenditure of the third family and D_3 be its disposable income. The consumption function for each family is as follows (the *C*s and *D*s are measured in thousands of dollars per year):

$$C_1 = 3 + 0.8D_1$$
$$C_2 = 2 + 0.8D_2$$
$$C_3 = 1 + 0.8D_3$$

a For the village as a whole, what is the marginal propensity to consume?

b Derive an equation for the consumption function in the village as a whole.

ANSWERS TO
TEST YOUR UNDERSTANDING

SECTION 1

TRUE OR FALSE: 1. False   2. False   3. True

SECTION 2

TRUE OR FALSE: 1. False   2. True   3. True

EXERCISES

1. 0.1. The marginal propensity to consume is unrelated to the income distribution, which is unrealistic.

2. a. $200 billion, b. 0.50, c. 0.50.

3. It varies.

SECTION 3

TRUE OR FALSE: 1. False

EXERCISES

1. This is untrue; firms can borrow.

2. a. Decrease; b. increase; c. increase; d. decrease; e. increase.

SECTION 4

TRUE OR FALSE: 1. True   2. False   3. False

EXERCISE

1. a. The complete table is:

GROSS DOMESTIC PRODUCT	INTENDED CONSUMPTION EXPENDITURE	INTENDED INVESTMENT	TOTAL INTENDED SPENDING
(millions of dollars)			
800	700	150	850
900	775	150	925
1,000	850	150	1,000
1,100	925	150	1,075

b. $1,000 million, since at this level of GDP total intended spending equals GDP.

c. $900 million minus $775 million, or $125 million.

d. When GDP equals $1,000 million, both intended saving and intended investment equals $150 million.

SECTION 5

TRUE OR FALSE: 1. True   2. False   3. True

SECTION 6

TRUE OR FALSE: 1. True   2. False   3. False

EXERCISES

1. $1 \div 0.2 = 5$.

2. The marginal propensity to save equals 0.25, and the multiplier equals 4.

SECTION 7

TRUE OR FALSE: 1. True   2. False

EXERCISE

1. GDP will increase by $2 billion, from $500 billion to $502 billion, as shown below.

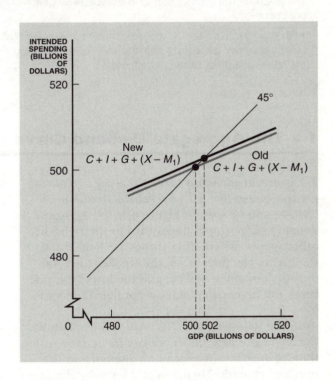

CHAPTER 4

Aggregate Demand and Supply Curves

Essentials of **Aggregate Demand and Supply Curves**

- The aggregate demand curve shows the level of real national output that will be demanded at each price level; the aggregate demand curve slopes downward to the right.

- The aggregate supply curve shows the level of real national output that will be supplied at each price level.

- In the short run, the equilibrium level of real national output and the equilibrium price level are given by the intersection of the aggregate demand curve and the short-run aggregate supply curve.

- In the long run, the aggregate supply curve is vertical, and the aggregate demand curve affects only the price level, not the level of real output. The level of real output equals its potential level regardless of the price level.

1 ■ The Aggregate Demand Curve

*The **aggregate demand curve** shows the level of real national output that will be demanded at each price level.* As can be seen in Figure 4.1, the aggregate demand curve slopes downward to the right. In other words, when other things are held equal, the higher the price level, the smaller the total output demanded will be; and the lower the price level, the higher the total output demanded will be.

In the following sections, you will learn how the aggregate demand curve can be derived, using the $C + I + G + (X - M_I)$ line discussed in the previous chapter. Then you will see why the aggregate demand curve slopes downward to the right.

EFFECTS OF CHANGES IN THE PRICE LEVEL ON THE $C + I + G + (X - M_I)$ LINE

The aggregate demand curve is intimately related to the $C + I + G + (X - M_I)$ line encountered in

Chapter 3. Recall that the $C + I + G + (X - M_I)$ line shows total intended spending at each level of GDP. To understand the relationship between the $C + I + G + (X - M_I)$ line and the aggregate demand curve, you must know one simple fact: *An increase in the price level lowers the* $C + I + G + (X - M_I)$ *line; a decrease in the price level raises the* $C + I + G + (X - M_I)$ *line.* The purpose of this section is to prove that this is true; in the next section you see how this fact can be used to derive the aggregate demand curve.

Suppose that the $C + I + G + (X - M_I)$ line is in position 1 in Figure 4.2. As we know from Chapter 3, this line is based on the assumption that the price level is constant. But suppose that the price level rises. Why will this lower the $C + I + G + (X - M_I)$ line (say from position 1 to position 2)? *One reason is that the increase in the price level will tend to push up interest rates.* In constructing the aggregate demand curve, it is assumed that the supply of money in the economy

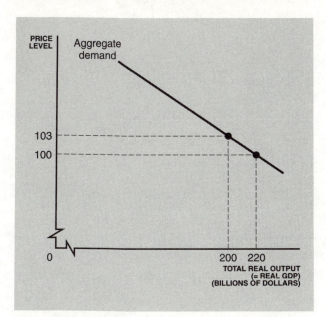

▪ **FIGURE 4.1**

Aggregate Demand Curve

The aggregate demand curve shows the level of total real output that will be demanded at each price level. If the price level is 100, a total real output of $220 billion will be demanded. If the price level is 103, a total real output of $200 billion will be demanded.

is fixed. An increase in the price level increases the average money cost of each transaction because the price of each good tends to be higher. Thus, if the price level increases considerably, people will have to hold more money in their wallets and checking accounts to pay for the items they want to buy. Since the supply of money is fixed, and the demand for money increases, there will be an increase in the price of money, which is the interest rate. (As pointed out in Chapter 3, the interest rate is the price paid to borrow money.)

When the interest rate goes up, firms that borrow money to invest in plant and equipment tend to cut down on their spending on these items. Due to the higher interest rates, the cost of borrowing money is greater, and hence some of these investment projects no longer seem prof-

itable. (Recall the discussion in Chapter 3.) Since I is reduced, $C + I + G + (X - M_I)$ must fall; this means that the $C + I + G + (X - M_I)$ line will shift downward. At each level of GDP, $C + I + G + (X - M_I)$ will be less than it was prior to the increase in the price level.

But the fact that an increase in the price level will tend to push up interest rates is not the only reason why it will lower the $C + I + G + (X - M_I)$ line. In addition, *the increase in the price level reduces the real value of the currency and government bonds held by the public.* Clearly, a $1,000 bank account represents less purchasing power if a hamburger costs $5 than if it costs $.50. Thus an increase in the price level reduces the real value of people's wealth, much of which is held in the form of assets (like currency, bank accounts, and government bonds) with a fixed dollar value. Such a reduction in people's wealth is likely to cause a downward shift in the consumption function. Since C is reduced, $C + I + G + (X - M_I)$ must fall, and the $C + I + G + (X - M_I)$ line will shift downward.

Still another reason why price level increases result in downward shifts in the $C + I + G + (X - M_I)$ line is as follows: *Increases in the price level tend to lower net exports because foreigners tend to respond to price increases by cutting back their purchases from you (and you purchase more from them).* For example, Europeans may be glad to buy U.S. computers at existing prices, but they may buy Japanese computers if prices double in the United States. Since $(X - M_I)$ is reduced, $C + I + G + (X - M_I)$ must fall, and the $C + I + G + (X - M_I)$ line will shift downward.

Just as an increase in the price level will shift the $C + I + G + (X - M_I)$ line downward (say from position 1 to position 2 in Figure 4.2), so a decrease in the price level will shift it upward (say from position 1 to position 3 in Figure 4.2). Why? Because a decrease in the price level will lower interest rates, and thus encourage investment spending. Also, the real value of the currency and government bonds held by the public will rise, and thus push up the consumption function. And net exports will tend to increase as foreigners step up their purchases from this country.

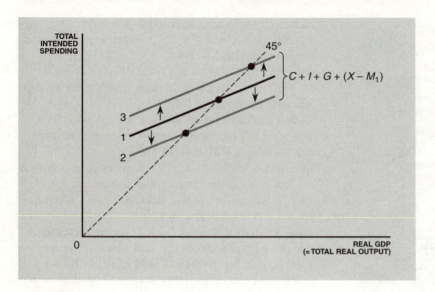

■ **FIGURE 4.2**

Effects of Changes in the Price Level on the $C + I + G + (X - M_I)$ **Line**

An increase in the price level (from OP_1 to OP_2) shifts the $C + I + G + (X - M_I)$ line downward (from position 1 to position 2). A decrease in the price level (from OP_1 to OP_3) shifts the $C + I + G + (X - M_I)$ line upward (from position 1 to position 3).

HOW TO DERIVE THE AGGREGATE DEMAND CURVE

On the basis of the analysis in the previous section, it is a simple matter to derive the aggregate demand curve—and to show how it is related to the $C + I + G + (X - M_I)$ line. Suppose that the price level is at its current level OP_1; this means that the $C + I + G + (X - M_I)$ line is in position 1 in the top panel of Figure 4.3. Clearly, the equilibrium level of real GDP is OQ_1, as shown there. What happens to real GDP if the price level rises to OP_2, which means that the $C + I + G + (X - M_I)$ line shifts to position 2 in the top panel in Figure 4.3? The equilibrium value of real GDP falls to OQ_2, as shown there. What happens to real GDP if the price level falls to OP_3, which means that the $C + I + G + (X - M_I)$ line shifts to position 3 in the top panel in Figure 4.3? The equilibrium value of real GDP rises to OQ_3, as shown there.

The bottom panel of Figure 4.3 shows the aggregate demand curve, which is derived from the shifts of the $C + I + G + (X - M_I)$ line in the top panel. To derive point A on the aggregate demand curve (which shows that real GDP is OQ_2 when the price level is OP_2), recall that when the price level is OP_2, the $C + I + G + (X - M_I)$ line is in position 2—and hence the equilibrium value of real GDP is OQ_2, according to the top panel. To derive point B on the aggregate demand curve (which shows that real GDP is OQ_1 when the price level is OP_1), recall that when the price level is OP_1, the $C + I + G + (X - M_I)$ line is in position 1—and hence the equilibrium value of real GDP is OQ_1, according to the top panel. To derive point C on the aggregate demand curve (which shows that real GDP is OQ_3 when the price level is OP_3), recall that when the price level is OP_3, the $C + I + G + (X - M_I)$ line is in position 3—and hence the equilibrium value of real GDP is OQ_3, according to the top panel.

REASONS FOR THE AGGREGATE DEMAND CURVE'S SHAPE

Take a close look at the bottom panel of Figure 4.3. Clearly, an increase in the price level (such as from OP_1 to OP_2) results in a reduction in total

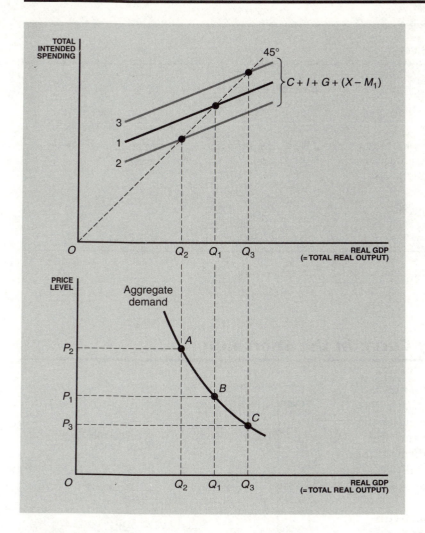

▪ FIGURE 4.3

▪ FIGURE 4.3

Derivation of the Aggregate Demand Curve

To derive point A on the aggregate demand curve, note that, if the price level equals OP_2, the $C + I + G + (X - M_I)$ line is in position 2, and equilibrium real GDP equals OQ_2. To derive point B, note that, if the price level equals OP_1, the $C + I + G + (X - M_I)$ line is in position 1, and equilibrium real GDP equals OQ_1

real output, and a decrease in the price level (such as from OP_1 to OP_3) results in a rise in total real output. Thus, on the basis of the analysis in the previous section, you find that the quantity of real national output that is demanded is inversely related to the price level. In other words, the aggregate demand curve slopes downward to the right, as shown in the bottom panel of Figure 4.3.

Basically, this is because increases in the price level lower the $C + I + G + (X - M_I)$ line, and decreases in the price level raise it.

In previous sections of this chapter, it was promised you would see why the aggregate demand curve slopes downward to the right. This discussion of Figure 4.3 provides the explanation.

TEST YOUR UNDERSTANDING

True or false?

_____ **1** The aggregate demand curve assumes that the money supply is fixed.

_____ **2** The aggregate demand curve slopes downward to the right for the same reason that a demand curve for an individual commodity slopes downward to the right.

_____ **3** An increase in the price level shifts the $C + I + G + (X − M_I)$ line upward.

Exercises

1 Give three reasons why, if the price level increases, the $C + I + G + (X − M_I)$ line will shift downward.

2 How does the aggregate demand curve differ from the demand curve for cotton?

2 ■ The Aggregate Supply Curve in the Short Run

The aggregate supply curve shows the level of real national output that will be supplied at each price level. Aggregate supply curves can pertain to either the short run or the long run. In the short run, the prices of all inputs are assumed to be fixed; in the long run, they are permitted to adjust fully to eliminate the unemployment or shortage of inputs (like labor).

As can be seen in Figure 4.4, the **short-run aggregate supply curve** slopes upward to the right. In other words, when other things are held equal, the higher the price level, the larger the total output supplied will be; and the lower the price level, the smaller the total output supplied will be.

WHY THE SHORT-RUN AGGREGATE SUPPLY CURVE SLOPES UPWARD TO THE RIGHT

To see why most economists believe that the short-run aggregate supply curve slopes upward to the right, let's begin by noting the obvious fact that firms are motivated to make profits. Because the profits earned by producing a unit of output equal the product's price minus the cost of producing it, increases in the product's price tend to

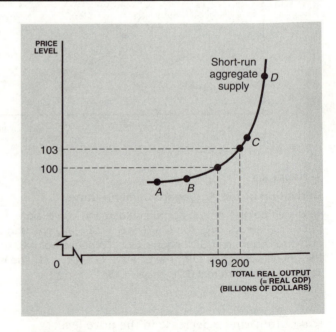

■ **FIGURE 4.4**

Short-Run Aggregate Supply Curve

The aggregate supply curve shows the level of total real output that will be supplied at each price level. If the price level is 100, a total real output of $190 billion will be supplied. If the price level is 103, a total real output of $200 billion will be supplied.

increase the firm's profits. (Why? Because the wages of workers and the prices of raw materials and other inputs are fixed in the short run.) Thus, *since increases in product prices tend to increase the profit per unit resulting from the production of the product, they tend to induce firms to produce more output.*

As an illustration, consider the Montgomery Corporation, which produces computer software that sells for $12 per unit. Suppose that it uses 1 hour of labor to produce 1 unit of software. If the wage rate is $10 per hour, and if you suppose for simplicity that Montgomery has no other costs, its profit per unit of output is

$$\$12 - \$10 = \$2.$$

Now suppose that the price of its software increases from $12 to $13 per unit. If the wage rate remains constant at $10 per hour, Montgomery's profit per unit of output increases to

$$\$13 - \$10 = \$3.$$

Given that production is more profitable than before the price increase, Montgomery is likely to increase its output.

WHY THE SHORT-RUN AGGREGATE SUPPLY CURVE GETS STEEPER

According to many economists, the short-run aggregate supply curve tends to be close to horizontal at relatively low levels of output, and tends to be steeper and steeper as output increases. To see why it is close to horizontal at relatively low output levels, note that there is likely to be considerable unutilized productive capacity under these conditions. If business picks up, firms are likely to increase their output by bringing this unutilized capacity back into operation. Since their costs per unit of output will not increase appreciably as their production rises, they will not raise price substantially. Thus the short-run aggregate supply curve will be close to horizontal.

On the other hand, at relatively high levels of output, production is pushing hard against capacity constraints, and it becomes increasingly difficult and costly for firms to increase their output further. Thus the short-run aggregate supply curve becomes steeper as output rises. Why? Because bigger and bigger increases in the price level are required to elicit a given additional amount of output. Moving from point B to point C to point D in Figure 4.4, the price level must go up by increasing amounts to elicit an additional billion dollars of real output. Eventually the short-run aggregate supply curve may become close to vertical.

Not all economists agree that the short-run aggregate supply curve has the shape indicated in Figure 4.4. The new classical macroeconomists (discussed in Chapter 2) argue that the short-run aggregate supply curve may be vertical if the changes in the price level that occur are expected. All that you should note at this point is that the shape of the short-run aggregate supply curve is a matter of controversy.

 TEST YOUR UNDERSTANDING

True or false?

_____ **1** The aggregate supply curve in the short run assumes that the prices of all inputs are variable.

_____ **2** In the horizontal range of the aggregate supply curve, it is assumed that there is little or no downward pressure on prices as output decreases because of the rigidity of wages and prices.

_____ **3** The vertical range of the aggregate supply curve is a simplification since it is generally possible to get a bit more output from any economic system.

Exercises

1 Why does the short-run aggregate supply curve become steeper and steeper as total real output increases?

2 How does the aggregate supply curve differ from the supply curve for cotton?

3 ▪ National Output and the Price Level

*In the short run, the **equilibrium level of real national output** and the **equilibrium price level** are given by the intersection of the aggregate demand curve and the short-run aggregate supply curve.* In Figure 4.5, the equilibrium level of real national output is $200 billion and the equilibrium price level is 103. Why? Because an equilibrium can occur only at a price level and level of real national output where aggregate demand equals aggregate supply.

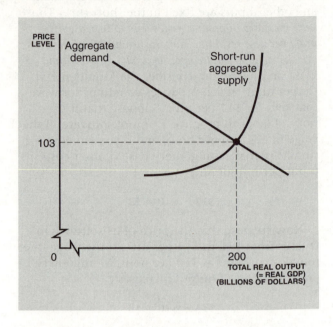

▪ **FIGURE 4.5**

Equilibrium Price Level and Total Real Output: Short Run

The equilibrium level of total real output and the equilibrium price level are given by the intersection of the aggregate demand and supply curves. Here the equilibrium price level is 103 and the equilibrium level of total real output is $200 billion.

 TEST YOUR UNDERSTANDING

True or false?

_____ **1** The aggregate demand curve is essentially the same in concept as the demand curve for a particular commodity like soap.

_____ **2** The aggregate supply curve is always a horizontal line.

Exercise

1 Why must an equilibrium occur only at a price level and level of national output where aggregate demand equals aggregate supply?

4 ▪ Shifts in the Aggregate Demand Curve

A host of factors can **shift the aggregate demand curve** to the right or the left. If firms demand more plant and equipment, perhaps because the expected profitability of additional productive capacity goes up or because interest rates go down, this will shift the aggregate demand curve to the right. If the government spends more money on goods and services, this too will shift it to the right. Or if the government reduces taxes, and thus provides consumers with more disposable income and encourages them to spend more on consumers' goods, this too will shift it to the right.

Anything that increases the amount of total real output demanded (when the price level is held constant) will shift the aggregate demand curve to the right. Thus developments abroad as well as at home can result in such a shift. For example, if the incomes of foreigners go up, this is likely to result in an increase in their demand for U.S. goods and serv-ices—and thus shift the aggregate demand curve to the right. Also, as you will see in subsequent chapters, if the government increases the money supply, this is likely to shift the aggregate demand curve to the right.

On the other hand, *anything that reduces the amount of total real output demanded (when the price level is held constant) will shift the aggregate demand curve to the left.* Thus, if firms demand less plant and equipment because the expected profitability of additional productive capacity goes down or because interest rates rise, this will shift the aggregate demand curve to the left. If the government spends less on goods and services, or if it raises taxes (and thus discourages consumer spending), this too will shift the aggregate demand curve to the left. And if the incomes of foreigners go down, this is still another reason why the aggregate demand curve may shift to the left.

 TEST YOUR UNDERSTANDING

True or false?

_____ **1** Regardless of the shape of the aggregate supply curve, a shift of the aggregate demand curve upward and to the right will result in inflation.

_____ **2** If the aggregate supply curve is very steep, a rightward shift of the aggregate demand curve will result in considerable inflation but a relatively small increase in real output.

_____ **3** Inflation generally is eliminated by a rightward shift of the aggregate demand curve.

_____ **4** In the horizontal range of the aggregate supply curve, a rightward shift of the aggregate demand curve has no effect on output.

_____ **5** In the vertical range of the aggregate supply curve, a leftward shift of the aggregate demand curve has no effect on the price level.

Exercise

1 Suppose that prices are rigid downward; that is, they can be increased but not decreased. The short-run aggregate supply curve (which is assumed here to have only a horizontal and a vertical range) is P_1BS, as shown on page 54. The aggregate demand curve shifts to the right (from D to D').

a. Will the movement of the aggregate demand curve from D to D' affect the short-run aggregate supply curve? If so, how and why?

b. If the aggregate demand curve were to return

to its original position (at *D*), would the short-run aggregate supply curve return to its original position? Why or why not?

c. Do the new classical macroeconomists assume that prices are rigid downward?

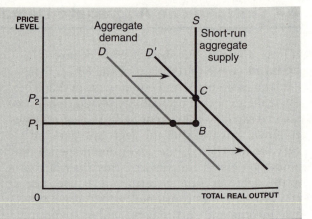

5 ▪ Shifts in the Short-Run Aggregate Supply Curve

Shifts occur in the short-run aggregate supply curve as well as in the aggregate demand curve. In this section, you consider the reasons for such shifts; in the next section, you analyze their effects.

THE WAGE RATE AND OTHER INPUT PRICES Input prices are held constant along a particular short-run aggregate supply curve. If they change, the curve shifts. Since the profit that a firm will make from a unit of output decreases as wage rates and other input prices go up, firms are likely to cut back on their output in response to increases in wage rates and other input prices. In other words, the aggregate supply curve is likely to shift to the *left* under these circumstances, as shown in Figure 4.6. On the other hand, if wage rates and other input prices go down, firms are likely to increase their output rate, since the profit that they will make from a unit of output will rise. In other words, the aggregate supply curve is likely to shift to the *right* under these circumstances.

TECHNOLOGY AND PRODUCTIVITY If improvements in technology occur, firms can produce more with a given set of resources, the result being that the profit from a unit of output increases. Consequently, firms are induced to produce more, the result being that the short-run aggregate supply curve shifts to the *right*.

AMOUNTS OF LABOR AND CAPITAL Clearly, the greater the amount of labor and capital available

in an economy, the more that can be produced. Thus, as the labor force grows and as firms invest in more and more capital, the short-run aggregate supply curve shifts to the *right*, since a greater output will be produced at each price level.

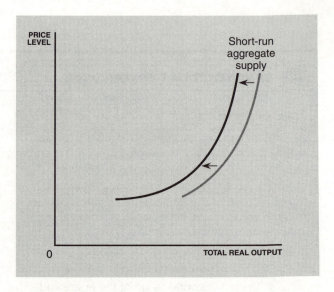

▪ **FIGURE 4.6**

Effect of an Increase in Wage Rates on the Short-Run Aggregate Supply Curve

If wage rates (or other input prices) increase, the short-run aggregate supply curve tends to shift to the left.

 TEST YOUR UNDERSTANDING

True or false?

_____ **1** The short-run aggregate supply curve is based on constant input prices.

_____ **2** If input prices increase, the short-run aggregate supply curve shifts to the right.

Exercises

1 What sorts of shifts in either the aggregate demand curve or the short-run aggregate supply curve (or both) would result in an increase in the price level but constant real output?

2 "One of the principal reasons why the short-run aggregate supply curve slopes upward to the right is that, as total real output increases, the quantity of money must increase as well; this means that the price level must rise, at least beyond some point." Do you agree?

3 Suppose that the aggregate demand curve is $P = 120 - Q$, where P is the price level and Q is real output (in billions of dollars). If the short-run aggregate supply curve (which is a horizontal line in the relevant range) shifts upward from $P = 102$ to $P = 104$, what will happen to real output?

4 Suppose that the Organization of Petroleum Exporting Countries (OPEC) raises oil prices by 50 percent in 1998. What effect will this have on the U.S. aggregate demand curve? On the U.S. short-run aggregate supply curve?

---

6 ▪ The Aggregate Supply Curve and Equilibrium in the Long Run

As pointed out earlier in this chapter, whereas input prices are fixed in the short run, in the long run they can adjust fully to eliminate the unemployment or shortage of inputs (like labor). Thus, _once these adjustments have been made, full employment will occur, and real national output will be at its potential level._ If the potential output of a particular economy is 100 billion (1997) dollars, this will be the amount of output supplied regardless of the price level.

In other words, _the aggregate supply curve is vertical in the long run._ Why? Because in the long run, wages and the prices of nonlabor inputs adjust. For example, there is time for old labor contracts to expire and for new ones to be negotiated. Shortages of raw materials are resolved. Unemployed workers find jobs. In the long run, input prices change by the same proportion as product prices, with the result that there is no incentive for firms to alter their output levels. When the price of everything changes by the

same proportion, the real value of everything is unchanged.

To see this, consider a firm that experiences a 10 percent increase in the price of its product. If this is due to a 10 percent increase in the general price level, this firm will in the long run pay 10 percent more for its inputs. Consequently, its profit per dollar of sales will be no different in the long run than it was before the 10 percent increase in the price level. Since this is the case, it has no incentive to produce more than it did before the increase in the price level.

Figure 4.7 shows the **long-run aggregate supply curve** for an economy with potential real GDP equal to OQ. It is a vertical line because the total quantity of goods and services produced when all inputs are efficiently and fully utilized does not depend on the price level. If the price level were to increase from 100 to 120 (and if wages and the prices of nonlabor inputs were to increase by the same proportion), the total quan-

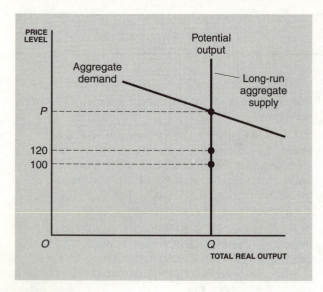

▪ **FIGURE 4.7**

Equilibrium Price Level and Total Real Output: Long Run

In the long run, the aggregate supply curve is vertical. The equilibrium level of total real output and the equilibrium price level are given by the intersection of the aggregate demand and supply curves. Here the equilibrium price level is *OP* and the equilibrium level of total real output is *OQ*.

tity of goods and services produced would remain equal to *OQ*.

In the long run, the equilibrium level of real national output and the equilibrium price level are given by the intersection of the aggregate demand curve and the long-run aggregate supply curve. Thus, in Figure 4.7, the equilibrium value of real GDP is *OQ*, and the equilibrium value of the price level is *OP*. Note that *the aggregate demand curve affects only the price level, not the level of real output, in the long run. The level of output equals its potential level regardless of the price level.* In Chapter 14, which deals with economic growth, you will study the factors determining the level of potential output—or, what amounts to the same thing, the factors determining the location of the long-run aggregate supply curve.

 TEST YOUR UNDERSTANDING

True or false?

_____ **1** The aggregate supply curve is horizontal in the long run.

_____ **2** In the long run, the aggregate demand curve affects only the price level, not the level of real output.

_____ **3** The level of output equals its potential level in the long run.

Exercises

1 Give the reason why, if the price level increases, the $C + I + G + (X - M_I)$ line will shift downward.

2 How does the aggregate demand curve differ from the demand curve for cotton?

■ CHAPTER REVIEW

KEY TERMS

aggregate demand curve

short-run aggregate supply curve

equilibrium real national output

equilibrium price level

shifts in aggregate demand curve

shifts in short-run aggregate supply curve

long-run aggregate supply curve

CHAPTER REVIEW

1 When an economy's resources are fully employed, its aggregate supply curve tends to be regarded as (horizontal, upward-sloping, vertical) _____. Further increases in the price level are not expected to result in _____ extra output.

2 A rightward shift of the aggregate demand curve will increase total output but not the price level if the economy is situated at the (horizontal, positively sloped, vertical) _____ range of the aggregate supply curve. It will increase the price level but not total output if the economy is situated at the (horizontal, positively sloped, vertical) _____ range of the aggregate supply curve. It will increase both the price level and total output if the economy is situated at the (horizontal, positively sloped, vertical) _____ range of the aggregate supply curve.

3 If the unemployment rate is very high, the government sometimes tries to shift the aggregate demand curve to the (right, left) _____. If inflation is a serious problem and the government wants to keep a tight lid on the price level, it sometimes tries to shift the aggregate demand curve to the (right, left) _____.

4 If the aggregate supply curve shifts to the right, the result is likely to be (increased, decreased) _____ total output and a (higher, lower) _____ price level. If the aggregate supply curve shifts to the left, the result is likely to be (increased, decreased) _____ total output and a (higher, lower) _____ price level.

5 A decrease in the price level (reduces, increases) _____ the real value of the currency and government bonds held by the public. This results in a(n) (decrease, increase) _____ in consumption expenditures. A decrease in the price level (increases, decreases) _____ the average money cost of a transaction, and thus (increases, decreases) _____ the demand for money; this will (increase, decrease)

ANSWERS TO COMPLETION QUESTIONS

vertical

considerable

horizontal

vertical

positively sloped

right

left

increased
lower

decreased
higher

increases

increase

decreases
decreases

_____ the interest rate. The aggregate demand curve slopes _____ to the _____.

decrease

downward, right

6 During the Great Depression, the aggregate demand curve shifted to the (left, right) _____. During World War II, the aggregate demand curve shifted to the (left, right) _____.

left

right

7 During the 1970s, the aggregate supply curve shifted to the (left, right) _____ because of the action of Arab and other oil-producing countries which (increased, decreased) _____ the price of oil substantially.

left

increased

NUMERICAL PROBLEMS

1 The aggregate demand curve for economy *A* is shown below.

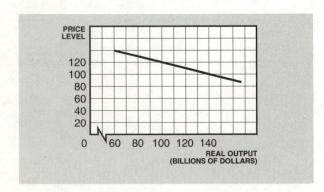

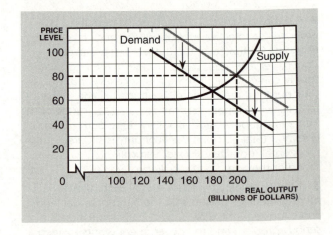

a If the aggregate supply curve is a vertical line at real output = $140 billion, what is the price level?

b If the aggregate supply curve is a horizontal line at price level = 120, what is real output?

c If the equation for the aggregate supply curve is $P = -40 + Q$, where P is the price level and Q is real output, what are the price level and real output?

2 The aggregate demand curve and the aggregate supply curve for economy *B* are shown on the right. As you can see, the aggregate demand curve shifts downward to the left.

a What is the effect of the shift of the aggregate demand curve on the price level? Specifically, what is the price level before and after the shift?

b What is the effect of the shift of the aggregate demand curve on real output? Specifically, what is real output before and after the shift?

c If economy *B* is devastated by an earthquake that reduces its productive capacity by 50 percent, how will the aggregate supply curve be affected?

3 Country *D*'s aggregate demand curve is $P = 1,000 - 2Q$, where P is the price level and Q is the total real output in billions of dollars. Country *D* is operating on the positively sloped range of its aggregate supply curve: When P increases by 1, Q increases by $1 billion. Suppose that the aggregate demand curve shifts to $P = 990 - 2Q$.

a Is this a shift of the aggregate demand curve to the left or to the right?

b What is the effect of this shift on the price level?

c What is the effect of this shift on total real output?

4 In Country E, the aggregate demand curve is $P = 5,000 - 5Q$, where P is the price level and Q is total real output (in billions of dollars). The aggregate supply curve (in the relevant range) is $P = 0.5Q$.

a What is the equilibrium value of the total real output?

b What is the equilibrium value of the price level?

 ANSWERS TO
TEST YOUR UNDERSTANDING

SECTION 1

TRUE OR FALSE: 1. True   2. False   3. False

EXERCISES

1. Increases in the price level will tend to push up interest rates, and this will lower investment. They will reduce the real value of currency and government debt held by the public, and thus reduce consumption expenditures. Also, they tend to lower net exports because foreigners cut back their purchases from us (and we purchase more from them).

2. The aggregate demand curve pertains to total real output, not the output of a particular good like cotton.

SECTION 2

TRUE OR FALSE: 1. False   2. True   3. True

EXERCISES

1. As production increases, it eventually pushes against capacity constraints, and it becomes increasingly difficult and costly for firms to increase their output further. Bigger and bigger increases in the price level are required to elicit an additional unit of output.

2. The aggregate supply curve pertains to total real output, not the output of a particular good like cotton.

SECTION 3

TRUE OR FALSE: 1. False   2. False

EXERCISE

1. Because an equilibrium can occur only at a price level and level of real national output where aggregate demand equals aggregate supply.

SECTION 4

TRUE OR FALSE: 1. False   2. True   3. False   4. False   5. False

EXERCISE

1. a. Yes. The movement of the aggregate demand curve from D to D' results in an increase in the price level from OP_1 to OP_2. Since the price level rises in this way, firms will be unwilling to supply the old amounts at the old prices. To supply the same amount of output as they formerly supplied when prices were OP_1, they now insist on prices of OP_2. Thus the short-run aggregate supply curve will shift from P_1BS to P_2CS.

b. No. Because prices are rigid downward, the short-run aggregate supply curve will remain at P_2CS (at least for a considerable period of time). Thus there is a "ratchet effect" whereby rightward shifts in the aggregate demand curve push the short-run aggregate supply curve upward, but leftward shifts in the aggregate demand curve do not push it back to its original position.[1]

c. No. They assume that wages and prices are completely flexible.

SECTION 5

TRUE OR FALSE: 1. True   2. False

EXERCISES

1. A leftward shift in the short-run aggregate supply curve, combined with a rightward shift in the aggregate demand curve, that kept their intersection at the same output level, would result in a constant real output but a higher price level.

2. No.

3. Q falls by $2 billion from $18 billion to $16 billion.

4. The principal effect will be on the short-run aggregate supply curve, which will shift upward and to the left. All other things equal, the result will be a higher price level and a lower real output level.

SECTION 6

TRUE OR FALSE: 1. False   2. True   3. True

EXERCISES

1. See Figure 4.2.

2. The aggregate demand curve pertains to total real output, not the output of a particular good like cotton.

---

[1] A ratchet is a device that permits a wheel to turn only one way.

CHAPTER 5

The Ups and Downs of the Economy

1 ■ Introduction

Practically everyone is interested in the ups and downs of the economy. Business executives must constantly be alert to increases and decreases in the market for their goods and services. Workers must be sensitive to whether the demand for their labor is growing or waning. Investors must forecast, as best they can, whether various firms will grow or decline. Government officials must try to head off the evils of unemployment and inflation. In this chapter, you look closely at the fluctuations that have occurred in recent decades in the U.S. economy.

2 ■ Anatomy of the Business Cycle

To illustrate what is meant by business fluctuations—or the business cycle—look at how national output has grown in the United States since World War I. Figure 5.1 shows the behavior of real GDP (in constant dollars) in the United States since 1919. It is clear that output has grown considerably during this period. Indeed, GDP is more than 6 times what it was 70 years ago. It is also clear that this growth has not been steady. On the contrary, although the long-term trend has been upward, there have been periods—like 1919–21, 1929–33, 1937–38, 1944–46, 1948–49, 1953–54, 1957–58, 1969–70, 1973–75, January–July 1980, 1981–82, and July 1990–March 1991—when national output has declined.

Recall that the potential GDP is the total amount of goods and services that could have been produced if there had been full employment. Figure 5.1 shows that national output tends to rise and approach (and perhaps exceed) its potential level (that is, its full-employment level), then falter and fall below this level, then rise to approach it once more, then fall below it again, and so on. For example, output remained close to its potential level in the prosperous mid-1920s, fell far below this level in the depressed 1930s, and rose again to this level once the United States entered World War II. This movement of national output is sometimes called the **business cycle,** but it must be recognized that these cycles are far from regular or consistent. On the contrary, they are very irregular.

Each cycle can be divided into four phases, as shown in Figure 5.2. The **trough** is the point where national output is lowest relative to its potential level (that is, its full-employment level). **Expansion** is the subsequent phase during which national output rises. The **peak** occurs when national output is highest relative to its potential level. Finally, **recession** is the subsequent phase during which national output falls.[1]

[1] More precisely, the peak and trough are generally defined in terms of deviations from the long-term trend of national output, rather than in terms of deviations from the potential (that is, the full-employment) level of national output. But the latter definition tends to be easier for beginners to grasp. Also, according to some people, a rough definition of a recession is at least two consecutive quarters of falling real GDP; it is not sufficient for output just to fall.

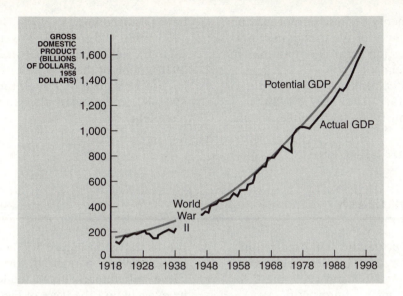

▪ **FIGURE 5.1**

Gross Domestic Product (in 1958 dollars), United States, 1919–1995, Excluding World War II

Real GDP has not grown steadily. Instead, it has tended to approach its potential level (that is, its full-employment level), then to falter and fall below this level, then to rise once more, and so on. This movement of national output is sometimes called the business cycle.

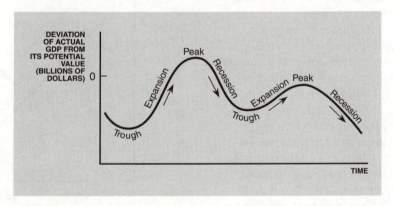

▪ **FIGURE 5.2**

Four Phases of Business Cycle

Each cycle can be divided into four phases: trough, expansion, peak, and recession.

Two other terms are frequently used to describe stages of the business cycle. A **depression** is a period when national output is well below its potential level; it is a severe recession. Depressions are, of course, periods of excessive unemployment. **Prosperity** is a period when national output is close to its potential level. Prosperity, if total spending is too high relative to potential output, can be a time of inflation. (Of course, in some business cycles, the peak may not be a period of prosperity because output may be below its potential level, or the trough may not be a period of depression because output may not be far below its potential level.)

From 1946 to 1995, peaks have occurred in 1948, 1953, 1957, 1960, 1969, 1973, 1980 (January), 1981, and 1990 (July), while troughs have occurred in 1949, 1954, 1958, 1961, 1970, 1975, 1980 (July), 1982 (November), and 1991 (March). Relative to the Great Depression of the 1930s, none of these recessions has been very long or very deep (although the 1974–75 and 1981–82 recessions resulted in substantial unemployment).

3 ■ The Great Crash

Now consider the fluctuations that occurred in the United States in recent decades. Begin with the late 1920s. During 1928 and 1929, the U.S. economy was in the midst of prosperity. As shown in Figure 5.1, gross domestic product was approximately equal to its potential value. Unemployment was low. Among the reasons for this prosperity was a relatively strong demand for machinery and equipment to produce new products (like the automobile, radio, telephone, and electric power) and to replace old machinery and equipment that had been worn out or outmoded during World War I and its aftermath.

The picture changed dramatically in 1929. After the stock market plummeted in October of that year, the economy headed down at a staggering pace. Real GDP fell by almost one-third between 1929 and 1933. Unemployment rose to an enormous 25 percent of the labor force by 1933. One important reason for this debacle was the severe contraction of gross private domestic investment. (Recall from Chapter 1 that gross private domestic investment is spending on tools, equipment, machinery, construction, and additional inventories.) Whereas gross private domestic investment was about $16 billion in 1929, it fell to about $1 billion in 1933. Another important factor was the decrease in the supply of money between 1929 and 1933. The money supply shrank from $26 billion in 1929 to $20 billion in 1933. This too tended to depress spending and output.

Put in terms of the aggregate demand and supply curves discussed in Chapter 4, the situation was as shown in Figure 5.3. For the reasons given in the previous paragraph, the aggregate demand curve shifted markedly to the left; and as would be expected on the basis of Figure 5.3, total real output and the price level fell between 1929 and 1933.

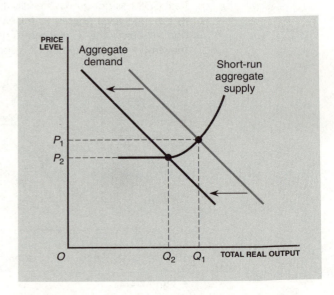

■ **FIGURE 5.3**

Shift of the Aggregate Demand Curve, 1929–1933

A marked shift to the left in the aggregate demand curve was the principal reason for the onset of the Great Depression. (For simplicity, assume that the aggregate supply curve remained fixed.) Output fell drastically (from OQ_1 to OQ_2); the price level fell too (from OP_1 to OP_2).

4 ▪ World War II and the Postwar Years

The United States remained mired in the Great Depression until World War II (and the mobilization period that preceded the war). To carry out the war effort, the government expanded the money supply and spent huge amounts on military personnel and equipment. One result of this increase in spending was a substantial increase in real GDP, which rose by about 75 percent between 1939 and 1945. Another result was a marked reduction in unemployment, as the armed forces expanded and as jobs opened up in defense plants (and elsewhere). Still another result was the appearance of serious inflationary pressures. While the aggregate demand curve marched to the right, there was severe upward pressure on the price level as increases in spending pushed national output close to its maximum. (See Figure 5.4.) To counter this pressure, the government instituted price controls and other measures that kept a temporary lid on prices; but when these controls were lifted after the termination of the war, the price level increased dramatically. Between 1945 and 1948, the Consumer Price Index rose by about 34 percent.

In 1948, the U.S. economy reached a peak, after which the unemployment rate increased to about 6 percent in 1949. But this recession was short lived, and expansion continued. In 1953, another recession began, but it was relatively mild. After the trough was reached in 1954, GDP rose substantially during the next several years, only to fall back once more in the recession of

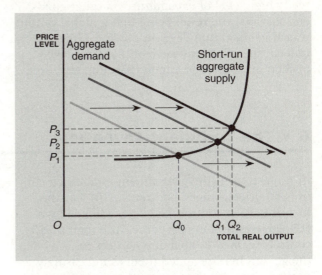

▪ **FIGURE 5.4**

Shifts of the Aggregate Demand Curve in World War II

When the United States entered World War II, the aggregate demand curve shifted to the right as military expenditures mushroomed. Output increased (from OQ_0 to OQ_1 to OQ_2), and inflationary pressures mounted. (For simplicity, assume that the aggregate supply curve remained fixed.) Much the same thing occurred during the Vietnam War.

1957–58. The fifties were characterized by relatively slow growth of real GDP and by a rising unemployment rate, both of which were the cause of considerable concern.

5 ▪ The Prosperous Sixties

As previous paragraphs have shown, the U.S. economy experienced recurring fluctuations prior to 1960. During the 1960s, this pattern seemed to change, as the United States entered a period of expansion which was uninterrupted until 1969. There were a variety of reasons for this extremely long expansion, including the tax cut of 1964, which (according to most economists) increased after-tax income and stimulated consumer spending and investment. The increases in the money supply during this period are also given credit for this long expansion.

While unemployment was being squeezed to minimal levels, inflation was heating up. An important factor here was the government's spending on the Vietnam War, which added to an already high level of expenditure on other goods and services, the result being that national output was at its maximum level in the late 1960s. Indeed, spending was so great that prices were pushed up at an increasingly alarming rate. And as prices rose, there was pressure for corresponding wage increases, which in turn pushed up firms' costs, and which were reflected in further price increases. By the end of the 1960s, inflation seemed to be the country's foremost economic problem.

6 ▪ The Turbulent Seventies

In August 1971, the government established controls on prices, wages, and rents. This was the first time such controls had been adopted by a U.S. government in peacetime. Although these controls seemed to hold down prices for a while, the government regarded them as increasingly unworkable, and they were phased out in 1973 and 1974. In early 1974, the price of oil was quadrupled by the OPEC countries. This, together with a hike in farm prices, spearheaded a severe inflationary spurt. (The Consumer Price Index rose by 12 percent during 1974.)

The middle and late 1970s were characterized by **stagflation,** a combination of high unemployment and high inflation. (The term stagflation was coined by putting together *stag*nation and in*flation*.) What caused this turn of events? According to many economists, it was because the short-run aggregate supply curve shifted upward and to the left. In their view, the situation was like that in Figure 5.5. This shift in the short-run aggregate supply curve both reduced national output and increased the price level. Since a reduction in national output means high unemployment and an increase in the price level means inflation, it is easy to see that such a shift in the short-run aggregate supply curve might result in stagflation.

But why did the short-run aggregate supply curve shift upward and to the left during the 1970s? The following reasons are among those frequently cited: (1) Food prices shot up, beginning in late 1972, because of bad crops around the world (and the disappearance of Peruvian anchovies, which caused a drop in the fish catch off the South American coast). (2) Many other raw-material prices increased rapidly, due to worldwide shortages. (3) As pointed out above, the price of crude oil increased greatly in 1974, 1979, and other years, due to the actions of Arab

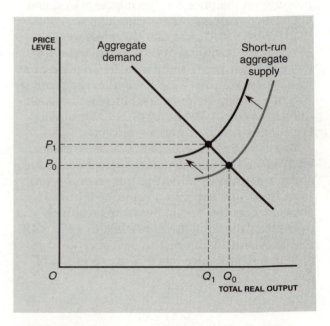

▪ **FIGURE 5.5**

Shift of the Short-Run Aggregate Supply Curve in the Seventies and Early Eighties

According to many economists, the stagflation of the late 1970s was due in considerable part to a shift of the short-run aggregate supply curve upward and to the left due to marked shortages and price increases for oil, food, and other materials. Assuming for simplicity that the aggregate demand curve remained fixed, output fell from OQ_0 to OQ_1, and the price level rose from OP_0 to OP_1.

and other oil-producing countries. Because of these factors, a given level of GDP could be produced only at a higher price level than was previ-

ously the case. That is, the short-run aggregate supply curve shifted upward and to the left.

7 ▪ The Eighties and Nineties

In the latter part of 1981, the economy slumped into another recession, and the unemployment rate increased considerably. By the middle of 1982, it was over 9 percent, and unemployment, not inflation, seemed to be the country's biggest economic problem. But this did not mean that inflation was quelled. The price level continued to rise, but at a less alarming rate.

November 1982 saw the trough of the recession. During 1983, real GDP grew by about 3.4 percent. Moreover, inflation continued to fall, the increase in the Consumer Price Index during 1983 being 3.2 percent. In 1984, the economy continued to show considerable strength, with real GDP growing at about 6.4 percent and inflation being held to about 4.3 percent. Throughout the rest of the 1980s, the growth of output continued, and became the longest peacetime expansion in U.S. history.

During 1990, many business executives, government officials, and ordinary citizens were con-

cerned that the economy was falling into a recession—and they were right. According to the Council of Economic Advisers, "After growing sluggishly for the first part of 1990, the economy entered a recession in the latter part of the year." During 1991, the government predicted that the recession would be short, but everyone recognized the fallibility of such predictions.

In fact, the trough occurred in March 1991, but it was followed by a slow recovery, and there was considerable attention devoted to this in the press and elsewhere. One casualty was George Bush, who lost the presidency in part for this reason. During 1993, the economy began to pick up steam and in 1994 there were unmistakable signs of rapid and unsustainable growth. Although inflation had not increased perceptibly, many observers were holding their breath. During 1995 and 1996, the boom continued, although many pundits were saying that it was looking old and tired.

8 ▪ Applying Economics: Forecasting

The following two problems are concerned with ways to forecast business fluctuations.

PROBLEM 5.1 Perhaps the simplest way to forecast business fluctuations is to use **leading indicators,** which are certain economic series that typically go down or up before national output does. The National Bureau of Economic Research, founded by Wesley C. Mitchell (1874–1948), has carried out detailed and painstaking research to examine the behavior of various economic variables over a long pe-

riod of time, in some cases as long as 100 years. The bureau has attempted to find out whether each variable goes down before, at, or after the peak of the business cycle, and whether it turns up before, at, or after the trough. Variables that go down before the peak and up before the trough are called **leading series.** Variables that go down at the peak and up at the trough are called **coincident series.** And variables that go down after the peak and up after the trough are called **lagging series.**

a. Would you expect new orders for durable

goods to be a leading indicator? Why or why not?

b. Would you expect stock prices to be a leading indicator? Why or why not?

c. Would you expect GDP to be a leading indicator? Why or why not?

d. If a large number of leading indicators turn down, this is viewed as a sign of a coming peak. If a large number turn up, this is thought to signal an impending trough. The Department of Commerce has published a composite index that is a weighted average of about a dozen leading indicators. The behavior of this index from 1950 to 1990 is shown in Figure 5.6. Does this index seem to be very reliable?

e. In 1952 and 1962, the index of leading indicators turned down. Were these signals correct?

PROBLEM 5.2   Leading indicators have been used primarily to spot turning points—peaks and troughs. They are of little or no use in predicting GDP. *One simple way of trying to forecast GDP is to treat certain components of total spending as given and to use these components to forecast the total.* This method is sometimes used by the president's Council of Economic Advisers, among others. For example, suppose that you decide to forecast investment spending, government expenditures, and net exports as a first step, after which you will use these forecasts to predict GDP. As you know from Chapter 1, investment spending is made up of three parts: expenditures on plant and equipment, residential construction, and changes in inventories. *To forecast expenditures on plant and equipment, the results of surveys of firms' expenditure plans for the next year are helpful.* The Department of Commerce and the Securities and Exchange Commission send out questionnaires (at the beginning of each year) to a large number of firms, asking them how much they plan to spend on plant and equipment during the year.

These surveys can help us forecast business expenditures on plant and equipment, but what about the other parts of investment spending—residential construction and changes in inven-

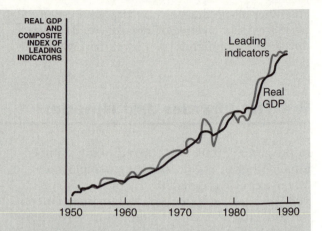

▪ **FIGURE 5.6**

Leading Indicators and Real GDP, United States, 1950–1990

Both GDP and the composite index of leading indicators are plotted against time, the scales of the two series being constructed so that they can readily be compared. As you can see, the leading indicators often give warnings of impending troughs or peaks.

tories? Lots of techniques are used to forecast them. *Some people use construction contracts and similar indicators as the basis for forecasts of residential construction. For inventory changes, some people watch surveys (like those that have been carried out by* Fortune *magazine and the Commerce Department) which ask companies about their inventory plans.*

Turning to government expenditures and net exports, there are ways to forecast them too, but they will not be described in detail here.

a. Suppose that your best estimate is that investment spending plus government expenditure plus net exports will equal $600 billion next year. Derive an equation relating next year's GDP to consumption expenditure next year.

b. If consumers in the past have devoted about 90 percent of their disposable income to consumption expenditure, and if disposable income has been about 70 percent of GDP, what is the relationship between consumption expenditure and GDP?

c. Using the results of parts a and b, forecast GDP next year.

d. What are the key assumptions underlying your forecast?

9 ▪ Applying Economics: Forecasting in Action

The following two problems deal with actual experience with forecasting techniques.

PROBLEM 5.3 Alan Greenspan, the chairman of the Federal Reserve Board, is a distinguished economist. In the Senate hearings prior to his confirmation, the accuracy of his forecasts was questioned by Senator William Proxmire of Wisconsin, who pointed out that Dr. Greenspan, when he served as chairman of former president Ford's Council of Economic Advisers, had published forecasts that overestimated the growth of GDP and underestimated the rate of inflation. When he left the Council of Economic Advisers, Dr. Greenspan returned to Townsend-Greenspan and Company, an economic forecasting firm, where his forecasts of the annual percentage change in GDP (in 1982 dollars) and of the rate of increase of the price level were as follows:

| | PERCENT INCREASE | | | |
| | IN REAL GDP | | IN PRICE LEVEL | |
YEAR	FORECAST	ACTUAL	FORECAST	ACTUAL
1978	4.8	3.3	6.5	7.3
1979	2.5	2.5	7.6	8.9
1980	− 1.6	− 0.2	8.4	9.0
1981	1.1	1.9	9.4	9.7
1982	− 1.0	− 2.5	8.4	6.4
1983	1.9	3.6	6.2	3.9
1984	5.8	6.4	4.9	3.8
1985	3.6	2.7	4.5	3.3
1986	2.9	2.5	4.4	2.7
1987	2.4	2.9	2.9	3.0

a. Did Dr. Greenspan anticipate that there would be a drop in real GDP in 1980 and 1982?

b. Did he foresee that there would be an increase in real GDP in 1983?

c. Did he anticipate the weaker (than in previous years) growth of the economy in 1985 and 1986?

d. Did he foresee the steep rise in inflation from 1978 to 1980?

e. Did he anticipate the marked decline in inflation during the 1980s?

PROBLEM 5.4 When World War II was coming to an end, government economists, using the forecasting techniques discussed in Problem 5.2, forecasted that GDP in 1946 would be about $170 billion. This forecast caused a severe chill in many parts of the government, as well as among business executives and consumers. A GDP of about $170 billion would have meant a great deal of unemployment. In fact, the GDP in 1946 turned out to be about $190 billion.

a. The economists who prepared this forecast assumed that the consumption function would be the same in 1946 as before the war. Were there any reasons to believe that the consumption function had shifted upward? (Hint: People had saved lots of money during the war, and there had been rationing of many goods.)

b. Suppose that the consumption function shifted upward by $8 billion. If the marginal propensity to save was 0.4, would this shift account for the forecasting error? Why or why not?

c. Under the circumstances described in part b, what would have been the multiplier?

d. Was unemployment in 1946 higher or lower than the government economists' forecast implied? Why?

e. Was this early forecast as accurate as those of Alan Greenspan 40 years later?

10 ■ Applying Economics: An Inflationary Gap

The following two problems deal with the nature of an inflationary gap and with how the economy, left to its own devices, would eliminate such a gap. Much more will be said about inflationary gaps in Chapter 6. This is just a beginning.

PROBLEM 5.5 The equilibrium value of real national product, in the short run, may not equal its potential value. In other words, equilibrium national output may not equal the level that would prevail if there were full employment. As shown in Figure 5.1, there frequently has been a gap between actual and potential GDP in the United States. In some periods, actual GDP exceeded potential GDP, due to an increase in aggregate demand when full employment had already been reached. For example, such a situation occurred in the late 1960s when the Vietnam War heated up. If such a situation exists, it is said that there is an inflationary gap.

a. In Figure 5.7, is there an inflationary gap if the short-run aggregate supply curve is S_1?

b. In such a situation, will jobs be plentiful? Will labor be in short supply?

c. Will unemployment be less than the normal frictional level?

d. Will unemployment be zero?

PROBLEM 5.6 The economy, if there is an inflationary gap, will tend to move toward full em-

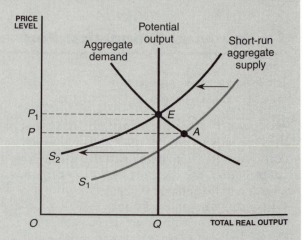

■ **FIGURE 5.7**

ployment. In the absence of government intervention, wage rates will be bid up, and firms' costs will rise. Inflation will occur.

a. In Figure 5.7, will the short-run aggregate supply curve tend to shift? If so, will it shift to the left or the right? Why?

b. Will real output tend to change? If so, will it increase or decrease?

c. In Figure 5.7, what is the eventual equilibrium point? Why?

d. Why do many policymakers desire to avoid this way of eliminating an inflationary gap?

11 ■ Applying Economics: A Recessionary Gap

The final two problems deal with a recessionary gap and with how the economy, left to its own devices, would eliminate such a gap. Recession-

ary gaps will be taken up in more detail in Chapter 6. The problems discussed here are only a start.

PROBLEM 5.7   If the short-run equilibrium value of real national product is below, not above, its potential value, it is said that there is a recessionary gap. In such a situation, the equilibrium value of real national output falls short of its potential value, the result being substantial unemployment.

a.   In Figure 5.8, is there a recessionary gap if the short-run aggregate supply curve is S_3?

b.   In such a situation, will there be a tendency for wage rates and other input prices to fall? If so, why?

c.   Will the short-run aggregate supply curve shift? If so, will it shift to the left or to the right?

d.   In Figure 5.8, what is the eventual equilibrium point?

e.   Why do many policymakers desire to avoid this way of eliminating a recessionary gap?

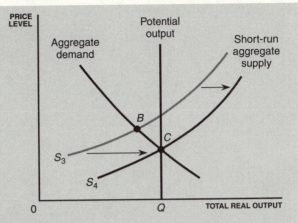

▪ **FIGURE 5.8**

PROBLEM 5.8   Suppose that prices are rigid downward; that is, they can be increased but not decreased. The short-run aggregate supply curve is P_1BS in Figure 5.9.

a.   If the aggregate demand curve is D, is there a recessionary gap? Why or why not?

b.   If the aggregate demand curve shifts from D to D', will this affect the short-run aggregate supply curve? If so, how and why?

c.   If the aggregate demand curve were to return to its original position (at D), would the short-run aggregate supply curve return to its original position? Why or why not?

d.   Is it realistic to suppose that prices are rigid downward? Why or why not?

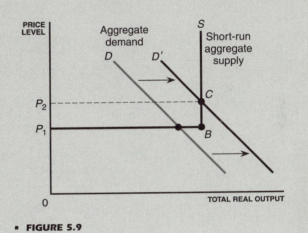

▪ **FIGURE 5.9**

12 ▪ Conclusion

Pick any major newspaper or television news show. Chances are that there will be a feature story on the ups or downs of the U.S. economy. To understand these stories—and equally important, to recognize errors, omissions, and biases in them—you have to know some economics. The material in Chapters 1 to 4 is essential; it is part of the alphabet of economics. Just as you wouldn't get very far without mastering the alphabet, it's a safe bet you won't get very far without mastering the ABCs of economics.

PART TWO

Fiscal Policy and Budget Deficits

CHAPTER 6
Fiscal Policy

Essentials of **Fiscal Policy**

- If the economy is suffering from excessive unemployment, and output is well below its potential level, a recessionary gap is said to exist.

- In response to a recessionary gap, governments often have increased their spending or have reduced taxes. Unfortunately, the effect has sometimes been inflationary pressure.

- If the economy is suffering from severe inflation, an inflationary gap is said to exist.

- In response to an inflationary gap, governments can cut their spending or raise taxes. Unfortunately, the result has sometimes been a rise in unemployment.

- Changes in taxes and government spending aimed at stabilizing the economy in the short run may not be most effective in promoting the long-term health of the economy.

1 ▪ Strategies for Dealing with a Recessionary Gap

Suppose that the economy is suffering from excessive unemployment and that output is well below its potential level; this means that there is a **recessionary gap.** In particular, assume that the situation is as shown in the left-hand panel of Figure 6.1. As you can see, the equilibrium value of total real output is OQ_1, which is well below OQ_0, the economy's potential output. Given this situation, there are several ways in which output can be pushed up to its potential level—so full employment can be restored. One way is to wait for wage rates and other input prices to fall in response to the high unemployment rate, and thus shift the short-run aggregate supply curve to the right, as shown in the middle panel of Figure 6.1. Although some economists believe that such a strategy is feasible, most believe that it would take too long because, in their view, wages tend to be quite sticky. In Chapter 12, you will review the controversies and evidence on this score. For now, it is sufficient to say that governments fre-

quently want to do what they can to hasten the movement toward full employment.

Another way to deal with the recessionary gap in the left-hand panel of Figure 6.1 is to wait for spending by the private sector to pick up, and thus shift the aggregate demand curve to the right, as shown in the right-hand panel of Figure 6.1. Here too the problem is that it may take a painfully long time for such a shift in the aggregate demand curve to occur. As you saw in Chapter 2, some recessions have gone on for years.

Still another strategy is for the government to increase its spending and/or to cut taxes, and thus shift the aggregate demand curve to the right. As in the case described in the previous paragraph, such a shift in the aggregate demand curve can push output up to its potential level, as shown in the right-hand panel of Figure 6.1. Governments eager to restore full employment often have used fiscal policy in this way. One problem has been that the stimulus resulting from their actions has sometimes been felt when spending by the private sector has picked up, the consequence being inflationary pressure because the aggregate de-mand curve has been pushed too far to the right. Much more will be said below and in subsequent chapters concerning the pros and cons of anti-recessionary fiscal policies.

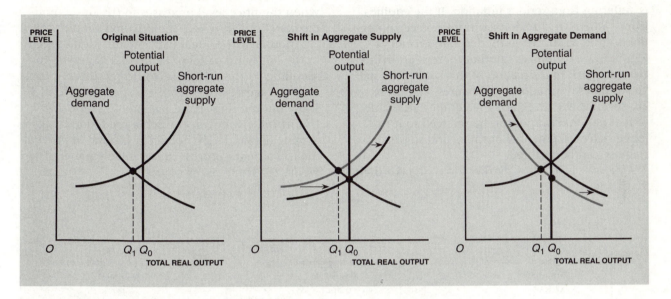

▪ **FIGURE 6.1**

Alternative Ways of Dealing with a Recessionary Gap

As shown in the left-hand panel, equilibrium output is OQ_1, which is well below the potential output of OQ_0. Thus there is a recessionary gap. One way to deal with this situation is to wait for wages and other input prices to fall, and thus push the short-run aggregate supply curve to the right, as shown in the middle panel. Another way is to wait for an increase in private-sector spending to push the aggregate demand curve to the right, as shown in the right-hand panel. Still another way is for the government to shift the aggregate demand curve to the right (as in the right-hand panel) by increasing its own spending and/or by cutting taxes.

 TEST YOUR UNDERSTANDING

True or false?

_____ **1** Increases in government spending have no effect on the equilibrium level of GDP.

_____ **2** If the government cuts taxes, it can shift the aggregate demand curve to the right, and thus help to reduce excessive unemployment.

_____ **3** Increased spending by the private sector can cure a recession, but it may take a long time to do so.

2 ▪ Strategies for Dealing with an Inflationary Gap

Having seen how fiscal policy has been used to deal with an economy suffering from excessive unemployment, turn to a case where an economy is suffering from serious inflation. If the equilibrium value of real national output exceeds potential output, as shown in the left-hand panel of Figure 6.2, economists say that there is an **inflationary gap.** In a situation of this sort, there will be substantial inflationary pressures, and there are several ways in which the equilibrium value of real national output can be reduced so it no longer exceeds potential output—and so price stability can be restored.

One way is to allow market forces to take their course. Wages and other input prices will be bid up, and thus shift the short-run aggregate supply curve to the left. The result will be inflation, but when the price level increases to OP_0 in the middle panel of Figure 6.2, the inflation should stop.

Another way to deal with the inflationary gap in the left-hand panel of Figure 6.2 is to wait for spending by the private sector to recede, and thus shift the aggregate demand curve to the left, as shown in the right-hand panel of Figure 6.2. Unfortunately, however, such a reduction in aggregate demand may not occur in time to prevent the inflationary process in the middle panel of Figure 6.2 from taking place.

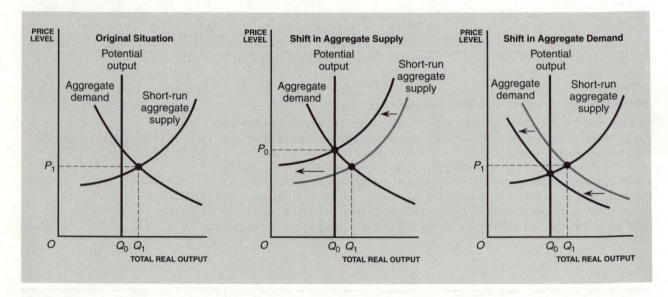

▪ **FIGURE 6.2**

Alternative Ways of Dealing with an Inflationary Gap

As shown in the left-hand panel, equilibrium output is OQ_1, which is well above the potential output of OQ_0. Thus there is an inflationary gap. One way to deal with this situation is to allow wages and other input prices to rise, and thus push the short-run aggregate supply curve to the left, as shown in the middle panel. Another way is to wait for a decrease in private-sector spending to push the aggregate demand curve to the left, as shown in the right-hand panel. Still another way is for the government to shift the aggregate demand curve to the left (as in the right-hand panel) by cutting its own spending and/or by raising taxes.

Still another strategy is for the government to cut its spending and/or raise taxes, and thus shift the aggregate demand curve to the left. As in the case described in the previous paragraph, such a shift in the aggregate demand curve can push output down to its potential level, as shown in the right-hand panel of Figure 6.2. Governments, eager to cut back inflationary pressures, often have used fiscal policy in this way. One problem is that the economic restraint resulting from their actions has sometimes been felt when spending by the private sector has receded, the consequence being that output has fallen below its potential level, and unemployment has risen. Much more will be said below and in subsequent chapters concerning the pros and cons of anti-inflationary fiscal policies.

☑ TEST YOUR UNDERSTANDING

True or false?

____ **1** If the equilibrium value of real national output exceeds potential output, there is a recessionary gap.

____ **2** One way to reduce an inflationary gap is to allow market forces to take their course.

____ **3** Another way to reduce an inflationary gap is for the government to reduce its spending.

Exercises

1 Suppose that the consumption function in a particular economy is given by the following table:

DISPOSABLE INCOME	CONSUMPTION EXPENDITURE
(billions of dollars)	
400	350
500	425
600	500
700	575
800	650

If taxes are 20 percent of GDP, fill in the blanks below.

GDP	CONSUMPTION EXPENDITURE
(billions of dollars)	
____	350
____	425
____	500
____	575
____	650

2 Use aggregate demand and supply curves to indicate how governments have used fiscal policy in their attempts to snuff out inflation.

---

3 ▪ Expansionary Fiscal Policy and Budget Deficits

Having seen how fiscal policy can be used in an attempt to stabilize the economy, you must recognize that expansionary fiscal policies—policies aimed at reducing recessionary gaps—frequently result in budget **deficits;** that is, government spending exceeds tax revenues. To meet the shortfall, the government has borrowed from the public. In other words, the government has sold bonds, notes, and other government IOUs of various kinds to the public. According to many economists, the government's demand for funds tends to raise interest rates, which is likely to reduce investment expenditures.

It is not hard to see why the government's demand for loanable funds will tend to raise interest rates. After all, the interest rate is the price paid for borrowing money. If the government increases the demand for loanable funds, the

price of loanable funds—the interest rate—would be expected to rise. A thorough discussion of the budget deficit is postponed to Chapters 7 and 8. For now, the important point to bear in mind is that *the government must somehow finance whatever deficits it runs.* And according to most economists, its financing of these deficits is likely to affect real GDP and the performance of the economy.

 TEST YOUR UNDERSTANDING

True or false?

____ **1** A deficit occurs when the government spends more than it collects in taxes.

____ **2** According to many economists, the government's demand for funds pushes up interest rates.

____ **3** The interest rate is the price of loanable funds.

4 ▪ Automatic Stabilizers

Governments, in their efforts to fight off serious unemployment or inflation, get help from some **automatic stabilizers:** structural features of the system of taxes and transfer payments that tend to stabilize national output. Although these economic stabilizers cannot do all that is required to keep the economy on an even keel, they help a lot. As soon as the economy turns down and unemployment mounts, they give the economy a helpful shot in the arm. As soon as the economy gets overheated and inflation crops up, they tend to restrain it. These stabilizers are automatic because they come into play without the need for new legislation or administrative decisions.

TAX REVENUES

Changes in income tax revenues are an important automatic stabilizer. The U.S. federal system relies heavily on the income tax. The amount of income tax collected by the federal government goes up with increases in GDP and goes down with decreases in GDP. This, of course, is just what you want to occur. When output falls off and unemployment mounts, tax collections fall

off too, so disposable income falls less than GDP. This means less of a fall in consumption expenditure, which tends to brake the fall in GDP. When output rises too fast and the economy begins to suffer from serious inflation, tax collections rise too; this tends to brake the increase in GDP. Of course, corporation income taxes, as well as personal income taxes, play a significant role here.

UNEMPLOYMENT COMPENSATION AND WELFARE PAYMENTS

Unemployment compensation is paid to workers who are laid off, according to a system that has evolved over many previous decades. When an unemployed worker goes back to work, he or she stops receiving unemployment compensation. Thus, when GDP falls off and unemployment mounts, the tax collections to finance unemployment compensation go down (because of lower employment), while the amount paid out to unemployed workers goes up. On the other hand, when GDP rises too fast and the economy begins to suffer from serious inflation, the tax collections to finance unemployment compensation go up, while the amount paid out goes down because there is much less unemployment. Again, this is just what you want to see happen. The fall in spending is moderated when unemployment is high, and the increase in spending is curbed when there are serious inflationary pressures. Various welfare programs have the same kind of automatic stabilizing effect on the economy.

 TEST YOUR UNDERSTANDING

True or false?

_____ **1** All the automatic stabilizers do is cut down on variations in unemployment and inflation, not eliminate them.

_____ **2** Changes in income tax revenues are an important automatic stabilizer.

_____ **3** When GDP rises too fast, tax collections to finance unemployment compensation go down.

---

5 ▪ Discretionary Fiscal Policy

The federal government frequently has changed tax rates—as well as expenditures—in an attempt to cope with unemployment and inflation. The following kinds of measures have been adopted.

1 THE GOVERNMENT HAS VARIED TAX RATES. When there has been considerable unemployment, the government sometimes has cut tax rates, as it did in 1975. Or if inflation has been the problem, the government sometimes has increased taxes, as it did in 1968 when, after considerable political maneuvering and buckpassing, the Congress was finally persuaded to put through a 10 percent tax surcharge to try to moderate the inflation caused by the Vietnam War. However, temporary tax changes are likely to have less effect than permanent ones, since consumption expenditure would be expected to be influenced less by transitory changes in income than by permanent changes.

2 THE GOVERNMENT HAS VARIED ITS EXPENDITURE FOR GOODS AND SERVICES. When increased unemployment seemed to be in the wind, it sometimes stepped up outlays on roads, urban reconstruction, and other public programs. Of course, these programs must be well thought out and socially productive. There is no sense in pushing through wasteful and foolish spending programs merely to make jobs. Or when, as in 1969, the economy has been plagued by inflation, the government sometimes has (as President Nixon ordered) stopped new federal construction programs temporarily.

3 THE GOVERNMENT HAS VARIED WELFARE PAYMENTS AND OTHER TYPES OF TRANSFER PAYMENTS. For example, when unemployment has been regarded as excessive, the federal government has sometimes helped the states to extend the length of time that the unemployed can receive unemployment compensation; this was expected to help reduce the unemployment rate.

PROBLEMS IN FORMULATING EFFECTIVE DISCRETIONARY FISCAL POLICY

While governments frequently carry out discretionary fiscal policies, it is important to recognize the many types of problems that can interfere with the effectiveness of such policies. *One of the big disadvantages of public works and similar spending programs is that they take so long to get started.* Plans must be made, land must be acquired, and preliminary construction studies must be carried out. By the time the expenditures are finally made and have an effect, the dangers of excessive unemployment may have given way to dangers of inflation, so that the spending, coming too late, may do more harm than good.

In recent years, there has been a widespread

feeling that government expenditures should be set on the basis of their long-run desirability and productivity. The optimal level of government expenditure is at the point where the value of the extra benefits to be derived from an extra dollar of government expenditure is at least equal to the dollar of cost. This optimal level is unlikely to change much in the short run, and it would be wasteful to spend more—or less—than this amount for stabilization purposes when tax changes could be used instead. Thus many economists believe that tax cuts or tax increases should be the primary fiscal weapons to fight unemployment or inflation.

However, *one of the big problems with tax changes is that it sometimes is difficult to get Congress to take speedy action.* There is often considerable debate over a tax bill, and sometimes it becomes a politi-

cal football. Another difficulty with tax changes is that it generally is much easier to reduce taxes than it is to get them back up again. To politicians, lower taxes are attractive because they are popular, and higher taxes are dangerous because they may hurt a politician's chance of reelection. In discussing fiscal policy (or most other aspects of government operations, for that matter), to ignore politics is to risk losing touch with reality.

Further, economists warn that, to the extent that discretionary fiscal policy involves reacting to short-term economic developments with little consideration of longer-term consequences, the result may be more harm than good. The point here is that changes in taxes and government spending aimed at stabilizing the economy in the short run may not be most effective in promoting the long-term health of the economy.

 TEST YOUR UNDERSTANDING

True or false?

_____ **1** Government discretionary programs like varying tax rates and welfare payments supplement the effects of the automatic stabilizers.

_____ **2** Public works programs can be started quickly.

_____ **3** Changes in taxes aimed at stabilizing the economy in the short run may not be best for the economy in the long run.

Exercises

1 "It is tempting to use fiscal policy in a reactive fashion, employing frequent discretionary changes in taxes and spending to alter economic activity temporarily and to counteract each aggregate fluctuation." What other strategies might be used?

2 "An important advantage of public works as a tool of fiscal policy is that they can be started quickly. An important advantage of tax rate changes is that they almost never get embroiled in partisan politics." Comment and evaluate.

3 "Even if the government spends a lot of money on a useless program, it will still create jobs, and hence be a good thing." Comment and evaluate.

4 According to the late Joseph Pechman of the Brookings Institute, "Among taxes, the federal individual income tax is the leading [automatic] stabilizer." He also says that "on the expenditure side, the major built-in stabilizer is unemployment compensation." Do you agree?

---

6 ▪ Supply-Side Economics

In the late 1970s and 1980s, some economists advocated tax reductions in order to stimulate national output. Their views came to be known

as **supply-side economics.** To stimulate rightward shifts of the aggregate supply curve, supply-siders favor the use of various financial incentives, particularly tax cuts. Why do they want to shift the aggregate supply curve to the right? Because this will increase total real output (without raising the price level). However, as shown in Figure 6.3, the increase in total real output will not be as large if the aggregate supply curve is relatively flat as it will be if it is vertical. In general, the supply-siders seem more inclined to accept the view that the aggregate supply curve is vertical (or close to it) than the Keynesian view that it is flat.

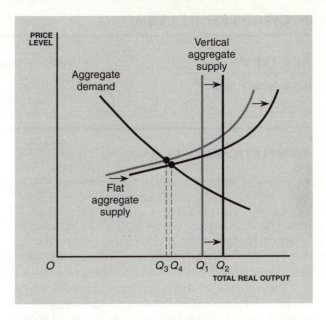

▪ **FIGURE 6.3**

Supply-Side Economics: The Effect of a Rightward Shift of the Aggregate Supply Curve

Supply-side economists advocate tax reductions to shift the aggregate supply curve to the right. If the aggregate supply curve is vertical (or close to it), such a shift will increase total real output by a much greater amount (from OQ_1 to OQ_2) than if it is relatively flat (in which case total real output will increase from OQ_3 to OQ_4).

 TEST YOUR UNDERSTANDING

True or false?

_____ **1** Supply-side economists are concerned primarily with influencing aggregate supply.

_____ **2** The goal of supply-side economists is to push the aggregate supply curve to the left.

▪ CHAPTER REVIEW

KEY TERMS

recessionary gap

inflationary gap
deficits

automatic stabilizers
supply-side economics

COMPLETION QUESTIONS

1 Two major economic targets the government should aim at are _____ and _____. If there is full employment but unacceptable inflation, the government should (increase, reduce) _____ spending. Structural features of our economy that tend to iron out business fluctuations and push in the direction of full employment at stable prices are called _____.

2 If the marginal propensity to consume is 0.75, and if the price level is constant, an extra $1 billion in government expenditure will increase equilibrium GDP by _____ billion. A reduction of $5 billion in government expenditure will reduce equilibrium GDP by _____ billion.

3 The amount of income tax collected by the federal government goes (down, up) _____ with increases in GDP and goes (down, up) _____ with decreases in GDP. Moreover, because the income tax is progressive, the average tax rate goes (down, up) _____ with increases in GDP, and goes (down, up) _____ with decreases in GDP.

4 When GDP falls off and unemployment increases, tax collections (fall, rise) _____, so _____ falls less than GDP; thus _____ falls less, and this tends to (cut, increase) _____ the fall in GDP. When GDP rises too quickly and the economy begins to suffer from serious inflation, tax collections (fall, rise) _____, which tends to (cut, increase) _____ the increase in GDP.

5 When GDP falls off and unemployment increases, the tax collections which finance unemployment compensation go (down, up) _____ because of (increased, lower) _____ employment. At the same time, the amount paid out to unemployed workers goes (down, up) _____. But when GDP rises too quickly and inflation besets the economy, the tax collections to finance unemployment compensation go (up, down) _____, while the amount paid out goes (up, down) _____ because there is much (less, more) _____ unemployment.

6 Because corporations generally maintain their dividends even though their sales fall off and also limit the

ANSWERS TO COMPLETION QUESTIONS

full employment, a stable price level

reduce

automatic stabilizers

$4

$20

up
down

up
down

fall, disposable income
consumption
cut

rise, cut

down
lower

up

up
down
less

increase in dividend payments even when their sales rise, their dividend policies tend to (stabilize, destabilize) _____ the economy. To the extent that consumers tend to be (fast, slow) _____ to raise or lower their spending in response to increases or decreases in their income, this too tends to (stabilize, destabilize) _____ the economy.

7 When there is high unemployment, the government may (cut, increase) _____ tax rates (as it did in 1981). If inflation is the problem, the government may (cut, increase) _____ taxes (as it did in 1968).

stabilize
slow

stabilize

cut

increase

NUMERICAL PROBLEMS

1 Suppose that the aggregate demand and supply curves are as shown in the graph below.

a Is there an inflationary gap?

b Is there a recessionary gap?

c If the government reduces taxes, is this likely to shift the aggregate demand curve? If so, how?

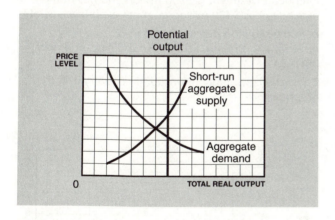

2 Suppose that the consumption function in country X is as follows:

DISPOSABLE INCOME	CONSUMPTION EXPENDITURE
(billions of dollars)	
900	750
1,000	800
1,100	850
1,200	900
1,300	950
1,400	1,000

a Suppose that intended investment is $200 billion and that government expenditure plus net exports is $100 billion. Plot the $C + I + G + (X - M_i)$ line and the 45-degree line in the following graph. (Assume that taxes are zero.)

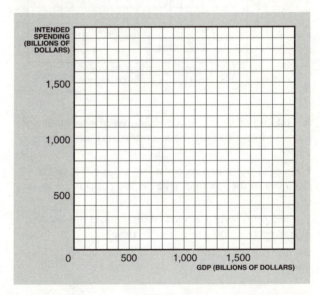

b If the price level is constant, what is the equilibrium value of GDP?

c Suppose that $1,400 billion is the full-employment GDP. Is there an inflationary gap? A recessionary gap?

d What sorts of measures can be taken by the government to promote full employment?

e What would be the effect on the equilibrium level of GDP of a $1 billion increase in government expenditure?

f What would be the effect on the equilibrium level of GDP of a $1 billion decrease in government expenditure?

g Plot the relationship between consumption expenditure and GDP if taxes equal 10 percent of GDP. Suppose that intended investment is $200 billion and that government expenditure plus net exports is $100 billion. Plot the $C + I + G + (X - M_i)$ line and the 45-degree line in the graph below. What is the equilibrium level of GDP?

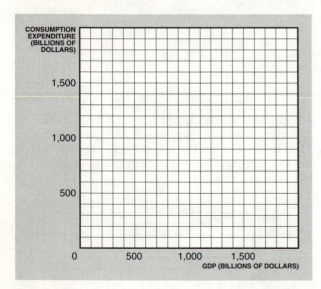

h Holding other factors constant, what effect will an increase in the tax rate have on the equilibrium level of GDP?

i Holding other factors constant, what effect will a decrease in the tax rate have on the equilibrium level of GDP?

j If the price level is not constant, should the analysis in this problem be altered? If so, how?

3a In country Y, the consumption function is as follows:

DISPOSABLE INCOME	CONSUMPTION
(millions of dollars)	
900	700
1,000	750
1,100	800
1,200	850
1,300	900

Suppose that intended investment is $100 million. If the price level is constant, what is the equilibrium level

of GDP if government expenditures are $200 million (and taxes and net exports are zero)?

b Suppose that country Y increases its government expenditures by $10 million. What will be the effect on its equilibrium GDP? Will GDP increase or decrease? By how much?

c Suppose that the government of country Y imposes a personal income tax which takes 16⅔ percent of everyone's pretax income. What now will be the relationship between GDP and consumption expenditure? Specifically, fill in the blanks below:

GDP	CONSUMPTION EXPENDITURE
(millions of dollars)	
_____	700
_____	750
_____	800
_____	850
_____	900

d What is the equilibrium value of country Y's GDP if intended investment is $100 million and government expenditure is $350 million (and net exports are zero)?

e In the situation described in part d, is country Y's government running a surplus or a deficit, and how big is it?

f Plot the consumption function in country Y in the graph below.

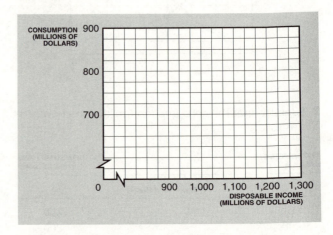

g Plot on the next page the relationship between consumption expenditure and GDP after country Y imposes the personal income tax.

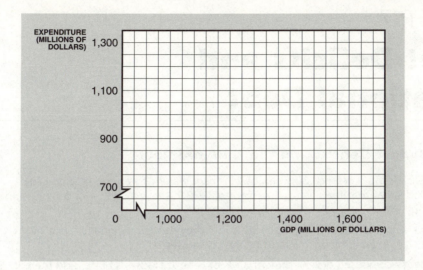

h In the graph above, plot the $C + I + G + (X - M)$ line for country Y under the conditions described in part d. Where does this line intersect the 45-degree line? What is the significance of this intersection point?

i Suppose that $1,100 million is the full-employment GDP. Is there an inflationary gap? A recessionary gap?

j If the price level is not constant, should the analysis in this problem be altered? If so, how?

ANSWERS TO
TEST YOUR UNDERSTANDING

SECTION 1

TRUE OR FALSE: 1. False   2. True   3. True

SECTION 2

TRUE OR FALSE: 1. False   2. True   3. True

EXERCISES

1. From top to bottom, the figures are 500, 625, 750, 875, 1,000.

2. See the right-hand panel of Figure 6.2.

SECTION 3

TRUE OR FALSE: 1. True   2. True   3. True

SECTION 4

TRUE OR FALSE: 1. True   2. True   3. False

SECTION 5

TRUE OR FALSE: 1. True   2. False   3. True

EXERCISES

1. The government might adopt certain rules regulating the behavior of taxes and/or government spending. As we shall see in Chapter 12, there is considerable controversy among economists over the roles that discretion and rules should play in determining fiscal and monetary policy.

2. Neither statement is generally true.

3. If the government spends money on a useless program, the result is waste. There is no sense in establishing wasteful and foolish spending programs merely to make jobs.

4. Yes.

SECTION 6

TRUE OR FALSE: 1. True   2. False

CHAPTER 7

Budget Deficits and the National Debt

Essentials of **Budget Deficits and the National Debt**

- The budget deficit is the difference between government expenditures and receipts. The deficit in the United States rose from about 1 percent of GDP in the 1960s to 4 or 5 percent in the 1980s and early 1990s.

- Two reasons for worrying about budget deficits is that they can create inflation and they can cause a substantial cut in investment spending by the private sector.

- The national debt—composed of government IOUs of various kinds—is huge, and there is considerable political support for balanced budgets.

- Most economists would not conclude that the government should balance its budget each year because it could make unemployment or inflation worse, not better.

1 ■ The Budget Deficit

The **budget deficit** is the difference between government expenditures and receipts. Obviously, the size of the deficit must be related to the size of the economy. A $200 billion deficit means one thing if a country's GDP is $100 billion, and quite another thing if its GDP is $10 trillion. Thus a deficit that would be huge for a tiny country like Monaco would be insignificant for a large country like the United States.

One way to relate the size of the deficit to GDP is to express the deficit as a percentage of GDP. Figure 7.1 shows that the deficit has increased from about 1 percent of GDP in the 1960s to about 2 percent in the 1970s to about 4 or 5 percent in the 1980s and early 1990s. Clearly, there was a substantial increase in the deficit, relative to GDP. In the late 1990s, President Clinton and

the Republican Congress revised policies so that, according to their estimates, the deficit would be reduced substantially.

However, not all economists believe that these measurements are correct. Robert Eisner of Northwestern University has argued that, when adjusted for inflation, the budget deficit is smaller than it appears when stated in nominal terms. For these and other reasons, he believes that fiscal policy has not been as effective as it could be. For example, in his view, the reported deficit in 1980 of $61 billion was actually an adjusted surplus of almost $8 billion. However, Eisner's views are controversial, and have failed to comfort the many people who are concerned about the size and persistence of recent federal budget deficits.

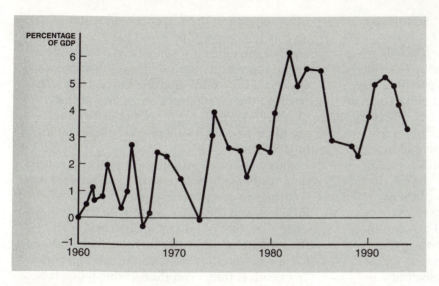

▪ **FIGURE 7.1**

Federal Deficit as a Percentage of GDP, 1960–1995

The federal deficit increased from about 1 percent of GDP in the 1960s to about 2 percent in the 1970s to about 4 or 5 percent in the 1980s and early 1990s.

 TEST YOUR UNDERSTANDING

True or false?

_____ **1** The federal deficit was less than 1 percent of GDP in 1990.

_____ **2** Robert Eisner has argued that the budget deficit is smaller than it appears.

---

2 ▪ Are Budget Deficits Inflationary?

One reason why the public is concerned about deficits is that they are often thought to cause inflation. Whether this is the case depends on how the deficits are financed. One way the government can finance a deficit is to print new money. In other words, the Federal Reserve (the Fed) can increase the money supply, and thus enable the government to use the additional money to pay for the portion of its expenditures not covered by tax revenues. If deficits are financed in this way, and if the resulting increases in the money supply are substantial, the result may be inflation. This follows from the fact stressed repeatedly in previous chapters that substantial increases in the money supply may cause inflation.

But recent deficits in the United States have been financed largely by government borrowing. Every so often, the Treasury sells a few billion dollars worth of bonds, notes, or bills. To sell its securities, the Treasury must offer potential buyers a high enough rate of return to make them an attractive investment. Suppose that the Treasury issues today $1 billion of 1-year securities to cover a deficit of $1 billion. If the rate of interest is 10 percent, it must pay the $1 billion plus interest of $100 million at the end of 1 year. To pay this $1.1 billion to the holders of these securities, it must borrow $1.1 billion a year from now. If it again has to pay 10 percent interest, it will owe $1.21 billion (the principal of $1.1 billion plus $.11 billion in interest) a year hence. Thus the amount that the government has to borrow to finance a $1 billion deficit today grows over time.

However, so long as the government does not create new money to finance the deficit, the result need not be inflationary. But Thomas Sargent of Stanford University and Neil Wallace of the University of Minnesota have pointed out that, even if deficits are not financed right away by the creation of new money, they may have inflationary consequences. As pointed out in the previous paragraph, the interest payments resulting from a growing national debt can become very large. Suppose that investors become convinced that at some point in the reasonably near future the level of government debt will have become so big that the interest payments will constitute a disturbingly large portion of the government's budget. If they think that the government will resort to the creation of new money at that time to finance all or part of the deficit, they are likely to fear that there will be substantial inflation then.

Faced with this prospect, investors may insist on a relatively high interest rate on government securities to compensate them for the anticipated inflation, and they may try to hold less money, since the value of money is expected to fall. At the same time, they may increase their demand for goods, and thus push up the price level now. The result is that, even though the deficit is not financed right away by the creation of new money, there may be inflation.

But if the deficit is kept within reasonable bounds, this situation need not occur. So long as the deficit is small enough so that investors remain convinced that the government is willing and able to keep the money supply under proper control, there need not be a problem of this sort. Even if the deficit is very large, it need not occur if people believe that deficits of this magnitude are only temporary and that in a relatively short time the budget will be brought into closer balance.

 TEST YOUR UNDERSTANDING

True or false?

_____ **1** If the Fed finances a deficit by printing new money, the result may be inflation.

_____ **2** Recent deficits in the United States have been financed largely by government borrowing.

_____ **3** Thomas Sargent and Neil Wallace point out that deficits, even if not financed right away by the creation of new money, may have inflationary consequences.

Exercise

1 The following table provides some information concerning a small country:

	(billions of dollars)
Gross domestic product (this year)	16.0
Gross domestic product (full-employment level)	20.0
Government expenditures on goods and services	1.8

According to experts on this country's economy, the government's tax receipts are equal to 10 percent of its GDP. Is the government of this country running a deficit or a surplus? (That is, are government expenditures greater than or less than tax receipts?)

3 ▪ Do Budget Deficits "Crowd Out" Private Investment?

Another reason why people are concerned about large budget deficits is that they fear that the government's deficit spending may result in a substantial cut in investment spending by the private sector. In other words, they fear that government budget deficits may crowd out private investment. Why may this occur? Because large government borrowing may push up the interest rate, and the higher interest rate may in turn cut private investment. (The interest rate is the price paid for the use of loanable funds.)

To illustrate how **crowding out** can occur, consider panel A of Figure 7.2, which shows the private sector's demand curve and supply curve for loanable funds. The demand curve for loanable funds, D_1, shows the total quantity of loanable funds demanded by firms and households at each interest rate. As would be expected, this demand curve slopes downward to the right, indicating that the quantity of loanable funds demanded goes up as the interest rate falls. The supply curve for loanable funds, S_1, shows the total quantity of loanable funds supplied by households, firms, and others at each interest rate. As would be expected, this supply curve slopes upward to the right, indicating that the quantity of loanable funds supplied goes up as the interest rate rises. The equilibrium level of the interest rate is 8 percent, where the quantity of loanable funds demanded equals the quantity supplied, and the equilibrium amount of funds borrowed for all purposes is $500 billion.

Now suppose that the government, which formerly did not have to borrow, increases its spending by $200 billion, and that the spending increase is financed entirely by borrowing. The result, as shown in panel A of Figure 7.2, is that the demand curve for loanable funds shifts to the right (from D_1 to D_2), reflecting the government's demand for the additional $200 billion of funds. Because of this shift of the demand curve, the equilibrium interest rate rises to 10 percent, and the quantity of funds borrowed increases to $600 billion. But $200 billion of these funds go to the government; this means that the private sector borrows only $400 billion. Thus the private sector borrows, and hence invests, $100 billion less than it did before the government entered the market for loanable funds to finance its $200 billion deficit.

However, this analysis may be incomplete. If the extra $200 billion of government expenditure increases national output (and disposable income), the amount of saving may increase. Consequently, the supply curve for loanable funds may shift to the right (from S_1 to S_2) as shown in panel B of Figure 7.2, the result being that the interest rate rises only to 9 percent, and the private sector borrows, and hence invests, $450 billion (rather than $400 billion in panel A). Thus the private sector invests $50 billion (rather than $100 billion in panel A) less than it did before the government set out to borrow $200 billion. Under these circumstances, a smaller amount of private investment is crowded out

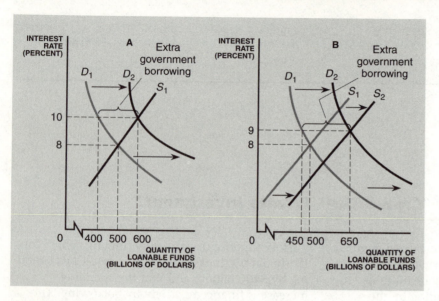

▪ **FIGURE 7.2**

How Government Borrowing Can Crowd Out Private Investment

If the government enters the market for loanable funds to finance its $200 billion deficit, the demand curve for loanable funds shifts to the right from D_1 to D_2, the result being that the interest rate rises from 8 to 10 percent and the quantity of funds borrowed by the private sector drops from $500 billion to $400 billion, as shown in panel A. If the extra government expenditure increases national output (and disposable income), the amount of saving may increase, and thus push the supply curve to the right from S_1 to S_2, as shown in panel B. The result is that the interest rate rises only to 9 percent, and the quantity of funds borrowed by the private sector falls only to $450 billion, not $400 billion.

than in panel A, where the increased government expenditure did not increase national output.

IS CROWDING OUT IMPORTANT?

Why does it matter if some private investment is crowded out? The answer is that, *if private investment is crowded out, the total amount of capital in the economy will be smaller than otherwise.* (Recall from Chapter 1 that net investment equals the change in the total amount of capital.) And a smaller capital stock means that the population will have fewer and poorer tools to work with—and thus less output. Consequently, large and persistent budget deficits really can harm future generations

because they may result in a smaller total amount of capital being passed on to the population's descendants.

In fact, however, private investment in the United States did not fall substantially in the face of the large deficits of the 1980s because foreigners provided much of the funds. For example, the Japanese purchased large amounts of our government securities. But what this means is that *future generations of Americans, while they will have a capital stock that is not much reduced, will owe a substantial amount to foreigners.* Obviously, when the government borrows from abroad, purchasing power is transferred from foreigners to us when the borrowing occurs, but purchasing power is transferred from us to foreigners when we pay interest on the debt and repay the principal.

Another effect of the high interest rates induced by large deficits has been an increase in the value of the dollar relative to other currencies. This is because foreign investors have had to buy dollars in order to purchase U.S. securities, which (because of high U.S. interest rates) have been attractive to them. Due to the swollen demand for dollars, the value of a dollar (relative to the Japanese yen or German mark) has tended to rise. One consequence of this has been that U.S. exports have tended to fall (because U.S. goods have become more expensive relative to foreign goods) and U.S. imports have tended to rise (because foreign goods have become cheaper relative to U.S. goods). Thus *large deficits have tended to depress our net exports.*

Finally, under certain circumstances, some economists believe that deficits can increase, not decrease, investment. This is known as the *crowding-in effect.* The idea is that, if the economy is experiencing considerable unemployment, the government's deficit spending may increase national output, and the higher national output may in turn increase investment. Of course, the magnitude of this effect depends on how sensitive real GDP is to the extra government spending and on how sensitive investment by the private sector is to whatever increase occurs (on this account) in real GDP. If the economy is at or close to full employment, it is unlikely that this effect will occur, but if the economy is at the pit of a depression, this effect, according to some economists, may overwhelm the crowding-out effect.

 TEST YOUR UNDERSTANDING

True or false?

_____ **1** Private investment in the United States did not fall substantially in the face of large deficits in the 1980s.

_____ **2** Foreigners purchased large volumes of our government securities.

_____ **3** Because of the crowding-in effect, deficits have reduced private investment in the United States.

Exercises

1 Explain how large budget deficits can discourage investment and inhibit the growth of a country's capital stock.

2 Did the large deficits of the 1980s have a devastating effect on the rate of growth of the U.S. capital stock?

---

4 ▪ The Structural Deficit

To see whether fiscal policy is expansionary (increasing aggregate demand) or contractionary (reducing aggregate demand), people often look at the size of the budget deficit. A large deficit frequently is viewed as more expansionary than

a small one (or a surplus). However, this can be quite misleading since budget deficits can occur because the economy is at less than full employment (defined as the lowest sustainable unemployment rate compatible with reasonable price stability). A better measure of whether fiscal policy is expansionary or contractionary is the **structural deficit,** which shows the difference between tax revenues and government expenditures that would result if gross domestic product were at its potential, not its actual, level.

To illustrate, go back several decades, and consider the situation in 1958 when the Eisenhower administration ran a deficit of about $10 billion. Basically, the reason for this deficit was that, with the unemployment rate at about 7 percent, there was a substantial gap between actual and potential output. Gross domestic product fell from 1957 to 1958, and, as a result, incomes and federal tax collections fell, and the government ran a deficit. But this $10 billion deficit was entirely due to the high level of unemployment the country was experiencing.

As shown in Figure 7.3, the structural deficit can differ substantially from the actual budget deficit. To understand whether fiscal policy is becoming more expansionary or contractionary, you must understand the difference.

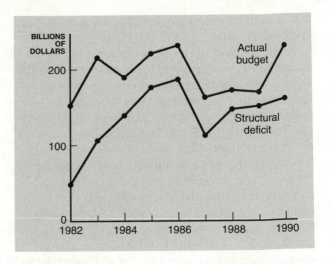

▪ **FIGURE 7.3**

Structural and Actual Budget Deficits, 1982–1990

The structural deficit shows the difference between tax revenues and government expenditures that would result if gross domestic product were at its potential level.

 TEST YOUR UNDERSTANDING

True or false?

_____ **1** Budget deficits that are large are always more expansionary than small ones.

_____ **2** The structural deficit is a better measure than the budget deficit of whether fiscal policy is expansionary or contractionary.

---

5 ▪ The National Debt: Size and Growth

As you have seen, when the federal government incurs a deficit, it generally borrows money to cover the difference. The **national debt**—composed of bonds, notes, and other government IOUs of various kinds—is the result of such borrowing. These IOUs are held by individuals, firms, banks, and public agencies. There is a large and very important market for government securities,

which are relatively riskless and highly liquid. If you look at the *New York Times* or *Wall Street Journal,* for example, you can find each day the prices at which each of a large number of issues of these bonds, notes, and bills are quoted.

How large is the national debt? In 1996, as shown in Figure 7.4, it was about $5 trillion. Without question, this is a huge amount, but it is

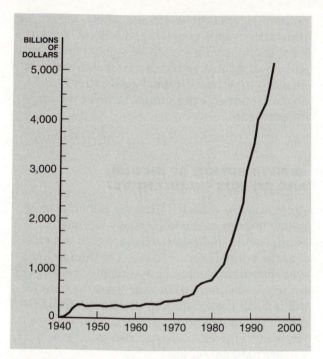

▪ **FIGURE 7.4**

Size of National Debt, United States, 1940–1996

The national debt, about $5.2 trillion in 1996, has been growing rapidly due to huge government deficits.

important to relate the size of the national debt to the size of our national output. After all, a $5 trillion debt means one thing if our annual output is $4 trillion, and another thing if our annual output is $400 billion. The debt—expressed as a percentage of output—is shown in Figure 7.5. Although the figures do not seem to provide any cause for immediate alarm, many economists have warned that there are problems in incurring large deficits of the kind that were responsible for the rapid rate of increase in the debt during the 1980s and 1990s.[1] These warnings have already been discussed in this chapter.

A BURDEN ON FUTURE GENERATIONS

Why have people been so agitated about the debt's size? One important reason has been that they have felt that the debt was a burden that was being thrust on future generations. To evaluate this idea, it is important to recognize that a public debt is not like your debt, which must be paid off at a certain time in the future. In prac-

[1] Note too that much of the public debt is in the hands of government agencies, not held by the public. For example, in 1996 only about $3.7 trillion was held by the public.

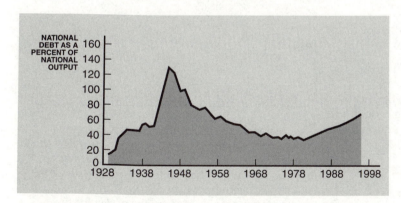

▪ **FIGURE 7.5**

National Debt as a Percent of National Output, United States, 1929–1996

As a percent of national output, the national debt declined steadily from World War II to about 1980. During the 1980s, it increased.

tice, new government debt is issued by the government to pay off maturing public debt. There never comes a time when you must collectively reach into your pockets to pay off the debt. And even if you did pay it off, the same generation would collect as the one that paid. However, as stressed above, the deficits that create the debt can put a burden on future generations if they crowd out private investment, and thus reduce the amount of capital turned over to future generations.

EFFECTS OF EXTERNALLY HELD DEBT

To the extent that the debt is held by foreigners, you must send goods and services overseas to pay the interest on it. This means that less goods and services are available for you and your fellow citizens. Thus, if you finance a particular government activity by borrowing from foreigners, the cost may be transferred to future generations, since they must pay the interest. But from the point of view of the world as a whole, the current generation sacrifices goods and services, since the lending country forgoes current goods and services. Also, it must be recognized that, if the debt is incurred to purchase capital goods, they may produce enough extra output to cover the interest payments.

REDISTRIBUTION OF INCOME AND EFFECTS ON INCENTIVES

Taxes must be collected from the public at large to pay interest to the holders of government bonds, notes, and other obligations. To the extent that the bondholders receiving the interest are wealthier than the public as a whole, there is some redistribution of income from the poor to the rich. To the extent that the taxes needed to obtain the money to pay interest on the debt reduce incentives, the result also may be a smaller national output.

☑ TEST YOUR UNDERSTANDING

True or false?

_____ **1** The national debt is smaller now than in 1950.

_____ **2** New government debt is issued by the government to pay off maturing public debt.

_____ **3** As the national debt grows, the payments required to meet interest charges grow too.

_____ **4** If buyers can be found for the government bonds that represent the national debt, there is no need to worry about the effects of the debt on a country's income distribution.

Exercise

1 The actual deficits of the U.S. government in selected years are shown at the right:

YEAR	(billions of dollars)
1954	1.2
1961	3.4
1967	8.7
1968	25.2
1975	53.2
1980	73.8
1990	220.4

a. Are all these deficits the result of spendthrift government spending?

b. In 1954, 1961, 1975, and 1980, there were drops in GDP which helped to cause tax revenue to fall below government expenditure. From the above figures alone, can you determine the extent to which a particular government deficit is due to high government spending or a weak economy?

c. Were the deficits in 1967 and 1968 the result of a weak economy? What information would you obtain to answer this question?

6 ▪ Alternative Policies Regarding the Federal Budget

SHOULD THE BUDGET BE BALANCED ANNUALLY?

At least three policies concerning the government budget are worthy of detailed examination. The first policy says that *the government's budget should be balanced each and every year.* This is the philosophy that generally prevailed, here and abroad, until a few decades ago. Superficially, it seems reasonable. After all, won't a family or firm go bankrupt if it continues to spend more than it takes in? Why should the government be any different? However, the truth is that the government has economic capabilities, powers, and responsibilities that are entirely different from those of any family or firm, and it is misleading—sometimes even pernicious—to assume that what is sensible for a family or firm is also sensible for the government.

If this policy of balancing the budget is accepted, the government cannot use fiscal policy as a tool to stabilize the economy. Indeed, if the government attempts to balance its budget each year, it may make unemployment or inflation worse rather than better. For example, suppose that severe unemployment occurs because of a drop in national output. Since incomes drop, tax receipts drop as well. Thus, if the government attempts to balance its budget, it must cut its spending and/or increase its tax rates, both of which may tend to lower, not raise, national output. On the other hand, suppose that inflation occurs because spending increases too rapidly. Since incomes increase, tax receipts increase too. Thus, for the government to balance its budget, it must increase its spending and/or decrease its tax rates, both of which may tend to raise, not lower, spending.

Despite these considerations, there has been a considerable amount of political support for a constitutional amendment to mandate a balanced federal budget. No doubt, the federal government, through inappropriate fiscal or monetary policies, has frequently been responsible for excessive inflation or unemployment. Some economists say that the real problem is how to prevent the government from creating disturbances,

rather than how to use the government budget (and monetary policy) to offset disturbances arising from the private sector. But for the reasons discussed above, most economists would not go so far as to conclude that the government should balance its budget each year.

SHOULD THE BUDGET BE BALANCED OVER THE BUSINESS CYCLE?

A second budgetary philosophy says that *the government's budget should be balanced over the course of each "business cycle."* As you have seen in previous chapters, the rate of growth of national output tends to behave cyclically. It tends to increase for a while, then drop, increase, then drop. Unemployment also tends to ebb and flow in a similar cyclical fashion. According to this second budgetary policy, the government is not expected to balance its budget each year, but is expected to run a big enough surplus during periods of high employment to offset the deficit it runs during the ensuing period of excessive unemployment. This policy seems to give the government enough flexibility to run the deficits or surpluses that, according to many economists, may be needed to stabilize the economy, while at the same time allaying any public fear of a chronically unbalanced budget. It certainly seems to be a neat way to reconcile the government's use of fiscal policy to promote noninflationary full employment with the public's uneasiness over chronically unbalanced budgets.

Unfortunately, however, it does contain one fundamental flaw. There is no reason to believe that the size of the deficits required to eliminate excessive unemployment will equal the size of the surpluses required to moderate the subsequent inflation. Suppose that national output falls sharply and causes severe and prolonged unemployment, and then regains its full-employment level only briefly, and then falls again. In such a case, the deficits incurred to get the economy back to full employment are likely to exceed by far the surpluses run during the brief period of full employment. Thus there would be no way to stabilize the economy without running an unbalanced budget over the course of this business cycle. If this policy were adopted, and if the government attempted to balance the budget over the course of each business cycle, many economists believe that this might interfere with an effective fiscal policy designed to promote full employment with stable prices.

SHOULD WE WORRY ABOUT BALANCING THE BUDGET?

Finally, a third budgetary policy says that *the government's budget should be set so as to promote whatever attainable combination of unemployment and inflation seems socially optimal,* even if this means that the budget is unbalanced over considerable periods of time. Proponents of this policy argue that, although it may mean a continual growth in the national debt, the problems caused by a moderate growth in the national debt are small when compared with the social costs of unemployment and inflation.

CHANGES IN PUBLIC ATTITUDES

Certainly, the history of the past sixty years has been characterized by enormous changes in the country's attitude toward the government budget. Sixty years ago, the prevailing attitude was that the government's budget should be balanced. The emergence of the Keynesian theory of the determination of national output and employment shook this attitude, at least to the point where it became respectable to advocate a balanced budget over the business cycle, rather than in each year. In many circles, persistent deficits of moderate size were viewed with no alarm. In the past twenty years, there has been some movement back toward earlier views favoring balanced budgets. Conservatives have emphasized the usefulness of the balanced budget as a device to limit government spending, which they regard as excessive. The public has tended to blame very high rates of inflation on large deficits. In 1997, President Clinton and the Republican Congress claimed that a balanced budget is on the way. All that can be said now is: "Wait and see."

 TEST YOUR UNDERSTANDING

True or false?

_____ **1** If the government's budget has to be balanced each year, the government can use fiscal policy to stabilize the economy.

_____ **2** Keynesian theory shook the belief that the budget should always be balanced.

_____ **3** In the mid-1990s, the federal government abandoned deficit financing.

Exercises

1 If the federal deficit rises, does this mean that fiscal policy is pushing real GDP upward? If the federal budget deficit falls, does this mean that fiscal policy is restraining real GDP? Explain.

2 Can large deficits have an adverse effect on a country's net exports? If so, how can this occur?

3 What are the arguments in favor of balancing the federal budget each year? What are the arguments against such a policy? Should the federal budget be balanced over the business cycle rather than during each year?

▪ CHAPTER REVIEW

KEY TERMS

budget deficit

crowding out
structural deficit

national debt

COMPLETION QUESTIONS

1 The _____ shows the difference between tax revenues and government expenditures that would result if gross domestic product were at its potential, not its actual, level.

2 During the 1980s and early 1990s, the federal budget deficit tended to be a (higher, lower) _____ percent of the GDP than during the 1970s.

3 If government accounting is corrected for the effects of _____, economists like _____ believe that the federal budget deficit is considerably smaller than it appears.

4 If deficits are financed by printing new money, the results are likely to be _____.

5 Thomas Sargent and Neil Wallace have pointed out that, even if deficits are not financed right away by the creation of _____, they may be inflationary.

6 If the government finances a deficit by borrowing, it is likely to push up _____, and thus _____ the amount of _____.

7 Government borrowing is likely to shift the demand curve for loanable funds to the _____.

8 Large deficits, because they increase _____, may induce foreign investors to purchase _____, the result being an increase in the _____ of the dollar, which tends to depress the _____ of the United States.

9 As a percentage of GDP, the national debt (grew substantially, did not grow substantially) _____ between 1939 and 1990.

10 If the government insists on balancing its budget each year, it is more apt to increase unemployment and inflation. For example, if severe unemployment occurs because of a drop in GDP, incomes drop and tax receipts (drop, increase) _____. If the government then attempts to balance its budget, it must (cut, increase) _____ spending and/or (cut, increase) _____ tax rates, both of which will tend to (cut, increase) _____ GDP.

11 Suppose that tax receipts and government expenditures on goods and services are related in the following way to GDP (all figures are in billions of dollars):

GDP	TAX RECEIPTS	GOVERNMENT EXPENDITURES
800	200	260
900	230	260
1,000	260	260
1,100	300	260

ANSWERS TO COMPLETION QUESTIONS

structural deficit

higher

inflation, Robert Eisner

inflationary

new money

interest rates
reduce, private investment

right

interest rates
U.S. securities
value
net exports

did not grow substantially

drop

cut
increase
cut

If GDP is $900 billion, the government runs a (deficit, surplus) _____ of $_____ billion. If the full-employment GDP is $1,100 billion, the (deficit, surplus) _____ at full employment is $_____ billion. For this economy to achieve full employment, intended investment must be $_____ billion (greater, less) _____ than intended saving at full employment. (Net exports equal zero.)

12 Borrowing is not the only method the government can use to finance a deficit. It can also create _____ to cover the difference between expenditures and revenues.

deficit, 30

surplus, 40

40
greater

money

NUMERICAL PROBLEMS

1 You are given the following information about an economy: GDP = $20 billion at full employment, GDP = $16 billion currently, taxes = .1(GDP), and government expenditures on goods and services = $1.8 billion.

a Is the government running a surplus or a deficit? Is the budget too expansionary? Why or why not?

b Suppose you learn that when GDP = $20 billion, intended saving + imports = $1.8 billion, and intended investment + exports = $1.5 billion. If tax rates cannot be changed, if the price level is fixed, and if government expenditures are altered to push the economy to full employment, will there be a surplus or deficit? How big?

2 Suppose that the government of Erewhon borrows $1 billion at 8 percent interest from U.S. and British banks. The money is invested in irrigation projects that

increase Erewhon's national output during the next 5 years by $300 million per year.

a Does this loan result in an increase in Erewhon's national debt? If so, by how much?

b Does this loan impose a net burden on the people of Erewhon? Why or why not?

3 Suppose that the government borrows $10,000 for a year, and that the rate of interest is 4 percent.

a At the end of the year, how much must the government pay the lender in principal?

b If the annual rate of inflation is 3 percent, does this amount (in part a) equal what was lent to the government?

c If there were zero inflation, what would be the interest cost during the year and the principal at the end of the year?

 ANSWERS TO
TEST YOUR UNDERSTANDING

SECTION 1

TRUE OR FALSE: 1. False   2. True

SECTION 2

TRUE OR FALSE: 1. True   2. True   3. True

EXERCISE

1. Government expenditures equals $1.8 billion. Tax receipts equal 10 percent of GDP, or $1.6 billion. Thus there is a deficit of $.2 billion. (That is, spending exceeds receipts by $.2 billion.)

SECTION 3

TRUE OR FALSE: 1. True   2. True   3. False

EXERCISE

1. Large budget deficits financed by government borrowing can push up the interest rate, and the higher interest rate can in turn cut private investment. Because of the cut in private investment, the country's capital stock may grow less rapidly than otherwise would be the case.

2. No.

SECTION 4

TRUE OR FALSE: 1. False   2. True

SECTION 5

TRUE OR FALSE: 1. False   2. True   3. True   4. False

EXERCISE

1. a. No. In some years, like 1954, 1961, 1975, and

1980, at least part of the reason for the deficit was a weak economy due to recession.

b. No. What one needs to know is the structural deficit or surplus in each year.

c. No. The unemployment rate is of use in indicating whether the economy was weak. Since the unemployment rate was less than 4 percent in 1967 and 1968, the economy certainly was not weak in these years. The structural deficit or surplus would help to answer this question.

SECTION 6

TRUE OR FALSE: 1. False   2. True   3. False

EXERCISE

1. If the federal budget deficit rises, but the structural deficit is falling, most economists would feel that fiscal policy is not becoming more expansionary. If the federal budget deficit falls, but the structural deficit is rising, most economists would feel that fiscal policy is not becoming more contractionary.

2. Large deficits financed by borrowing can push up the interest rate, and the higher interest rate will tend to increase the value of the dollar relative to other currencies. Thus, U.S. exports will tend to fall (because U.S. goods will become more expensive relative to foreign goods) and U.S. imports will tend to rise (because foreign goods will become cheaper relative to U.S. goods). Consequently, net exports will tend to fall.

3. Supporters of a balanced budget say that it would help curb government spending (which they regard as excessive). Opponents say that, if the government had to balance its budget, it could not use fiscal policy to help stabilize the economy.

CHAPTER 8

What Should Be Done about the Federal Deficit?

1 ■ Introduction

An enormous amount of attention has been directed at the federal deficit and whether it should be reduced and, if so, how. This chapter presents eight multipart problems, which analyze selected aspects of this topic as well as other questions concerning fiscal policy. To provide the background information required to understand and do these problems, we begin with a very brief thumbnail sketch of fiscal policy in the United States. No attempt is made to provide a complete, continuous history of fiscal policy; instead, the focus is on about a half-dozen key episodes, beginning in 1953.

When Dwight Eisenhower took office as president in 1953, he inherited a prosperity that had been bubbling along since the postwar boom. But by August 1953, there were signs that the economy was headed for a recession. By 1954 the unemployment rate was 6 percent, the highest since the Great Depression. Although Eisenhower remained outwardly confident, there was concern behind the scenes about the deepening recession and a debate about what the government should do. Because the recession reduced tax revenues,

the government was running a deficit, and some people felt that taxes should be raised to snuff out the deficit.

But President Eisenhower was getting other advice. In 1954 the Committee for Economic Development (composed largely of top business executives) urged the president to forget about balancing the budget and to leave the economy alone. As 1954 wore on and the Democrats and the labor unions demanded action, the economy stumbled, sputtered, then took off in an upward direction. The first Republican recession since 1929 had come and gone, and even dedicated Democrats had to admit that the country had survived. But it survived by the government's doing nothing. And in hindsight, nothing turns out to have been just the thing to do.

The Council of Economic Advisers, chaired by Arthur F. Burns, played a major role in this event. Ironically, in 1952 Congress had tried to kill the council by cutting off its funding. By the end of 1954 it was clear that the council, its chairman, and its stabilizing budget policy had passed a major test with honors.

2 ■ Fiscal Policy in the Late 1950s

1958 was a recession year in the United States. Tax revenues declined. Unemployment compensation payments rose. The budget deficit for the year approached $10 billion. According to many economists, the large deficit helped to get the

recovery going, but when the recession was over President Eisenhower set out to recoup his losses by balancing the budget. As the president forged ahead with his plan for a budget surplus, voices were raised in warning. Some of these warnings came from the Committee for Economic Development, the group of top business executives cited above.

Another person urging caution in the drive for a big surplus was Vice President Richard Nixon. During the recession of 1958, Nixon had urged a tax cut to stimulate the economy. His advice was not heeded. Now, as he prepared to run for president in 1960, he urged a more expansionary budget policy. Again his advice was rejected because the administration was more concerned about fighting inflation. Eisenhower in his last year in office was willing to take the political risk of pinching off growth. He assumed that the next administration would be able to carry on with the expansionary policy—a next administration that was expected to be Republican.

By the summer of 1960, the recovery had ground to a halt, stopping well short of the goal of full employment. As the ranks of the jobless increased, Democratic presidential candidate John Kennedy was helped politically, while Richard Nixon watched the economy slide back into recession and victory slip through his fingers. Historians still argue whether it was the budget surplus and the unexpected recession that cost him the victory; but many economists seem to agree that a budget deficit in 1960 would have generated more jobs and more growth in the economy.

3 ▪ The Kennedy Tax Cut

When the Kennedy administration took office in 1961, it was confronted with a relatively high unemployment rate—about 7 percent in mid-1961. By 1962, although unemployment was somewhat lower (about 6 percent), the president's advisers, led by Walter W. Heller, chairman of the Council of Economic Advisers, convinced the president to propose a tax cut to reduce unemployment further.

The proposed tax bill was a victory for Heller and the CEA. Even though it would mean a deliberately large deficit, the president had been convinced to cut taxes to push the economy closer to full employment. But Congress was not so easily convinced. Many members of Congress labeled the proposal irresponsible and reckless.

Others wanted to couple tax reform with tax reduction. It was not until 1964, after President Kennedy's death, that the tax bill was enacted.

The effects of the tax cut are by no means easy to measure, in part because the rate of growth of the money supply increased at the same time, which (as we shall see in Chapter 9) should also affect GDP. But consumption expenditure did increase sharply during 1964. Moreover, the additional consumption expenditure undoubtedly induced additional investment. According to some estimates, the tax cut resulted in an increase in GDP of about $24 billion in 1965 and more in subsequent years. Most economists seemed to regard the tax cut of 1964 as a success.

4 ▪ Biting the Bullet

In late July 1965, President Lyndon Johnson announced that the United States would send 50,000 more troops to Vietnam. From fiscal 1965 to fiscal 1966, defense expenditures rose from $50 billion to $62 billion—a large increase in government expenditure, and one that took place at a time of relatively full employment. Such an increase in government expenditure would be expected to cause inflationary pressures. The Council of Economic Advisers recognized this danger, and recommended in late 1965 that the president urge Congress to increases taxes. Johnson was reluctant. The inflationary pressures mounted during 1966, and little was done by fiscal policymakers to quell them.

Even in 1967, Congress was unwilling to raise

taxes. The case for fiscal restraint was, it felt, not clear enough. As for the president, he said, "It is not a popular thing for a president to do . . . to ask for a penny out of a dollar to pay for a war that is not popular either." Finally, in mid-1968, a 10 percent surcharge on income taxes, together with some restraint in government spending, was enacted. Economists tended to regard this increase in taxes as the right medicine, but it was at least two years too late, and its effects were delayed and insufficient.

5 ■ The Tax Cut of 1975

In late 1974, the unemployment rate began to mount. Whereas it was 5.5 percent in August, it reached 7.2 percent in December. Although economists were rather slow to recognize that the economy was slumping into a severe recession, by early 1975 it was felt that some stimulus was needed. Inflation, which President Gerald Ford had labeled public enemy number one in the fall of 1974, continued to be a problem, but most policymakers felt that unemployment rates were reaching intolerable levels.

In early 1975, President Ford proposed a $16 billion tax cut. As his Council of Economic Advisers stated, its purpose was "to halt the decline in production and employment so that growth of output can resume and unemployment can be reduced." Congress passed a $23 billion tax cut in March 1975, only a relatively few months before the recovery was well under way. The tax cut had less impact than some economists predicted because consumers did not spend, but instead saved, much of the tax reduction. Because the tax reduction was temporary, it had less effect on consumption expenditure than if it was permanent.

6 ■ The Reagan Tax Cut

When the Reagan administration took office in 1981, it was committed to cut both government expenditures and taxes. In August 1981 the administration pushed through Congress a huge tax cut for both individuals and businesses. At the same time, it reduced federal expenditures (relative to the level that former president Jimmy Carter had proposed). However, the tax cuts were far in excess of the spending cuts, particularly since reductions in GDP in late 1981 also tended to reduce tax receipts. Thus the administration was faced with record deficits of over $100 billion in fiscal 1982 and about $200 billion in fiscal 1983. In early 1982 President Ronald Reagan said he would try to cut spending further in an attempt to soak up some of the red ink. But the economy was in a recession (with an unemployment rate of 9 percent) and there was little sympathy on Capitol Hill for further spending cuts. Since inflation had fallen to well under double digits, unemployment once again seemed to be public enemy number one.

In November 1982 the economy pulled out of the recession, and the expansion began. Economists of all schools, but particularly supply-side economists—who advocated the 1981 tax cut to increase incentives for work and saving, and thus to shift the aggregate supply curve to the right— gave the 1981 tax cut considerable credit for increasing real GDP and reducing unemployment. From 1983 to 1986, all years of healthy expansion, the federal government ran huge deficits of about $200 billion per year. President Reagan vowed that he would not raise taxes, and proposed cuts in nonmilitary government expenditures, whereas his critics asked for tax increases and reductions in military spending. In 1986, Congress passed a major tax reform bill that lowered tax rates and broadened the tax base by reducing loopholes. In late 1987, after the sharp stock market decline, President Reagan and congressional leaders met to try to find a mutually agreeable way to cut the huge deficits, but limited progress was made.

7 ▪ The Bush Years

In November 1988, George Bush, then vice president, was elected to the presidency on a platform of "no new taxes." Many critics, here and abroad, doubted that the federal deficit could be reduced without additional tax revenue. During 1989 and 1990, the deficit continued to be about $200 billion. In late 1990, Congress and President Bush agreed to a fiscal package that would reduce the deficit, but by no means eliminate it. Included were additional taxes, including increased tax rates for high-income families and bigger taxes on cigarettes, beer, and wine. After an expansion of record length, the U.S. economy entered a recession in late 1990, and some observers questioned whether it was a good time to raise taxes.

8 ▪ Clinton's Fiscal Policies

In the election of 1992, Bill Clinton promised to stimulate the economy and promote the creation of more high-paying jobs. After his election, he proposed a fiscal stimulus package, but it was not passed by Congress. As in previous years, there was a widespread feeling that the deficit was too large and that a stimulus package might only make it worse. Moreover, many observers felt that the recovery was picking up steam and that extra stimulus was not required.

The Clinton administration raised taxes considerably on the highest-income segments of the population. According to Clinton, income tax rates were raised "for only the top 1.2 percent of taxpayers, the group of Americans who gained the most during the 1980s and are most able to pay higher taxes to help reduce the deficit."[1]

[1] *Economic Report of the President* (Washington, D.C.: Government Printing Office, 1994), p. 4.

In 1996, Clinton's Council of Economic Advisers said that "Deficit reduction done the wrong way will reduce living standards and worsen inequality. Cutting spending to reduce the deficit requires hard choices. . . . Some proposed budget cuts, such as those that would reduce equality of educational opportunity, represent attacks on fundamental American values. Others, such as in programs that protect the environment and Americans' health and safety, would have adverse effects on living standards in the future. . . "[2]

In 1997, Clinton and the Republican Congress reached a deal on balancing the budget, although many of the detailed provisions will have to be worked out in the future.

[2] *Economic Report of the President*, 1996, p. 37.

9 ▪ Applying Economics: What to Do about Deficits

The following two problems are concerned with federal budgetary deficits in the United States.

PROBLEM 8.1 Some economists, like Nobel laureate James Buchanan and Milton Friedman, favor an amendment to the Constitution of the United States requiring the federal government to balance the budget. In their view, this would enable Congress to resist more effectively the political pressures to spend what they regard as excessive amounts. Other people are dubious of the wisdom of such a policy, as we saw in the previous chapter. While this proposal has not passed, it has received a notable amount of support. For example, on March 1, 1994, the U.S. Senate nearly approved such a measure, with 63 senators voting for it. If four more votes had been cast in its favor, it would have gotten through the Senate. A major step would have been taken toward its approval.

a. Senator Harry Byrd of Virginia took his oath of office as Senator the same day that Franklin D. Roosevelt took his as President—March 4, 1933. On May 4, 1955, after over 20 years in the Senate, he said the following about federal deficits: "Year by year, nearly in direct ratio to deficit spending, the purchasing power of the dollar has declined. Beginning with a 100-cent dollar in 1940, the value of the dollar had declined to 52 cents in 1954. . . . As proof of the fact that deficit spending is directly responsible for cheapening the dollar, let me mention that in 1942, when we spent $19 billion in excess of revenue, the dollar in that one year declined 10 cents in value."[3] Do you agree that budget deficits are bound to result in inflation? If so, explain why this is the case. If not, explain why budget deficits may not produce inflation and give examples.

b. On June 11, 1962, President John F. Kennedy made the commencement address at Yale University in which he said: "The myth persists that federal deficits create inflation and budget surpluses prevent it. Yet sizable budget surpluses after the war did not prevent inflation, and persistent deficits for the last several years have not upset our basic price stability. Obviously deficits are sometimes dangerous—and so are surpluses. But honest assessment plainly requires a more sophisticated view than the old and automatic cliché that deficits automatically bring inflation."[4] Is it true that surpluses can be dangerous? If so, under what circumstances is this true and why?

c. Many people favor a balanced budget because they think it will keep a lid on excessive government spending. In 1959, Maurice Stans, a federal budget director, said, "[F]ederal programs are not only large . . . but have a built-in durability—a staying power with which

we must reckon as a fact of life."[5] Critics of government spending cite cases like the B-1 bomber, which cost about $25 billion (for 100 airplanes), despite the allegation that it is slow, sluggish, and limited in range. There are problems, which may never be fully corrected, in the plane's electronic defensive systems. In 1987, one of the first B-1 bombers crashed; another crashed in 1988. When war broke out in the Persian Gulf in 1991, critics pointed out that the Pentagon did not make use of the airplane. What factors stand in the way of canceling programs like the B-1 bomber? Why is it so difficult to phase out government programs when they seem to have outlived their usefulness or have gotten into trouble?

d. According to the Republican members of Congress's Joint Economic Committee, "nearly 24 percent of economic output is devoted to federal spending, compared to 19 percent in the early 1960s. The rise of the deficits reflects an underlying unwillingness to control congressional spending."[6] As evidence they point to Figure 8.1. Do you agree? Why or why not?

e. In his 1994 Economic Report, President Clinton said: "For more than a decade, the Federal Government has been living well beyond its means—spending much more than it has taken in, and borrowing the difference. The resulting deficits have been huge, both in sheer magnitude and as a percentage of the Nation's output. Since 1981 the Federal debt has been growing faster than the economy, reversing the trend of the previous three decades. As a consequence. . . , Federal budget deficits have been gobbling up an inordinate share of the Nation's savings, driving up real long-term interest rates, discouraging private investment, and impeding long-run private sector growth."[7] Do you agree that the deficit increases real long-term interest rates? (See Figure 8.2.) If so, why does it do so?

[3] *Congressional Record,* May 5, 1955.

[4] John F. Kennedy, "Mythology vs. Economic Knowledge," in Arthur Okun (ed.), *The Battle Against Unemployment* (New York: Norton, 1965), p. 2.

[5] Maurice Stans, "The Need for Balanced Federal Budgets," ibid., p. 116.

[6] Joint Economic Committee, *The 1993 Joint Economic Report* (Washington, D.C.: Government Printing Office, April 1, 1993), p. 104.

[7] *Economic Report of the President,* 1994, p. 3.

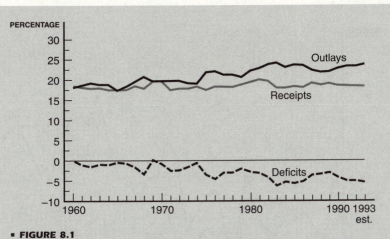

▪ **FIGURE 8.1**

Federal Outlays, Receipts, and Deficits (as a Percentage of GDP), 1960–1993

SOURCE: Executive Office of the President, Office of Management and Budget, *Budget Baselines, Historical Data*, January 1993.

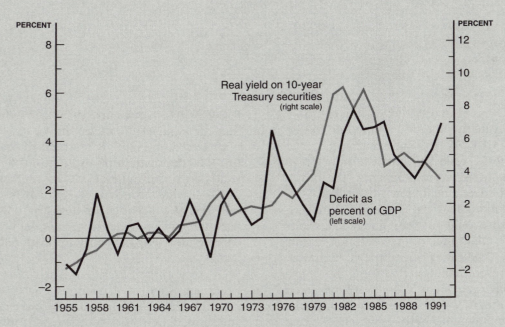

▪ **FIGURE 8.2**

Federal Deficits and Real Interest Rates, 1995–1991

SOURCE: *Economic Report of the President*, 1994, p. 31.

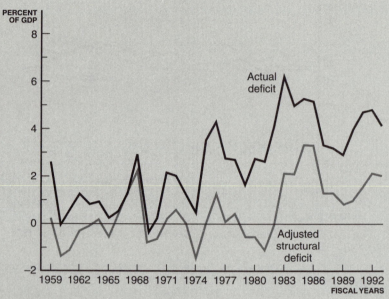

▪ **FIGURE 8.3**

Actual and Structural Deficits, 1959–1993 (Percent of GDP)

* The structural deficit has been adjusted for inflation.

SOURCE: *Economic Report of the President*, 1994.

If it increases interest rates, is it likely to reduce private investment and the rate of growth of GDP? Why or why not?

f. In 1994, President Clinton's Council of Economic Advisers said it opposed "the balanced budget amendment to the Constitution for many reasons. First and foremost, the amendment would put fiscal policy in a straitjacket that might imperil macroeconomic stability, thereby abdicating one of the government's principal responsibilities and raising the specter of mass unemployment."[8] Do you think that the amendment would make it more difficult to fight unemployment? Why or why not?

PROBLEM 8.2   Actual and structural deficits of the federal government are shown in Figure 8.3.

a. Based on Figure 8.3, which shows the Clinton administration's estimates of the structural deficit, were the deficits in 1968 and 1985 due to a weak economy? Why or why not?

b. What concept of the deficit would you use to determine whether fiscal policy is becoming more expansionary or more restrictive? Why?

c. According to President Bush's Council of Economic Advisers, "economists agree almost unanimously that deficits *should* increase during and immediately after recessions."[9] Why?

[8] Ibid., p. 39.

[9] *Economic Report of the President*, 1993, p. 246.

10 ▪ Applying Economics: The Pros and Cons of Discretionary Fiscal Policy

The following two problems are concerned with the extent to which discretionary fiscal policy of various kinds can and should be adopted.

PROBLEM 8.3 In 1962, President Kennedy's Council of Economic Advisers argued as follows in favor of discretionary fiscal policy: "Discretionary budget policy, e.g., changes in tax rates or expenditure programs, is indispensable—sometimes to reinforce, sometimes to offset, the effects of the stabilizers. To be effective, discretionary budget policy should be flexible. In order to promote economic stability, the Government should be able to change quickly tax rates or expenditure programs, and equally able to reverse its actions as circumstances change. Failure to arrest quickly a downturn in income, production, and employment may shake the faith of firms and households in prompt recovery and thereby lead to a cumulative decline. Delay in countering inflationary pressures may permit the development of a self-propelling speculative boom, with disruptive consequences to the domestic economy. . . . "[10]

a. Nobel laureate James Tobin of Yale University has argued that "Recoveries from almost every previous postwar recession have had the help of fiscal stimulus. The much-touted 1983–88 recovery was driven by fiscal demand stimulus massively greater than any previous peacetime fiscal expansion. It took two main forms: consumption by affluent taxpayers enjoying lower tax rates and a rapid build-up of defense spending."[11] Doesn't this indicate that discretionary fiscal policy is called for? Why or why not?

b. In 1989, Lee Hamilton, chairman of the Joint Economic Committee of Congress, was asked: "At this stage of the business cycle,

shouldn't we normally be generating a budget surplus rather than a growing deficit?" His reply was: "That's exactly what economists have been telling us in the Joint Economic Committee hearings. The federal government ought to be running a substantial surplus in the budget."[12] Why should the government have been running a surplus in 1989? To do so, was it necessary that discretionary fiscal policy be adopted? Why or why not?

c. According to President Bush's Council of Economic Advisers, "in its extreme form, discretionary policy involves reacting to short-term developments, with little attempt to consider and communicate intentions for future actions."[13] Why should the government consider and communicate intentions for future actions? Why not pay heed to the old maxim: Sufficient to the day is the evil thereof?

d. President Bush's advisers also stated that "programs of fiscal stimulus can lead, over time, to long-run government spending that exceeds the level implied by an assessment of the costs and benefits of the programs themselves."[14] How can this occur? Do you think that this is a real danger? Why or why not?

PROBLEM 8.4 The federal budget is a statement of the government's anticipated expenditures and revenues. The federal budget is for a fiscal year, from October 1 to September 30. About 15 months before the beginning of a particular fiscal year, the various agencies of the federal government begin to prepare their program proposals for that year. Then they make detailed budget requests which the president, with his Office of Management and Budget (OMB), goes over. Since the agencies generally

[10] *Economic Report of the President*, 1962, pp. 71–72.

[11] James Tobin, "Thinking Straight About Fiscal Stimulus and Deficit Reduction," *Challenge*, March–April 1993, p. 18.

[12] Lee Hamilton, "Can We Break the Budget Deadlock?" *Challenge*, July–August 1989.

[13] *Economic Report of the President*, 1990, p. 64.

[14] Ibid.

want more than the president wants to spend, he usually cuts down their requests.

In January (preceding the beginning of the fiscal year), the president submits his budget to Congress, which then spends many months in intensive deliberation and negotiation. Congressional committees concerned with particular areas like defense or education recommend changes in the president's budget. The Congressional Budget Office makes various types of economic analyses to help senators and representatives evaluate alternative programs. The process by which decisions are reached is influenced by the push and shove of partisan politics, as well as by economic factors. Eventually, however, decisions regarding the expenditures of the huge federal government are made.

a. According to President Bush's Council of Economic Advisers, "Because the Federal budget process begins well in advance of actual spending, and because downturns are difficult to forecast, annual appropriations are usually not an effective means of fighting recessions."[15] Suppose that it takes the federal government a year to formulate and approve spending plans and actually spend the money. If a downturn can be recognized only 3 months before it occurs, what are the difficulties in using federal expenditures for antirecessionary purposes?

b. According to Wilfred Lewis, an economist at OMB, the "successful use of public works to counter recessions requires a shelf of approved, planned projects ready to start, and such a shelf requires either a slowing down once the recession is over, or at least the ability to stop short of actually constructing useful public works that have been fully planned."[16] Why is it necessary to stop short of constructing public works once they have been fully planned? Why not go ahead and complete them? Surely it is better to do so than to abandon a project that is incomplete.

c. The tax legislative process in the United States is complex. Frequently the major initiative leading to a change in the tax laws comes

15 Ibid., p. 111
16 Wilfred Lewis, "The Limitations of Public Works," in Okun, *The Battle Against Unemployment*, p. 124.

from the president, who requests tax changes in his State of the Union message, his budget message, or a special tax message. Much of the spadework underlying his proposals will have been carried out by the Treasury Department.

The proposal of a major tax change generally brings about considerable public debate. Representatives of labor, industry, agriculture, and other economic and social groups present their opinions. Newspaper articles, radio shows, and television commentators analyze the issues. By the time Congress begins to look seriously at the proposal, the battle lines between those who favor the change and those who oppose it are generally pretty clearly drawn. The tax bill incorporating the change is first considered by the Ways and Means Committee of the House of Representatives, a very powerful committee composed of members drawn from both political parties. After public hearings, the committee goes into executive session and reviews each proposed change with its staff and with the Treasury staff. After careful study, the committee arrives at a bill it recommends—though this bill may or may not conform to what the president asked for. Then the bill is referred to the entire House of Representatives for approval. Only rarely is a major tax bill recommended by the committee turned down by the House.

Next, the bill is sent to the Senate. There it is referred to the Finance Committee, which is organized like the House Ways and Means Committee. The Finance Committee also holds hearings, discusses the bill at length, makes changes in it, and sends its version of the bill to the entire Senate, where there frequently is considerable debate. Ultimately, it is brought to a vote. If it does not pass, that ends the process. If it does pass (and if it differs from the House version of the bill, which is generally the case), then a conference committee must be formed to iron out the differences between the House and Senate versions. Finally, when this compromise is worked out, the result must be passed by both houses and sent to the president. The president rarely vetoes a tax bill, although it has occasionally been done.

Suppose that there is evidence that a recession is about to occur. What are the problems involved in using tax changes to fight it? Do you think that these problems are more severe than those involved in using tax changes to fight inflation? Why or why not?

d. In its 1993 annual report, President Bush's Council of Economic Advisers said that "a temporary income tax cut will affect consumption less than a permanent cut. . . . Given current concerns about large budget deficits, unless income tax cuts are linked to reductions in future government spending, people may be more likely to believe any current tax cut will be offset by higher taxes in the future. If so, tax cuts will have little effect on current spending."[17] Why will a temporary tax cut affect consumption expenditure less than a permanent cut? If you were a member of Congress, would you expect that tax cuts would have little effect on current spending unless government spending is to be cut? Why or why not?

[17] *Economic Report of the President,* 1993, p. 113.

11 ▪ Applying Economics: The Effects of Fiscal Policy

The following two problems deal with the effects of fiscal policy and the differences between open and closed economies in the extent of these effects.

PROBLEM 8.5 Suppose that the full-employment level of GDP is $300 billion in a particular country. At a level of disposable income of $200 billion, consumers save zero; the marginal propensity to consume is 3/4 at all levels of disposable income. The government spends $40 billion and collects $40 billion in taxes from consumers; there are no other taxes and no transfer payments. This country has a closed economy; that is, there are no exports or imports. In the relevant range (up to full employment), the short-run aggregate supply curve is horizontal.

a. For an equilibrium to occur, must GDP equal desired spending on final goods and services? That is, must it equal desired consumption expenditure plus planned investment plus government expenditure? Why or why not?

b. If planned investment in the economy equals $10 billion, will there be an inflationary gap? A recessionary gap? Why or why not?

c. Can full employment be achieved by changes in the level of government expenditure? If so, how large must these changes be? Will the government run a budget deficit or surplus, and how big will it be?

d. If government expenditures remain at $40 billion, can full employment be achieved by changes in the level of taxes? If so, how large must these changes be? Will the government run a budget deficit or surplus, and how big will it be?

e. Is it realistic to assume that the short-run aggregate supply curve is horizontal? Why or why not?

f. Is the assumption that the short-run aggregate supply curve is horizontal in accord with the simple Keynesian model?

PROBLEM 8.6 Practically all human beings realize that they are not islands unto themselves, and that they benefit from living with, working with, and trading with other people. Exactly the same is true of countries. They too must interact with one another, and they too benefit from trade with one another. In 1995, the exports of the United States amounted to about $810 billion, and our imports were about $900 billion. Without foreign trade, the United States, like other countries, would be worse off economically.

Given that foreign trade occurs, people must exchange one country's currency for that of another country. The value of a particular country's currency in terms of foreign currencies can vary considerably from one period of time to another. For example, in 1985 a dollar was worth about 3 German marks, whereas in 1991 it was worth only about 1.6 German marks. When the value of a country's currency goes down, it encourages exports (because this country's goods become cheaper to foreigners) and discourages imports (because other countries' goods become more expensive to this country's people and firms).

a. Suppose an economy is closed (that is, no exports and imports), and that the government decides to use fiscal policy to stimulate the economy; that is, it cuts taxes or increases spending. If this expansionary fiscal policy shifts the aggregate demand curve from D_1 to D_2 in Figure 8.4, what effect will this expansionary fiscal policy have on real GDP? What effect will it have on the price level?

b. In contrast to part a, suppose that the economy is not closed. In this case, what will be the effect of this expansionary fiscal policy on the interest rate, particularly if this policy results in increased government borrowing? Will the interest rate be pushed up or down? Why?

c. Given the change in the interest rate discussed in part b, what will be the effect on the value of the dollar relative to other currencies like the Japanese yen or the German mark? Will the dollar become more or less valuable? Why?

d. What will be the effect of the change in the value of the dollar (discussed in part c) on the aggregate demand curve? Will it push the aggregate demand curve to the right or the left?

(Hint: What will be the effect on net exports?)

e. What will be the effect of the change in the value of the dollar (discussed in part d) on the aggregate supply curve? Will it push the aggregate supply curve to the right or the left? (Hint: Will imported inputs be cheaper or more expensive?)

f. If the economy is not closed, will this expansionary fiscal policy have more or less effect on real GDP than if the economy is closed? Why?

g. If the economy is not closed, will this expansionary fiscal policy have more or less effect on the price level than if the economy is closed? Why?

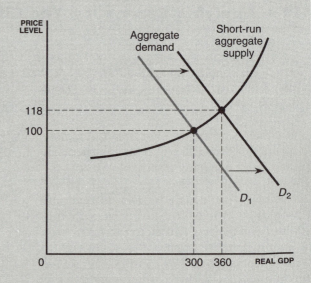

■ **FIGURE 8.4**

Effects of Expansionary Fiscal Policy

12 ■ Applying Economics: The Peace Dividend and the Clinton Stimulus Package

The final two problems are concerned with the so-called peace dividend, which was an important issue in the Bush administration, and the Clinton administration's proposals for fiscal stimulus in early 1993.

PROBLEM 8.7 Reduced military tensions after the fall of the Berlin Wall brought a cut in military spending and a lot of discussion during the Bush years of a "peace dividend." Some felt that the money that was spent on defense should be used for other government programs such as education, law enforcement, and the environment. But President Bush, among others, disagreed. "When I hear 'peace dividend,'" he said, some people think, "if you cut defense spending by $10 billion, we can take that money and spend it on something else. They all have a wide variety of programs. We can't do that. We've got enormous budget problems."[18]

a. According to experts, there was no surge in aggregate demand or productivity after the Korea or Vietnam Wars. Would you have expected such a surge from the military build-down of the 1990s? Why or why not?

b. Defense's share of GDP was about 5 percent in the early 1990s (Figure 8.5), as contrasted with about 10 percent in the late 1960s and almost 20 percent in the early 1950s.[19] Would you expect that a given percentage reduction in U.S. military capabilities would have as big an effect on aggregate demand and output in the 1990s as at the end of the Korea or Vietnam Wars? Why or why not?

c. According to *Business Week* magazine, "Whatever the size of the [defense] cuts, they appear certain to bring an eventual peace dividend to the U.S. in the form of lower inflation and interest rates, a declining budget deficit, and faster growth."[20] Do you agree? Why or why not?

d. The geographical distribution of defense spending on goods and services and of spending on military R and D in 1989 is shown in Table 8.1. Which areas are particularly likely to be hit hard by defense cuts? If you were a congressional representative of one of these districts, would you resist the cuts and fight for aid to the affected areas? If so, how would you carry out such a fight?

e. According to DRI/McGraw-Hill, a leading economic forecasting firm, a 20 percent defense cut in the period 1991 to 1994 would have had

[18] "Peace Dividend from Winding Down Cold War Would Disappear into Sinkhole of U.S. Deficit," *Wall Street Journal,* December 4, 1989.

[19] Edwin Mansfield and Nariman Behravesh, *Economics USA,* (4th ed.; New York: Norton, 1995), p. 261.

[20] *Business Week,* December 11, 1989.

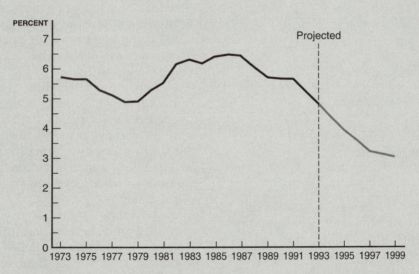

▪ **FIGURE 8.5**

National Defense Purchases as Percentage of Gross Domestic Product, 1973–1993

SOURCE: *Economic Report of the President,* 1994, p. 58.

▪ **TABLE 8.1**

Percent of Defense Spending on Goods and Services, by Geographical Area, 1989

AREA	PERCENT
Los Angeles–Long Beach, California	7.2
Washington, D.C. and vicinity	4.2
Norfolk–Virginia Beach–Newport News	4.2
St. Louis and Illinois	3.8
Boston	3.1
Nassau–Suffolk, New York	3.0
San Jose, California	2.7
Philadelphia and New Jersey	2.2
Fort Worth–Arlington, Texas	2.1
Anaheim–Santa Ana, California	2.1
Seattle, Washington	1.7
Dallas, Texas	1.6
Denver, Colorado	1.5

SOURCE: *Business Week*, December 11, 1989.

the following effects on output in selected industries:[21]

INDUSTRY	PERCENT CHANGE
Cement	62
Autos	20
Primary metals	10
Household appliances	10
Machine tools	10
Office and computing equipment	2
Electronic components	−3
Aircraft	−21
Communication equipment	−24

Why would such a cut cause a substantial reduction in the output of aircraft and communications equipment? Why would it cause a substantial increase in the output of cement? (Hint: Housing starts might increase.)

PROBLEM 8.8 In the first quarter of 1991, the recession ended in the United States, and the

[21] Ibid.

expansion began, but it was a slower expansion than usual. In the first year after the trough of a recession, real national output generally increases by about 6 percent; in this case, real national output in the first year grew by less than 2 percent. Moreover, employment did not increase at all for a year after the trough (see Figure 8.6). Thus, while recovery occurred in 1991 and 1992, some called it a "jobless recovery."

In late 1992 and early 1993, members of the incoming Clinton administration considered what steps should be taken. In February 1993, the Joint Economic Committee of Congress held hearings to examine the state of the U.S. economy and the economic challenges confronting Bill Clinton and his new administration. Among the participants were Nobel laureates James Tobin of Yale and Robert Solow of MIT, as well as Allan Meltzer of Carnegie-Mellon University.

a. James Tobin recommended "stimulus of $60 billion a year for the two years 1993 and 1994, about 1 percent of GDP, capable thanks to secondary "multiplier" effects of adding 1.5 percent to GDP demand, a modest amount relative to the 6 percent shortfall of GDP from its potential."[22] What value of the multiplier was Tobin using? How can one measure potential GDP? If you had been a member of the Joint Economic Committee, what questions would you have put to Tobin?

b. Robert Solow testified "that 4-plus percent GDP growth in 1993 is a fairly conservative target for policy. That would require a stimulus package near $35 billion. . . . "[23] What did Solow mean by a "stimulus package"? If you had been a member of the Joint Economic Committee, what questions would you have put to Solow?

c. According to Allan Meltzer, "Much current discussion suggests that the most urgent necessity is to reduce the deficit while increasing spending to provide short-term stimulus. I

[22] James Tobin, "Policy for Recovery and Growth," Testimony before the Joint Economic Committee of Congress, February 11, 1993.

[23] Robert Solow, Testimony before the Joint Committee of Congress, February 11, 1993.

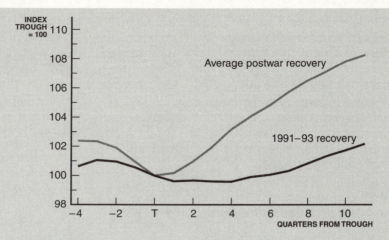

▪ **FIGURE 8.6**

Recovery Pattern of Nonfarm Payroll Employment Average Postwar Recovery and 1991–1993 Recovery

SOURCE: *Economic Report of the President,* 1994, p. 57.

do not share that view. The recovery will continue without additional short-run stimulus."[24]

[24] Allan Meltzer, "The Economy and Policy as 1993 Begins," Testimony before the Joint Committee of Congress, February 11, 1993.

Did it matter how quickly recovery continued? Why or why not? If you had been a member of the Joint Economic Committee, what questions would you have put to Professor Meltzer?

d. Figure 8.7 shows the changes in defense

▪ **FIGURE 8.7**

Defense Spending: Actual and Trend, 1989–1993

SOURCE: *Economic Report of the President,* 1994, p. 72.

spending from 1989 to 1993. Does it appear that military cutbacks could have been responsible for the relatively slow recovery? Why or why not?

e. The period 1991 to 1993 saw the lowest rates of growth of output in foreign industrial countries in over thirty years. Output growth averaged only 0.6 percent per year in the European Community (which includes Germany, France, Italy, and the United Kingdom, among others), 1.7 percent per year in Japan, and 0.2 percent per year in other industrial countries (see Table 8.2). Was this responsible in part for the relatively slow recovery? Why or why not?

f. If you were a member of Congress, would you have supported or opposed a short-run fiscal stimulus package in early 1993? Why or why not?

▪ **TABLE 8.2**

Foreign Country Real GDP Growth, 1989–1992

	ANNUAL PERCENTAGE GROWTH			
	1989	**1990**	**1991**	**1992**
European Community	3.5	3.0	0.8	1.1
Japan	4.7	4.8	4.0	1.3
Other industrial countries	3.2	1.1	−1.1	0.6
Developing countries	4.1	3.7	4.5	5.8

SOURCE: *Economic Report of the President*, 1994, p. 59.

13 ▪ Conclusion

The huge federal deficit has had an overwhelming influence on government decision making and on the discussion of public issues in the United States in recent years. Regardless of whether a public official or a TV commentator has been discussing health care, Social Security, education, the environment, or a host of other topics, he or she has been likely to refer, at least in passing, to the deficit and its implications for the topic under discussion. In this chapter, you have considered the following questions: Should the Constitution be amended to require a balanced budget? If not, how far should the government go toward a balanced budget? Should discretionary fiscal policy be abandoned? These questions are extremely important, and you should understand them. While economics alone cannot provide you with all the answers, it can clarify the issues enormously. In this chapter, you have seen how the concepts presented in previous chapters can shed valuable new light on these issues.

PART THREE

Monetary Policy

CHAPTER 9

Money and the Economy

Essentials of **Money and the Economy**

- Money acts as a medium of exchange, a standard of value, and a store of value.

- The sum total of coins, currency, demand deposits, and other checkable deposits is called the money supply (narrowly defined).

- With GDP constant, the amount of money demanded by individuals and firms is inversely related to the interest rate. The higher the interest rate, the smaller the amount of money demanded.

- In recent decades, governments have tried to manipulate the money supply in order to close (or at least reduce) recessionary and inflationary gaps.

- Monetarists emphasize the money supply in explaining the determination of output, employment, and prices.

- Classical economists propounded the crude quantity theory of money and prices, which states that the price level will be proportional to the money supply.

1 ▪ What Is Money?

You may be inclined to say that money consists of bills of a certain size and color with certain words and symbols printed on them, as well as coins of a certain type. But this definition would be too restrictive, since money in other societies has consisted of whale teeth, wampum, and a variety of other things. Thus it seems better to define money by its functions than by its physical characteristics. Like beauty, money is as money does.

MEDIUM OF EXCHANGE

Money acts as a medium of exchange. People exchange their goods and services for something called money, and then use this money to buy the goods and services they want. To see how important money is as a medium of exchange, suppose that it did not exist. To exchange the goods and services they produce for the goods

and services they want to consume, people would have to resort to *barter*, or direct exchange. If you were a wheat farmer, you would have to go to the people who produce the meat, clothes, and other goods and services you want, and swap some of your wheat for each of these goods and services. This would be a very cumbersome procedure.

STANDARD OF VALUE

Money acts as a standard of value. It is the unit in which the prices of goods and services are measured. How do you express the price of coffee or tea or shirts or suits? In dollars and cents. Thus money prices tell you the rates at which goods and services can be exchanged. If the money price of a shirt is $45 and the money price of a tie is $15, a shirt will exchange for 3 ties. Put differently, a shirt will be "worth" 3 times as much as a tie.

STORE OF VALUE

Money acts as a store of value. A person can hold on to money and use it to buy things later. You often hear stories about people who hoard a lot of money under their mattresses or bury it in their back yards. These people have an overdeveloped appreciation of the role of money as a store of value. But even those who are less miserly use this function of money when they carry some money with them, and keep some in the bank to make future purchases.

 TEST YOUR UNDERSTANDING

True or false?

____ **1** Without money, people would resort to barter.

____ **2** Money prices indicate the rates at which goods and services can be exchanged.

____ **3** Money is not useful as a store of value.

Exercises

1 "Money, in and of itself, has no value whatsoever. It is valuable only because of what it can buy." Comment and evaluate.

2 Explain in detail why the following items are not money: (a) government bonds, (b) General Motors stock, (c) gold, (d) uranium.

---

2 ▪ The Money Supply, Narrowly Defined

In practice, it is not easy to draw a hard-and-fast line between what is money and what is not money, for reasons discussed below. But everyone agrees that coins, currency, demand deposits, and other checkable deposits are money. And the sum total of coins, currency, demand deposits, and other checkable deposits is called the money supply, narrowly defined.[1]

COINS AND CURRENCY

Coins are a small proportion of the total quantity of money in the United States. This is mainly because coins come in such small denominations.

[1] In addition, travelers checks are included in the money supply, narrowly defined, since you can pay for goods and services about as easily with travelers checks as with cash. As indicated in Table 9.1, travelers checks are only about 1 percent of the money supply, narrowly defined. Since they are so small a percentage of the money supply, you can ignore them in the following discussion.

It takes a small mountain of pennies, nickels, dimes, quarters, and half-dollars to make even a billion dollars. Of course, the metal in each of these coins is worth less than the face value of the coin; otherwise people would melt them down and make money by selling the metal. In the 1960s, when silver prices rose, the government stopped using silver in dimes and quarters to prevent coins from meeting this fate.

Currency—paper money like the $5 and $10 bills everyone likes to have on hand—constitutes a second and far larger share of the total money supply than coins. Together, currency and coins outstanding totaled about $393 billion in 1996, as shown in Table 9.1. The Federal Reserve System, described in the next chapter, issues practically all U.S. currency in the form of Federal Reserve notes. Before 1933, it was possible to exchange currency for a stipulated amount of gold, but this is no longer the case. (The price of gold on the free market varies; thus the amount of gold you

▪ **TABLE 9.1**

Money Supply, November 1996

TYPE OF MONEY	AMOUNT (billions of dollars)
Demand deposits	400
Currency and coins[a]	393
Other checkable deposits[b]	274
Travelers checks[c]	9
Total	1,076

[a] Only currency and coins outside bank vaults (and the Treasury and Federal Reserve) are included.

[b] Includes ATS and NOW balances at all institutions, credit union, share draft, and other minor items.

[c] See footnote 1.

can get for a dollar varies too.) All U.S. currency (and coin) is presently "fiat" money. It is money because the government says so and because the people accept it. There is no metallic backing of the currency anymore. But this does not mean that you should be suspicious of the soundness of our currency, since gold backing is not what gives money its value. (In fact, to some extent, cause and effect work the other way. The use of gold to back currencies has in the past increased the value of gold.) Basically, the value of currency depends on its acceptability by people. And the government, to ensure its acceptability, must limit its quantity.

DEMAND DEPOSITS AND OTHER CHECKABLE DEPOSITS

Demand deposits—bank deposits subject to payment on demand—are another part of the narrowly defined money supply. They are larger than currency and coins, as shown in Table 9.1. At first you may question whether these demand deposits—or checking accounts, as they are commonly called—are money at all. In everyday speech, they often are not considered money. But economists include demand deposits as part of the money supply, and for good reason. After all, you can pay for goods and services just as easily by check as with cash. Indeed, the public pays for

more things by check than with cash. This means that checking accounts are just as much a medium of exchange—and just as much a standard of value and a store of value—as cash. Thus, since they perform all of the functions of money, they should be included as money.

Other **checkable deposits** include negotiable order of withdrawal (NOW) accounts and other accounts that are very close to being demand deposits. A *NOW account* is essentially an interest-bearing checking account at banks, savings banks and other thrift institutions. First created in 1972 by a Massachusetts savings bank, such accounts became legal in more and more states, particularly in the northeast. In 1980, Congress passed a financial reform act that permitted federally chartered thrift institutions to have NOW accounts. Banking innovations like NOW accounts have blurred the distinction between checking and savings accounts. Since many savings and loan associations, mutual savings banks, and credit unions are now providing accounts against which checks can be drawn, it would make no sense to include as money only demand deposits in commercial banks. Instead, all such checkable deposits are included.

The narrowly defined money supply—the sum total of coins, paper currency, demand deposits, and other checkable deposits—has generally increased from one year to the next. However, the rate of increase of the quantity of money has by no means been constant. In some years, like 1990, the quantity of money increased by about 4 percent; in others, like 1986, it increased by over 10 percent. A great deal will be said later about the importance and determinants of changes in the quantity of money.

THE MONEY SUPPLY, BROADLY DEFINED

The narrowly defined money supply (which includes coins, currency, demand deposits, and other checkable deposits) is not the only definition of the money supply that is used by economists. There is also the money supply, broadly defined, which includes savings and small time deposits (deposits under $100,000 with a specific maturity, for example, one year) and money market mutual fund balances and money market deposit accounts, as well as coins, currency, demand deposits, and other checkable deposits. The money supply, narrowly defined, is often called

M1, while the money supply, broadly defined, is often called M2. Figure 9.1 shows how the broadly defined money supply has behaved in recent decades.

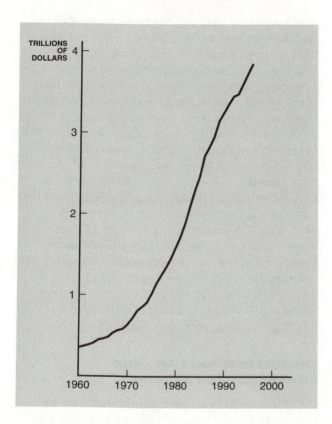

 FIGURE 9.1

Behavior of Money Supply (Broadly Defined), United States, 1960–1996

The money supply, broadly defined, about $4 trillion in 1996, has increased from year to year, but the rate of increase has by no means been constant.

✔ TEST YOUR UNDERSTANDING

True or false?

_____ **1** The value of currency does not depend on its acceptability by people.

_____ **2** The narrowly defined money supply includes coins, currency, demand deposits, and other checkable deposits.

_____ **3** M1 increases at a constant annual rate.

Exercise

1 Give some reasons why savings accounts should be regarded as money. Give some reasons why they should not. Which side of the argument do you find more convincing?

3 ▪ The Demand for Money

Let's now look in detail at how changes in the quantity of money affect gross domestic product. The first step in doing this is to discuss the demand for money. Why does a family or firm want to hold money? Certainly, a family can be wealthy without holding much money. You all know stories about very rich people who hold very little money, since virtually all their wealth is tied up in factories, farms, and other nonmonetary assets. Given that people and firms obtain a much higher return from other kinds of assets than from money, why do they want to hold money, rather than other kinds of assets? Two of the most important reasons are the following.

TRANSACTIONS DEMAND FOR MONEY   To carry out most transactions, money is required. Thus people and firms have to keep some money on their person and in their checking accounts to buy things. The higher a person's income—in real terms—the more goods and services that person probably will want to purchase, and hence the more money he or she will want to hold for transactions purposes. For example, in 1997, when a doctor made about $100,000 a year, the average physician would want to keep more money on hand for transactions purposes than in the days—many years ago—when a doctor made perhaps $10,000 a year. Because the quantity of money demanded by a household or firm increases with its income, it follows that the total quantity of money demanded for transactions purposes in the economy as a whole is directly related to real gross domestic product. That is, the higher (lower) the level of real GDP, the greater (less) the quantity of money demanded for transactions purposes.

In addition, the total quantity of money demanded for transactions purposes is directly related to the price level. That is, the higher (lower) the price level, the greater (less) the quantity of money demanded for transactions purposes. Obviously, if the price level were to double tomorrow, you would want to keep more money on hand for transactions purposes. In order to purchase the same goods and services as before, you would need more money.

PRECAUTIONARY DEMAND FOR MONEY   Besides the transactions motive, households and firms like to hold money because of uncertainty in the timing and size of future disbursements and receipts. Unpredictable events often require money. People get sick, and houses need repairs. Also, receipts frequently do not come in exactly when expected. To meet such contingencies, people and firms like to put a certain amount of their wealth into money and near-money. In the economy as a whole, the total quantity of money demanded for precautionary purposes (like the quantity demanded for transactions purposes) is likely to vary directly with real GDP and the price level. If GDP goes up, households and firms will want to hold more money for precautionary purposes, because their incomes and sales will be higher than before the increase in GDP. If the price level goes up, they will want to hold more money to offset the reduced purchasing power of the dollar.[2]

THE INTEREST RATE AND THE DEMAND CURVE FOR MONEY

Up to this point, you have considered why individuals and firms want to hold money. But you must recognize that there are disadvantages, as well as advantages, in holding money. One is that the real value of money will fall if inflation occurs. Another is that an important cost of holding money is the interest or profit you lose, since

[2] Still another motive for holding money is the speculative motive. People like to hold some of their assets in a form in which they can be sure of its monetary value and can take advantage of future price reductions. The amount of money individuals and firms will keep on hand for speculative reasons will vary with their expectation concerning future price movements. In particular, if people feel that the prices of bonds and stocks are about to drop soon, they are likely to demand a great deal of money for speculative reasons. By holding money, they can obtain such securities at lower prices than at present.

instead of holding money, you might have invested it in assets that would have yielded interest or profit. For example, the annual cost of holding $5,000 in money if you can obtain 6 percent on existing investments is $300, the amount of interest or profit forgone.[3]

With GDP constant, the amount of money demanded by individuals and firms is *inversely* related to the interest rate. *The higher the interest rate, the smaller the amount of money demanded. The lower the interest rate, the greater the amount of money demanded.* This is because the cost of holding money increases as the interest rate or yield on existing investments increases. For example, if the interest rate were 7 percent rather than 6

percent, the cost of holding $5,000 in money for one year would be $350 rather than $300. Thus, as the interest rate or profit rate increases, people try harder to minimize the amount of money they hold. So do firms. Big corporations like IBM or General Motors are very conscious of the cost of holding cash balances (see Figure 9.2).

[3] For simplicity, assume that money yields no interest or profit. This is not true because, as you saw earlier, the money supply includes some interest-bearing checkable deposits. But this makes no real difference to the present argument. Even if money yields some interest, it yields a much smaller return than alternative investments like bonds. Thus there is an opportunity cost involved in holding money.

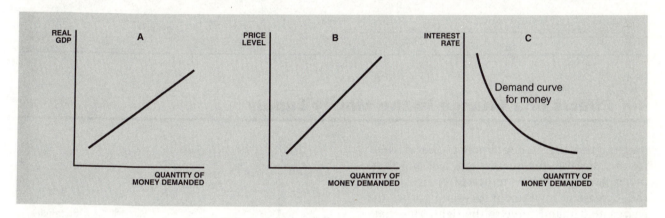

▪ **FIGURE 9.2**

The Demand for Money

Holding the interest rate and the price level constant, the quantity of money demanded is *directly* related to real GDP, as shown in panel A. Holding the interest rate and real GDP constant, the quantity of money demanded is *directly* related to the price level, as shown in panel B. Holding real GDP and the price level constant, the quantity of money demanded is *inversely* related to the interest rate, as shown in panel C. This last relationship is known as the demand curve for money.

 TEST YOUR UNDERSTANDING

True or false?

____ **1** The higher a person's income, the more money he or she tends to hold for transaction purposes.

____ **2** The total quantity of money demanded for

precautionary purposes is likely to be inversely related to real GDP.

____ **3** The higher the interest rate, the smaller the amount of money demanded.

Exercises

1 Why is the interest rate regarded as the "price" of holding money? What factors will shift the demand curve for money to the right? To the left?

2 Stephen Goldfeld of Princeton University has found that a 1 percent increase in real GDP or a 1 percent increase in interest rates has had the following effect on the real quantity of money demanded (that is, the quantity of money demanded divided by the price level):

	EFFECT OF 1 PERCENT INCREASE IN REAL GDP	EFFECT OF 1 PERCENT INCREASE IN INTEREST RATE
	(percent)	
Short run	+0.19	−0.045
Long run	+0.68	−0.160

a. The short-run effects are the effects after three months; the long-run effects are the effects after a few years. Why are the effects in the long run greater than in the short run?

b. If real GDP increases by 10 percent, what is the effect on the real quantity of money demanded in the long run?

c. If the interest rate increases from 8 to 10 percent, what is the effect on the real quantity of money demanded in the short run?

d. Goldfeld also found that the quantity of money demanded is proportional to the price level. Why do you think that this is the case?

4 ■ Effects of a Change in the Money Supply

Suppose that the money supply increases, the result being that the interest rate falls and that investment goes up. As indicated in Figure 9.3, the increase in investment spending pushes the aggregate demand curve to the right. This makes sense, since the quantity of total real output demanded (at the existing price level) goes up.

What will be the effect of this increase in the money supply? The answer depends heavily on the shape of the aggregate supply curve. If the economy is fully employed and the aggregate supply curve is vertical (or close to it), increases in the money supply will result in inflation, but little or no extra real output. However, if the intersection of the aggregate demand and supply curves prior to the increase in the money supply occurred in the upward-sloping range of the aggregate supply curve, as in Figure 9.3, the effect is an increase in real GDP from OY_0 to OY_1 and an increase in the price level from OP_0 to OP_1. Thus the increase in the money supply raises both total real output and the price level. (Of course, if the intersection occurred in the horizontal range of the aggregate supply curve, the price level would be constant.)

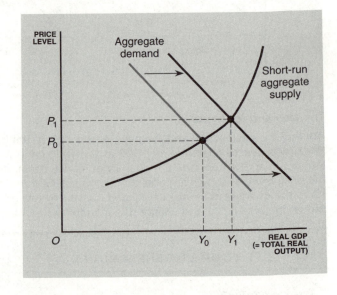

■ **FIGURE 9.3**

Effect of an Increase in the Money Supply on Real GDP and the Price Level

An increase in the money supply pushes the aggregate demand curve to the right, and thus increases real GDP from OY_0 to OY_1 and raises the price level from OP_0 to OP_1.

Just as an increase in the money supply pushes the aggregate demand curve to the right, so a decrease in the money supply pushes it to the left. A decrease in the money supply results in an increase in the interest rate, which results in a decrease in investment. Since the quantity of total real output demanded (at each price level) goes down, the aggregate demand curve shifts to the left. If the aggregate supply curve is vertical (or close to it), the result will be a reduction in the price level, but little or no cut in real output. But if the economy is operating in the upward-sloping range of the aggregate supply curve, the result will be a reduction in both the price level and real output.

 TEST YOUR UNDERSTANDING

True or false?

_____ **1** An increase in the money supply pushes the aggregate demand curve to the right.

_____ **2** A decrease in the money supply pushes the aggregate demand curve to the right.

_____ **3** An increase in investment pushes the aggregate demand curve to the right.

---

5 ▪ Closing a Recessionary Gap

In recent decades, governments throughout the world have tried to manipulate the money supply in order to close (or at least reduce) recessionary and inflationary gaps. Suppose that the economy is in the short-run equilibrium position shown in Figure 9.4. There is a recessionary gap, as evidenced by the fact that the equilibrium level of real national output, OQ_1, is less than its potential

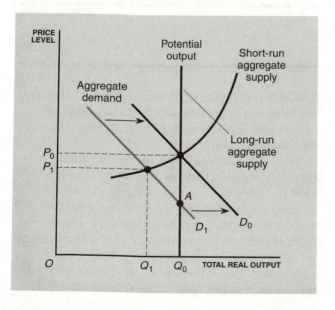

▪ **FIGURE 9.4**

Increasing the Money Supply to Close a Recessionary Gap

Initially there is a recessionary gap, since the equilibrium level of output, OQ_1, is less than the potential level, OQ_0. One way to close this gap may be to increase the money supply, and thus shift the aggregate demand curve from position D_1 to position D_0. Although this increases output to its potential level, there are inflationary consequences: the price level increases from OP_1 to OP_0.

level, OQ_0. (Recall that potential output is the amount of output that would be produced if there were full employment.) One way to deal with this situation is to leave things alone. As you know from previous chapters, a recessionary gap of this sort will eventually cure itself. As wages and prices eventually fall, the short-run aggregate supply curve will shift to the right, and the equilibrium level of real output will rise toward the potential level, OQ_0. Eventually the economy will move to point A, where the aggregate demand curve intersects the long-run aggregate supply curve, which is the vertical line at OQ_0.

But as Keynes and his followers pointed out, this process may take a long time to work itself out—and the pain inflicted on the unemployed and others may be substantial. Thus many economists have recommended that governments increase the money supply to help close a reces-

sionary gap. For example, in Figure 9.4, the government might increase the money supply so as to push the aggregate demand curve from its initial position (D_1) rightward to D_0, the result being that total real output will be raised from OQ_1 to its potential level, OQ_0. In this way, the recessionary gap will be closed.

However, one undesirable side effect is that the increase in the money supply raises the price level from OP_1 to OP_0. In other words, there are inflationary consequences. As pointed out in the previous section, the extent of the inflationary consequences depends on the steepness of the short-run aggregate supply curve. If the short-run aggregate supply curve is close to vertical, the inflationary consequences may be very great; but if the short-run aggregate supply curve is close to horizontal, they may be quite moderate.

 TEST YOUR UNDERSTANDING

True or false?

_____ **1** One way to close a recessionary gap is to increase the money supply.

_____ **2** One way to close a recessionary gap is to leave things alone, which will result in a rise in wages and prices.

_____ **3** One undesirable side effect of an increase in the money supply may be an increase in inflation.

6 ■ Closing an Inflationary Gap

Turning from a recessionary gap to an inflationary gap, suppose that the economy is in the short-run equilibrium position shown in Figure 9.5. There is an inflationary gap, as indicated by the fact that the equilibrium level of real national output, OQ_2, is greater than the potential level, OQ_0. Here, as in the case of a recessionary gap, one way to deal with the situation is to leave things alone. As you know from previous chapters, an inflationary gap of this sort will eventually cure itself. As wages and prices are bid up, the short-run aggregate supply curve shifts to the left. Eventually the economy will move to point

B, where the aggregate demand curve intersects the long-run aggregate supply curve, and the equilibrium level of real national output equals the potential level, OQ_0.

However, this leftward shift of the short-run aggregate supply curve will result in inflation until the price level rises to OP_3, in Figure 9.5. Given the many undesirable consequences of such inflation (detailed in Chapter 2), many economists have recommended that governments cut back on the money supply to help close an inflationary gap. For example, in Figure 9.5, the government might reduce the money supply so as to push the aggregate demand curve from its initial position (D_2) leftward to D_0, the result being that the price level will be OP_0, rather than OP_3. In this way, the government closes the inflationary gap.

Unfortunately, one side effect may be that unemployment will increase. Although this increase in unemployment will not be permanent, many economists believe that it can be substantial and prolonged.

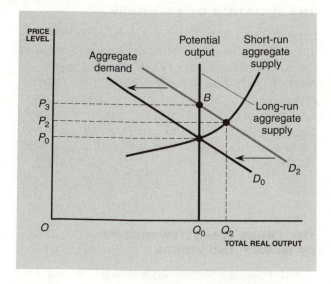

▪ **FIGURE 9.5**

Reducing the Money Supply to Close an Inflationary Gap

Initially there is an inflationary gap, since the equilibrium level of output, OQ_2, exceeds the potential level, OQ_0. One way to close this gap may be to reduce the money supply, and thus shift the aggregate demand curve from position D_2 to position D_0. This will result in the price level's equaling OP_0, which is lower than OP_3, which it would have equaled without the shift in the aggregate demand curve.

 TEST YOUR UNDERSTANDING

True or false?

____ **1** A reduction in the money supply will shift the aggregate demand curve to the right.

____ **2** When there is an inflationary gap, the equilibrium level of output exceeds the potential output.

____ **3** If the government cuts back on the money supply to help close an inflationary gap, unemployment may increase.

7 ▪ Monetarism

Some prominent economists, led by Milton Friedman of Stanford University's Hoover Institution, share a point of view known as monetarism; hence, they are called monetarists. During the 1950s and 1960s (and to a lesser extent during the 1970s and 1980s), there was a continuing (and sometimes bitter) controversy between the monetarists and the Keynesians. Monetarists regard the rate of growth of the money supply as the principal determinant of nominal GDP. (**Nominal GDP** means GDP in money, not real terms. In other words, nominal GDP is GDP measured in current, not constant, dollars.) At heart, the argument between the monetarists and the Keynesians was over what determines the level of output, employment, and prices. The Keynesians put more emphasis on the federal budget than the monetarists did; the monetarists put more emphasis on the money supply than did the Keynesians.

THE VELOCITY OF MONEY

The monetarists revived interest in the so-called quantity theory of money, which was developed many years ago by such titans of economics as Alfred Marshall of Cambridge and Irving Fisher at Yale. To understand this theory, it is useful to begin by defining a new term: the velocity of circulation of money. The **velocity of circulation of money** is the rate at which the money supply is used to make transactions for final goods and services. That is, it equals the average number of times per year that a dollar is used to buy the final goods and services produced by the economy. In other words.

$$V = \frac{\text{GDP}}{M}, \qquad (9.1)$$

where V is velocity, GDP is the nominal gross domestic product, and M is the money supply. For example, if the nominal gross domestic product is $1 trillion and the money supply is $200 billion, the velocity of circulation of money is 5; this means that, on the average, each dollar of money consummates $5 worth of purchases of gross domestic product.

Nominal gross domestic product can be expressed as the product of real gross domestic product and the price level. In other words,

$$\text{GDP} = P \times Q, \qquad (9.2)$$

where P is the price level—the average price at which final goods and services are sold—and Q is gross domestic product in real terms. For example, suppose that national output in real terms consists of 200 tons of steel. If the price of a ton of steel is $100, then nominal GDP equals $P \times Q$, or $100 × $200, or $20,000.

If you substitute $P \times Q$ for GDP in Equation (9.1), you have

$$V = \frac{P \times Q}{M}, \qquad (9.3)$$

That is, velocity equals the price level (P) times the real GDP (Q) divided by the money supply (M). This is another way to define the velocity of circulation of money—a way that will prove very useful.

THE EQUATION OF EXCHANGE

Now that you have a definition of the velocity of circulation of money, your next step is to consider the so-called equation of exchange. The **equation of exchange** is really nothing more than a restatement, in somewhat different form, of the definition of the velocity of circulation of money. To obtain the equation of exchange, all you have to do is multiply both sides of Equation (9.3) by M. The result is

$$MV = PQ. \qquad (9.4)$$

THE CRUDE QUANTITY THEORY OF MONEY AND PRICES

The classical economists discussed in Chapter 2 assumed that both V and Q were constant. They believed that V was constant because it was determined by the population's stable habits of holding money, and they believed that Q would remain constant at its full employment value. On the basis of these assumptions, they propounded the **crude quantity theory** of money and prices, a theory that received a great deal of attention and exerted considerable influence in its day.

If these assumptions hold, it follows from the equation of exchange—Equation (9.4)—that the price level (P) must be proportional to the money supply (M), because V and Q have been assumed to be constant. (In the short run, the full-employment level of real gross domestic product will not change much.) Thus you can rewrite Equation (9.4) as

$$P = \frac{V}{Q} M, \qquad (9.5)$$

where V/Q is a constant. So P must be proportional to M if these assumptions hold.

The conclusion reached by the crude quantity theorists—namely, *that the price level will be propor-*

tional to the money supply—is very important if true. To see how they came to this conclusion, you must recognize that they stressed the transaction motive for holding money. Recall from an earlier section that, on the basis of this motive, you would expect the quantity of money demanded to be directly related to the level of nominal GDP. Further, the demand for money was assumed to be stable, and little or no attention was paid to the effect of the interest rate on the demand for money. Indeed, the crude quantity theorists went so far as to assume that the quantity of money demanded was *proportional* to the level of nominal GDP. This amounted to assuming that velocity was constant.

Suppose there is a 10 percent increase in the quantity of money. Why would the crude quantity theorists predict a 10 percent increase in the price level? To begin with, they would assert that, since the quantity of money has increased relative to the value of nominal GDP, households and firms now hold more money than they want to hold. Further, they would argue that households and firms will spend their excess money balances on commodities and services, and that the resulting increase in total intended spending will increase the nominal value, but not the real value of GDP (since full employment is assumed). In other words, the increase in aggregate demand

will bid up prices. More specifically, they would argue that prices will continue to be bid up until they have increased by 10 percent, since only then will the nominal value of GDP be big enough so that households and firms will be content to hold the new quantity of money.

EVALUATION OF THE CRUDE QUANTITY THEORY

The crude quantity theory is true to its name: it is only a crude approximation to reality. One important weakness is its assumption that velocity is constant. Another is its assumption that the economy is always at full employment, which you know from previous chapters to be far from true. But despite its limitations, the crude quantity theory points to a very important truth: If the quantity of money increases by a large percentage, the price level is very likely to increase greatly as well. Thus, if the money supply is increased tenfold, there will be a marked increase in the price level. If you take the crude quantity theory at face value, you would expect a tenfold increase in the price level; but that is a case of spurious accuracy. Perhaps the price level will go up only eightfold. Perhaps it will go up twelvefold. The important thing is that it will go up a lot.

 TEST YOUR UNDERSTANDING

True or false?

_____ **1** If the velocity of money is increasing at 2 percent per year and the economy's potential real GDP is growing at 3 percent per year, the money supply should grow at 6 percent to maintain a constant price level.

Exercises

1 If the value of GDP (in money terms) increases 10 percent and the money supply remains fixed,

does velocity increase? Why, or why not? What are some of the factors that might cause an increase in velocity?

2 "The history of the United States is an account of one inflation after another. The currency is being debased further and further. Soon we may experience a runaway inflation." Comment and evaluate.

3 Describe how the quantity of money influences nominal and real GDP according to (a) the simple Keynesian model and (b) the crude quantity theory.

■ CHAPTER REVIEW

KEY TERMS

coins

currency

demand deposits

checkable deposits

M1

M2

nominal GDP

velocity of circulation of money

equation of exchange

crude quantity theory

COMPLETION QUESTIONS

1 If the short-run aggregate supply curve is close to vertical, an increase in the money supply will increase the _____ and have little effect on _____.

2 If the velocity of money is 5, and the money supply equals $200 billion, nominal GDP equals _____. If the velocity of money remains constant at 5, a $10 billion increase in the money supply results in a _____ increase in nominal GDP, and a $5 billion decrease in the money supply results in a _____ decrease in nominal GDP.

3 If the demand curve for money is a vertical line, the interest rate (does, does not) _____ influence the quantity of money demanded. One reason why such a demand curve for money seems (likely, unlikely) _____ is that there are _____ costs of holding money, and these costs increase as the interest rate (rises, falls) _____.

4 One of the most important costs of holding money is the loss of _____.

5 The _____ of money is the rate at which the money supply is used to make transactions for final goods and services.

6 The _____ assumes that full employment exists, and states that the price level must be proportional to the money supply.

7 The _____ shows the relationship between the interest rate and the money supply.

8 Excessive increases in the quantity of money may result in serious _____, whereas inadequate increases in the quantity of money may result in excessive _____.

9 The three principal types of money included in M1 are _____, _____, and _____.

ANSWERS TO COMPLETION QUESTIONS

price level, real output

$1 trillion

$50 billion
$25 billion

does not

unlikely, opportunity

rises

interest or profit

velocity of circulation

crude quantity theory

demand curve for money

inflation

unemployment

coins, currency, demand (and other checkable) deposits

10 _____ is the debt of the government, whereas _____ are the debts of the commercial banks.

Currency
demand deposits

11 The amount of money held by individuals and firms is inversely related to the _____.

interest rate

NUMERICAL PROBLEMS

1 The aggregate demand and supply curves in a particular country are shown below:

a If an increase occurs in the money supply, how will this graph change?

b If a decrease occurs in the money supply, how will this graph change?

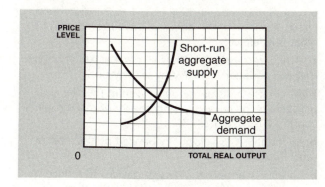

2 In country *A*, the price level during various years is as follows:

YEAR	PRICE LEVEL (1950 = 100)
1950	100
1960	120
1970	140
1980	200
1990	300
2000	350

a Plot the relationship between the price level and time in the graph at the top of the next column.

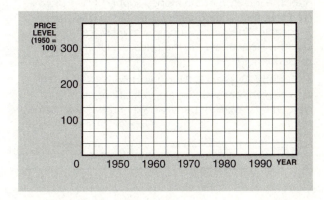

b By what percentage does the value of money decline in country *A* from 1980 to 1990? From 1950 to 1980?

c If your grandfather invested in a 40-year, $1,000 bond in country *A* in 1950, and if he held it until maturity in 1990, how much did he receive in principal in 1990 dollars? In 1950 dollars?

d Do you think that your grandfather was wise to invest in this bond? Why or why not?

3 Suppose that in the country of South Isthmus, the relationship between the interest rate and the quantity of money demanded, holding real GDP and the interest rate constant, is

$$i = 20 - 2M,$$

where *i* is the interest rate (in percentage points) and *M* is the quantity of money (in trillions of dollars).

a What is the name often given to this relationship?

b What is the interest rate in South Isthmus if the quantity of money demanded equals $5 trillion?

c Suppose that GDP in South Isthmus increases. Will the relationship between *i* and *M* remain constant? If not, in what direction will it shift?

4a If nominal GDP in South Isthmus increased by 20 percent between 1989 and 1994, while the money supply increased by 10 percent, what change occurred in the velocity of circulation of money?

b If nominal GDP in South Isthmus increased by 20 percent between 1992 and 1994, while velocity increased by less than 20 percent, did the money supply increase during this period, or did it decrease?

5 In the country of North Isthmus, suppose that the quantity of money increased considerably during 1997. After the increase in the money supply, it was discovered that the crude quantity theory of money was applicable. The money supply was increased by 10 percent. How much did the price level increase as a consequence?

6 Country Q's real GDP increased from 1992 to 1995 by 3 percent per year, and its velocity of money increased by 2 percent per year. Fill in the blanks below.

YEAR	PRICE LEVEL	MONEY SUPPLY
	(1992 = 100)	
1992	100	100
1993	___	101
1994	100	___
1995	100	___

7 The following data come from the 1979 and 1991 *Economic Reports of the President:*

YEAR	M1	M2	NOMINAL GDP
	(billions of dollars)		
1967	187.4	350.0	816.4
1969	209.0	392.5	963.9
1971	234.0	471.9	1,102.7
1973	270.5	571.4	1,359.3
1975	295.2	664.7	1,598.4
1977	338.5	809.5	1,990.5

Using M2 rather than M1, was velocity more stable during this time period? Do you think that velocity in the United States was the same in 1990 as during the above period?

8 What factors influence the velocity of circulation of money?

9 Suppose that the quantity of money demanded in country X (denoted by M) is related in the following way to nominal GDP (denoted as Y) and the interest rate (denoted by i):

$$M = \frac{Y(30 - 2i)}{50},$$

where M and Y are in trillions of dollars and i is in percentage points.

a Is the demand curve for money in this country a straight line?

b Does an increase in GDP from 1 to 2 trillion dollars affect the slope of the demand curve for money? If so, what is its effect?

c If the interest rate exceeds 15 percent, do you think that this equation holds? Why or why not?

10a On the basis of the data given in the previous problem, is the crude quantity theory of money valid in country X? Explain.

b In country X, is velocity influenced by the interest rate? Explain.

c Country X adopts a variety of devices to reduce the cost of transferring money balances from saving to checking accounts. Will this affect the validity of the equation in the previous problem? If so, what effect is it likely to have?

 ## ANSWERS TO
TEST YOUR UNDERSTANDING

SECTION 1

TRUE OR FALSE: 1. True   2. True   3. False

EXERCISES

1. The paper content of a dollar has little value. Money derives value from its ability to be exchanged for goods and services, because it is a unit of account, and because it acts as a store of value.

2. They do not act as a medium of exchange, a standard of value, and a store of value.

SECTION 2

TRUE OR FALSE: 1. False   2. True   3. False

EXERCISE

1. Savings accounts can be transformed into a medium of exchange, currency, by savings withdrawal. They represent a store of value. But the traditional argument against including them in the money supply has been that, in most instances, you could not pay directly for anything with them.

SECTION 3

TRUE OR FALSE: 1. True   2. False   3. True

EXERCISES

1. Because when you hold money, you give up the interest on it that could be earned.

2. a. Because it takes time for households and business firms to recognize and adapt to changing conditions. In the short run, they tend to be locked in to existing patterns of behavior, and it takes time to adjust.

b. The real quantity of money demanded will increase by about 6.8 percent.

c. Since the interest rate increases by 25 percent (from 8 to 10 percent), the real quantity of money demanded will fall by about 25×0.045, or 1.125 percent.

d. People demand money to pay for things. As the price level goes up, they require more money to pay for the same things. In other words, as the price level goes up, more money is demanded in order to have the same purchasing power as before.

SECTION 4

TRUE OR FALSE: 1. True   2. False   3. True

SECTION 5

TRUE OR FALSE: 1. True   2. False   3. True

SECTION 6

TRUE OR FALSE: 1. False   2. True   3. True

SECTION 7

TRUE OR FALSE: 1. False

EXERCISES

1. Yes, according to $MV = PQ$, V must increase by 10 percent. If people and firms conserve on the use of cash because of higher interest rates or the use of new technologies and payment methods, velocity will increase.

2. There is an inflationary bias in the U.S. economy, but it is not likely that the United States will experience a runaway inflation in the near future.

3. a. Simple Keynesian model: Changes in the money supply influence total spending through interest rates.

b. Crude quantity theory: The quantity of money affects the price level, but not real output, thereby influencing nominal GDP.

CHAPTER 10

The Federal Reserve and the Banking System

Essentials of **the Federal Reserve and the Banking System**

▪ The Federal Reserve System has control over the quantity of money in the U.S. economy.

▪ Commercial banks can and do create money.

▪ To determine how much money the banking system can create, divide the amount of excess reserves by the legally required ratio of reserves to deposits.

▪ If the banking system has a deficiency of reserves, the banking system as a whole will reduce demand deposits.

1 ▪ The Federal Reserve System

Any country must exercise control over the quantity of money. In the United States, the Federal Reserve System is charged with this responsibility. The Federal Reserve System—or Fed, as it is often called—plays a central role in the economy as a whole. After a severe financial panic in 1907, when a great many banks failed, there was strong public pressure to do something to strengthen the U.S. banking system. At the same time, there was great fear of centralized domination of the country's banks. The result—after six years of negotiation and discussion—was the establishment by Congress of the **Federal Reserve System** in 1913.

COMMERCIAL BANKS

As shown in Figure 10.1, the organization of the Federal Reserve System can be viewed as a triangle. At the base are the commercial banks. Congress has given the Federal Reserve very substantial powers over all banks and over nonbank depository institutions, even those that do not belong to the Federal Reserve System.

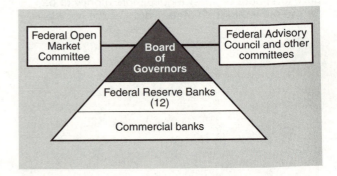

▪ FIGURE 10.1

Organization of the Federal Reserve System

The Federal Reserve System contains the commercial banks, the 12 regional Federal Reserve Banks, and the Board of Governors, as well as the Federal Open Market Committee and various advisory councils and committees.

FEDERAL RESERVE BANKS

In the middle of the triangle in Figure 10.1 are the 12 Federal Reserve Banks, each located in a Federal Reserve district. The entire country is divided into 12 Federal Reserve districts, with Federal Reserve Banks in New York, Chicago, Philadelphia, San Francisco, Boston, Cleveland, St. Louis, Kansas City, Atlanta, Richmond, Minneapolis, and Dallas. Each of these banks is a corporation owned by the commercial banks, but, despite this fact, the commercial banks do not in any sense act as owners of the Federal Reserve Bank in their district. Instead, each Federal Reserve Bank is a public agency. These Federal Reserve Banks act as "bankers' banks," performing much the same sorts of functions for commercial banks that commercial banks perform for the public. That is, they hold the deposits of banks and make loans to them. In addition, the Federal Reserve Banks perform a function no commercial bank can perform: They issue Federal Reserve notes, which are the country's currency.

THE BOARD OF GOVERNORS

At the top of the triangle in Figure 10.1 is the Board of Governors of the Federal Reserve System. Located in Washington, this board—generally called the Federal Reserve Board—has seven members appointed by the president for 14-year terms. The board, which coordinates the activities of the Federal Reserve System, is supposed to be independent of partisan politics and to act to promote the country's general economic welfare. It is responsible for supervising the operation of the money and banking system of the United States. The board is assisted in important ways by the Federal Open Market Committee, which establishes policy concerning the purchase and sale of government securities. The Federal Open Market Committee is composed of the board plus the presidents of five Federal Reserve Banks. The board is also assisted by the Federal Advisory Council, a group of 12 commercial bankers that advises the board on banking policy.

FUNCTIONS OF THE FEDERAL RESERVE

The Federal Reserve Board, with the 12 Federal Reserve Banks, constitutes the central bank of the United States. Every major country has a central bank. England has the Bank of England, and France has the Bank of France. **Central banks**

are very important organizations, whose most important function is to help control the quantity of money. One interesting feature of the United States's central bank is that its principal allegiance is to Congress, not to the executive branch of the federal government. This came about because Congress wanted to protect the Fed from pressure by the president and the Treasury Department. Thus the Fed was supposed to be independent of the executive branch. In fact, although the Fed has sometimes locked horns with the president, it has generally cooperated with him and his administration.

To repeat, a central bank's most important function is to control the money supply. But this is not its only function. A central bank also handles the government's own financial transactions, and coordinates and controls the country's commercial banks. Specifically, the Federal Reserve System is charged with the following responsibilities.

BANK RESERVES The Federal Reserve Banks hold deposits, or reserves, of the banks. As you will see, these reserves play an important role in the process whereby the Fed controls the quantity of money.

CHECK COLLECTION The Federal Reserve System provides facilities for check collection. In other words, it enables a bank to collect funds for checks drawn on other banks.

CURRENCY The Federal Reserve Banks supply the public with currency through the issuance of Federal Reserve notes.

GOVERNMENT FISCAL AGENT The Federal Reserve Banks act as fiscal agents for the federal government. They hold some of the checking accounts of the U.S. Treasury, and aid in the purchase and sale of government securities.

BANK SUPERVISION Federal Reserve Banks supervise the operation of the commercial banks. More will be said about the nature of bank supervision and regulation later in the chapter, and much more will be said about the functions of the Federal Reserve in the next chapter.

TEST YOUR UNDERSTANDING

True or false?

____ **1** The Federal Reserve System includes the commercial banks.

____ **2** The Federal Reserve Banks hold some deposits of commercial banks and make loans to them.

____ **3** The Federal Reserve Bank has 14 members appointed by the president for seven-year terms.

2 ■ Commercial Banks in the United States

There are thousands of commercial banks in the United States. This testifies to the fact that, in contrast to countries like England, where a few banks with many branches dominate the banking scene, the United States has promoted the growth of a great many local banks. In part, this has stemmed from a traditional suspicion in this country of "big bankers." ("Eastern bankers" are a particularly suspect breed in some parts of the country.)

Commercial banks have two primary functions. First, *banks hold demand deposits and permit checks to be drawn on these deposits.* This function is familiar to practically everyone. Most people have a checking account in some commercial bank, and draw checks on this account. Second, *banks lend money to industrialists, merchants, homeowners, and other individuals and firms.* At one time or another, you will probably apply for a loan to finance some project for your business or home. Indeed, it is quite possible that some of the costs of your college education are being covered by a loan to you or your parents from a commercial bank.

THE BALANCE SHEET OF AN INDIVIDUAL BANK

A good way to understand how a bank operates is to look at its balance sheet. The left-hand side of a firm's balance sheet shows the nature of its

assets; the right-hand side of a firm's balance sheet shows the firm's *liabilities* (that is, its debts) and its *net worth* (the value of the firm's owners' claims against the firm's assets). Since a firm's net worth is defined as the difference between its assets and its liabilities, the sum of the items on the left-hand side of a balance sheet must equal the sum of the items on the right-hand side. Table 10.1 shows the balance sheet of a particular bank as of the end of 1996.

THE LEFT-HAND SIDE The left-hand side shows that the total assets of the bank were $110.7 billion, and that these assets were made up as follows: $7.8 billion in cash, $6.9 billion in bonds and other securities, $85.8 billion in loans, and $10.2 billion in other assets. In particular, note that the loans included among the assets of this bank are the loans it made to firms and individuals. As we

■ **TABLE 10.1**

Balance Sheet, Hypothetical Bank, December 31, 1996 (Billions of Dollars)

ASSETS		LIABILITIES AND NET WORTH	
Cash	7.8	Deposits	92.3
Securities	6.9	Other liabilities	12.0
Loans	85.8	Net worth	6.4
Other assets	10.2		
Total	110.7	Total	110.7

have emphasized, lending money is one of the major functions of a commercial bank.

THE RIGHT-HAND SIDE The right-hand side of the balance sheet says that the total liabilities—or debts—of this bank were $104.3 billion, and that these liabilities were made up of $92.3 billion in deposits and $12.0 billion in other liabilities. Note that the deposits at this bank are included among its liabilities, since this bank owes the depositors the amount of money in their deposits. It will be recalled that maintaining these deposits is one of the major functions of a commercial bank. Returning to the bank's balance sheet, the difference between its total assets and its total liabilities—$6.4 billion—is its net worth, which is the value of the bank's owners' claims against the bank's assets.

LEGAL RESERVE REQUIREMENTS

The Federal Reserve requires every commercial bank (whether or not it is a member of the Federal Reserve System) to hold a certain percentage of its deposits as reserves. Most of these reserves are held in the form of deposits by banks at the Federal Reserve. Thus, for example, a great deal of the Bank of America's reserves are held in its deposit with the Federal Reserve. In addition, some of any bank's reserves are held in cash on the bank's premises. However, its legal reserves are less than the "cash" entry on its balance sheet since its deposits with other banks do not count as legal reserves. The most important reason for legal reserve requirements is to control the money supply, as indicated in the following chapter.

 TEST YOUR UNDERSTANDING

True or false?

_____ **1** If bank X's loans and securities are higher than bank Y's, bank X's legally required reserves are higher than bank Y's.

_____ **2** The most important reason for legal reserve requirements is to keep banks from failing.

_____ **3** The safety of a bank depends entirely on the level of its legal reserves.

_____ **4** One noteworthy characteristic of any bank's balance sheet is the fact that a very large percentage of its liabilities must be paid on demand.

---

3 ▪ How Banks Can Create Money

To see how banks can create money, imagine the following scenario. First, suppose that someone deposits $10,000 of newly printed money in bank A, and that the legal reserve requirement is that 1/6 of a bank's deposits must be held as reserves. Second, suppose that bank A lends Ms. Smith $8,333, and that Ms. Smith uses this money to purchase some equipment from Mr. Jones, who deposits Ms. Smith's check in his account at bank B. Third, bank B buys a bond (a security that is an IOU of the firm or government that issues it) for $6,944 from Ms. Stone, who uses the money to pay Mr. Green for some furniture. Mr. Green deposits the check to his account at bank C.

Admittedly, this is a somewhat complicated plot with a substantial cast of characters, but life is like that.

MONEY CREATION AT BANK A

The first step in our drama occurs when someone deposits $10,000 in newly printed money in bank A. The effect of this deposit is shown in the first panel of Table 10.2: Bank A's demand deposits and its reserves both go up by $10,000. Thus, it makes a loan of $8,333, since this is the amount of its **excess reserves** (those in excess of legal requirements). Because of the $10,000 increase in

▪ **TABLE 10.2**

Changes in Bank A's Balance Sheet (Dollars)

	ASSETS		**LIABILITIES AND NET WORTH**	
Bank	Reserves	+10,000	Demand deposits	+10,000
receives	Loans and			
deposit	investments	No change	Net worth	No change
	Total	+10,000	Total	+10,000
	Reserves	No change	Demand deposits	+ 8,333
Bank	Loans and			
makes loan	investments	+ 8,333	Net worth	No change
	Total	+ 8,333	Total	+ 8,333
Ms. Smith	Reserves	− 8,333	Demand deposits	− 8,333
spends	Loans and			
$8,333	investments	No change	Net worth	No change
	Total	− 8,333	Total	− 8,333
	Reserves	+ 1,667	Demand deposits	+10,000
Total	Loans and			
effect	investments	+ 8,333	Net worth	No change
	Total	+10,000	Total	+10,000

its deposits, its legally required reserves increase by $10,000/6, or $1,667. (Recall that $1 in reserves must be held for every $6 in deposits.) Thus, if it had no excess reserves before, *it now has excess reserves of $10,000 − $1,667, or $8,333.* When Ms. Smith asks one of the loan officers of the bank for a loan to purchase equipment, the loan officer approves a loan of $8,333. Ms. Smith is given a checking account of $8,333 at bank A.

How can bank A get away with this loan of $8,333 without winding up with less than the legally required reserves? The answer is given in the rest of Table 10.2. The second panel of this table shows what happens to bank A's balance sheet when bank A makes the $8,333 loan and creates a new demand deposit of $8,333. Obviously, both demand deposits and loans go up by $8,333. Next, look at the third panel of Table 10.2, which shows what happens when Ms. Smith spends the $8,333 on equipment. As pointed out above, she purchases this equipment from Mr. Jones. Mr. Jones deposits Ms. Smith's check to his account in bank B which presents

the check to bank A for payment. After bank A pays bank B (through the Federal Reserve System), the result—as shown in the third panel—is that bank A's deposits go down by $8,333 since Ms. Smith no longer has the deposit. Bank A's reserves also go down by $8,333 since bank A has to transfer these reserves to bank B to pay the amount of the check.

As shown in the bottom panel of Table 10.2, the total effect on bank A is to increase its deposits by the $10,000 that was deposited originally and to increase its reserves by $10,000 minus $8,333, or $1,667. In other words, reserves have increased by one-sixth as much as demand deposits. This means that bank A will meet its legal reserve requirements. To see this, suppose that before the deposit of $10,000, bank A had demand deposits of $X and reserves of $X/6. Then after the full effect of the transaction occurs on bank A's balance sheet, bank A's demand deposits will equal ($X + $10,000), and its reserves will equal ($X/6 + $10,000/6), since $1,667 = $10,000/6. Thus bank A continues to hold $1 in reserves for every $6 in demand deposits, as required by the Fed.

It is important to recognize that *bank* A *has now created $8,333 in new money.* To see this, note that Mr. Jones winds up with a demand deposit of this amount that he didn't have before; and this is a net addition to the money supply, since the person who originally deposited the $10,000 in currency still has her $10,000, although it is in the form of a demand deposit rather than currency.

MONEY CREATION AT BANK B

The effects of the $10,000 deposit at bank A are not limited to bank A. Instead, as you will see, other banks can also create new money as a consequence of the original $10,000 deposit at bank A. Let's begin with bank B. Recall from the previous section that the $8,333 check made out by Ms. Smith to Mr. Jones is deposited by the latter in his account at bank B. This is a new deposit of funds at bank B. As pointed out in the previous section, bank B gets $8,333 in reserves from bank

A when bank A pays bank B to get back the check. Thus the effect on bank B's balance sheet, as shown in the first panel of Table 10.3, is to increase both demand deposits and reserves by $8,333.

Bank B is in much the same position as was bank A when the latter received the original deposit of $10,000. Bank B can make loans or investments equal to its excess reserves, which are $6,944. (The way we derive $6,994 is explained in the footnote below.)[1] Specifically, it decides to buy a bond for $6,944 from Ms. Stone, and credits her checking account at bank B for this amount. Thus, as shown in the second panel of Table 10.3, the effect of this transaction is to increase bank B's investments by $6,944 and to increase its demand deposits by $6,944. Ms. Stone writes a check for $6,944 to Mr. Green to pay for some furniture. Mr. Green deposits the check in

[1] Since bank B's deposits increase by $8,333, its legally required reserves increase by $8,333/6, or $1,389. Thus $1,389 of its increase is legally required, and the rest ($8,333 − $1,389 = $6,944) is excess reserves.

▪ **TABLE 10.3**

Changes in Bank B's Balance Sheet (Dollars)

	ASSETS		LIABILITIES AND NET WORTH	
Bank receives deposit	Reserves	+8,333	Demand deposits	+8,333
	Loans and investments	No change	Net worth	No change
	Total	+8,333	Total	+8,333
	Reserves	No change	Demand deposits	+6,944
Bank buys bond	Loans and investments	+6,944	Net worth	No change
	Total	+6,944	Total	+6,944
Mr. Green deposits money in Bank C	Reserves	−6,944	Demand deposits	−6,944
	Loans and investments	No change	Net worth	No change
	Total	−6,944	Total	−6,944
Total effect	Reserves	+1,389	Demand deposits	+8,333
	Loans and investments	+6,944	Net worth	No change
	Total	+8,333	Total	+8,333

bank C. Bank B's demand deposits and its reserves are decreased by $6,944 when it transfers this amount of reserves to bank C to pay for the check. When the total effects of the transaction are summed up, bank B, like bank A, continues to meet its legal reserve requirements, since its increased reserves ($1,389) equal one-sixth of its increased demand deposits ($8,333).

Bank B has also created some money—$6,944 to be exact. Mr. Green has $6,944 in demand deposits that he didn't have before; and this is a net addition to the money supply since the person who originally deposited the currency in bank A still has her $10,000, and Mr. Jones still has the $8,333 he deposited in bank B.

THE TOTAL EFFECT OF THE ORIGINAL $8,333 IN EXCESS RESERVES

How big an increase in the money supply can the entire banking system support as a consequence of the original $8,333 of excess reserves arising from the $10,000 deposit in bank A? Clearly, the effects of the original injection of excess reserves into the banking system spread from one bank to another, since each bank hands new reserves (and deposits) to another bank, which in turn hands them to another bank. For example, bank C now has $6,944 more in deposits and reserves and so can create $5,787 in new money by making a loan or investment of this amount.[2] This process goes on indefinitely, and it would be impossible to describe each of the multitude of steps involved. Fortunately, it isn't necessary to do so. You can figure out the total amount of new money the entire banking system can support as a consequence of the original excess reserves at bank A without going through all these steps.

You do this by computing how much new money each bank creates. Bank A creates $8,333, which is the amount of excess reserves provided by the $10,000 deposit. Then bank B creates an additional $6,944, which is five-sixths of $8,333. Then bank C creates an additional $5,787—five-

[2] Why $5,787? Because it must hold $6,944/6 = $1,157 as reserves to support the new demand deposit of $6,944. Thus it has excess reserves of $5,787, and it can create a new demand deposit of this amount.

sixths of $6,944, or (5/6)(5/6) of $8,333, which is $(5/6)^2$ of $8,333. The amount of money created by each bank is less than that created by the previous bank, so that the total amount of new money created by the original injection of $8,333 of excess reserves—$8,333 + $6,944 + $5,787 + ⋯— tends to a finite limit as the process goes on and on. Elementary algebra tells us what this sum of terms will be. When the process works itself out, the entire banking system can support $50,000 in new money as a consequence of the original injection of $8,333 of excess reserves.[3] For a further explanation of this fact, see Figure 10.2, which describes the cumulative expansion in demand deposits. (Table 10.4 shows the amount of new demand deposits created at each stage of this process.)

[3] The proof of this is as follows. The total amount of new money supported by the $8,333 in excess reserves is $8,333 + $6,944 + $5,787 + ⋯, which equals $8,333 + (5/6) × $8,333 + $(5/6)^2$ × $8,333 + $(5/6)^3$ × $8,333 + ⋯, which equals

$$\$8,333 \times \left[1 + \frac{5}{6} + \left(\frac{5}{6}\right)^2 + \left(\frac{5}{6}\right)^3 + \cdots \right]$$

$$= \$8,333 \times \frac{1}{1 - 5/6} = \$50,000,$$

since $\quad 1 + \dfrac{5}{6} + \left(\dfrac{5}{6}\right)^2 + \left(\dfrac{5}{6}\right)^3 + \cdots = \dfrac{1}{1 - 5/6}$.

▪ **TABLE 10.4**

Increase in Money Supply Resulting from $8,333 in Excess Reserves

SOURCE	AMOUNT (dollars)
Created by bank A	8,333
Created by bank B	6,944
Created by bank C	5,787
Created by bank D	4,823
Created by bank E	4,019
Created by bank F	3,349
Created by bank G	2,791
Created by bank H	2,326
Created by bank I	1,938
Created by bank J	1,615
Created by other banks	8,075
Total	50,000

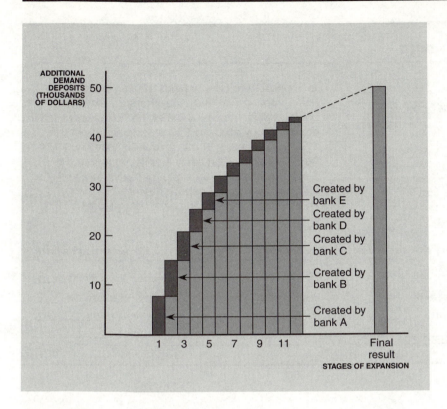

▪ **FIGURE 10.2**

Cumulative Expansion in Demand Deposits on the Basis of $8,333 of Excess Reserves and Legal Reserve Requirement of 16⅔ Percent

The original deposit was $10,000, which resulted in excess reserves of $8,333. In the first stage of the expansion process, bank *A* created an additional $8,333. In the second stage, bank *B* created an additional $6,944.

Suppose bank *C* lent $5,787 to Mr. White, who used the money to buy a truck from Mr. Black, who deposited Mr. White's check to his account at bank *D*. If so, bank *C* created an additional $5,787.

Suppose that bank *D* lent Ms. Cohen $4,823, which Ms. Cohen used to buy some lumber from Mr. Palucci, who deposited Ms. Cohen's check to his account at bank *E*. If so, bank *D* created an additional $4,823.

The process goes on until the final result is $50,000 of additional demand deposits.

TEST YOUR UNDERSTANDING

True or false?

_____ **1** If Marcia Jones pays back a $1,000 loan from her cousin, this results in a $1,000 decline in the money supply.

Exercises

1 Suppose that John Smith deposits $50,000 in newly printed currency to his account at bank *A*. What is the effect on bank *A*'s balance sheet?

ASSETS	LIABILITIES AND NET WORTH
(dollars)	
Reserves_____	Demand deposits _____
Loans and investments____	Net worth_____
Total_____	Total _____

2 Suppose that bank *A* lends the Bugsbane Music Box Company $30,000. After the Bugsbane Music Box Company receives the $30,000 loan, it uses the money to buy a new piece of equipment from the XYZ Tool Company. The XYZ Tool Company deposits Bugsbane's check on bank *A* to its account at the Bank of America. What is the total effect on bank *A*'s balance sheet of the deposit described in Exercise 1, and the loan and the purchase described here? Fill in the blanks below.

ASSETS	LIABILITIES AND NET WORTH
(dollars)	
Reserves_____	Demand deposits _____
Loans and investments____	Net worth_____
Total_____	Total _____

4 ▪ The Effect of Excess Reserves: A General Proposition

If a certain amount of excess reserves is made available to the banking system, the banking system as a whole can increase the money supply by an amount equal to the amount of excess reserves multiplied by the reciprocal of the required ratio of reserves to deposits. In other words, to obtain the total increase in the money supply that can be achieved from a certain amount of excess reserves, multiply the amount of excess reserves by the reciprocal of the required ratio of reserves to deposits—or, what amounts to the same thing, *divide the amount of excess reserves by the legally required ratio of reserves to deposits*. Putting it in still another way, the banking system as a whole can increase the money supply by $1/r$ dollars—where r is the required ratio of reserves to deposits—for every $1 in excess reserves.

Suppose that the banking system gains excess reserves of $10,000 and that the required ratio of reserves to deposits is 1/6. To determine how much the banking system can increase the money supply, you must divide the amount of the excess reserves—$10,000—by the required ratio of reserves to deposits—1/6—to get the answer: $60,000. If the required ratio of reserves to deposits is 1/10, by how much can the banking system increase the money supply? Dividing $10,000 by 1/10, you get the answer: $100,000. Note that the higher the required ratio of reserves to deposits, the smaller the amount by which the banking system can increase the money supply on the basis of a given amount of excess reserves. More will be said about this in the next chapter.

TEST YOUR UNDERSTANDING

True or false?

_____ **1** To obtain the total increase in demand deposits that can result from a certain amount of excess reserves, divide the amount of excess reserves by the legally required ratio of reserves to deposits.

_____ **2** The banking system as a whole can increase the money supply by *r* dollars—where *r* is the required ratio of reserves to deposits—for every $1 in excess reserves.

Exercise

1 The public is free to decide how much money it wants to hold in the form of currency (and coins) and how much it wants to hold in the form of demand deposits. Suppose that the relationship between the amount it wants to hold in currency (and coins) and the amount it wants to hold in demand deposits is as follows:

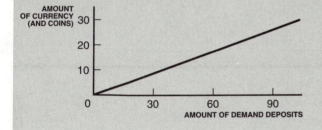

The reserve requirement is 20 percent, and commercial banks hold no excess reserves. For simplicity, assume that there are no checkable deposits other than demand deposits.

a. If the Federal Reserve wants to reduce the quantity of money by $2 billion, how much of a decrease must occur in demand deposits?

b. To obtain this decrease in demand deposits, by how much must banks' legal reserves decline?

c. In fact, the ratio of currency (and coins) to demand deposits increased during the 1970s in the United States. Was this consistent with the above graph?

d. Some people attribute the rise in this ratio to an increase in tax evasion and the growth of the underground economy. Why?

5 ▪ The Effect of a Deficiency of Reserves

If the banking system has a deficiency of reserves of a certain amount, the banking system as a whole will reduce demand deposits by an amount equal to the deficiency in reserves multiplied by the reciprocal of the required ratio of reserves to deposits.

In other words, to obtain the total decrease in demand deposits resulting from a deficiency in reserves, *divide the deficiency by the legally required ratio of reserves to deposits.* Putting it another way, the banking system as a whole will reduce demand deposits by 1/*r* dollars—where *r* is the required ratio of reserves to deposits—for every $1 deficiency in reserves. Although there is often a simultaneous contraction of money on the part of many banks, just as there is often a simultaneous expansion, this doesn't affect the result.

Apply this proposition to a particular case. Suppose that the banking system experiences a deficiency in reserves of $8,333 and that the required ratio of reserves to deposits is 1/6. Applying this rule, you must divide the deficiency in reserves—$8,333—by the required ratio of reserves to deposits—1/6—to get the answer, which is a $50,000 reduction in demand deposits.

Note that the effect if a $1 deficiency in reserves is equal in absolute terms to the effect of $1 in excess reserves. Both result in a $1/*r* change in demand deposits.

TEST YOUR UNDERSTANDING

True or false?

_____ **1** In absolute terms, the effect of a $1 deficiency in reserves is the same as the effect of $1 in excess reserves.

Exercises

1 "Banks do not create money. After all, they can only lend out money that they receive from depositors." Comment and evaluate.

2 Suppose that the legally required ratio of reserves to deposits is 1/10. If $100 million in excess reserves are made available to the banking system, by how much can the banking system increase the money supply? What is the answer if the legally required ratio of reserves to deposits is 1/6 rather than 1/10?

3 A bank often requires business borrowers to maintain a compensating balance in the bank. For example, a firm may have to keep 20 percent of its currently outstanding loans from the First National Bank as a demand deposit in the bank. Suppose that the First National Bank makes a $100,000 loan to the Acme Corporation at 10 percent interest with a 20 percent minimum compensating balance requirement.

a. How much of the loan can the Acme Corporation actually use?

b. How much interest does the Acme Corporation pay each year on the loan?

c. Based on your answers to parts a and b, what is the interest rate that the Acme Corporation is paying on the amount of money it borrows *and can use*?

CHAPTER REVIEW

KEY TERMS

central banks

excess reserves

COMPLETION QUESTIONS

1 The sum of the items on the _____ side of a balance sheet must equal the sum of the items on the _____ side.

2 A commercial bank can lend the amount by which its reserves are in excess of the _____.

3 The higher the required ratio of reserves to deposits is, the (larger, smaller) _____ is the amount by which the banking system can increase the money supply on the basis of a given amount of excess reserves.

4 If there is a $10,000 decrease in reserves (and the

ANSWERS TO COMPLETION QUESTIONS

left-hand

right-hand

legally required reserves

smaller

required ratio of reserves to deposits is 1/6), the entire banking system will reduce demand deposits by _____ if there are no excess reserves.

5 The _____ can influence the money supply by influencing the amount of reserves and the legal reserve requirements.

6 When excess _____ are made available to the banking system, the system as a whole can increase _____ by an amount equal to the amount of excess reserves multiplied by the _____ of the required ratio of reserves to deposits. For instance, if the banking system has excess reserves of $10,000 and the required ratio of reserves to deposits is 1/6, to determine how much the banking system can increase demand deposits, we divide _____ by _____. The increase in demand deposits is _____.

7 If the banking system has a deficiency of reserves, the system as a whole will reduce _____ by an amount equal to the deficiency in reserves multiplied by the _____ of the required ratio of reserves to deposits.

8 To obtain the total decrease in demand deposits resulting from a deficiency in reserves, divide the deficiency in reserves by the _____.

$60,000
Federal Reserve System

reserves

demand deposits
reciprocal

$10,000, 1/6
$60,000

demand deposits

reciprocal

legally required ratio of reserves to deposits

NUMERICAL PROBLEMS

1 Suppose that the balance sheet of Crooked Arrow National Bank is currently as follows:

ASSETS		LIABILITIES AND NET WORTH	
	(millions of dollars)		
Reserves	0.5	Demand deposits	2.5
Loans and securities	3.0	Net worth	1.0

The bank is legally required to hold reserves equal to at least 20 percent of its demand deposits.

a Suppose the depositors withdraw $100,000. Indicate what the individual items on the bank's balance sheet will be after this withdrawal:

ASSETS		LIABILITIES AND NET WORTH	
	(millions of dollars)		
Reserves	____	Demand deposits	____
Loans and securities	____	Net worth	____

b Will the bank have the required legal reserves after the withdrawal? If not, what courses of action are open to it?

2 Suppose that depositors deposited $100,000 of new money in the Crooked Arrow National Bank, rather than withdrew $100,000.

a What effect will this have on the bank's reserves? By how much can the bank increase its loans?

b Suppose that Crooked Arrow National Bank lends out the maximum amount that it can, under these circumstances. It lends this amount to John Brown, who uses it to buy a piece of equipment from the Ace Machine Tool Company, which deposits it in the First National Bank. Show the effect of this transaction together with the $100,000 deposit on the balance sheet of the Crooked Arrow National Bank by filling in the blanks below.

Crooked Arrow National Bank

Change in reserves _____

Change in demand deposits _____

Change in loans and securities _____

Change in net worth _____

c Show the effect of the transaction in part b on the balance sheet of the First National Bank by filling in the blanks below.

First National Bank

Change in reserves _____

Change in demand deposits _____

Change in loans and securities _____

Change in net worth _____

d Can the First National Bank increase its loans? By how much?

e Suppose that the First National Bank lends the maximum amount (according to part d) to William Cooper, who buys land from Jean Jones, who deposits the amount to her account at the Second National Bank. Show the effect of this transaction together with Brown's deposit on the balance sheet of the First National Bank by filling in the blanks below.

First National Bank

Change in reserves _____

Change in demand deposits _____

Change in loans and securities _____

Change in net worth _____

f Show the effect of the transaction in part e on the balance sheet of the Second National Bank by filling in the blanks below.

Second National Bank

Change in reserves _____

Change in demand deposits _____

Change in loans and securities _____

Change in net worth _____

g Can the Second National Bank increase its loans? By how much?

h How much bank money can the banking system as a whole support on the basis of the $100,000 of new reserves described in part a?

3a Suppose that the Federal Reserve reduces the reserve requirement from 20 to 15 percent while the bank's balance sheet is as shown in Problem 1. After the reduction, will the bank have excess reserves? If so, how much?

b Suppose that the Federal Reserve increases the reserve requirement from 20 to 25 percent while the bank's balance sheet is as shown in Problem 1. After the increase, will the bank be short of the legally required reserves? If so, by how much?

4 Bank *C* lends $5,000 to a depositor, Mary Monroe, by crediting her checking account balance with a $5,000 deposit.

a What is the effect of this transaction on the bank's assets?

b What is the effect of this transaction on the country's money supply (defined as M1)? What is its effect on M2?

c If Mary Monroe transfers the $5,000 from her checking account to her savings account at the bank, what is the effect on M1? What is the effect on M2?

5 Suppose that commercial bank reserves are $50 billion, the legal reserve requirement is 20 percent, and currency (and coins) in the hands of the public is $10 billion.

a If there are no excess reserves, what does M1 equal?

b If commercial bank reserves fall to $49 billion while currency in the hands of the public increases to $11 billion, what would M1 be if the other assumptions remain valid?

c Suppose that the reserve requirement increases to 25 percent (but that the other assumptions in part b remain valid). What is M1?

☑ ANSWERS TO
TEST YOUR UNDERSTANDING

SECTION 1

TRUE OR FALSE: 1. True   2. True   3. False

SECTION 2

TRUE OR FALSE: 1. False   2. False   3. False   4. True

SECTION 3

TRUE OR FALSE: 1. False

EXERCISES

1. Reserves, demand deposits, total assets and total liabilities rise by $50,000. Loans and investments and net worth are unchanged.

2. Effect on balance sheet:

ASSETS		LIABILITIES AND NET WORTH	
		(dollars)	
Reserves	+20,000	Demand deposits	+50,000
Loans	+30,000	Net worth	0
Total	+50,000	Total	+50,000

SECTION 4

TRUE OR FALSE: 1. True   2. False

EXERCISE

1. a. The graph indicates that the public wants to hold $1 in currency (and coins) for every $3 in demand deposits. Thus, if demand deposits decrease by $1.5 billion, currency (and coin) will decrease by $.5 billion, the total decrease in the money supply being $2.0 billion.

b. Since legal reserves equal 20 percent of demand deposits (because no excess reserves are held), legal reserves must decrease by $.3 billion (that is, 20

percent of $1.5 billion) if demand deposits decrease by $1.5 billion.

c. No.

d. Because the underground economy tends to be based on the use of currency (which is not traceable) rather than deposits (which are traceable).

SECTION 5

TRUE OR FALSE: 1. True

EXERCISES

1. The loans made by banks within the limits of reserve requirements do create money.

2. If the reserve ratio is 1/10, the system can support an additional $1,000 million with $100 million in excess reserves. If the reserve requirement is 1/6, $100 million in excess reserves can support a $600 million increase in the money supply.

3. a. $80,000.   b. $10,000.   c. 12½%.

Monetary Policy

Essentials of **Monetary Policy**

- The Federal Reserve can influence the money supply by managing the reserves of the banking system.

- The most important means the Federal Reserve has to control the quantity of bank reserves (and thus the quantity of excess reserves) are open market operations (the purchase and sale by the Fed of U.S. government securities in the open market).

- The Federal Reserve can also influence the money supply by changing the amount of reserves banks must hold for every dollar of demand deposits.

- The Federal Reserve also influences the money supply through changes in the discount rate, the interest rate the Fed charges banks for loans.

1 ■ What Is Monetary Policy?

Monetary policy is the exercise of the central bank's influence over the quantity of money and interest rates to promote the objectives of national economic policy. Increases in the money supply tend to push up real GDP and the price level, whereas decreases in the money supply tend to push them down. The extent to which the effect is on the price level rather than real GDP depends on the steepness of the short-run aggregate supply curve. The steeper it is, the greater the effect on the price level and the smaller the effect on real GDP. In the long run, increases in the money supply raise only the price level, not real GDP, and decreases in the money supply lower the price level, not real GDP.

When a recession seems imminent and business is soft, the central bank often increases the money supply and pushes down interest rates. That is, it "eases money" and "eases credit," as the newspapers put it. This tends to push the aggregate demand curve to the right. On the other hand, when the economy is in danger of overheating and serious inflation threatens, the central bank often reins in the money supply and pushes up interest rates. That is, in newspaper terms, it "tightens money" and "tightens credit." This tends to push the aggregate demand curve to the left, thus curbing the upward pressure on the price level.

In formulating monetary policy, the government's objectives generally are to attain or maintain reasonably full employment without excessive inflation. As you will see, not all economists agree that the sorts of discretionary policies described in the previous paragraph are most likely to achieve these objectives, but we now postpone a consideration of this controversy. Regardless of how you think the central bank should behave, it is important that you understand the ways in which it can increase or decrease the money supply.

A country's monetary authorities can influence the money supply by managing the reserves of the banking system. Suppose that the monetary authorities want to increase the money supply more rapidly than they would otherwise. How can they realize this objective? By providing the banks with plenty of excess reserves. As you saw in the previous chapter, excess reserves enable the banks to increase the money supply. Indeed, you learned that if there were no desired excess reserves and no currency withdrawals, the banks could increase the money supply by $6 for every $1 of excess reserves.[1] (The ways in which the monetary authorities can increase the reserves of the banking system—and thus provide excess reserves—are discussed at length in subsequent sections.)

On the other hand, suppose that the monetary authorities decide to cut back on the rate of increase of the money supply. To do so, they can slow down the rate of increase of bank reserves. As you saw in the previous chapter, this will force the banks to curtail the rate of growth of their demand deposits, by easing off on the rate of growth of their loans and investments. Indeed, if the monetary authorities go so far as to reduce the reserves of the banking system, this will tend to reduce the money supply. Under the assumptions made in the previous chapter, the banks must cut back the money supply by $6 for every $1 deficiency in reserves.

MAKERS OF MONETARY POLICY

Who establishes the United States's monetary policy? Who decides that, in view of the current and prospective economic situation, the money supply should be increased (or decreased) at a certain rate? As in the case of fiscal policy, this is not a simple question to answer; many individuals and groups play an important role. Certainly, however, *the leading role is played by the* **Federal Reserve Board** *and the* **Federal Open Market Committee.** The chairman of the Federal Reserve Board is the chief spokesperson for the Federal Reserve System. The recent chairmen— Alan Greenspan, Paul A. Volcker, G. William Miller, Arthur F. Burns, and William McChesney Martin—undoubtedly have had considerable influence over monetary policy.

---

[1] This assumes that the legal reserve requirement is 16⅔ percent. If the legal reserve requirement were 10 percent, a $10 increase in the money supply could be supported by $1 of excess reserves. However, a much smaller increase in the money supply may result from a dollar of reserves if banks want to hold excess reserves and if currency is withdrawn.

Although the Federal Reserve is responsible to Congress, Congress has established no clear guidelines for its behavior. Thus the Federal Reserve has had wide discretionary powers over monetary policy. But the Federal Reserve System is a huge organization, and it is not easy to figure out exactly who influences whom and who decides what. Formal actions can be taken by a majority of the board and of the Federal Open Market Committee (which is composed of the 7 members of the board plus 5 of the presidents of the 12 regional banks). However, this obviously tells only part of the story.

To get a more complete picture, it is essential to note too that many agencies and groups other than the Fed have an effect on monetary policy, although it is difficult to measure their respective influences. The Treasury frequently has an important voice in the formulation of monetary policy. The Fed must take into account the problems of the Treasury, which is faced with the task of selling huge amounts of government securities each year. Also, congressional committees hold hearings and issue reports on monetary policy and the operations of the Federal Reserve. These hearings and reports cannot fail to have some effect on Fed policy. In addition, beginning in 1975, Congress has stipulated that the Fed must publish its long-term targets for growth in the money supply, the purpose being to establish somewhat more control over monetary policy. Finally, the president may attempt to influence the Federal Reserve Board. To keep the board as free as possible from political pressure, members are appointed for long terms—14 years—and a term expires every 2 years. But since members frequently do not serve out their full terms, a president may be able to name more than two members during each of his terms in office. (President Carter was able to name four members in his first few years in office.)

THE FEDERAL RESERVE BANKS: THEIR CONSOLIDATED BALANCE SHEET

As you know from the section before last, the Federal Reserve influences the money supply largely by controlling the quantity of bank reserves. To understand how the Federal Reserve can control the quantity of bank reserves, you must begin by examining the consolidated balance sheet of the 12 regional Federal Reserve Banks. Such a consolidated balance sheet is shown in Table 11.1. It pertains to September 30, 1996.

As shown in Table 11.1, the assets of the Federal Reserve Banks are largely of three kinds: gold certificates, securities, and loans to commercial banks. Each is explained below.

1 *Gold certificates* are warehouse receipts issued by the Treasury for gold bullion. For present purposes, this item is less important than securities or loans to commercial banks.

2 The *securities* listed on the Federal Reserve Banks' balance sheet are U.S. government bonds, notes, and bills. By buying and selling these securities, the Federal Reserve exercises considerable leverage on the quantity of bank reserves (as you will see below).

3 The *loans to commercial banks* listed on the Federal Reserve Banks' balance sheet are loans of reserves that the Fed has made to commercial

banks. As pointed out in the previous chapter, the Fed can make such loans if it wants to. The interest rate charged for such loans—the discount rate—is discussed below.

According to the right-hand side of the balance sheet in Table 11.1, the liabilities of the Federal Reserve Banks are largely of three kinds: outstanding Federal Reserve notes, Treasury deposits, and reserves of banks. Each is explained below.

1 The *outstanding Federal Reserve notes* are the paper currency that you use. Since these notes are debts of the Federal Reserve Banks, they are included among the Banks' liabilities.

2 *Treasury deposits* are the deposits which the U.S. Treasury maintains at the Federal Reserve banks. The Treasury draws checks on these deposits to pay its bills.

3 The *reserves of banks* have been discussed in some detail in the previous chapter. Although these reserves are assets from the point of view of the commercial banks, they are liabilities from the point of view of the Federal Reserve Banks.

▪ **TABLE 11.1**

Consolidated Balance Sheet of the 12 Federal Reserve Banks, September 30, 1996 (Billions of Dollars)

ASSETS		LIABILITIES AND NET WORTH	
Gold certificates	11	Reserves of banks	21
Securities	391	Treasury deposits	8
Loans to commercial banks and		Outstanding Federal Reserve notes	407
other assets	50	Other liabilities and net worth	16
Total	452	Total	452

SOURCE: *Federal Reserve Bulletin*, 1996.

 TEST YOUR UNDERSTANDING

True or false?

_____ **1** The Federal Reserve influences the money supply largely by controlling the quantity of bank reserves.

_____ **2** Although the Federal Reserve is responsible to Congress, Congress has established no clear guidelines for its behavior. Thus, the Federal Reserve has had wide discretionary powers over monetary policy.

_____ **3** The commercial banks that are members of the Federal Reserve System can borrow from the Federal Reserve when their reserves are low (if the Fed is willing).

Exercises

1 According to Beryl Sprinkel, chairman of the Council of Economic Advisers in the Reagan administration, the annual rate of change of the money supply (as a ratio of real national output) from 1955 to 1968 was as follows in various Latin American countries. Also, the annual rate of increase of the consumer price index was as follows.

	ANNUAL RATE OF INCREASE (percent)	
COUNTRY	**MONEY SUPPLY ÷ REAL NATIONAL OUTPUT**	**CONSUMER PRICE INDEX**
Argentina	22.6	26.6
Brazil	35.3	37.9
Chile	29.0	27.6
Colombia	11.2	10.4
Ecuador	4.4	2.3
Mexico	3.8	3.6
Peru	7.7	9.0

Are these results in accord with the crude quantity theory of money?

2 Do these results seem to imply that velocity in each country is relatively constant over time?

3 Do these results imply that velocity is approximately the same in one country as in another?

2 ▪ Open Market Operations

Table 11.1 shows that government securities constitute a large proportion of the assets held by the Federal Reserve Banks. The market for government securities is huge and well developed, and the Federal Reserve is part of this market. Sometimes it buys government securities, sometimes it sells them. Whether it is buying or selling—and how much—can have a heavy impact on the quantity of bank reserves. Indeed, the most important means the Federal Reserve has to control the quantity of bank reserves (and thus the quantity of excess reserves) are **open market operations,** which is the name given to the purchase and sale by the Fed of U.S. government securities in the open market.

BUYING SECURITIES

Suppose that the Federal Reserve buys $1 million worth of government securities in the open market, and that the seller of these securities is General Motors.[2] To determine the effect of this transaction on the quantity of bank reserves, look at the effect on the balance sheet of the Fed and on the balance sheet of the Chase Bank, General Motors' bank.[3] In this transaction, the Fed receives $1 million in government securities and gives General Motors a check for $1 million. When General Motors deposits this check to its account at the Chase Bank, the bank's demand deposits and reserves increase by $1 million.

Thus, as shown in Table 11.2, the left-hand side of the Fed's balance sheet shows a $1 million increase in government securities, and the right-

[2] Large corporations often hold quantities of government securities.

[3] For simplicity, assume that General Motors has only one bank, the Chase Bank. Needless to say, this may not be the case, but it makes no difference to the point being made here. You will make a similar assumption regarding the investment firm of Merrill Lynch in the next section.

▪ **TABLE 11.2**

Effect of Fed's Purchasing $1 Million of Government Securities (Millions of Dollars)

A. Effect on Fed's balance sheet:

ASSETS		LIABILITIES AND NET WORTH	
Government securities	+1	Bank reserves	+1

B. Effect on balance sheet of the Chase Bank:

ASSETS		LIABILITIES AND NET WORTH	
Reserves	+1	Demand Deposits	+1

hand side shows a $1 million increase in bank reserves. The left-hand side of the Chase Bank's balance sheet shows a $1 million increase in reserves and the right-hand side shows a $1 million increase in demand deposits. Clearly, *the Fed has added $1 million to the banks' reserves.* The situation is somewhat analogous to the $10,000 deposit at bank *A* in the previous chapter.

SELLING SECURITIES

Suppose that the Federal Reserve sells $1 million worth of government securities in the open market. They are bought by Merrill Lynch, Pierce, Fenner, and Smith, a huge brokerage firm. What effect does this transaction have on the quantity of bank reserves? To find out, look at the balance sheet of the Fed and the balance sheet of Merrill Lynch's bank, which again is assumed to be the Chase Bank. When Merrill Lynch buys the government securities from the Fed, the Fed gives Merrill Lynch the securities in exchange for Merrill Lynch's check for $1 million. When the Fed presents this check to the Chase Bank for

payment, Chase's demand deposits and reserves decrease by $1 million.

Thus, as shown in Table 11.3, the left-hand side of the Fed's balance sheet shows a $1 million decrease in government securities, and the right-hand side shows a $1 million decrease in reserves. The left-hand side of the Chase Bank's balance sheet shows a $1 million decrease in reserves, and the right-hand side shows a $1 million decrease in demand deposits. Clearly, *the Fed has reduced the reserves of the banks by $1 million.*

THE FEDERAL OPEN MARKET COMMITTEE

As indicated above, open market operations are the Fed's most important means of controlling the money supply. The Federal Reserve adds to bank reserves when it buys government securities and reduces bank reserves when it sells them. Obviously, the extent to which the Federal Reserve increases or reduces bank reserves depends in an important way on the amount of government securities it buys or sells. The greater the amount,

▪ **TABLE 11.3**

Effect of Fed's Selling $1 Million of Government Securities (Millions of Dollars)

A. Effect on Fed's balance sheet:

ASSETS		LIABILITIES AND NET WORTH	
Government securities	−1	Bank reserves	−1

B. Effect on balance sheet of the Chase Bank:

ASSETS		LIABILITIES AND NET WORTH	
Reserves	−1	Demand Deposits	−1

the greater the increase or decrease in bank reserves.

The power to decide on the amount of government securities the Fed should buy or sell at any given moment rests with the Federal Open Market Committee. This group wields an extremely powerful influence over bank reserves and the country's money supply. Every three or four weeks, the Federal Open Market Committee meets to discuss the current situation and trends, and gives instructions to the manager of the Open Market Account at the Federal Reserve Bank of New York, who actually buys and sells the government securities.

☑ TEST YOUR UNDERSTANDING

True or false?

_____ **1** If the Federal Reserve buys government securities in the open market, this reduces bank reserves.

_____ **2** If the Federal Reserve sells government securities in the open market, this increases bank reserves.

Exercises

1 Suppose that the Federal Reserve buys $5 million worth of government securities from General Motors. Insert the effects in the blanks on the right above.

Effects on Fed's balance sheet:

Securities _____ Bank reserves _____

Effects on balance sheet of General Motors' bank:

Reserves _____ Demand deposits _____

2 Suppose that the Federal Reserve sells $5 million worth of government securities to General Motors. What is the effect on the quantity of bank reserves?

3 If the Federal Reserve buys $500 million worth of government securities, will this tend to shift the aggregate demand curve to the right? To the left?

---

3 ▪ Changes in Legal Reserve Requirements

Open market operations are not the only means the Federal Reserve has to influence the money supply. Another way is *to* **change the legal reserve requirements.** In other words, *the Federal Reserve Board can change the amount of reserves banks must hold for every dollar of demand deposits.* In 1934, Congress gave the Federal Reserve Board the power to set—within certain broad limits—the legally required ratio of reserves to deposits. From time to time, the Fed uses this power to change legal reserve requirements. For example, in 1958 it cut the legally required ratio of reserves to deposits in big city banks from 17½ to 16½ percent, and the ratio remained there until 1968, when it was raised to 17 percent. Table 11.4 shows the legal reserve requirements in 1996.

EFFECT OF AN INCREASE IN RESERVE REQUIREMENTS

The effect of an increase in the legally required ratio of reserves to deposits is that banks must hold larger reserves to support the existing amount of demand deposits. This in turn means that banks with little or no excess reserves will have to sell securities, refuse to renew loans, and reduce their demand deposits to meet the new reserve requirements. For example, suppose that a bank has $1 million in reserves and $6 million in demand deposits. If the legal reserve requirement is 16 percent, it has excess reserves of $1 million minus $960,000 (0.16 × $6 million), or $40,000. It is in good shape. If the legal reserve

▪ TABLE 11.4

Legal Reserve Requirements of Depository Institutions, 1996

TYPE AND SIZE OF DEPOSITS	RESERVE REQUIREMENTS (percent of deposits)
Net transaction accounts	
Up to $52 million	3
Over $52 million	10
Nonpersonal time deposits	0

SOURCE: *Federal Reserve Bulletin*, February 1996.

requirement is increased to 20 percent, this bank now needs $1.2 million (0.20 × $6 million) in reserves. Since it only has $1 million in reserves, it must sell securities or refuse to renew loans.

Consider now what happens to the banking system as a whole. Clearly, an increase in the legally required ratio of reserves to deposits means that, with a given amount of reserves, the banking system can maintain less demand deposits than before. For example, if the banking system has $1 billion in total reserves, it can support $1 billion/0.16, or $6.25 billion, in demand deposits when the legal reserve requirement is 16 percent. But it can support only $1 billion/0.20, or $5 billion, in demand deposits when the legal reserve requirement is 20 percent (see Table

11.5).[4] Thus *increases in the legal reserve requirement tend to reduce the amount of demand deposits—bank money—the banking system can support.*

EFFECT OF A DECREASE IN RESERVE REQUIREMENTS

What is the effect of a decrease in the legally required ratio of reserves to deposits? It means that banks must hold less reserves to support the existing amount of demand deposits, which in turn means that banks will suddenly find themselves with excess reserves. If the banking system has $1 billion in reserves and $10 billion in demand deposits, there are no excess reserves when the legal reserve requirement is 10 percent. But suppose the Federal Reserve lowers the legal reserve requirement to 9 percent. Now the amount of legally required reserves is $900 million (0.09 × $10 billion), so that the banks have $100 million in excess reserves; this means that they can increase the amount of their demand deposits. Thus *decreases in the legal reserve requirements tend to increase the amount of demand deposits—bank money—the banking system can support.*

[4] Assume arbitrarily in Table 11.5 that the total net worth of the banks is $2 billion. Obviously, this assumption concerning the amount of total net worth makes no difference to the point being made here. Also, for simplicity, ignore checkable deposits other than demand deposits here and below.

▪ TABLE 11.5

Consolidated Balance Sheet of All Banks, before and after an Increase (from 16 to 20 Percent) in the Legal Reserve Requirement (Billions of Dollars)

A. Before the increase in the legal reserve requirement:

ASSETS		LIABILITIES	
Reserves	1.00	Demand deposits	6.25
Loans and investments	7.25	Net worth	2.00
Total	8.25		8.25

B. After the increase in the legal reserve requirement:

ASSETS		LIABILITIES	
Reserves	1.00	Demand deposits	5.00
Loans and investments	6.00	Net worth	2.00
Total	7.00		7.00

Changes in legal reserve requirements are a rather drastic way to influence the money supply—they are to open market operations as a cleaver is to a scalpel, and so are made infrequently. For example, for about ten years—from April 1958 to January 1968—no change at all was made in legal reserve requirements for demand deposits in city banks. Nonetheless, the Fed can change legal reserve requirements if it wants

to. And there can be no doubt about the potential impact of such changes. Large changes in reserve requirements can rapidly alter bank reserves and the money supply. When the Fed eased credit in December 1990, it eliminated the 3 percent reserve requirement on certificates of deposit held by corporations with maturities of less than 18 months—and quickly added billions of dollars to bank reserves.

 TEST YOUR UNDERSTANDING

True or false?

_____ **1** An increase in the legal reserve requirement tends to reduce the amount of demand deposits the banking system can support.

_____ **2** A decrease in the legal reserve requirement tends to lower the amount of demand deposits the banking system can support.

Exercise

1 "When the Fed increases legal reserve requirements, it loosens credit, because the banks have more reserves." Comment and evaluate.

---

4 ▪ Changes in the Discount Rate

Still another way that the Federal Reserve can influence the money supply is through changes in the discount rate. As shown by the balance sheet of the Federal Reserve Banks (in Table 11.1), commercial banks can borrow from the Federal Reserve when their reserves are low (if the Fed is willing). This is one of the functions of the Federal Reserve. The interest rate the Fed charges the banks for loans is called the **discount rate,** and the Fed can increase or decrease the discount rate whenever it chooses. Increases in the discount rate discourage borrowing from the Fed, whereas decreases in the discount rate encourage it.

The discount rate can change substantially and fairly often (Table 11.6). Take 1980. The discount rate was increased from 12 to 13 percent in early 1980, then reduced to 12 percent in May, 11 percent in June, and 10 percent in July, after which it was raised back up to 13 percent by December

1980. When the Fed increases the discount rate (relative to other interest rates), it makes it more expensive for banks to augment their reserves in this way; hence it tightens up a bit on the money supply. On the other hand, when the Fed decreases the discount rate, it is cheaper for banks to augment their reserves in this way, and hence the money supply eases up a bit. Thus, in December 1990, the Fed, trying to stimulate a weak economy, reduced the discount rate from 7 to 6.5 percent.

The Fed is largely passive in these relations with the banks. It cannot make the banks borrow. It can only set the discount rate and see how many banks show up at the "discount window" to borrow. Also, the Fed will not allow banks to borrow on a permanent or long-term basis. They are expected to use this privilege only to tide themselves over for short periods, not to borrow

TEST YOUR UNDERSTANDING

True or false?

_____ **1** The discount rate is the rate of interest that the state governments pay member banks on their reserves kept with the Fed.

_____ **2** A reduction in the discount rate has a direct effect on member bank reserves; it increases them in much the same way that open market purchases of government securities by the Fed increases them.

_____ **3** Banks are expected to borrow from the Federal Reserve only for short periods.

▪ **TABLE 11.6**

Average Discount Rate, 1965–1996

YEAR	DISCOUNT RATE (percent)	YEAR	DISCOUNT RATE (percent)
1965	4.04	1981	13.41
1966	4.50	1982	11.02
1967	4.19	1983	8.50
1968	5.17	1984	8.80
1969	5.87	1985	7.69
1970	5.95	1986	6.33
1971	4.88	1987	5.66
1972	4.50	1988	6.20
1973	6.45	1989	6.93
1974	7.83	1990	6.98
1975	6.25	1991	5.45
1976	5.50	1992	3.25
1977	5.46	1993	3.00
1978	7.46	1994	3.60
1979	10.28	1995	5.21
1980	11.77	1996	5.02

SOURCE: _Economic Report of the President,_ 1997.

in order to relend at a profit. To discourage banks from excessive use of the borrowing privilege, the discount rate is kept relatively close to short-term market interest rates.

Most economists agree that changes in the discount rate have relatively little direct impact, and that the Fed's open market operations can and do offset easily the amount the banks borrow. Certainly changes in the discount rate cannot have anything like the direct effect on bank reserves of open market operations or changes in legal reserve requirements. _The principal importance of changes in the discount rate lies in their effects on people's expectations._ When the Fed increases the discount rate, it is generally interpreted as a sign that the Fed will tighten credit and the money supply. A cut in the discount rate is generally interpreted as a sign of lower interest rates and easier money.

Exercise

1 Suppose that you have $5,000 to invest. At a restaurant you overhear someone saying that the Fed is almost certain to increase the discount rate dramatically. If this rumor is correct, do you think that you should invest now, or wait until after the increase in the discount rate? Or doesn't it matter? Be sure to explain the reasons for your preference (or lack of it) in this regard.

5 ▪ When Is Monetary Policy Tight or Easy?

Everyone daydreams about being powerful and important. It is a safe bet, however, that few people under the age of 21 daydream about being members of the Federal Reserve Board or the Federal Open Market Committee. Yet the truth is that the members of the board and the committee are among the most powerful people in the country. Suppose you were appointed to the Federal Reserve Board. As a member, you would have to decide—month by month, year by year—exactly how much government securities the Fed should buy or sell, as well as whether and when changes should be made in the discount rate, legal reserve requirements, and other instruments of Federal Reserve policy. How would you go about making your choices?

Obviously you would need lots of data. Fortunately, the Fed has a very large and able research staff to provide you with plenty of the latest information about what is going on in the economy. But what sorts of data should you look at? One thing you would want is some information on the extent to which monetary policy is inflationary or deflationary—that is, the extent to which it is **"easy"** or **"tight."** This is not simple to measure, but there is general agreement that the members of the Federal Reserve Board—and other members of the financial and academic communities—look closely at short-term interest rates and the rate of increase of the money supply.

THE LEVEL OF SHORT-TERM INTEREST RATES

Keynesians have tended to believe that changes in the quantity of money affect aggregate demand via their effects on the interest rate. High interest rates tend to reduce investment, which in turn reduces GDP. Low interest rates tend to increase investment, which in turn increases GDP. Because of their emphasis on these relationships, Keynesians tend to view monetary tightness or ease in terms of the behavior of interest rates. High interest rates are interpreted as meaning that monetary policy is tight. Low interest rates are interpreted as meaning that monetary policy is easy.

According to many economists, the *real interest rate,* not the *nominal interest rate,* is what counts in this context. The *real* interest rate is the percentage increase in *real* purchasing power that the lender receives from the borrower in return for making the loan. The *nominal* interest rate is the percentage increase in *money* that the lender receives from the borrower in return for making the loan. The crucial difference between the real rate of interest and the nominal rate of interest is that the former is *adjusted for inflation* whereas the latter is not.

Suppose that a firm borrows $1,000 for a year at 12 percent interest, and that the rate of inflation is 9 percent. When the firm repays the lender $1,120 at the end of the year, this amount of money is worth only $1,120 ÷ 1.09, or about $1,030, when corrected for inflation. Thus the real rate of interest on this loan is 3 percent, not 12 percent (the nominal rate). Why? Because the lender receives $30 in constant dollars (which is 3 percent of the amount lent) in return for making the loan. The real rate of interest is of importance in investment decisions because it measures the real cost of borrowing money.[5]

THE RATE OF INCREASE OF THE MONEY SUPPLY

Monetarists have tended to link changes in the quantity of money directly to changes in GDP. Consequently, they have tended to view monetary tightness or ease in terms of the behavior of

the money supply. When the money supply is growing at a relatively slow rate (much less than 4 or 5 percent per year), this is interpreted as meaning that monetary policy is tight. A relatively rapid rate of growth in the money supply (much more than 4 or 5 percent per year) is taken to mean that monetary policy is easy.

Another measure stressed by the monetarists is the **monetary base,** which by definition equals bank reserves plus currency outside banks. The monetary base is important because the total money supply is dependent on—and made from—it. A relatively slow rate of growth in the monetary base (much less than 4 or 5 percent per year) is interpreted as a sign of tight money. A relatively rapid rate of growth (much more than 4 or 5 percent per year) is taken to mean that monetary policy is easy.

[5] Expressed as an equation, $i_r = i_n - p$, where i_r is the real rate of interest, i_n is the nominal rate of interest, and p is the rate of inflation. In the example in the text, $i_n = 12$ percent and $p = 9$ percent; thus $i_r = 3$ percent.

 TEST YOUR UNDERSTANDING

True or false?

_____ **1** An attempt by the Federal Reserve to keep interest rates on U.S. government securities constant would be in accord with the wishes of the monetarists since it would stabilize the rate of growth of the quantity of money.

_____ **2** In setting the appropriate money supply, the Federal Reserve must bear in mind changes in the velocity of money.

Exercises

1 "The Fed should keep interest rates low to promote prosperity. Unfortunately, however, it is dominated by bankers who like high interest rates because they increase bank profits." Comment and evaluate.

2 "The Fed is like a driver whose steering wheel

takes about a minute to influence the car's wheels." Comment and evaluate.

3 According to economist Sherman Maisel, William McChesney Martin, former chairman of the Federal Reserve Board, felt "that the primary function of the Federal Reserve Board was to determine what was necessary to maintain a sound currency. . . . [To Martin] it is as immoral for a country today to allow the value of its currency to fall as it was for kings of old to clip coinage." Do you agree with Martin's views? Why, or why not?

4 An enormous amount of statistical and economic research has been carried out to determine how quickly an unanticipated recession can be combated by monetary policy. According to Robert Gordon of Northwestern University, the total lag between the occurrence of such an unanticipated slowdown in economic activity and the impact of monetary policy is about 14 months. In other words, it takes about 14 months for the Federal Reserve to become aware of the slowdown, to take the appropriate actions, and to have these actions affect real GDP.

a. On the average, how long do you think it takes for a slowdown to be reflected in the government's economic data?

b. How long do you think it takes for the Fed to pay attention to the signal and change monetary policy?

c. Once a change has been made in the rate of increase of the money supply, how long do you think it takes until real GDP is affected?

d. What problems result from the long lag between a change in economic conditions and the impact of monetary policy?

▪ CHAPTER REVIEW

KEY TERMS

monetary policy

Federal Reserve Board

Federal Open Market Committee

open market operations

change in legal reserve requirements

discount rate

"easy"

"tight"

monetary base

COMPLETION QUESTIONS

1 When a serious inflation seems imminent, the monetary authorities are most likely to (increase, decrease) _____ the rate of growth of the money supply and to (increase, decrease) _____ interest rates.

2 If the monetary authorities think that a recession is developing, they tend to (increase, decrease) _____ the reserves of the banks.

3 Increases in the legal reserve requirement are likely to (increase, reduce) _____ the amount of demand deposits the banking system can support.

4 If the demand curve for money shifts _____ and to the _____, the Fed must increase the quantity of money if interest rates are to remain constant.

5 Bank reserves plus currency outside banks equals the _____.

6 (Monetary, Fiscal) _____ authorities can react much more quickly to changed economic conditions than can (monetary, fiscal) _____ authorities.

ANSWERS TO COMPLETION QUESTIONS

decrease
increase

increase

reduce

upward
right

monetary base
Monetary

fiscal

7 If the short-run aggregate supply curve is close to horizontal, increases in the money supply tend to (increase, decrease) _____ real national product, and decreases in the money supply tend to (increase, decrease) _____ real national product, with little or no effect on the _____ level.

increase

decrease
price

8 If the short-run aggregate supply curve is upward sloping, increases in the money supply tend to affect the _____ level, as well as real _____. If the aggregate supply curve is vertical, increases in the money supply result in (increases, decreases) _____ in the price level, since real output cannot (increase, decrease) _____ appreciably.

price, output

increases
increase

9 If the banking system has $1 billion in _____, it can support $6.25 billion in demand deposits when the legal reserve requirement is 16 percent. It can only support $5 billion in demand deposits when the legal reserve requirement is 20 percent. Thus, increases in the legal reserve requirements tend to (increase, decrease) _____ the amount of demand deposits the banking system can support.

total reserves

decrease

10 If the banking system has $1 billion in reserves and $5 billion in demand deposits, there are no _____ when the legal reserve requirement is 20 percent. If the Federal Reserve lowers the legal reserve requirement to 16 percent, the amount of legally required reserves is _____ million. The banks then have _____ million in excess reserves; this means that they can (increase, decrease) _____ the amount of their demand deposits.

excess reserves

$800
$200
increase

11 Experts disagree about which of the available measures—such as _____ rates, the rate of increase of the _____ supply, or the rate of increase of the _____ base—is the best measure of how tight or easy monetary policy is.

interest
money
monetary

NUMERICAL PROBLEMS

1 Suppose that on May 1, 1998, the Federal Reserve sells $100 million of U.S. government securities to the public, which pays for them by check.

a Show at right the effect of this sale on the balance sheets of the Federal Reserve and the commercial banks:

FEDERAL RESERVE	
ASSETS	**LIABILITIES**
Government securities ____	Member bank reserves ____

COMMERCIAL BANKS (balance sheet for all banks combined)	
ASSETS	**LIABILITIES**
Reserves ____	Demand deposits ____

b Does this transaction have any effect on the balance sheets of the members of the public who bought the bonds? If so, what is the effect?

c If the commercial banks had no excess reserves before the sale of these bonds, do they have any excess reserves after the sale? Do they have less than the legally required reserves after the sale?

d Suppose that the Fed bought, rather than sold, $100 million of U.S. government securities, and that these securities were bought from the general public. Would this transaction result in an increase or decrease in member bank reserves? By how much would reserves increase or decrease? Is this the sort of result that the Fed would have desired during the period in 1981 when it was trying hard to fight inflation?

2 Suppose that the banking system has no excess reserves, total reserves are $50 billion, and total demand deposits are $200 billion. Suppose that the graph below shows the net amount that the banking system will borrow (that is, net of repayments) from the Federal Reserve if the discount rate equals the levels shown there.

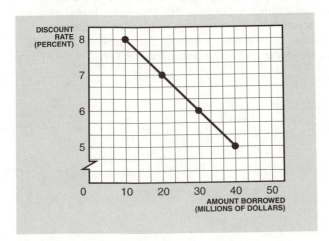

a How much will the banking system borrow if the discount rate is 7 percent? 5 percent? What is the legal reserve requirement?

b If the Fed wants to increase the money supply by $40 million, what discount rate should it set? (Assume that banks maintain no excess reserves.)

c If the Fed wants to have the same effect on bank reserves as if it bought $20 million worth of govern-

ment securities in the open market, what discount rate should it set?

3 From the following figures, construct the consolidated balance sheet of the 12 Federal Reserve banks. (All figures are in billions of dollars.)

Gold certificates	10	Reserves of member banks	30
Other liabilities and net worth	5	Other assets	10
Securities	100	Treasury deposits	5
Outstanding Federal Reserve notes	90	Loans to commercial banks	10

4 Given the consolidated balance sheet which you have constructed in Problem 3, what effect will each of the following transactions (taken by itself) have on this balance sheet?

a The Federal Reserve sells $100 million in securities to the public (which pays by check).

b The Federal Reserve lowers the discount rate, which results in member banks borrowing $50 million from the Fed.

c The U.S. government buys $1 billion worth of aerospace equipment, which is paid for by checks on the Treasury's deposits at the Fed.

5 Given that each of the transactions described in Problem 4 occurs (separately), what is the effect in each case on the potential money supply, if the legal reserve requirement is 20 percent?

6 Suppose that the Federal Reserve purchases $100 million of U.S. government securities from *commercial banks.*

a What will be the effect on the balance sheet of the Federal Reserve banks?

b What will be the effect on the balance sheet of the commercial banks?

c What is the effect on the potential money supply if the legal reserve requirement is 20 percent?

7 Suppose that the Federal Reserve sells $100 million of U.S. government securities to *commercial banks.*

a What will be the effect on the balance sheet of the Federal Reserve banks?

b What will be the effect on the balance sheet of the commercial banks?

c What is the effect on the potential money supply if the legal reserve requirement is 10 percent?

ANSWERS TO
TEST YOUR UNDERSTANDING

SECTION 1

TRUE OR FALSE: 1. True   2. True   3. True

EXERCISES

1. Yes
2. Yes
3. No

SECTION 2

TRUE OR FALSE: 1. False   2. False

EXERCISES

1. All entries should be +$5 million.
2. They are reduced.
3. To the right.

SECTION 3

TRUE OR FALSE: 1. True   2. False

EXERCISE

1. This statement is incorrect.

SECTION 4

TRUE OR FALSE: 1. False   2. False   3. True

EXERCISE

1. You probably should wait to invest as a dramatic increase in the discount rate is likely to mean higher interest rates and lower bond prices.

SECTION 5

TRUE OR FALSE: 1. False   2. True

EXERCISES

1. Keeping interest rates low in no way guarantees prosperity. In fact, such a policy could lead to serious inflation at times when the economy is becoming overheated.

2. It is true that the Fed's policies take time to have a considerable impact.

3. This is a matter of political choice; some may agree, while others may not.

4. a.–c. According to Gordon, the average lags are approximately as follows:

LAG	MONTHS
From slowdown to reflection in economic data	2
From reflection in economic data to change in money supply	3
From change in money supply to effect on real GDP	9
Total	14

d. By the time the effects of the expansionary monetary policy are felt, the economy may not need additional stimulus. Suppose that you were driving a car in which the wheels respond to turns of the steering wheel with a substantial lag. The problems would be analogous to those confronting the Fed.

■ CHAPTER 12

Controversies over Stabilization Policy

Essentials of **Controversies over Stabilization Policy**

▪ The new classical macroeconomists question the extent to which the government can use monetary and fiscal policies to close recessionary and inflationary gaps because the expectations of firms and individuals (concerning their incomes, job prospects, and other relevant variables) are influenced by government policies.

▪ Real business cycle theorists believe that business fluctuations are the natural (indeed efficient) response of the economy to changes in technology and the availability of resources.

▪ The new Keynesians do not believe that markets clear continuously. Like the old Keynesians, they believe that prices or wages, or both, tend to adjust slowly in the short run, with the result that the quantity of output, more than price, tends to adjust to changes in aggregate demand.

1 ▪ The New Classical Macroeconomists

The **new classical macroeconomists,** led by Nobel laureate Robert Lucas, Thomas Sargent, and Neil Wallace, came to prominence in the 1970s. Their theory of macroeconomics was based on three assumptions. First, they assumed that markets cleared; in other words, prices of inputs and outputs varied so as to equate the quantity supplied to the quantity demanded. Second, they assumed that people and firms have imperfect information. Third, they assumed that the expectations of people and firms conform to the theory of rational expectations.

RATIONAL EXPECTATIONS

The theory of rational expectations has had a substantial impact on economic analysis and policy. Basically, what it says is that individuals and firms do not make systematic errors in forecasting the future. In other words, forecasts, *on the average,* are assumed to be correct. Of course, this

does not mean that forecasters are always right. Obviously, this is far from true. Instead, the new classical macroeconomists assume that forecasting errors are purely random. By assuming that people's expectations are on the average correct, they also assume in effect that these expectations are determined as part of the model and are genuinely forward looking. Consequently, the announcement or anticipation that a particular event will occur results in immediate effects on the economy, even before the anticipated event actually occurs.

UNEMPLOYMENT AND BUSINESS FLUCTUATIONS

According to the new classical macroeconomists, high rates of unemployment are not evidence of a gap between actual and potential output that can be reduced; instead, output fluctuations result from random forecasting errors. Markets are as-

159

sumed to work efficiently; and firms, acting to maximize their profits, are assumed to make the best possible decisions. According to Lucas, since unemployed workers have the option of accepting pay cuts to get jobs, excess unemployment is essentially voluntary.

Fluctuations in aggregate demand are due principally to erratic and unpredictable government policy, in his view. Changes in the quantity of money induce cyclical fluctuations in the economy. But the power of policy changes to affect real GDP is limited. People come to learn the way in which policy is made, and only unanticipated government policy changes can have a substantial impact on output or employment. Once firms and individuals learn of any systematic rule for adjusting government policy to events, the rule will have no effect.

CAN STABILIZATION POLICIES WORK?

On the basis of their theories, the new classical macroeconomists conclude that the *government cannot use monetary and fiscal policies to close recessionary and inflationary gaps in the way described in Chapters 6 and 11, because the models presented in those chapters do not recognize that the expectations of firms and individuals concerning their incomes, job prospects, sales, and other relevant variables are influenced by government policies.* If firms and individuals formulate their expectations rationally, they will tend to frustrate the government's attempts to use activist stabilization policies.

To illustrate what these economists are saying, suppose that the economy is in a recession and that the government, trying to close the recessionary gap in the ways described in Chapters 6 and 11, increases the amount that it spends on goods and services and increases the money supply. Because prices tend to move up while wages do not, profits tend to rise and firms find it profitable to expand. But this model is based on the supposition that labor is not smart enough to foresee that prices are going to go up and that labor's real wage is going to diminish. If labor does foresee this (that is, if its expectations are rational), it will insist on an increase in its money wage, which will mean that firms will not find it

profitable to expand, and the government's anti-recession policy will not work as expected.

REACTIONS PRO AND CON

These views have received considerable attention in academic and policy circles. For example, in one of its annual reports, the Federal Reserve Bank of Minneapolis stated:

> The [new classical] view conjectures that some amount of cyclical swing in production and employment is inherent in the micro-level processes of the economy that no government macro policies can, or should attempt to, smooth out. Expected additions to money growth certainly won't smooth out cycles, if the arguments in this paper are correct. Surprise additions to money growth have the potential to make matters worse. . . . One strategy that seems consistent with the significant, though largely negative, findings of [the new classical macroeconomists] would have monetary policy focus its attention on inflation and announce, and stick to, a policy that would bring the rate of increase in the general price level to some specified low figure.[1]

Given the fact that the new classical macroeconomists have challenged the core of the theory underlying discretionary stabilization policies, it is not surprising that many economists, particularly liberals, have attacked their conclusions. Franco Modigliani, for instance, has claimed that their model is inconsistent "with the evidence; if it were valid, deviations of unemployment from the natural rate would be small and transitory—in which case [Keynes's] *General Theory* would not have been written."[2] Since Lucas's theory makes excess unemployment the result of purely unexpected events, one would think that unemployment would fluctuate randomly around its equilibrium level if this theory is true. Critics point out that recessions sometimes last quite a long time.

[1] Federal Reserve Bank of Minneapolis, *Rational Expectations—Fresh Ideas that Challenge Some Established Views of Policy Making,* Minneapolis, 1977, pp. 12–13.

[2] F. Modigliani, "The Monetarist Controversy, or, Should We Forsake Stabilization Policies," *American Economic Review,* March 1977, p. 6.

Critics also claim that the new classical macro-economics neglects the inertia in wages and prices. Contracts are written for long periods of time. Workers stick with firms for considerable periods. Consequently, wages and prices do not adjust as rapidly as is assumed by the new classical macroeconomists. According to the critics, most empirical analysis does not support the view that wages and prices adjust rapidly. On the contrary, wage and price movements show only slow and adaptive changes.

One of the most serious criticisms has centered on the new classical macroeconomists' contention that business fluctuations would be eliminated if firms and consumers had accurate current infor-

mation about the aggregate price level. Given that the Consumer Price Index is widely disseminated with a relatively short lag, this does not seem very plausible. As Northwestern's Robert Gordon put it, "With monthly and even weekly data on the money supply available, people could make expectational errors about monetary changes lasting for only a few weeks, not nearly enough to explain business cycles lasting an average of four and one-half years in the postwar era, and twelve years for the period of high unemployment between 1929 and 1941."[3]

[3] R. Gordon, *Macroeconomics*, (5th ed.; Glenview, Ill.: Scott Foresman, 1990), p. 202.

 TEST YOUR UNDERSTANDING

True or false?

_____ **1** The new classical macroeconomists believe that fluctuations in aggregate demand are due principally to erratic and unpredictable government policy.

_____ **2** According to Robert Lucas, people come to learn the way in which policy is made, and only unanticipated government policy changes can have a substantial effect on output or employment.

_____ **3** According to Lucas, excess unemployment is essentially voluntary.

Exercises

1 According to the new classical macroeconomists, any unemployed worker has the opportunity to work, but refuses to do so because, given his or her expectations concerning inflation, the expected real wage rate is too low. Does this seem reasonable? Why, or why not?

2 Robert Gordon has stated that "the weakness of the new classical model lies not in the assumption of rational expectations, but rather in its assumption of continuous market clearing." What does "continuous market clearing" mean? Do you agree with Gordon? Why, or why not?

2 ▪ Real Business Cycle Models

In contrast to the models described in the previous section, some new classical macroeconomists, such as Edward Prescott of the University of Minnesota, argue that business fluctuations are due predominantly to "real" rather than "monetary" factors. These economists, whose influence within the new classical camp has grown substantially in the late 1980s and early 1990s, are called

real business cycle theorists. In their view, business fluctuations are the natural (indeed *efficient*) response of the economy to changes in technology and the availability of resources. Thus business fluctuations are due largely to shifts in the aggregate supply curve, not the aggregate demand curve.

To illustrate what they have in mind, consider

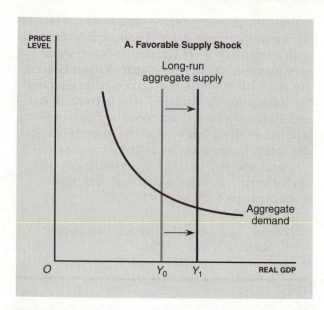
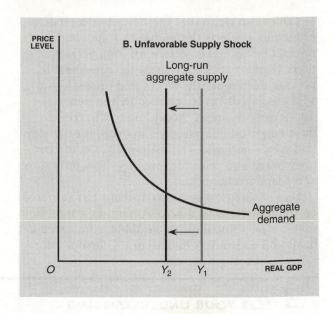

▪ **FIGURE 12.1**

Favorable and Unfavorable Supply Shocks

In panel A, a favorable supply shock (technological advance) shifts the aggregate supply curve to the right and increases real GDP from OY_0 to OY_1. In panel B, an unfavorable supply shock (oil cutback) shifts the aggregate supply curve to the left and decreases real GDP from OY_1 to OY_2.

Figure 12.1. Suppose that technological change shifts the long-run aggregate supply curve to the right, with the result that real GDP increases from OY_0 to OY_1. Then suppose that OPEC cuts back on the supply of oil, causing a shift of the aggregate supply curve to the left, with the result that real GDP falls from OY_1 to OY_2. These output fluctuations are due to shifts in the aggregate supply curve, not the aggregate demand curve. According to real business cycle models, this is the way that business fluctuations in the real world tend to occur.

What are the factors that shift the aggregate supply curve, and thus cause business fluctuations? Among the most important are new products, new methods of production, new sources of raw materials, changes in the price of raw materials, and good or bad weather. These factors are sometimes called **supply shocks.** The effects of a *favorable* supply shock (that is, one that pushes the aggregate supply curve to the right) may per-

sist for several years, after which an *unfavorable* supply shock (one that pushes the aggregate supply curve to the left) may be felt. For example, in Figure 12.1, the technological advance that increases real GDP from OY_0 to OY_1 is a favorable supply shock, which is succeeded by an unfavorable supply shock—the cutback of oil from OPEC—which reduces real GDP from OY_1 to OY_2.

As in the other new classical models discussed earlier in this chapter, real business cycle models assume that equilibrium is achieved in all markets. In other words, markets clear. Each firm produces the amount of output it desires, and hires the quantity of labor it wants. Workers get as much work as they want; there is no involuntary unemployment. Prices and wages respond flexibly to changing economic conditions. This is in contrast to the new Keynesian models, taken up in succeeding sections, which assume that there are many factors that prevent markets from clearing. Also, it is in contrast to the original

Keynesian model which assumed that wages were inflexible.

THE EFFECT OF A SUPPLY SHOCK

To illustrate in more detail how supply shocks can cause business fluctuations, suppose that there is a temporary decline in agricultural productivity due to bad weather, and that this productivity decline reduces real income in agriculture. This cut in real income leads farmers to decrease their consumption of goods and services, but they do not decrease their consumption levels all at once. Instead, they spread the reduction of consumption over time. Thus a supply shock of this sort would be expected to spread from one sector of the economy to another. As farmers cut back their consumption levels, nonagricultural indus-

tries—like clothing and automobiles—may feel the pinch. Also, the effects of such a supply shock would be expected to persist for some time. Since farmers cut back their consumption spending gradually, the adverse effects on the sales of other industries—like clothing and automobiles—are likely to continue for some time.

An unfavorable supply shock—such as this decline in agricultural productivity—leads firms to want fewer workers at the prevailing wage. Thus, according to real business cycle models, real wages will fall, as the demand curves for labor shift to the left. The fact that these models predict that real wages will tend to fall when real GDP falls—and that real wages will tend to rise when real GDP rises—is in accord with past experience, according to some observers, but not according to others.

 TEST YOUR UNDERSTANDING

True or false?

_____ **1** Real business cycle models assume that prices and wages are flexible and markets clear.

Exercise

1 Critics of real business cycle theories question whether any conceivable supply shock could explain the huge drop in output in the Great Depression. (Real GDP fell by about 30 percent between 1929 and 1933.) What is a supply shock?

3 ▪ The New Keynesians

Just as there is a new classical macroeconomics, so there is a new Keynesianism. Like the original Keynesians, the new Keynesians do not believe that markets clear continuously; in other words, they do not believe that the quantity demanded of a good or input always equals the quantity supplied. Instead, they believe that, if there is a sudden shift in the demand or supply curve, prices will fail to adjust quickly enough to equate the quantity demanded to the quantity supplied.

In their view, the economy can stay in a state of disequilibrium for years if prices adjust slowly enough.

As we know from previous sections, this is a quite different view from that held by the new classical macroeconomists, who assume that markets clear continuously because prices adjust quickly. The new Keynesians, like the old Keynesians, say that their view is the more realistic one. They argue that it is unrealistic to assume that workers who are unemployed during recessions are voluntarily unemployed. Ask such a worker, they say, whether he or she would refuse a job offer at the prevailing wage. In their view, it is very likely that he or she would say no, and thus shed doubt on whether the labor market actually clears. Turning to product markets, they ask whether a firm in a recession is selling all that it would desire. In their view, such a firm would be likely to say it was not, and thus shed doubt on whether the product market actually clears.

Like the new classical macroeconomists, the new Keynesians have adopted the theory of rational expectations. For example, MIT's Stanley Fisher has shown that, if the public has rational expectations, systematic monetary policy can stabilize the economy. But his theory assumes that wages are inflexible, whereas the new classical macroeconomists assume that they are flexible. This is a fundamental difference.

HOW DO NEW KEYNESIANS DIFFER FROM OLD KEYNESIANS?

Both old and new Keynesians assume that prices or wages or both tend to adjust slowly in the short run, with the result that the quantity of output, more than price, tends to adjust to changes in aggregate demand. But whereas old Keynesians merely assumed that wages tend to be rigid and that prices are sticky, new Keynesians have developed theories that help to explain why such wage and price stability can be expected, given the rational behavior of individuals and firms. In other words, new Keynesians have tried to construct a microeconomic foundation for Keynesianism that old Keynesians failed to provide.

Basically, the focus of new Keynesians has been on the reasons for wage and price rigidities. As you will see, some rigidities of this sort can be temporary: output adjusts slowly, but eventually gets to the unique optimal level. In other cases, however, these rigidities can be permanent: because the model has more than one equilibrium, the economy can be caused to move to an entirely different equilibrium with different levels of employment and output.

MENU COSTS AND STICKY PRICES

To explain why prices adjust slowly, the new Keynesians assume that markets are not perfectly competitive. In other words, firms are assumed to have some control over the prices of their products. For many products, like computers, oil, or beer, this is a reasonable assumption. Going a step further, they also assume that a firm incurs costs when it changes its price. Such a cost is called a **menu cost.** Why? Because it is the same sort of cost that a restaurant incurs when it changes its prices—and thus must print new menus.

As an illustration, consider the Jefferson Company, a producer of a wide variety of hand tools. If it changes its price schedule, it must print new catalogs, spend a considerable amount to inform its customers of the price changes, change many aspects of its billing system, and so forth. Its accountants figure that it costs Jefferson $40,000 every time it changes its price schedule.

Suppose that there is an upward shift in the demand curve for Jefferson's product. Given this increase in demand, Jefferson's president suspects that it may be wise to raise the firm's prices. According to the firm's accountants, the firm's sales, costs, and profits will be as shown in Table 12.1, if it raises or does not raise its prices. Clearly, the president is right; Jefferson would make higher profits if it increased its prices. However, the figures in Table 12.1 do not take into account the $40,000 cost of changing prices. When these menu costs are taken into account, it is not profitable for Jefferson to increase its prices.

In the next few months, the upward shift in the demand curve for Jefferson's product contin-

■ TABLE 12.1

Jefferson Company's Profit If It Raises or Does Not Raise Its Prices, Original Situation

	PRICES ARE RAISED	PRICES ARE NOT RAISED
Sales	$1,095,000	$1,070,000
Costs	840,000	850,000
Profit	$ 255,000	$ 220,000

▪ TABLE 12.2

Jefferson Company's Profit If It Raises or Does Not Raise Its Prices, Subsequent Situation

	PRICES ARE RAISED	PRICES ARE NOT RAISED[a]
Sales	$1,120,000	$1,080,000
Costs	860,000	870,000
Profit	$ 260,000	$ 210,000

[a] Note that, if prices are not raised, sales and costs differ from what they would have been in Table 12.1 if prices were not raised. This is because Table 12.2 pertains to a later situation than does Table 12.1.

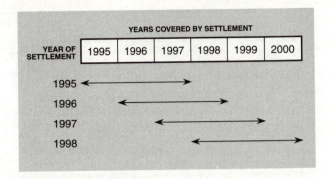

▪ FIGURE 12.2

Overlapping Three-Year Labor Contracts

Not all contracts come up for renewal at the same time; instead they overlap, one consequence being that wages adjust slowly, and with a substantial lag, to changes in aggregate demand.

ues, and its president wonders once again whether the firm should raise its prices. The firm's accountants estimate that its sales, costs, and profits will be as shown in Table 12.2, if it now raises or does not raise its prices. At this point, is it profitable for Jefferson to change its price schedule? The answer is yes, because Table 12.2 shows that the increase in profit— $260,000 − $210,000 = $50,000—is more than sufficient to cover the menu cost of $40,000.

The point here is that, according to the new Keynesians, prices can be sticky because of the existence of menu costs. This is one way that they explain why prices adjust slowly, and why markets do not clear continually.

LONG-TERM LABOR CONTRACTS AND STICKY WAGES

Like prices, wages can be sticky, according to the new Keynesians, and this is due in part to long-term labor contracts. In the United States, formal labor contracts prevail in heavily unionized industries like steel, automobiles, rubber, and electrical machinery. Those contracts influence the level of wages in other industries, since they tend to be imitated elsewhere. Many contracts extend for three years; the contract calls for specified increases in wage rates each year plus (in some instances) extra wage increases that offset whatever changes occur in the Consumer Price Index.

Not all contracts come up for renewal at the same time. Instead, as shown in Figure 12.2, some contracts come up for renewal each year. Assuming for simplicity that all contracts are negotiated at the beginning of the year, and that all last for three years, the contracts negotiated in 1995 cover 1995, 1996, and 1997; those negotiated in 1996 cover 1996, 1997, and 1998; and so on. One important consequence of these multi-year labor contracts is that wages adjust slowly, and with a substantial lag, to changes in aggregate demand.

Given that long-term contracts tend to slow the rate of adjustment of wages, it is interesting to ask why workers and firms prefer to enter into such agreements. One reason is that each wage negotiation costs both workers and firms a considerable amount of time and money, since each side must prepare its case thoroughly. Thus both sides are happy if these negotiations only take place every few years. Also, if labor and management do not come to an agreement, a strike may occur, with substantial potential losses to both sides. Neither side really wants a strike (except in very unusual circumstances), and if there are wide time intervals between negotiations, there also are likely to be wide time intervals between strikes.

TEST YOUR UNDERSTANDING

True or false?

_____ **1** New Keynesians claim that the new classical macroeconomics neglects the inertia in wages and prices and is inconsistent with the evidence.

_____ **2** Both the new classical macroeconomists and the new Keynesians often assume that the expectations of people and firms conform to the theory of rational expectations.

_____ **3** According to the new Keynesians, wages can be sticky.

Exercises

1 According to the new Keynesians, some unemployment is involuntary. It is their view that some

unemployed workers would like jobs at the going wage rate, but cannot find them. Does this seem reasonable? Why, or why not?

2 In Japan, labor contracts tend to extend for one year, not the three-year period that is common in the United States. Does this affect how rigid wages are?

3 If wages and prices were sticky before 1930, can this be attributed to long-term labor contracts between unions and firms? Why, or why not?

4 In 1914, Henry Ford reduced the length of the working day from 9 to 8 hours, and raised the minimum daily wage from $2.34 to $5.00. He afterward said this "was one of the finest cost-cutting moves we ever made." How is it possible that an increase in the wage rate can reduce costs?

4 ▪ Policy Activism: Pro and Con

Much of the debate between the new Keynesians and the new classical macroeconomists is really over policy activism. The new Keynesians—like the old Keynesians—tend to be policy activists; they believe that discretionary monetary and fiscal policies are required to keep the economy on a reasonably even keel. The new classical macroeconomists tend to be very skeptical about how much stabilization policies of this sort can achieve. The debate over the pros and cons of policy activism has been going on for decades. Although it is hazardous to try to summarize the views of each side (since there is considerable disagreement within each camp), the disagreements between policy activists and their opponents tend to be along the following lines.

STABILITY OF PRIVATE SPENDING

Many opponents of policy activism tend to believe that, if the government's economic policies did not destabilize the economy, private spending would be quite stable. Personal consumption expenditures change relatively slowly as households adjust

their estimates of their long-term income prospects. Policy activists, on the other hand, believe that business and consumer spending represent a substantial source of economic instability that should be offset by monetary and fiscal policy.

FLEXIBILITY OF PRICES

Even if intended private spending is not entirely stable, flexible prices tend to stabilize it, according to nonactivists. The policy activists reply that prices are relatively inflexible downward; in their view, the length of time that would be required for the economy to get itself out of a severe recession would be intolerably long. Their opponents seem more inclined than policy activists to believe that high unemployment will cause wages and input prices to fall, shifting the aggregate supply curve downward and increasing output in a reasonable period of time.

RULES VERSUS ACTIVISM

Opponents of policy activism tend to believe that, even if intended private spending is not entirely stable, and if prices are not entirely flexible, activist monetary and fiscal policies to stabilize the economy are likely to do more damage than good. They sometimes favor a rule stipulating that the money supply should grow steadily at a constant rate, because of the difficulties in forecasting the future state of the economy and because of the long and variable time lag in the effect of changes in the quantity of money on output and prices. The policy activists, while admitting that monetary and fiscal policies have sometimes been destabilizing, are much more optimistic about the efficacy of such policies in the future.

DIVERGENT POLITICAL BELIEFS

One final and very important point: While economics is a science, not a mere reflection of the economist's political beliefs, it nonetheless is impossible to divorce an economist's views of the economy from his or her political feelings, where policy issues are involved. To a considerable extent, the differences between the policy activists and their opponents stem from divergent political beliefs. The policy activists tend to be optimistic concerning the extent to which the government can be trusted to formulate and carry out a responsible set of monetary and fiscal policies. They recognize that some politicians are willing to win votes in the next election by destabilizing the economy, but they nonetheless believe that discretionary action by elected officials will generally be more effective than automatic rules. Opponents of policy activism, on the other hand, are skeptical of the willingness of politicians to do what is required to stabilize the economy, rather than what is politically expedient. Since this aspect of the debate is difficult to resolve (in any scientific way), a complete resolution of this controversy is not likely any time soon.

 TEST YOUR UNDERSTANDING

True or false?

____ **1** Opponents of activist monetary and fiscal policies sometimes favor a rule for the money supply.

____ **2** Policy activists tend to be optimistic concerning the extent to which the government can be trusted.

Exercise

1 As stated repeatedly, if wages are inflexible, involuntary unemployment is likely to occur. According to the new Keynesians, long-term union contracts are one of the factors that make wage rates downwardly inflexible, at least in the short run. Martin Weitzman of MIT has proposed a way to increase the downward flexibility of wage rates, and thus reduce the amount of involuntary unemployment. Put baldly, the proposal is that some part of a worker's wage rate should be tied directly to his or her employer's profits; in other words, workers should get part of their compensation in the form of **profit sharing.**

Suppose that a worker receives $2 per hour in wages for every million dollars in profits of his or her employer. In addition, suppose that he or she receives a guaranteed hourly wage of $5, regardless of what the employer's profits may be. Then the following graph shows the relationship between the worker's hourly wage rate and the employer's annual profits:

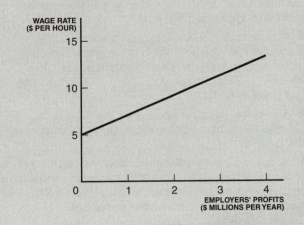

a. If the employer earns profits of $4 million per year, what will the worker's hourly wage rate be?

b. If the employer earns profits of $1 million per year, what will the worker's hourly wage rate be?

c. Suppose that the employer's profits drop from $4 million to $1 million because of the onset of a recession. Is the employer as likely to lay off workers under the profit-sharing system described above as under the traditional wage-setting arrangement

where the hourly wage rate is $10 (say), regardless of the employer's profits?

d. Some people argue that this sort of profit sharing distributes the burden of recession more equitably than the traditional wage-setting arrangement. In what way is the burden distributed differently?

e. Weitzman's proposal has been criticized by many groups, including unions. What concerns might workers and others have about the adoption of such a profit-sharing plan?

▪ CHAPTER REVIEW

KEY TERMS

new classical macroeconomists

real business cycle theorists

supply shocks

menu cost

profit sharing

COMPLETION QUESTIONS

1 According to the new classical macroeconomists, high rates of unemployment (are, are not) _____ evidence of a gap between actual and _____ output that can be reduced; instead, output fluctuations result from _____ errors.

2 One of the most serious criticisms of the new classical macroeconomists has centered on their contention that _____ would be eliminated if firms and consumers had up-to-date and accurate information about the aggregate price level.

3 According to real business cycle theories, output fluctuations are due to shifts in the aggregate supply curve. Among the factors causing shifts in this curve are new _____, new _____ of production, and good or bad _____.

4 A favorable supply shock pushes the _____ curve to the right; an unfavorable supply shock pushes this curve to the _____.

5 _____ contracts tend to slow the adjustment of wages. Workers and firms enter into such contracts because each wage negotiation _____ both workers and firms a considerable amount of _____ and _____.

ANSWERS TO COMPLETION QUESTIONS

are not

potential

random forecasting

business fluctuations

products, methods

weather

aggregate supply

left

Long-term labor

costs

time, money

ANSWERS TO
TEST YOUR UNDERSTANDING

SECTION 1

TRUE OR FALSE: 1. True   2. True   3. True

EXERCISES

1. Critics of the new classical macroeconomics maintain that many unemployed workers would be willing to work if offered a job at a reasonable wage. They say that, if you ask the unemployed workers or actually offer them jobs, you'll see that this is true. The new classical macroeconomists deny this.

2. Market clearing means that the quantity supplied equals the quantity demanded in each market. Critics of the new classical macroeconomics deny that markets continually clear in this way.

SECTION 2

TRUE OR FALSE: 1. True

EXERCISE

1. Something that causes a shift in the aggregate supply curve.

SECTION 3

TRUE OR FALSE: 1. True   2. True   3. True

EXERCISES

1. Critics of this view maintain that unemployed workers sometimes are unwilling to take jobs that would pay them in accord with their worth to potential employers and that, if they were willing to settle for a reasonable wage, they could get a job. The new Keynesians, on the other hand, believe that wages tend to be sticky, and that the quantity of labor supplied may exceed the quantity of labor demanded, particularly in recessions.

2. It may tend toward less rigidity.

3. No. The rise of trade unions in the United States occurred largely in the 1930s and 1940s. Thus, it seems very unlikely that long-term labor contracts between unions and firms could explain the stickiness of wages and prices—or the existence of business fluctuations—before 1930.

4. Because it may increase labor productivity.

SECTION 4

TRUE OR FALSE: 1. True   2. True

EXERCISE

1. a. $13 per hour.

b. $7 per hour.

c. No. Since a worker will receive only $7 per hour during the recession, rather than $10 per hour, the employer is less likely to lay him or her off, because it is more likely that the worker's services are worth $7 per hour than $10 per hour.

d. Under profit sharing, all workers (covered by profit sharing) take a cut in pay during a recession, but fewer are laid off than under the traditional arrangement. Thus the burden is shared more equally than under the traditional arrangement, in which most workers suffer no pay cut during a recession, but the minority who are laid off experience a severe reduction in earnings.

e. Some unions are concerned that the average wage rate (averaged over the various phases of the business cycle) may be much lower than under the traditional arrangement. Also, there is the question of whether workers will be willing to trade more jobs and greater stability of employment for a weaker and reduced wage guarantee.

CHAPTER 13

Why Did the Fed Hike Interest Rates in Late 1994?

1 ■ Introduction

On November 16, 1994, the headline of the *New York Times* trumpeted: "Federal Reserve Increases Interest Rates by 3/4 Point; Jump Is Largest Since 1981." It was the sixth time during 1994 that the Federal Reserve had nudged interest rates higher, and the effects were showing up throughout the U.S. economy. For example, whereas interest rates on 30-year mortgages were available at about 7 percent at the beginning of the year, they had increased to over 9 percent by November.

Only one day after the increase in interest rates, the Bureau of Labor Statistics reported that consumer prices in October 1994 had gone up by 1/10 of a percentage point, a very small rise. The result was sharp criticism of the Fed. In the words of the *New York Times*, "The Federal Reserve's decision this week to raise interest rates in order to ward off inflation was, as expected, criticized from all corners."[1] Take Marvin Lohr, a restaurant owner in Frederick, Maryland, who said, "I know there's this fear about inflation, but I still think they are ahead of the game."[2] The purpose of this chapter is to indicate the factors influencing the Fed when it made this decision, as well as to discuss other Fed policies in the past.

2 ■ The Carter Years

To begin with, it is essential to review briefly the recent history of monetary policy in the United States. During the Carter years inflation was a particular problem; and in his 1976 presidential campaign, President Carter belabored Arthur F. Burns, the chairman of the Federal Reserve, for increasing the money supply too slowly. Once Carter became president, there was speculation that he and Burns might clash. During 1977 the narrowly defined money supply (M1) grew by about 7 percent, and the broadly defined money supply (M2) grew by about 9 percent. Interest rates increased somewhat, but monetary policy in 1977 was not restrictive.

In 1978 the rate of inflation once again approached double-digit levels. As many observers predicted, President Carter did not reappoint Arthur F. Burns as chairman of the Fed; instead, the job went to G. William Miller, an industrialist. In late 1978 the Fed, led by Miller, raised the discount rate to an all-time high of 9 1/2 percent. Some reserve requirements were also increased. The narrowly defined money supply (M1) grew by about 7 percent, and the broadly defined money supply (M2) grew by about 4 percent in 1978.

In August 1979 Miller resigned as Fed chairman (to become secretary of the Treasury) and

---

[1] *New York Times*, November 17, 1994, p. A24.

[2] *New York Times*, November 20, 1994, p. 26.

was succeeded by Paul Volcker, formerly president of the Federal Reserve Bank of New York. In his first months in office, Volcker was viewed as a more determined foe of inflation than his predecessor. Interest rates were pushed to record highs.

Yet the rate of inflation, which was widely regarded as the country's number-one economic problem, stubbornly remained at well above 10 percent.

3 ■ The Reagan Years

During 1981, the prime rate was pushed up to about 20 percent, and the general public as well as the financial community was getting the message that the Fed meant business in its fight against inflation. The widespread expectation that inflation would continue unchecked began to disappear. During 1982, the Consumer Price Index rose by about 4 percent, which was high relative to 20 years before, but low relative to the late 1970s. The money supply grew by about 8 or 9 percent in 1982 and 1983, and interest rates fell substantially. By early 1985, the prime rate was about 11 percent.

During 1985 and 1986, the money supply grew at a very rapid clip, reflecting the Federal Reserve's desire to extend the recovery. Interest rates fell substantially. In 1987, Alan Greenspan replaced Paul Volcker as Fed chairman. The Fed began to tighten money somewhat to prevent the dollar from falling further against other currencies, but after the stock market crash in October 1987, it loosened money again.

4 ■ The Bush Years

The U.S. economy continued to grow during 1988 and 1989, but there was increased concern about inflation. In 1990, with the U.S. military buildup in Iraq and higher oil prices, the Fed feared that it might have to contend with serious inflationary pressures. At the same time, it was worried that the economy would fall into a recession.

In late 1990, more and more economists and other observers felt that a recession had already begun. In response, the Fed lowered the discount rate and loosened money. While the concern over inflation had not gone away, the main thrust of Federal Reserve policy in early 1991 was toward stimulating the economy. When the economy was slow to recover from the recession, the Fed pushed short-term interest rates below the rate of inflation, and kept them there.

5 ■ The Clinton Years

In 1993, short-term interest rates were essentially constant, and monetary policy was not restrictive. Because the broad monetary aggregates like M2 tended to behave in atypical ways, the Fed placed much less emphasis on them than in previous decades. According to President Clinton's Council of Economic Advisers, "Some of the change in behavior of the monetary aggregates stems from massive portfolio shifts by American households. For example, the sharp decline in interest rates on bank certificates of deposit [a form of savings account] led many households to shift money into stock and bond funds."[3]

According to many economists, the Fed kept monetary policy expansive in 1992 and 1993 even though the economy was strengthening

[3] *Economic Report of the President*, 1994, p. 70.

considerably. In 1993 and even 1994, the Fed seemed to underestimate the economy's strength. By November 1994, there was little evidence that the Fed's actions had dampened the expansion, which was proceeding at a rapid pace. In early 1997, the Fed increased interest rates slightly.

6 ■ Applying Economics: Fighting Unemployment

The following two problems are concerned with the use of monetary policy to fight unemployment in the early 1990s.

PROBLEM 13.1 In July 1990, a recession began in the United States. As shown in Figure 13.1, the unemployment rate increased during late 1990 and 1991. In his Economic Report to the Congress, President George Bush said in February 1992 that "1991 was a challenging year for the American economy.

Output was stagnant and unemployment rose. The recession, which began in the third quarter of 1990, following the longest peacetime expansion in the nation's history, continued in 1991."[4]

a. Table 13.1 shows the changes in interest rates between 1990 and 1992. Are these changes in the direction you would expect? Why or why not?

[4] *Economic Report of the President*, February 1992, p. 3.

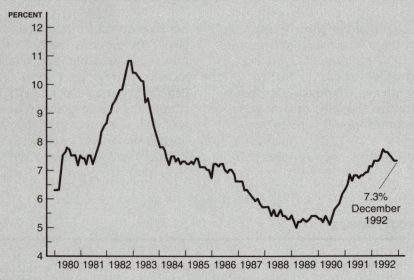

■ **FIGURE 13.1**

Civilian Unemployment Rate, 1980–1992

SOURCE: *Economic Report of the President*, 1993, p. 43.

▪ **TABLE 13.1**

Interest Rates, 1990 to 1992

YEAR	PRIME RATE CHARGED BY BANKS	DISCOUNT RATE
1990	10.01	6.98
1991	8.46	5.45
1992	6.25	3.25

SOURCE: *Economic Report of the President,* 1993.

▪ **TABLE 13.2**

Growth Rates of M1 and M2 during 1990 to 1993

YEAR	PERCENTAGE GROWTH RATE OF: M1	M2
1990	4.1	3.5
1991	8.7	3.0
1992	14.2	1.4
1993	10.2	1.6

SOURCE: *Economic Report of the President,* 1994.

b. Figure 13.2 shows the behavior of real and nominal short-term interest rates. What is the difference between real and nominal interest rates? Why are real interest rates of importance?

c. Between 1990 and 1992, did real short-term interest rates change in the direction you would expect? Why or why not?

d. Table 13.2 shows the growth rates of M1 and M2. Were the changes from 1990 to 1992 in the growth rate of M1 in the direction you would expect? Why or why not?

e. Between 1990 and 1992, were the changes in the growth rate of M2 in the direction you would expect? Why or why not?

PROBLEM 13.2 Both during the fight against unemployment in 1991–92 and during subsequent years, the Federal Reserve down-played the significance of the growth of the quantity of money as an indicator of how easy or tight monetary policy is. For example, John LaWare, one of the members of the Federal Reserve Board, said in 1994: "I get a feel for what I think is going on based on the information—not only the anecdotal information

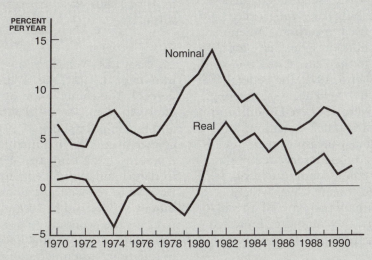

▪ **FIGURE 13.2**

Real and Nominal Short-Term Interest Rates, 1970–1992

SOURCE: *Economic Report of the President,* 1993, p. 100.

in the press and the statistical information assembled and compiled by the staff here, but also from the general tone of the markets. I'm probably least sensitive to the money figures because I don't know what they mean anymore."[5]

a. As pointed out above by President Clinton's Council of Economic Advisers, many people have moved their money from savings accounts to mutual funds. Are savings accounts part of the money supply as measured by M2? Are mutual funds part of the money supply as measured by M2? Has this

[5] *New York Times,* February 28, 1994, p. D1.

movement of funds tended to reduce the usefulness of M2 as an indicator of how easy or tight monetary policy is? Why or why not?

b. Some members of the Federal Reserve Board say that they use as indicators measures of expected inflation, such as long-term interest rates and commodity prices. Why are these measures regarded as relevant?

c. The Federal Reserve also looks at the behavior of gold prices. Why is this regarded as relevant?

d. Still another measure that receives attention is capacity utilization by the country's factories. Why is this of relevance?

7 ▪ Applying Economics: Fighting Inflation

The following two problems deal with the steps taken to fight inflation in the late 1970s and early 1980s.

PROBLEM 13.3 In 1979 the inflation rate began to hit double digits. In the second quarter of 1979 the money supply began to rise sharply. Financial managers here and abroad issued statements that inflation was reaching dangerous levels. Fiscal policy was not used to curb this inflation. Consequently, much of the responsibility for fighting inflation fell to the Federal Reserve.

On Saturday, October 6, 1979, the Federal Open Market Committee held a special meeting where the members were quartered in different hotels to avoid attracting public attention. Feeling that extraordinary measures were required, the committee raised reserve requirements and increased the discount rate from 11 to 12 percent, even though it was widely believed that the economy had entered a recession. At the same time, the committee indicated that it would try to reduce the rate of growth of the money supply.

a. Why did the Federal Open Market Committee raise the legal reserve requirements?

b. Why was the discount rate increased from 11 to 12 percent?

c. Why did the committee try to reduce the rate of growth of the money supply?

d. In the last quarter of 1979, the rate of growth of the money supply fell to about 5 percent. The prime rate (the interest rate banks charge their best customers) rose from about 13 percent in September 1979 to about 20 percent in April 1980. Was monetary policy tight during this period?

PROBLEM 13.4 When President Reagan came into office in 1981, the inflation rate was 11 percent. The combination of President Carter's efforts to stimulate the economy in 1977–78 and the oil price shock of 1979 had apparently created an underlying inflation rate of about 8 percent. In his campaign, Reagan had promised to reduce inflation by encouraging the Federal Reserve to reduce the rate of growth of the money supply and by creating greater incentives for the economy to produce more goods. He would therefore attack the traditional causes of inflation, "too much money chasing too few goods," from both sides.

By the 1980s, most economists believed that people's expectations about the possible effects of future government policies could affect how well the policies worked. For example, if the government tried to stimulate the economy by increasing the rate of growth of the money supply, its policy would fail if firms and labor unions simply raised prices and wages in expectation of higher inflation. The additional money supplied to the economy would go into higher prices rather than toward stimulating more production.

a. One group of economists felt that it would take a long time to get business and labor to reduce their expectations of future inflation. Why do you think that they believed this? If true, why was this of significance?

b. Another group of economists felt that inflation could be reduced without a large increase in unemployment if the government's resolve to stick to inflation-fighting policies was credible. Why did they believe that the government's anti-inflation policies were not credible?

c. The Fed adhered to a tight money policy in 1981. It was not until October 1982 that the Fed eased up. By that time the rate of inflation had fallen from the 11 percent level of early 1981 to 3.5 percent. Was the Fed successful in achieving its objectives?

d. What were the social costs of the Fed's fight against inflation?

8 ▪ Applying Economics: Problems in Formulating Monetary Policy

The following two problems deal with some of the problems faced by the Fed in formulating monetary policy.

PROBLEM 13.5 Suppose that the existing money supply equals $300 billion, and that the public's demand curve for money shifts upward and to the right, as shown in Figure 13.3. That is, at each level of the rate of interest, the public demands a greater amount of money than before. If the interest rate remains at 12 percent, the quantity of money demanded by the public will exceed $300 billion, the existing quantity supplied. Thus the level of interest rates will rise from 12 to 14 percent, as shown in Figure 13.3.

a. Under these circumstances, will it appear to some economists—those who favor the use of interest rates as an indicator of monetary tightness or ease—that monetary policy has tightened? Why or why not?

b. The Fed can push the level of interest rates back down by increasing the quantity of money. The equilibrium value of the interest rate is the one where the quantity of money demanded equals the quantity of money supplied. If the demand curve for money remains fixed at its new higher level, the Fed can push

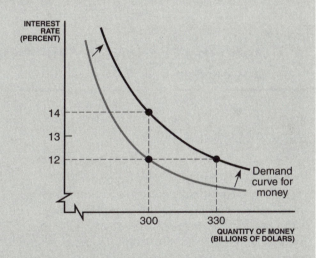

▪ **FIGURE 13.3**

Effect of a Shift in the Demand Curve for Money

If the demand curve for money shifts upward and to the right, as shown here, the equilibrium value of the interest rate will increase from 12 to 14 percent if the quantity of money supplied remains $300 billion. If the Fed wants to push the equilibrium level of the interest rate back to 12 percent, it must increase the quantity of money supplied to $330 billion.

the interest rate back down to 12 percent by increasing the quantity of money to $330 billion. With this quantity of money, the equilibrium interest rate is 12 percent, as shown in Figure 13.3. Under these circumstances, will it appear to some economists —those who favor the growth rate of the quantity of money as an indicator of monetary tightness or ease—that monetary policy has eased? Why or why not?

c. Can the Fed avoid both increasing the rate of growth of the quantity of money and raising interest rates? Why or why not? If the answer is no, what problems may this cause?

PROBLEM 13.6 An enormous amount of statistical and econometric research has been carried out to determine how quickly an unanticipated recession can be combated by monetary policy. According to Robert Gordon of Northwestern University, the total lag between the occurrence of such an unanticipated slowdown in

economic activity and the impact of monetary policy is about 14 months. In other words, it takes about 14 months for the Federal Reserve to become aware of the slowdown, to take the appropriate actions, and to have these actions affect real GDP.

a. On the average, how long do you think it takes for a slowdown to be reflected in the government's economic data?

b. How long do you think it takes for the Fed to pay attention to the signal and change monetary policy?

c. Once a change has been made in the rate of increase of the money supply, how long do you think it takes until real GDP is affected?

d. What problems result from the long lag between a change in economic conditions and the impact of monetary policy?

9 ■ Applying Economics: The Fed's Discussion on November 15, 1994

In the final two problems, we return to the decision by the Federal Reserve in late 1994 to increase interest rates.

PROBLEM 13.7 Investors and other decision makers are continually concerned about whether interest rates will go up, down, or stay the same; thus, they must continually try to guess what the Fed will do. For example, consider the situation in October 1994. According to *Business Week*, "within the secretive Fed, a spirited debate has erupted over the state of the economy. A group of inflation hawks—regional [Federal Reserve] bank president Robert T. Parry of San Francisco, J. Alfred Broaddus, Jr., of Richmond, and Jerry L. Jordan of Cleveland—want an immediate rate increase. They fear a pickup in retail sales, rising commodity prices, and tight industrial capacity portend an overheating economy and a coming inflation surge unless the Fed moves decisively. At the other end is

Vice-Chairman Alan S. Blinder, who . . . argues that past Fed tightenings haven't been felt yet and will eventually slow the economy."[6]

a. In late October, data issued by the U.S. Department of Commerce indicated that in the third quarter of 1994, GDP grew at an annual rate of 3.4 percent, well in excess of the 2.5 percent growth rate that many people regarded as the maximum that could occur without causing increased inflation. Do you think that this increased the probability that the Fed would raise interest rates?

b. The National Association of Purchasing Management reported strong factory activity and higher prices in October. Do you think that this increased the probability that the Fed would raise interest rates?

c. The Federal Reserve's own survey of regional economies on November 2 indicated

[6] *Business Week*, October 31, 1994, p. 57.

price increases for manufacturers' materials. Do you think that this increased the probability that the Fed would raise interest rates?

d. In its November 14 issue, *Business Week* stated that "the Fed is sure to raise [interest rates] when it meets on November 15. . . . [A] move will shift monetary policy from neutral to one that's outright restrictive"[7] If you accepted this forecast, would you expect bond prices to fall? Why or why not?

PROBLEM 13.8 At its November 15, 1994 meeting, the Federal Open Market Committee raised the discount rate by ¾ percentage point. This decision occurred about 5 hours after it was reported that U.S. factories operated at 84.9 percent of capacity in October, the highest level in almost 15 years. Retail sales were also in-

creasing rapidly; and the Federal Reserve Bank of Atlanta reported price rises in the Southeast. According to James Annable, chief economist at the First Chicago Corporation, "This is a very, very robust economy. . . . It's growing too fast."[8]

a. According to Henry Kaufman, a respected Wall Street money manager and economist, "This increase [in interest rates] is entirely justified, but it is not the last one in this cycle. At some point in the next three months, they will have to act again. The economy is too strong to be greatly affected or slowed by the present level of rates."[9] Figure 13.4 shows the rate of capacity utilization and the inflation rate since 1972. When capacity utilization exceeds 83 percent, does inflation tend to increase? Given that capacity utilization was about 85 percent in

[7] *Business Week,* November 14, 1994, p. 31.

[8] *New York Times,* November 16, 1994, p. D6.
[9] Ibid., p. A1.

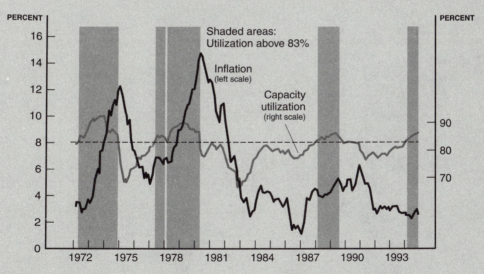

▪ **FIGURE 13.4**

Capacity Utilization Rate and Inflation Rate, 1972–1994

All figures are seasonally adjusted and plotted monthly. **Inflation** is the monthly change in the Consumer Price Index at an annual rate. **Unemployment** is the civilian unemployment rate. **Capacity utilization** is total output as a percentage of the economy's productive capacity.

SOURCE: *New York Times,* November 17, 1994.

October 1994, did Kaufman's statement seem justified?

b. Figure 13.5 shows the unemployment rate and the inflation rate since 1972. When the unemployment rate is below 6 percent, does inflation tend to increase? Given that the unemployment rate was 5.7 percent in October 1994, did Kaufman's statement seem justified?

c. Jerry Jasinowski, president of the National Association of Manufacturers, opposed the Fed's decision. In his view, "The Fed is fundamentally misreading the American economy. They ought to get out from behind their desks and see what is really happening in plants and on factory floors across the country."[10] According to the National Association of Manufacturers, U.S. factories were likely to have more capacity than existing statistics indicated. Why would that be of relevance?

d. Would an increase in interest rates be

[10] Ibid.

likely to reduce the sales of manufacturers? If so, would this help to explain why the National Association of Manufacturers opposed the Fed's decision?

e. Organized labor also criticized the Federal Reserve. John Zalusky, an economist at the AFL-CIO, was reported to have said, "What they are doing is coming down on the side of the bloody bondholders who don't want inflation to undermine the value of their bonds."[11] Are bondholders the only group that is fearful of inflation? Why or why not?

f. The *New York Times* reported that Alan Greenspan, chairman of the Fed, testified in the summer of 1994 that "the central bank should err, if at all, on the side of raising rates too much. It is easier to reverse an unexpected drop in economic output by lowering interest rates than it is to stop an inflationary spiral

[11] Ibid.

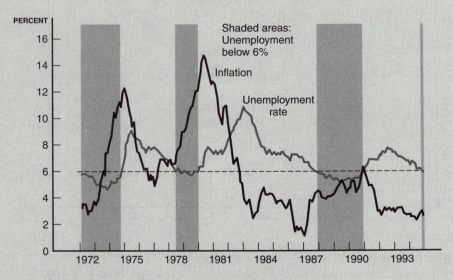

▪ **FIGURE 13.5**

Unemployment Rate and Inflation Rate, 1972–1994

SOURCE: *New York Times*, November 17, 1994.

with higher rates. . . ."[12] Do you agree? Why or why not?

g. The Clinton administration was reported to be somewhat more antagonistic to this increase in interest rates than earlier ones. Would the effects of this interest hike have been likely to be felt close to the 1996 election? If so, why might Bill Clinton have been concerned?

[12] Ibid., p. D6.

10 ▪ Conclusion

The Federal Reserve has a widespread and important impact on Americans, as illustrated by the following brief account in *Business Week* of the effect of the Fed's decision on November 15, 1994: "In barely an hour, banks bumped their prime [interest] rates from 7.75 to 8.5 percent. The dollar rallied strongly. . . . Stocks dipped, however, on fears that higher rates would cut profits."[13] To understand what is going on in the economy and why, it is essential that you know the material in Chapters 9 to 12. Without such knowledge, it is impossible even to read newspapers like the *New York Times* or *Wall Street Journal*. Lacking such knowledge, you are cut off from meaningful discussion of the U.S. economy.

[13] *Business Week,* November 28, 1994, p. 43.

PART FOUR

Economic
Growth

■ CHAPTER 14
Basics of Economic Growth

Essentials of **Economic Growth**

■ The production possibilities curve shows all efficient combinations of output an economy can produce. A country's potential output increases when its production possibilities curve shifts outward.

■ According to Thomas Malthus, the human population was in danger of outrunning its food supply. Malthus underestimated the effects of technological change.

■ So long as the economy sustains noninflationary full employment and the capital-output ratio remains constant, the rate of growth of national output will be directly related to the percent of GDP devoted to investment.

■ The rate of technological change is perhaps the most important single determinant of a country's rate of economic growth.

1 ■ The Production Possibilities Curve

There are two common measures of the rate of **economic growth.** The first is the rate of growth of a nation's real gross domestic product, which tells you how rapidly the economy's total real output of goods and services is increasing. The second is the rate of growth of per capita real gross domestic product, which is a better measure of the rate of increase of a country's standard of living. The second measure will be used here unless stated otherwise.

To represent the process of economic growth, it is convenient to use the production possibilities curve which shows all efficient combinations of output an economy can produce. For example, suppose that a society produces only two goods: food and tractors. If this society has at its disposal a fixed amount of resources and if technology is fixed, the production possibilities curve (like the one in Figure 14.1) shows the maximum quantity of food that can be produced, given each amount of tractors produced.

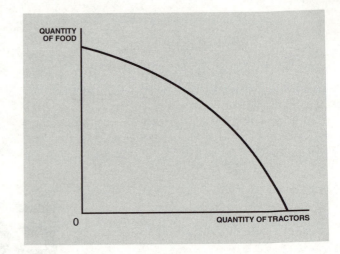

■ **FIGURE 14.1**

Production Possibilities Curve

The production possibilities curve shows all efficient combinations of output an economy can produce.

SHIFTS OF THE PRODUCTION POSSIBILITIES CURVE

A country's potential output increases when its production possibilities curve shifts outward, as from position *A* to position *B* in Figure 14.2. This happens because the society can produce (and consume) more of one good without having to produce (and consume) less of the other good. Thus its productive capacity must be greater. If the production possibilities curve shifts outward, if the economy is efficient, and if population remains constant, per capita GDP increases and economic growth occurs. Moreover, the faster the production possibilities curve shifts outward, the greater the rate of economic growth.

NO SHIFT OF THE PRODUCTION POSSIBILITIES CURVE

Even if a country's production possibilities curve does not shift outward, economic growth can occur if unemployment or inefficiency is reduced. If a country allows some of its resources to be unemployed or underutilized because of an insufficiency of intended spending, this will cause the economy to operate at a point *inside* the production possibilities curve rather than *on* the curve.

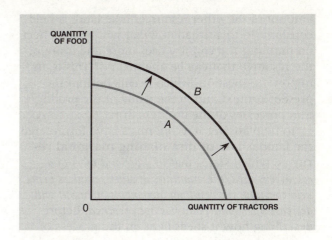

▪ **FIGURE 14.2**

Outward Shift of Production Possibilities Curve

A country's potential output increases when its production possibilities curve shifts outward from position *A* to position *B*.

The same thing will happen if a country allocates its resources inefficiently. Clearly, a country can achieve some economic growth by getting closer to the production possibilities curve through a reduction in unemployment or inefficiency.

 TEST YOUR UNDERSTANDING

True or false?

____ **1** A country's potential output increases when its production possibilities curve is shifted inward.

____ **2** Economic growth can occur even if a country's production possibilities curve does not shift outward.

____ **3** Unemployment results in an economy's being at a point inside the production possibilities curve.

---

2 ▪ The Law of Diminishing Marginal Returns

If a country's land, labor, and capital increase, you would certainly expect its output to increase as well. But suppose the country cannot increase the amount used of all of its resources at the same rate. Instead, suppose it can increase the quantity of one resource, say labor, while the amount of the other resources, like land, is held constant. In this situation, what will be the effect on output if the country uses more and more of the resource that can be augmented? This is an important question, which occurs both in the present context and in the study of the production processes of the business firm.

To help answer it, economists have formulated the famous **law of diminishing marginal returns,** which states that, *if more and more of a resource is used, the quantities of other resources being held constant, the resulting increments of output will decrease after some point has been reached.* Before describing how it sheds light on the process of economic growth, consider the nature of this law.

Suppose that you obtain data concerning the amounts of output resulting from the utilization of various amounts of one resource, holding constant the amounts of other resources. For example, suppose that data are obtained concerning the amounts of output resulting from various amounts of labor, holding constant the amounts of capital and land. Then suppose that you determine the *extra* amount of output resulting from the addition of each *extra* unit of labor. According to the law of diminishing marginal returns, this extra amount of output will eventually *decrease,* as more and more labor is utilized with the fixed

amounts of capital and land. In other words, beyond some point, *an additional unit of labor will add less and less to total output.*

AN AGRICULTURAL EXAMPLE

To illustrate the workings of this law, consider Table 14.1, which shows the total output—or GDP—of a simple agricultural society under a set of alternative assumptions concerning the number of hours of labor used. For simplicity, assume that this society produces only one product, corn, so that total output can be measured in bushels of corn. Also, assume that the amount of land and capital that can be used is fixed in quantity. Column 1 in the table shows various alternative numbers of hours of labor that can be used with this fixed amount of land and capital. Column 2 shows the total output in each case.

Column 3 shows the additional output resulting from the addition of an extra hour of labor; this is called the **marginal product of labor.** For example, if the quantity of labor is between 2 million hours and 3 million hours, the marginal product of labor is 2.5 bushels per hour of labor, because each extra hour of labor results in an extra 2.5 bushels of output.

■ TABLE 14.1

The Law of Diminishing Marginal Returns

(1) HOURS OF LABOR	(2) BUSHELS OF CORN	(3) MARGINAL PRODUCT OF LABOR	(4) AVERAGE PRODUCT OF LABOR
(millions)		(bushels per hour)	
1	1.5		1.50
		2.0	
2	3.5		1.75
		2.5	
3	6.0		2.00
		3.0	
4	9.0		2.25
		2.0	
5	11.0		2.20
		2.0	
6	13.0		2.17
		1.0	
7	14.0		2.00
		0.0	
8	14.0		1.75

In Table 14.1, the marginal product of labor increases as more and more labor is used, but only up to a point. Beyond 4 million hours of labor, the marginal product of labor goes down as more and more labor is used. Specifically, the marginal product of labor reaches a maximum of 3.0 bushels per hour when between 3 and 4 million hours of labor are used. Then it falls to 2.0 bushels per hour when between 4 and 5 million hours of labor are used, remains at 2.0 bushels per hour when between 5 and 6 million hours of labor are used, and falls once again to 1.0 bushel per hour when between 6 and 7 million hours of labor are used.

Thus, as predicted by the law of diminishing marginal returns, *the marginal product of labor eventually declines.* Moreover, as shown in column 4 of Table 14.1, the **average product of labor,** which is defined as total output per hour of labor, also falls beyond some point as more and more labor is used with a fixed amount of other resources. This too stems from the law of diminishing marginal returns.

REASONS FOR DIMINISHING RETURNS

It is easy to see why the law of diminishing marginal returns must be true. For example, imagine what would happen in the simple economy of Table 14.1 if more and more labor were applied to a fixed amount of land. Beyond a point, as more and more labor is used, the extra labor has to be devoted to less and less important tasks. If enough labor is used, it even becomes increasingly difficult to prevent the workers from getting in one another's way! For such reasons, one certainly would expect that, beyond some point, extra amounts of labor would result in smaller and smaller increments of output.

Finally, note two important things about this law. First, at least one resource must be fixed in quantity. The law of diminishing marginal returns does not apply to cases in which there is a proportional increase in all resources. Second, technology is assumed to be fixed. The law of diminishing marginal returns does not apply to cases in which technology changes.

 TEST YOUR UNDERSTANDING

True or false?

_____ **1** The law of diminishing marginal returns applies when all inputs are increased.

Exercises

1 Suppose that a society produces only two goods, food and tractors, and that its production possibilities curve in 1997 and 1998 is as follows:

QUANTITY OF FOOD (millions of tons)	QUANTITY OF TRACTORS (thousands of tractors)
0	9
1	8
2	7
3	5
4	3
5	0

If this society produces 4 thousand tractors and 3 million tons of food in 1997 and 5 thousand tractors and 3 million tons of food in 1998 (its population remaining constant), has any economic growth occurred between 1997 and 1998? If so, to what is it due?

2 Suppose that the society in Exercise 1 produces 6 thousand tractors and 3 million tons of food in 1999 (its population remaining the same as in 1998). Has any economic growth occurred between 1998 and 1999? If so, is it due to a shift in the production possibilities curve?

3 Suppose that a society produces only one commodity, wheat, and that its production function is:

HOURS OF LABOR	BUSHELS OF WHEAT
(millions)	
0	0
1	2
2	4
3	6
4	7
5	7

What is the marginal product of labor when between 1 and 2 million hours of labor are used? When between 2 and 3 million hours of labor are used? When between 4 and 5 million hours of labor are used? Do the results conform to the law of diminishing marginal returns? Why, or why not?

3 ▪ Thomas Malthus and Population Growth

A country's rate of economic growth depends on, among other things, how much the quantities of inputs of various kinds increase. To illuminate the growth process, consider the effect on the rate of economic growth of increasing each kind of input, holding the others constant. Begin by looking at the effects of changes in the quantity of labor. Economists have devoted a great deal of attention to the effects of **population growth** on the rate of economic growth. The classic work was done by Thomas Malthus (1776–1834), a British parson who devoted his life to academic research. The first professional economist, he taught at a college established by the East India Company to train its administrators—and was called "Pop" by his students behind his back. Whether "Pop" stood for population or not, Malthus's fame is based on his theories of population growth.

Malthus believed that the population tends to grow at a geometric rate. In his *Essay on the Principle of Population*, published in 1798, he pointed out the implications of such a constant rate of growth:

If any person will take the trouble to make the calculation, he will see that if the necessities of life could be obtained without limit, and the number of people could be doubled every twenty-five

years, the population which might have been produced from a single pair since the Christian era, would have been sufficient, not only to fill the earth quite full of people, so that four should stand in every square yard, but to fill all the planets of our solar system in the same way, and not only them but all the planets revolving around the stars which are visible to the naked eye, supposing each of them . . . to have as many planets belong to it as our sun has.[1]

In contrast to the human population, which tends to increase at a geometric rate, the supply of land can increase slowly if at all.[2] And land, particularly in Malthus's time, was the source of food. Consequently, it seemed to Malthus that the human population was in danger of outrunning its food supply: "Taking the whole earth," he wrote, ". . . and supposing the present population to be equal to a thousand millions, the human species would increase as the numbers, 1, 2, 4, 8, 16, 32, 64, 128, 256, and subsistence as 1, 2, 3, 4,

[1] T. Malthus, *Essay on the Principle of Population*, as quoted by R. Heilbroner, *The Worldly Philosophers* (5th ed.; New York: Simon and Schuster, 1980). p. 71.

[2] Of course, it does not matter to Malthus's argument whether the population doubles every 25 years or every 40 years. The important thing is that it increases at a geometric rate.

5, 6, 7, 8, 9. In two centuries, the population would be to the means of subsistence as 256 to 9; in three centuries as 4096 to 13, and in two thousand years the difference would be incalculable."[3]

A BLEAK PROSPECT

Certainly, Malthus's view of humanity's prospects was bleak, as he himself acknowledged (in a masterpiece of British understatement) when he wrote that "the view has a melancholy hue." According to Malthus, the prospect for economic progress was very limited. Given the inexorable increase in human numbers, the standard of living will be kept at a minimum level required to keep body and soul together. If it exceeds this level, the population will increase, and drive the standard of living back down. On the other hand, if the standard of living is less than this level, the population will decline because of starvation. Certainly, the long-term prospects were anything but bright. Thomas Carlyle, the famous historian and essayist, called economics "the dismal science." To a considerable extent, economics acquired this bad name through the efforts of Parson Malthus.

Malthus's theory can be interpreted in terms of the law of diminishing marginal returns. Living in what was still largely an agricultural society, he emphasized the role of land and labor as resources, and assumed a relatively fixed level of technology. Since land is fixed, increases in labor—due to population growth—will eventually cause the marginal product of labor to get smaller and smaller because of the law of diminishing marginal returns. In other words, because of this law, the marginal product of labor will behave as shown in Figure 14.3, with the result that continued growth of the labor force will ultimately bring economic decline—that is, a reduction in output per worker. This happens because, as the marginal product of labor falls with increases in the labor force, the average product of labor will eventually fall as well—and the average product of labor is another name for output per worker.

[3] T. Malthus, "The Principle of Population Growth," reprinted in E. Mansfield, *Principles of Macroeconomics: Readings, Issues, and Cases*, 4th ed.

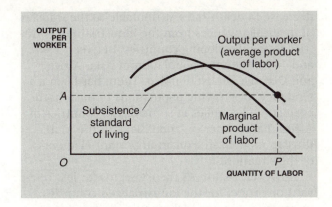

■ FIGURE 14.3

Diminishing Marginal Returns and the Effect of Population Growth

According to Malthus, the labor force will tend to *OP* because, if output per worker exceeds *OA*, population will increase, and if output per worker is less than *OA*, starvation will reduce the population.

Of course, Malthus recognized that various devices could keep the population down—war, famine, birth-control measures, among others. In fact, he tried to describe and evaluate the importance of various checks on population growth. For example, suppose that population tends to grow to the point where output per worker is at a subsistence level—just sufficient to keep body and soul together. If this is the case, and if the subsistence level of output per worker is *OA*, then the labor force will tend to equal *OP* in Figure 14.3. Why? Because, as noted above, Malthus believed that if the standard of living rises appreciably above *OA*, population will increase, and thus force it back toward *OA*. On the other hand, if the standard of living falls below *OA*, some of the population will starve, and thus push it back toward *OA*.

EFFECTS OF POPULATION GROWTH

Was Malthus right? Among some of the developing countries of the world, his analysis seems very relevant today. During the past sixty years, the population of the developing countries has grown very rapidly, in part because of the decrease in death rates attributable to the transfer of medical advances from the industrialized countries to the developing countries. Between 1940 and 1970, the total population of Asia, Africa, and Oceania almost doubled. There has been a tendency for growing populations to push hard against food supplies in some of the countries of Africa, Latin America, and Asia; and the Malthusian model can explain important elements of the situation.

However, Malthus's theory seems far less relevant or correct for the industrialized countries. In contrast to his model, population has not increased to the point where the standard of living has been pushed down to the subsistence level. On the contrary, the standard of living has increased dramatically in all the industrialized countries. The most important mistake Malthus made was to underestimate the extent and importance of technological change. Instead of remaining fixed, the marginal-product-of-labor curve in Figure 14.3 moved gradually to the right, as new methods and new products increased the efficiency of agriculture. In other words, the situation was shown in Figure 14.4. Thus, as popula-

tion increased, the marginal product of labor did not go down. Instead, technological change prevented the productivity of extra agricultural workers from falling.

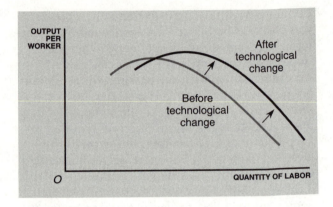

▪ **FIGURE 14.4**

Shift over Time in the Marginal Product of Labor

Technological change has shifted the marginal-product-of-labor curve to the right.

 TEST YOUR UNDERSTANDING

True or false?

_____ **1** Malthus believed that the population tends to grow at a geometric rate.

_____ **2** Malthus underestimated the importance of technological change.

Exercise

1 Some observers have suggested that a country's population might be controlled through the use of the price system. For example, the government might say that each couple should be allowed two "free births." After that, the couple would have to buy a certificate granting the right to have an additional child. The government would issue a fixed amount of certificates or "birth rights," each certificate enabling a woman to have a child. The available certificates would be sold to the highest bidders.

a. What would the supply curve for these certificates look like?

b. Using a diagram, show how the equilibrium price of a certificate would be determined.

c. What factors would determine the location and shape of the demand curve for certificates?

d. What social, political, and religious objections can you see to such a scheme?

4 ▪ Capital Formation and Economic Growth

To understand the role of investment in the process of economic growth, let's extend the simple model discussed in Chapter 3. Ignore the government (and the rest of the world) and consider only the private sector of the economy. Suppose that the full-employment, noninflationary GDP this year is $1,000 billion, and that the consumption function is such that consumption expenditure is $900 billion if GDP is $1,000 billion. If intended investment this year is $100 billion, with the result that GDP is in fact $1,000 billion, *next year's full-employment GDP will increase because this year's investment will increase the country's productive capacity.* In other words, this year's investment increases next year's full employment GDP. The amount of the increase in full-employment GDP depends on the **capital-output ratio,** which is the number of dollars of investment (or extra capital goods) required to produce an extra dollar of output. For example, if the capital-output ratio is 2, $2 of investment is required to increase full-employment GDP by $1.

Consider the effect of investment on full-employment GDP more closely. If the capital-output ratio is 2, full employment GDP will increase by $50 billion as a consequence of the $100 billion of investment. Thus full-employment GDP next year is $1,050 billion. On the other hand, suppose that this year's investment is $200 billion rather than $100 billion, and that the consumption function is such that consumption expenditure is $800 billion rather than $900 billion if GDP is $1,000 billion. What will full-employment GDP be next year? If the capital-output ratio is 2, it will be $1,100 billion. Why? Because the $200 billion in investment will increase full-employment GDP by $100 billion—from $1,000 billion to $1,100 billion.

Thus the full-employment GDP will be larger if investment is $200 billion than if it is $100 billion. Similarly, the full-employment GDP will be larger if investment is $300 billion than if it is $200 billion. If the capital-output ratio is 2, the full-employment GDP will be $1,150 billion next year if investment is $300 billion. Why? Because the $300 billion in investment will increase full-employment GDP by $150 billion—from $1,000 to $1,150 billion.

In general, the greater the percent of GDP that the society devotes to investment this year, the greater will be the increase in its full-employment GDP. Thus, *so long as the economy sustains noninflationary full employment and the capital-output ratio remains constant, the rate of growth of national output will be directly related to the percent of GDP devoted to investment.*[4]

SOME EVIDENCE CONCERNING THE EFFECTS OF INVESTMENT

Certainly, this result seems sensible enough. If a country wants to increase its growth rate, it should produce more blast furnaces, machine tools, and plows, and less cosmetics, household furniture, and sports cars. But all this is theory. What do the facts suggest? Table 14.2 shows the rate of investment and the growth rate in six major industrialized countries of the non-Communist world in the 1970s. The investment rate was highest in Japan; so was the growth rate. The investment rates were lowest in the United States and the United Kingdom, and their growth rates were among the lowest. Of course, this does not prove that there is any simple cause-and-effect relationship between the investment rate

---

[4] It can be shown that the rate of growth of GDP equals s/b, where s is the proportion of GDP that is saved (and invested), and b is the capital-output ratio, assuming that both s and b are constant and that full employment is maintained. For example, if b is 2 and $s = 0.10$, GDP will grow at 5 percent per year, since $0.10/2 = 0.05$. This result is part of the so-called Harrod-Domar growth model developed by Sir Roy Harrod of Oxford and Evsey Domar of MIT. Although useful, this result must be used with caution since it is based on highly simplified assumptions.

▪ **TABLE 14.2**

Rate of Growth of Output (1978–1980) and Investment as Percentage of Output (1970–1977)

COUNTRY	ANNUAL AVERAGE RATE OF GROWTH OF OUTPUT	OUTPUT INVESTED
	(percent)	
France	2.8	18.8
Germany	3.3	18.7
Canada	2.4	19.3
Japan	5.0	26.7
United Kingdom	1.0	17.6
United States	2.6	14.5

SOURCE: *Economic Report of the President.*

and the growth rate, but it certainly is compatible with the view that investment influences growth.

As revealed in the historical record of the United States, between 1929 and 1947 the amount of U.S. plant and equipment increased at about the same rate as the labor force. On the other hand, between 1947 and 1965, the amount of U.S. plant and equipment increased much more rapidly than the labor force. These facts would lead you to expect that the rate of economic growth would be more rapid in the latter period; and, in keeping with the theory, this turns out to be true. Again, you must be cautious about interpreting such comparisons. Lots of other things besides the investment rate were different from 1947 to 1965 than from 1929 to 1947, and these other things, not the investment rate, may have been responsible for the difference in growth rates. However, it seems likely that the difference in investment rates was at least partially responsible.

THE ROLE OF HUMAN CAPITAL

A country's rate of economic growth is influenced by the rate at which it invests in human capital as well as physical capital. It may seem odd to speak of *human* capital, but every society builds up a certain amount of human capital through investments in formal education, on-the-job training, and health programs. You often hear people talk about investing in their children's future by putting them through college. For the economy as a whole, the expenditure on education and public health can also be viewed—at least partly—as an investment, because consumption is sacrificed in the present in order to make possible a higher level of per capita output in the future.

The United States invests in human capital on a massive scale. In 1987, it devoted roughly $500 billion to gross investment in formal education. In addition, $100 billion was spent on worker training, excluding informal efforts to improve skills and performance. These enormous and rapidly growing investments in human capital have unquestionably increased the productivity, versatility, and adaptability of our labor force. They have certainly made a major contribution to economic growth.

Income tends to rise with a person's education. Using this relationship to measure the influence of education on a person's productivity, some economists, notably the University of Chicago's Nobel laureates Theodore Schultz and Gary Becker, have tried to estimate the profitability, both to society and to the individual, of an investment in various levels of education. Becker has tried to estimate the rate of return from a person's investment in a college education. According to his estimates, the typical urban white male received about a 10 percent return (after taxes) on his investment in tuition, room, books, and other college expenses (including the earnings he gave up by being in college rather than at work). This was a relatively high return—much higher, for example, than if the student (or his family) simply put the equivalent amount of money in a savings bank or in government bonds.

During the 1970s and early 1980s, rates of return from investments in schooling were estimated to be 10 to 13 percent for secondary education and 8 to 10 percent for higher education. However, because it is so difficult to adjust for differences among people in ability and effort, these results should be viewed with caution.

TEST YOUR UNDERSTANDING

True or false?

_____ **1** The greater the percent of GDP that the society devotes to investment, the greater will be the increase in full-employment GDP.

_____ **2** A country's rate of economic growth is not influenced by the rate at which it invests in human capital.

Exercises

1 Suppose that a society's full-employment GDP increases between 1995 and 1996 by $100 billion. During the same period, its corporations paid $20 billion in salaries to corporate executives, and it invested $200 billion. What is the capital-output ratio in this society? Will the capital-output ratio in this society always be the same? Why, or why not?

2 Suppose that a society's capital-output ratio is 3 and that it invests 10 percent of its GDP. If full employment is maintained, by what percentage will its GDP grow?

5 ▪ The Role of Technological Change

A country's rate of economic growth depends on the rate of technological change, as well as on the extent to which quantities of inputs of various kinds increase. Indeed, the rate of technological change is perhaps the most important single determinant of a country's rate of economic growth. Recall that technology is knowledge concerning the industrial and agricultural arts. Thus **technological change** consists of new methods of producing existing products; new designs that make it possible to produce goods with important new characteristics; and new techniques of organization, marketing, and management.

Consider the computer, one of the most important technological advances of the twentieth century. Computers have increased production, decreased waste, improved quality control, and reduced the chance of damage to equipment. In banking, for example, they have made possible much faster processes for sorting checks, balancing accounts, and computing service charges.

You have already seen that technological change can shift the curves in Figure 14.4, and

thus ward off the law of diminishing marginal returns. But note that new knowledge by itself has little impact. _Unless knowledge is applied, it has little effect on the rate of economic growth._ A change in technology, when applied for the first time, is called an **innovation,** and the firm that first applies it is called an **innovator.** Innovation is a key stage in the process leading to the full evaluation and utilization of a new process or product. The innovator must be willing to take the risks involved in introducing a new and untried process, good, or service; and in many cases, these risks are high. Once a change in technology has been applied for the first time, the **diffusion process**—the process by which the use of the innovation spreads from firm to firm and from use to use—begins. How rapidly an innovation spreads depends heavily on its economic advantages over older methods or products. The more profitable the use of the innovation is, the more rapidly it will spread.

Joseph Schumpeter, Harvard's distinguished economist and social theorist, stressed the important role played by innovators in the process of economic growth. In Schumpeter's view, innovators are the mainspring of economic progress, the people with the foresight to see how new things can be brought into being and the courage and resourcefulness to surmount the obstacles to change. For their trouble, innovators receive profit; but this profit eventually is whittled down by competitors who imitate the innovators. For example, one innovator introduces vacuum tubes, a later innovator introduces semiconductors; one innovator introduces the steam locomotive, a later innovator introduces the diesel locomotive. This process goes on and on—and is a main source of economic growth.

 TEST YOUR UNDERSTANDING

True or false?

_____ **1** Technological change has shifted the marginal-productivity-of-labor curve to the right.

_____ **2** How rapidly an innovation spreads depends heavily on its economic advantage over older methods or products. The more profitable the use of the innovation is, the more rapidly it will spread.

_____ **3** Schumpeter stressed the important role played by the innovator in the process of economic growth.

---

6 ▪ The Gap between Actual and Potential Output

Up to this point, the consideration of economic growth has centered on the factors that determine how rapidly a country's potential output grows—factors like technological change, increased education, investment in plant and equipment, and increases in the labor force. In other words, you have focused on the factors responsible for rightward shifts of the long-run aggregate supply curve. Although you have not paid much attention in this chapter to the gap between actual and potential output, this does not mean that increases in output per capita cannot be achieved by reducing this gap. Obviously, they can be.

However, only so much can be achieved by squeezing the slack out of the economy. For example, if there is a 7 percent unemployment rate, output per capita can be increased by perhaps 6 percent simply by reducing the unemployment rate to 5 percent. *But this is a one-shot improvement.* To get any further increase in output per capita, the country must increase its potential output. This doesn't mean that it isn't important to maintain a high level of employment in the economy. Of course, it is, for reasons discussed at length in Chapter 2. But the point is that, once the economy gets to full employment, no further increase in output per capita can occur by this route. If a country wants further increases in output per capita over the long haul, it must influence the factors responsible for the rate of growth of potential output.

TEST YOUR UNDERSTANDING

True or false?

____ **1** Increase in per capita output cannot be achieved by reducing the gap between actual and potential output.

____ **2** National governments under peacetime conditions have few opportunities to push actual output close to potential output.

7 ▪ Developing Countries

Both the industrialized countries and the developing countries themselves want to raise the income levels in the developing countries. A country is defined here as a developing country if its per capita income is less than $5,000. Well over half the world's population live in the developing countries, which include many of the countries in Asia, Africa, and Latin America. In recent years, there has been a great increase in the expectations and material demands of the people in these countries.

The developing countries vary greatly, but they generally devote most of their resources to the production of food, are composed of two economies (one market oriented, the other subsistence), and often have relatively weak, unstable governments and a relatively high degree of income inequality.

One obvious reason why income per capita is so low is that the people in the developing countries have so little capital to work with. The developing countries, with their low incomes, do not save much, they lack entrepreneurs, and the climate for investment (domestic or foreign) often is not good.

Some developing countries suffer from overpopulation; and as total output has increased, these gains have been offset by population increases. Modern medical techniques have reduced the death rate, while the birth rate has remained high. The result has been a population explosion.

An important issue facing the governments of most developing countries is the extent to which they want to promote a balance between the agricultural and industrial sectors of the economy. Without question, the developing countries are expanding industry relative to agriculture. In some cases, more balance—less emphasis on industry, more on agriculture—would have been preferable. Moreover, some countries have put too much emphasis on substituting their own production for imports, even when their own production is uneconomic.

The United States has been involved in a number of major aid programs to help the developing countries. In recent years, these aid programs have sometimes come under attack, because of a feeling in Congress and elsewhere that they have not been working well. The World Bank, established by the major powers in 1944, also has channeled major amounts of capital into the developing countries.

Now over fifty years old, the World Bank makes loans to people or governments with sound investment projects who have been unable to get private financing. Moreover, by floating its own bond issues it can lend money above and beyond what was originally put up by the major powers. In other words, the World Bank sells its own IOUs, which are considered safe by investors because they are guaranteed by member countries. In addition, it helps developing countries get loans from private lenders by insuring the loans. That is, the World Bank can tell the lender that if the loan goes sour, it will see that the lender is paid back.

This movement of capital from the capital-rich countries to the capital-poor countries should prove beneficial for both rich and poor. The poor countries are enabled to carry out projects that will result in economic returns high enough to pay off the lender with interest and have some net benefits left over. The rich countries are enabled to invest their capital at a higher rate of return than they could obtain at home. Thus both parties benefit, as long as the loans are economically sound.

 TEST YOUR UNDERSTANDING

True or false?

_____ **1** There has been a tendency for growing populations to push hard against food supplies in some of the countries of Africa, Latin America, and Asia; and the Malthusian model can explain important elements of the situation.

_____ **2** A country's rate of economic growth is not influenced by the rate at which it invests in human capital.

Exercises

1 Governments of developing countries sometimes force industrialization, even though many of their people would prefer a different strategy. Suppose that a particular country's production possibilities curve is as shown below:

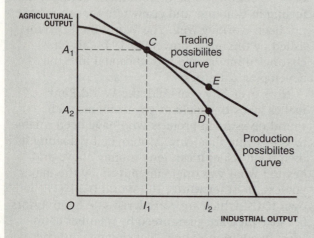

This country's government wants to increase its industrial output from OI_1 to OI_2.

a. If its industrial output is increased in this way (and if the society remains on this production possibilities curve), what will be the cost to consumers?

b. How can the government push the society from point C to point D on the production possibilities curve?

c. Suppose that this country can trade its agricultural output for industrial goods in world markets. Its trading possibilities curve, which shows the various amounts of agricultural and industrial output that the country can end up with if it specializes in agricultural output and trades it for industrial output, is as shown above. Is there a way to reduce the cost of obtaining the extra $(OI_2 - OI_1)$ of industrial goods? If so, what is it?

d. If the price of agricultural goods rises relative to the price of industrial goods in world markets, how will this affect the trading possibilities curve? Will it affect the cost of obtaining the extra $(OI_2 - OI_1)$ of industrial goods? If so, how?

2 According to a famous theory put forth by Nobel Laureate W. Arthur Lewis of Princeton University, the supply curve of unskilled labor in some developing countries is a horizontal line, as shown on page 195. In other words, unlimited supplies of unskilled labor are available in this country at the existing wage rate, OW. Suppose that the value of the marginal product of each amount of unskilled labor in this country is as shown on page 195. For example, the value of the marginal product (which equals the price of the product times labor's marginal product) is L_1B when OL_1 workers are employed.

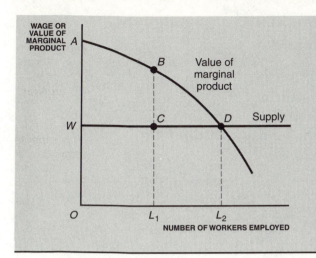

a. How many unskilled workers will be employed in the country?

b. How much profit will be realized by hiring the OL_1th worker?

c. If firms invest their profit (from hiring the first, second, . . . , OL_2th workers) in plant and equipment, what effect will this have on the value-of-marginal-product curve?

d. If the value-of-marginal-product curve shifts, will this affect the equilibrium wage rate?

▪ CHAPTER REVIEW

KEY TERMS

economic growth

law of diminishing marginal returns

marginal product of labor

average product of labor

population growth

capital-output ratio

technological change

innovation

innovator

diffusion process

COMPLETION QUESTIONS

1 The additional output resulting from the addition of an extra unit of labor is called the _____.

2 The _____ process, in which the use of an innovation spreads, begins once a change in technology has been applied for the first time.

3 A country's output under full employment is its _____.

4 The two most common measures of the rate of _____ growth are (1) the rate of growth of a country's _____, which tells us how rapidly the economy's total real output of goods and services is increasing, and (2) the rate of growth of _____, which is a better measure of the rate of increase of a country's standard of living.

ANSWERS TO COMPLETION QUESTIONS

marginal product of labor

diffusion

potential output

economic
real gross domestic product

per capita real gross domestic product

5 To achieve a more rapid rate of growth, consumers must frequently be willing to give up some _____ now so that they can have (more, less) _____ goods and services in the future. A country's potential output increases when its production possibilities curve shifts (inward, outward) _____.

consumption
more

outward

6 A country's rate of economic growth depends on the extent of the changes in the amounts of the various _____ used, as well as on the rate of _____ change.

inputs
technological

7 If the capital-output ratio is 2, full-employment GDP will increase by $50 billion as a consequence of _____ billion of investment.

$100

NUMERICAL PROBLEMS

1 In a highly industrialized economy, suppose that the relationship between hours of labor and production of steel is as follows:

HOURS	TONS OF STEEL
	(millions)
1	2
2	4
3	7
4	9
5	10
6	9

a At what point does the marginal product of labor decline? At what point does the average product of labor decline?

b Suppose that an advance in technology allows this economy to obtain twice as many tons of steel (as shown above) for each number of hours of labor. Under these conditions, what is the marginal product of labor when between 4 and 5 million hours of labor are used? What is the average product of labor when 6 million hours are used?

c If the economy produced 4 million tons of steel before the technological advance and 8 million tons after the technological advance, by what percentage did labor productivity—output per hour of labor—increase?

d Plot the average product curve for labor, before the technological change in the graph below:

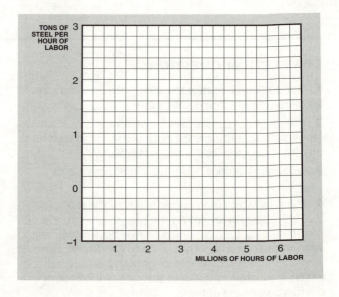

2 Suppose that the relationship between output per worker and the quantity of labor in Bangladesh is as shown below:

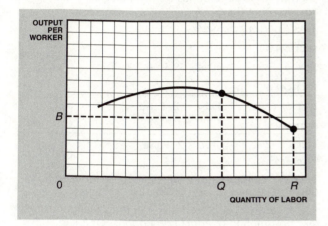

a Suppose the current labor force is such that the quantity of labor is *OQ*. If the subsistence level of output per worker is *OB*, what would the Malthusian theory predict about the change in population in Bangladesh?

b Suppose that Bangladesh's labor force is *OR* rather than *OQ*. What would the Malthusian theory predict about the change in population in Bangladesh?

3a If the capital-output ratio is 3 in Bangladesh, what effect will $10 million in investment have on Bangladesh's full-employment GDP?

b If Bangladesh saves 5 percent of GDP, and if the capital-output ratio is 3, what will be the rate of growth of full-employment GDP?

c Under the circumstances described in part b, what will be the effect on the rate of growth of full-employment GDP if Bangladesh saves 10 percent (rather than 5 percent) of GDP?

d If Bangladesh's population increases by 4 percent per year, what is the rate of increase of per capita full-employment GDP under the circumstances described in part b? Under the circumstances described in part c?

4 Assume that the capital-output ratio is 2 in a certain developing country, and that its full-employment GDP is $20 billion. For simplicity, assume that there is no government or foreign trade. The consumption function, *CC'*, is plotted in the graph above on the right.

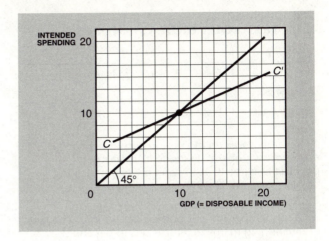

a How much investment must there be this year if there is full employment?

b If there is full employment this year, what will be the full-employment value of GDP next year?

c Next year, how much investment must there be to maintain full employment? (Hint: The marginal propensity to consume is 1/2.)

5 The following table shows the output of an economy where various amounts of capital are employed. The amounts of all other resources used are held constant. Fill in the blanks.

AMOUNT OF CAPITAL (billions of dollars)	TOTAL OUTPUT	AVERAGE PRODUCT OF CAPITAL	MARGINAL PRODUCT OF CAPITAL
0	0	——	
			——
1	100	——	
			——
2	210	——	
			——
3	310	——	
			——
4	400	——	
			——
5	480	——	
			——
6	540	——	

ANSWERS TO
TEST YOUR UNDERSTANDING

SECTION 1

TRUE OR FALSE: 1. False   2. True   3. True

SECTION 2

TRUE OR FALSE: 1. False

EXERCISES

1. Yes, there was an increase in output per capita. The economy was operating inside its production possibilities curve in 1997, and on its production possibilities curve in 1998.

2. Yes. Yes.

3. 2 bushels per hour; 2 bushels per hour; 0. The law of diminishing marginal returns sets in beyond 3 million hours of labor input.

SECTION 3

TRUE OR FALSE: 1. True   2. True

EXERCISE

1. a. The supply curve would be a vertical line since the quantity of certificates supplied is fixed.

b. The diagram is as shown below, and the equilibrium price is *OP*.

c. The demand curve would be influenced by how much people want children, and how much they are willing to pay for the right to have them.

d. Obviously, many people would feel that such a program would be a major violation of their freedom, particularly since there are strong religious feelings and beliefs involved. People who wanted children and who were too poor to pay for a certificate would certainly object strenuously. There is no serious support for such a system in the United States.

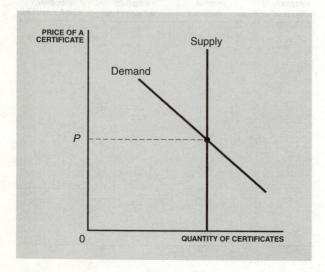

SECTION 4

TRUE OR FALSE: 1. True   2. False

EXERCISES

1. The capital-output ratio is 2. No, this ratio can change; its value depends on technological change, among other things.

2. $3\frac{1}{3}$ percent per year.

SECTION 5

TRUE OR FALSE: 1. True   2. True   3. True

SECTION 6

TRUE OR FALSE: 1. False   2. False

SECTION 7

TRUE OR FALSE: 1. True   2. False

EXERCISES

1. a. Agricultural output will have to be reduced from OA_1 to OA_2.

b. It can subsidize production of industrial goods and tax consumption of agricultural goods. Or it can intervene directly to increase industrial output and reduce agricultural output.

c. The country can move from point *C* to point *E* by trading its agricultural goods for industrial goods in world markets. Since point *E* lies above point *D*, the cost (that is, the reduction in agricultural goods) of the extra industrial goods is less than at point *D*.

d. It will reduce the slope of the trading possibilities curve, which will be closer to horizontal. The cost of obtaining the extra industrial goods will fall, since point *E* will be raised.

2. a. OL_2 workers, since this is the point where the supply curve intersects the value-of-marginal-product curve. So long as the value of the marginal product of an extra worker exceeds his or her wage, it pays firms to hire the extra worker. Thus extra workers will be hired up to the point where employment is OL_2.

b. The profit earned from the hiring of each extra worker equals the difference between the value of this worker's marginal product and this worker's wage. Thus the profit realized by hiring the OL_1th worker equals L_1B minus *OW*, or *CB*.

c. The value-of-marginal-product curve will shift to the right. With more plant and equipment, the marginal product of a particular amount of labor will increase.

d. No, because the value-of-marginal-product curve will still intersect the supply curve at a wage of *OW*.

■ CHAPTER 15

What Should U.S. Policy toward Civilian Technology Be?

1 ■ Introduction

Although it is very difficult to measure international differences in technological levels, the available evidence suggests that the United States long has been a leader in technology. Scattered impressionistic evidence indicates that this was true in many fields before 1850. After 1850, the available quantitative evidence indicates that productivity was higher in the United States than in Europe, that the United States had a strong export position in technically progressive industries, and that Europeans tended to imitate U.S. techniques. The existence of such a gap in the nineteenth century would not be surprising, since this was a heyday of U.S. invention. (Among the key U.S. inventions of the period was the system of interchangeable parts.) Needless to say, the United States did not lead in all fields, but it appears that we held a technological lead in many important parts of manufacturing.

After World War II, there was a widespread feeling that this technological gap widened, due in part to the wartime devastation of many countries in Europe and elsewhere. In the 1960s, Europeans expressed considerable concern over the technology gap. They asserted that superior know-how stemming from scientific and technical achievements in the United States had allowed U.S. companies to obtain large shares of European markets in fields like aircraft, space equipment, computers, and other electronic products. In 1966, Italy's foreign minister, Amintore Fanfani, went so far as to call for a "technological Marshall Plan" to speed the flow of U.S. technology across the Atlantic.

The factors responsible for these technological gaps were difficult to sort out and measure. A host of factors—the social climate, the educational system, the scientific community, the amount and quality of industrial research, the nature of domestic markets, the quality of management, and government policies, among others—influence a country's technological position. In addition, the large government expenditures on research and development (R and D) in the United States played an important role.

During the past twenty years, the U.S. technological lead has been reduced in a great many areas. The annual rate of growth of output per hour of labor in the United States has tended to lag behind that in countries like Japan and Germany. In industries like steel and automobiles, the United States has yielded the technological lead to others, notably the Japanese. Even in relatively new industries born largely in the United States, such as semiconductors, many have faulted U.S. firms for lagging behind Japan.

Confronted with this trend, the federal government under both Democratic and Republican administrations has tried to establish appropriate policies. This chapter discusses and analyzes these attempts, beginning with some background material concerning the patent system and various federal proposals and initiatives, after which we present six multipart problems, which analyze selected aspects of technology policy in the United States and elsewhere. These problems provide the students with valuable practice in applying economic concepts and techniques.

2 ▪ The Patent System

One of the oldest U.S. laws regarding civilian technology is the patent law, which grants inventors exclusive control over their inventions for 20 years from initial filing. That is, inventors are given a temporary monopoly over the use of their inventions. Since Congress passed the original patent act in 1790, the arguments used to justify the existence of the patent laws have not changed very much. First, *these laws are regarded as an important incentive to induce the inventor to put in the work required to produce an invention.* Particularly in the case of the individual inventor, it is claimed that patent protection is a strong incentive. Second, *patents are regarded as a necessary incentive to induce firms to carry out the further work and make the necessary investment in pilot plants and other items that are required to bring the invention to commercial use.* If an invention became public property when made, why should a firm incur the costs and risks involved in attempting to develop, debug, and perfect it? Another firm could watch, take no risks, and duplicate the process or product if it were successful. Third, it is argued that because of the patent laws, *inventions are disclosed earlier than otherwise, the consequence being that other inventions are facilitated by the earlier dissemination of the information.* The resulting situation is often contrasted with the intense secrecy about processes which characterized the medieval guilds and which undoubtedly retarded technological progress and economic growth.

Not all economists agree that the patent system is beneficial. A patent represents a monopoly right, although, as many inventors can testify, it may be a very weak one. Critics of the patent system stress the social costs arising from the mo-nopoly. After a new process or product has been discovered, it may cost very little for other persons who could make use of this knowledge to acquire it. The patent gives the inventor the right to charge a price for the use of the information, with the result that the knowledge is used less widely than is socially optimal. Critics also point out that patents have been used to create monopoly positions, which were sustained by other means after the original patents had expired. They cite as examples the aluminum, shoe machinery, and plateglass industries. In addition, the cross-licensing of patents often has been used by firms as a vehicle for joint monopolistic exploitation of their market.

Critics also question the extent of the social gains arising from the system. They point out that the patent system was designed for the individual inventor, but that over the years most research and development has been institutionalized. They assert that patents are not really important as incentives to the large corporation, since it cannot afford to fall behind in the technological race, whether or not it receives a patent. Also, they say that because of long lead times, most of the innovative profits from many innovations can be captured before imitators have a chance to enter the market, whether or not the innovator is granted a patent. Finally, they claim that firms keep secret what inventions they can, and patent those they cannot. These questions concerning the effects and desirability of the patent system have proved extremely difficult to settle. But most observers seem to agree that, despite its faults, it is hard to find a realistic substitute for the patent system.

3 ▪ Federal Proposals and Initiatives during the 1960s

Many, but not all, policymakers feel that the patent laws alone will not induce private industry to do enough research and development. During the 1960s, some attempts were made to institute a federal program to support civilian technology.

According to the Council of Economic Advisers, "in a number of industries the amount of organized private research undertaken is insignificant, and the technology of many of these low-research industries has notably failed to keep pace with advances elsewhere in the economy."[1] In 1963, the Department of Commerce proposed a Civilian Industrial Technology program to encourage and support additional R and D in industries that it regarded as lagging. It proposed that support be given to important industries, from the point of view of employment, foreign trade, and so forth, which have "limited or dispersed technological resources." Examples cited by the department included textiles, building and construction, machine tools and metal fabrication, lumber, foundries, and castings. The proposal met with little success on Capitol Hill. Industrial groups opposed the bill because they feared that government sponsorship of industrial R and D could upset existing competitive relationships.

There was also concern about the diffusion of new technology. In 1965, the State Technical Services Act was passed by Congress. It authorized a program for industry somewhat analogous to the agricultural extension service—universities and technical schools throughout the country distributing technological information to local firms and serving as economic planning centers for their areas. The major purpose of this industrial extension service was to increase the rate of

diffusion for new technology. Some firms, particularly small ones, are slow to adopt new techniques because they are unable to comprehend and evaluate technical information. The industrial extension service provided demonstrations, short courses, and conferences, as well as referral to specialized consultants and experts. In this way, it hoped to narrow the gap between average and best practice.

The industrial extension service faced problems that were absent in the case of the agricultural extension service. Whereas the latter could deal with a relatively homogeneous group of clients, the former could not; whereas it was possible in earlier days for an agricultural extension agent to be familiar with most relevant aspects of agricultural technology, it is impossible now for anyone to be familiar with most aspects of industrial technology; and whereas individual farmers seldom view each other as competitors, in manufacturing, one firm's gain in productivity and sales may be partly at the expense of another. In addition, it was more difficult in the case of the industrial extension service to delineate the set of appropriate clients. The firms that were most eager to use the service and those that were easiest to persuade to adopt new techniques were not necessarily those for whom the service could do the most good. Eventually, the program was discontinued.

[1] Council of Economic Advisers, *Annual Report*, 1964, p. 105.

4 ▪ The Domestic Policy Review on Industrial Innovation

Another attempt to formulate a federal civilian technology program was made in 1978 and 1979, when the federal government carried out a Domestic Policy Review on Industrial Innovation. The Industry Advisory Subcommittee involved in this review prepared draft reports on federal procurement; direct support of R and D; environmental, health, and safety regulations; industry structure; economic and trade policy; patents; and information policy. These drafts were discussed and criticized by the Academic and Public Interest Subcommittees involved in the review. Further, the Labor Subcommittee presented a report, as did each of a large number of government agencies. The overall result was a large and far-flung effort to come up with policy recommendations.

One theme that ran through the Industry Advisory Subcommittee's reports was that many aspects of environmental, health, and safety regulations deter innovation. There was a strong feeling that this was the case in a number of industries, although it was recognized that we lack very dependable or precise estimates of the effects of particular regulatory rules on the rate of innovation. However, the recommendations of the Industry Advisory Subcommittee with respect to regulatory changes were met with considerable hostility by the Labor and Public Interest Subcommittees. Another theme found in some of the Industry Advisory Subcommittee's reports was that tax credits for R and D expenditures should be considered seriously. Other groups, including the U.S. Treasury Department, did not warm to this proposal.

On October 31, 1979, President Carter put forth a number of proposals, based on the Domestic Policy Review. He asked Congress to establish a consistent policy with respect to patents arising from government R and D, and advocated exclusive licenses for firms that would commercialize inventions of this sort. Also, he asked the Justice Department to write guidelines indicating the conditions under which firms in the same industry could carry out joint research projects without running afoul of the antitrust laws. Further, to reduce regulatory uncertainties, he asked environmental, health, and safety agencies to formulate a five-year forecast of what rules they thought would be adopted.

In addition, President Carter proposed the creation of four "generic technology centers" at universities or other sites in the private sector to develop and transfer technologies where the social returns far exceed the private returns. Each center would be jointly financed by industry and government. Also, he proposed a new unit at the National Technical Information Service to improve the transfer of technology from government laboratories to private industry, and he proposed that the National Science Foundation and several other agencies expand an existing program of grants to firms and universities that carry out collaborative research. He also asked that a program to support innovative small businesses (currently under way at the National Science Foundation) be expanded.

5 ▪ R and D Tax Credits

When the Reagan administration took office in 1981, it established R and D tax credits to induce firms to increase their expenditures on research and development. The nature of these R and D tax credits will be described in Problem 15.5. For now, the important things to understand are what R and D is, how much of it is done in the United States, and who pays for it.

Research and development consists of activities carried out to gain new knowledge and to use this knowledge to improve products and processes. The total amount of R and D carried out by industry, government, universities, and other organizations in the United States grew considerably during the late 1970s and early 1980s, but remained relatively constant from 1985 to 1993 (Figure 15.1). In part, this was due to the apparent conclusion of the Cold War (which meant less defense R and D) and the sluggishness of the U.S. economy (which depressed firms' profits and made them less inclined to invest in R and D). According to some observers, it was important that R and D spending grow more rapidly; others disagreed.

Over 40 percent of the country's R and D is funded by the federal government, mainly for defense, health, space, energy, and general science. The Department of Defense, National

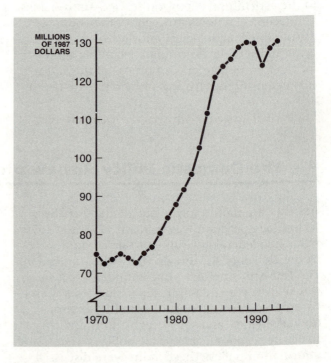

▪ **FIGURE 15.1**

Total Expenditures for Research and Development, United States

SOURCE: *Science and Engineering Indicators* (Washington, D.C.: National Science Foundation, 1993).

Institutes of Health, National Aeronautics and Space Administration, Department of Energy, and National Science Foundation are the federal agencies with the biggest R and D budgets (Table 15.1). Over 50 percent of the country's R and D is funded by industry, the biggest spenders being the transportation equipment, electrical equipment, machinery, and chemical (including drug) industries (Table 15.2).

Colleges and universities perform only about 13 percent of the country's R and D, but their role is important, particularly in fundamental research. In industries like drugs, information processing, and instruments, research carried out at colleges and universities has provided new theoretical and empirical findings and new types of instrumentation that have been essential for the development of some very significant new products and processes.

In absolute terms, the United States spends far more on R and D than any other country. Indeed, it spent more in 1991 than Japan, Germany, and France combined. Even if only nondefense R and D is considered, it spends more than any other country, Japan being in second place. However, as a percent of GDP, nondefense R and D expenditures in the United States are lower than in Japan or Germany (Table 15.3).

▪ **TABLE 15.1**

Federal Obligations for R and D and R and D Plant, 1994

AGENCY	(billions of dollars)	AGENCY	(billions of dollars)
Department of Agriculture	1.4	Department of Transportation	.7
Department of Commerce	.7	Department of Veterans Affairs	.3
Department of Defense	37.6	Agency for International Development	.3
Department of Education	.2	Environmental Protection Agency	.5
Department of Energy	5.9	National Aeronautics and Space Administration	8.6
National Institutes of Health	10.1	National Science Foundation	2.2
Department of Interior	.6	Nuclear Regulatory Commission	.1

SOURCE: *Science and Engineering Indicators* (Washington, D.C.: National Science Foundation, 1993).

▪ **TABLE 15.2**

Industrial R and D Expenditures, 1991

INDUSTRY	(billions of dollars)	INDUSTRY	(billions of dollars)
Food and tobacco	1.4	Stone, clay, and glass	.9
Textiles and apparel	.2	Primary metals	.8
Lumber	.2	Fabricated metal products	.6
Paper	.7	Machinery	14.0
Chemicals	13.1	Electrical equipment	12.5
Petroleum refining	2.2	Transportation equipment	15.9
Rubber	.7	Instruments	6.5

SOURCE: *Science and Engineering Indicators*, 1993.

▪ **TABLE 15.3**

R and D Expenditures, by Country, 1991

	TOTAL	R AND D EXPENDITURES NONDEFENSE	TOTAL	NONDEFENSE
	(billions of 1987 dollars)		(percent of GDP)	
United States	123	96	2.6	1.9
Japan	61	60	3.0	3.0
Germany	30	28	2.8	2.7
France	21	17	2.4	1.9
United Kingdom	16	13	2.1	1.7
Italy	11	11	1.4	1.3
Canada	6	6	1.4	1.4

SOURCE: *Science and Engineering Indicators*, 1993.

6 ▪ Technology Policy in the Clinton Administration

In 1993, the Clinton administration took office. Its technology policy, which differed considerably from that of the Reagan and Bush administrations, was described as follows by his Council of Economic Advisers:

An enduring American approach to promoting technology development and diffusion evolved just after the Second World War. The United States channeled public investment into basic research at universities and government laboratories, then supported the initial application of the results in products and production processes procured by public agencies. New technologies first developed for (and procured by) the Department of Defense, the Department of Energy, or the National Aeronautics and Space Administration (NASA), or supported by the National Science Foundation or the National Institutes of Health (NIH), would then diffuse, or "spin off," into commercial use. In this manner, the Federal Government supported the development and diffusion of jet aircraft and engines, semiconductor microelectronics, computers and computer-controlled machine tools, pharmaceuticals and biotechnology, advanced energy and environmental technologies, advanced materials, and a whole host of other commercially successful technologies.

This system worked well as long as military systems represented the leading-edge applications of

new industrial technologies and as long as foreign competitors, with direct support from their own governments, did not pose a significant competitive challenge. In many areas of basic research supported outside the defense establishment, including biomedical research and the development of pharmaceuticals, biotechnology, and medical diagnostic devices, the system continues to work well. But the circumstances that allowed the United States to rely primarily on a defense-led model have changed. With the end of the cold war, demand for new defense systems is now less than it was. Commercial product spinoffs from military research have also diminished from their heyday of the 1950s and 1960s, and American companies face intense international competition from increasingly capable foreign firms. On the other hand, these changes also create exciting new opportunities: Innovative defense technologies are now more likely to emerge first in commercial products and production techniques, and American companies are taking advantage of expanded opportunities in foreign markets. Accordingly, the Administration's technology initiatives are shifting the composition of Federal R&D from military to civilian concerns, and the composition of military R&D toward the development of so-called dual-use technologies—those with applications to both military and commercial products."[2]

[2] *Economic Report of the President*, 1994, pp. 193–94.

7 ▪ Applying Economics: Productivity Growth and the U.S. Technological Edge

The following two problems are concerned with productivity growth in the United States and its technological edge over other countries.

PROBLEM 15.1 Productivity is generally defined as output per hour of labor. In 1984, *Business Week* said: "The growth of productivity in the private sector, which averaged around 3% in the two decades after World War II, slid to an anemic rate of less than 2% from 1970–78 and was virtually flat from 1978 through 1982, the worst performance since the early days of the Depression."[3] Five years later, *Fortune* magazine said: "The best barometer of living standards is total output per person. . . . Other nations are

laboring hard to catch [up with the United States], and more power to them. But America's growth is lethargic these days—and that is something to worry about."[4]

a. Table 15.4 provides data regarding the changes from one year to the next in output per hour of labor in the U.S. business sector. Has the growth rate of productivity in the late 1980s and 1990s returned to the relatively high levels of 1948 to 1968? If not, is it really something to worry about? Why or why not?

b. Output per hour of labor tends to be relatively low among women and among new entrants into the labor force, in part because of

[3] *Business Week,* February 13, 1984.

[4] *Fortune,* November 6, 1989.

▪ TABLE 15.4

Percentage Change from Previous Year in Output per Hour of All Persons, Business Sector, United States, 1948–1992

YEAR	PERCENTAGE CHANGE	YEAR	PERCENTAGE CHANGE	YEAR	PERCENTAGE CHANGE
1948	4.5	1963	4.1	1978	0.6
1949	1.6	1964	4.3	1979	−1.1
1950	8.5	1965	2.7	1980	−0.8
1951	3.6	1966	2.8	1981	1.3
1952	3.7	1967	2.6	1982	0.1
1953	3.2	1968	3.0	1983	2.3
1954	2.5	1969	0.6	1984	2.4
1955	3.4	1970	1.4	1985	1.4
1956	1.3	1971	3.3	1986	2.1
1957	2.8	1972	3.2	1987	1.0
1958	3.2	1973	2.5	1988	1.0
1959	2.5	1974	−1.9	1989	−0.7
1960	1.6	1975	2.4	1990	0.7
1961	3.8	1976	3.0	1991	1.0
1962	3.5	1977	1.7	1992	3.3

SOURCE: *Economic Report of the President,* 1994.

their limited experience and training and the sort of work they get. During the late 1960s, women and new entrants increased as a proportion of the labor force. Did this help to cause the productivity slowdown in the late 1960s? If so, how?

c. During 1948 to 1973, relatively high rates of private investment resulted in a growth of the capital-labor ratio of almost 3 percent per year. After 1973, relatively low rates of investment resulted in the growth of the capital-labor ratio by only 1¾ percent per year. Did this help to cause the productivity slowdown in the late 1970s? If so, how?

d. A variety of new environmental, health, and safety regulations affected industry during the 1970s. Could this have helped to cause the productivity slowdown in that period? If so, how?

e. In recent years, many observers have asserted that the rate of introduction of new products and processes in the United States has fallen. Could this have helped to cause the productivity slowdown? If so, how?

f. As a percentage of GDP, expenditures on research and development in the United States fell from 1964 to 1978. Could this have helped to cause the productivity slowdown during this period? If so, how?

PROBLEM 15.2 United States policymakers worried in the 1980s that the U.S. economy might be losing its competitive edge. As the *New York Times* put it, "Hardly a day goes by without somebody voicing concern about America's deteriorating ability to compete in world markets. Japan and other Pacific Rim countries now dominate the manufacture of videocassette recorders, cameras and many other consumer electronics goods. Japanese companies make about one-quarter of the cars sold in the United States. Is the United States falling behind in the race to develop new products and methods of making them? Have research and development been sacrificed for the sake of short-term profits?"[5]

a. If the United States had been losing its technological edge over Japan and other countries, does this mean that the rate of technological change in the United States had been decreasing? Why or why not?

b. Table 15.5 shows the average rate of growth of industrial expenditures on research and development during 1973 to 1980, 1980 to 1985, and 1985 to 1990 in the United States, Germany, France, Italy, Japan, and the United Kingdom. Do these data suggest that the United States may have been falling behind its rivals in this regard?

c. Pharmaceuticals is an important high-technology industry. Table 15.6 shows the

[5] *New York Times,* June 4, 1989.

■ **TABLE 15.5**

Average Growth Rate of Industrial Research and Development, Major Countries, 1973–1990

COUNTRY	1973–1980	1980–1985	1985–1990
		(percentages)	
United States	2.7	8.1	1.0
Japan	5.4	11.2	8.0
Germany	6.1	4.6	3.4
France	3.7	5.4	5.2
United Kingdom	2.6	1.3	3.6
Italy	4.2	9.3	6.9

SOURCE: *Science and Engineering Indicators,* 1993.

▪ **TABLE 15.6**

Production of Drugs and Medicines and Electrical Machinery, Major Countries, 1981, 1986, and 1992

	DRUGS AND MEDICINES			ELECTRICAL MACHINERY		
	1981	1986	1992	1981	1986	1992
	(millions of 1980 dollars)					
United States	18	22	27	60	64	69
Japan	13	15	20	48	64	94
Germany	8	9	11	36	43	59
France	3	3	3	16	19	25
United Kingdom	5	7	8	14	17	21
Italy	3	4	5	12	14	17

SOURCE: *Science and Engineering Indicators*, 1993.

output of pharmaceuticals in various major countries in 1981, 1986, and 1992. Does it appear that the United States has been able to compete? Why or why not?

d. Electrical machinery is an important high-technology industry. Table 15.6 shows the output of electrical machinery in various major countries in 1981, 1986, and 1992. Does it appear that the United States has been able to compete? Why or why not?

e. According to Paul Krugman of MIT, "One might assume, naively, that . . . competitiveness can be measured by the ability of a country to sell more abroad than it buys."[6] Why is this a naive belief?

f. If the United States's technological edge over other countries is declining in a particular industry, should the federal government subsidize more R and D in this industry? Why or why not?

[6] Paul Krugman, "Competitiveness: A Dangerous Obsession," *Foreign Affairs,* March–April 1994, p. 31.

8 ▪ Applying Economics: Technology Policy

The following two problems deal with the much-debated question of how activist government policy toward civilian technology should be.

PROBLEM 15.3 Many new technologies result in external economies—benefits that cannot be appropriated by the firms that develop them. For example, Bell Telephone Laboratories invented the transistor, but was unable to garner more than a small fraction of the social benefits from its invention. Also, as pointed out by President Clinton's Council of Economic Advisers, "The development of refrigerated steamships at the end of the nineteenth century increased the availability of perishable agricultural products throughout the world. Most of this benefit ultimately accrued to farmers and consumers rather than to the inventors of refrigerated steamships. Similarly, the principle of interchangeable parts in manufacturing, originally developed for the production of firearms, soon was adopted for use in the fabrication of clocks, hardware, sewing machines, and other manufactured products."[7]

[7] *Economic Report of the President,* 1994.

a. If an R and D project can be expected to result in a new technology that will result in external economies, does this mean that the government should fund the project? Why or why not?

b. If the investment in an R and D project can be expected to yield a high rate of return to society as a whole, does this mean that the government should fund the project? Why or why not?

c. If the investment in an R and D project can be expected to yield a high rate of return to society as a whole, but if any private firm or individual that made this investment could not make any money from it, does this mean that the government should fund the project? Why or why not?

d. The National Advisory Committee on Aeronautics carried out research and development concerning wind tunnels, aircraft fuels, aircraft design, and other fundamental matters regarding aviation. No individual firm had much incentive to do such work because it could appropriate only a small share of the benefits. But because the benefits to the economy as a whole were substantial, the government intervened to finance work of this sort. Was this justified? Why or why not?

e. The federal government provided much of the early funding for R and D concerning computers. Until at least 1951 to 1954, all the significant R and D in this area was funded by the government because firms were not convinced that a commercial market existed for computers. Were government expenditures of this sort economically justified? Why or why not?

PROBLEM 15.4 According to President George Bush's Council of Economic Advisers,

> Governments in the United States and elsewhere have shown themselves to be less able than private businesses to pick specific technologies that will be commercially successful. They have often supported fashionable technologies with powerful advocates, rather than those that are economically productive. . . . Moreover, in many cases governments have continued to support technologies in which they have invested, even if those technologies have been long since demonstrated to be economically unsound by market and technological developments. . . . The best way to support development of civilian technology is through improving private incentives for applied research and development, not by attempting the impossible job of second-guessing private-sector investments.[8]

a. On April 12, 1981, the maiden flight of the space shuttle *Columbia* began, about nine years after President Nixon gave the go-ahead for NASA's development of the space shuttle in early 1972. Table 15.7 compares NASA's esti-

[8] *Economic Report of the President,* 1990, p. 117.

▪ **TABLE 15.7**

Performance and Cost Characteristics of the Space Shuttle, Estimated and Actual

PERFORMANCE OR COST CHARACTERISTIC	ESTIMATE IN EARLY 1970S	ACTUAL
Maximum payload capacity (pounds)	65,000	53,000
Turnaround time (hours)	160	1,240
Number of flights in 1984	60	22
Average cost of a 1984 launch (millions of dollars)	16	140
Cost per payload-pound in 1984 (dollars)	246	2,641

SOURCE: J. Banks, "The Space Shuttle," in L. Cohen and R. Noll, *The Technology Pork Barrel* (Washington, D.C.: Brookings Institution, 1991), p. 198.

mates of the cost and performance of the space shuttle in the early 1970s with its actual cost and performance. Did the space shuttle perform as expected? Was it more or less costly than expected?

b. There was tremendous political interest in Congress and elsewhere in the shuttle program. One careful observer of the program stressed "the particularly superb way that the pork got carved up on the shuttle program. Every major space technology firm got a juicy contract, and furthermore, NASA's reputation for big contracts had been well established in the Apollo program. Thus, the primary contractors formed a permanent support group (a space-industrial complex) in favor of big space projects."[9] Did this process of building political support for the shuttle program get in the way of making economically sound decisions? If so, how?

c. Another major government R and D program in the 1970s that received considerable criticism was the Clinch River breeder reactor project. In 1975 congressional hearings on this project, which was being challenged on environmental and economic grounds, Chairman Pastore said: "We have to make sure about the environment, I grant you that. We have to make sure about the cost-benefits aspects of the program. We have to look into that. How will we ever know those questions until we get a demonstration plant?"[10] If a demonstration plant costs several billion dollars, should these questions be dealt with before or after its construction?

d. In 1979 hearings on the Clinch River breeder reactor project, Representative Michael Myers said: "If we were back at the point now of first making a decision as to whether or not we should enter into fast breeder reactor research, then we would be more inclined toward [canceling the project]. But there has been so much invested, more than ten years of research in the project that we are now talking about, that we are way past the point of making that decision."[11] Do you agree with Representative Myers' proposition? Why or why not?[12]

[9] Jeffrey Banks, "The Space Shuttle," in Linda Cohen and Roger Noll, *The Technology Pork Barrel* (Washington, D.C.: Brookings Institution, 1991), p. 212.

[10] Ibid., p. 237.

[11] Ibid., p. 233.

[12] In fact, appropriations for the Clinch River breeder reactor project were cut off in fiscal 1984.

9 ▪ Applying Economics: Research and Development

The following two problems deal with research and development; the first takes up R and D tax credits in the United States, while the second is concerned with research and development in the developing countries.

PROBLEM 15.5 Beginning in July 1981, U.S. taxpayers could reduce their tax bills by 25 percent of the amount by which their R and D expenditures exceeded the average of the previous three years. This new R and D tax credit was one of the provisions of the major tax cut introduced by the Reagan administration. A number of countries, including Canada and Sweden, had already adopted such R and D tax credits. The purpose of this R and D tax credit was to induce firms to increase their expenditures on research and development. In subsequent years, there was continual controversy over the effectiveness of the U.S. R and D tax credit, and it was altered in a variety of ways in the 1980s and 1990s, until it ended in June 1995.

a. Suppose that a firm's R and D expenditures in 1979 to 1981 were as follows:

1979	$10 million
1980	$11 million
1981	$12 million

If this firm spent $13 million on R and D in 1982, by how much would the R and D tax credit reduce its tax bill then?

b. Why should a tax credit of this sort induce increases in the amount spent by a firm on R and D?

c. According to studies made by the General Accounting Office, the extra amount of R and D induced by the R and D tax credit from 1981 to 1985 was between $1 billion and $2.5 billion, whereas the loss in tax revenue was about $7 billion.[13] Does this mean that the R and D tax credit was not worthwhile?

d. One of the big problems in administering an R and D tax credit is to define what is and what is not research and development. According to *Forbes* magazine, "The current statute is so vague that it unwittingly encourages companies to misuse the credit. . . . R

[13] General Accounting Office, "The Research Tax Credit Has Stimulated Some Additional Research Spending," Washington, D.C., September 1989.

and D credits have been claimed by film production companies, car importers, and, reportedly, even restaurants—for developing new menus."[14] Why is it so difficult to define research and development? What difference does it make if many of the expenditures for which the credit is claimed are, strictly speaking, not research and development?

PROBLEM 15.6 Developing countries tend to do relatively little research and development, and they rarely produce products or processes that are fundamentally new to the world. Instead, they rely heavily on the industrialized countries like the United States for new technology, which they adapt to the local environment. Even in Brazil, India, and South Korea, the design capabilities of the most sophisticated firms are still relatively limited. But this does not mean that R and D is unimportant in developing countries. Without R and D facilities and personnel, it is very difficult for developing countries to monitor technological advances and to choose which new technologies to obtain and assimilate.

a. Table 15.8 shows the sources of R and D funding and nature of R and D performers in

[14] *Forbes*, February 25, 1985, p. 130.

▪ **TABLE 15.8**

Sources of R and D Funding and Nature of R and D Performers, Selected Countries

COUNTRY	PERCENT OF R AND D FUNDING				PERCENT OF R AND D PERFORMANCE		
	GOVERNMENT	INDUSTRY	FOREIGN	OTHER	INDUSTRY	UNIVERSITIES	GOVERNMENT
Argentina	95	0	1	4	41	22	37
Brazil	67	20	5	8	30	17	53
India	87	3	0	0	26	0	74
Mexico	15	1	1	83	30	51	19
South Korea	19	81	0	0	67	11	22
Japan	21	79	0	0	67	20	13
United States	47	50	0	3	73	12	15

SOURCE: C. Dahlman and C. Frischtak, *National Systems Supporting Technical Advance in Industry: The Brazilian Experience* (Washington, D.C.: World Bank, June 1990).

seven major countries (Argentina, Brazil, India, Japan, Mexico, South Korea, and the United States). Government tends to be a much more important source of R and D funding than industry in the developing countries. From the point of view of stimulating economic growth, what are the disadvantages of this arrangement?

b. In these developing countries, industry tends to perform a much smaller percentage of all R and D than in the developed countries. From the point of view of stimulating economic growth, what are the disadvantages of this arrangement?

c. The Council for Scientific and Industrial Research, a public agency, has accounted for a large share of industrial R and D in India. According to Stanford's Nathan Rosenberg, most R and D projects were chosen by the scientists themselves who had little detailed information about the needs of the public and private sector firms that would be the ultimate

users of their output.[15] From the point of view of stimulating economic growth, what are the disadvantages of this arrangement?

According to Yale's Gustav Ranis, the fast-growing East Asian countries like South Korea have forced scientific institutes to be "useful to the marketplace. . . . Institutes were assisted in this process by budgetary pressures which forced them to rely increasingly on private sector contracts in place of government subsidies."[16] Aren't all scientific institutes bound to be useful to the market place? Why or why not? Why were these budgetary pressures of assistance in this regard?

[15] N. Rosenberg, "Science and Technology Policy for the Asian NICs: Lessons from Economic History," in R. Evenson and G. Ranis (eds.), *Science and Technology: Lessons for Development Policy* (Boulder, Col.: Westview, 1990).

[16] G. Ranis, "Science and Technology Policy: Lessons from Japan and the East Asian NICs," ibid., pp. 172–73.

10 ▪ Conclusion

Every president, at least from John F. Kennedy on, has wrestled with the problem of what, if anything, the federal government should do to support civilian technology in the United States. Kennedy, Carter, and Clinton opted for more activist programs than did Reagan or Bush. Regardless of whether you are a Democrat or a Republican (or an independent), it is important that you understand the issues and controversies

in this area, and it is evident from the present chapter that, to achieve such an understanding, you must know the elementary principles of economics, discussed in the previous chapter. Without a knowledge of the determinants of economic growth, it would be hopeless to try to understand government policies toward research and development.

PART FIVE

International Economics

■ CHAPTER 16

International Trade

Essentials of **International Trade**

■ A country has a comparative advantage in producing those products in which its efficiency relative to other countries is high.

■ So long as a country has a comparative advantage in the production of some commodities and a comparative disadvantage in the production of others, it can benefit from specialization and trade with other countries.

■ A tariff is a tax that the government imposes on imports, its purpose being to protect domestic industry and workers from foreign competition.

■ A quota is a limit that the government imposes on the amount of certain commodities that can be imported annually.

■ Tariffs and quotas tend to reduce trade, raise prices, protect domestic industry from foreign competition, and reduce the standard of living of the country as a whole.

1 ■ Advantages of Trade

Why do we trade with other countries? To clarify the benefits of trade, consider the following example. Suppose that the United States can produce 2 computers or 5,000 cases of wine with 1 unit of resources. Suppose that France can produce 1 computer or 10,000 cases of wine with 1 unit of resources. Given the production possibilities in each country, are there any advantages in trade between the countries? And if so, what commodity should each country export, and what commodity should each country import? Should France export wine and import computers, or should it import wine and export computers?

To answer these questions, assume that the United States is producing a certain amount of computers and a certain amount of wine—and that France is producing a certain amount of computers and a certain amount of wine. If the United States shifts 1 unit of its resources from producing wine to producing computers, it will increase its production of computers by 2 com-

puters and reduce its production of wine by 5,000 cases of wine. If France shifts 1 unit of resources from the production of computers to the production of wine, it will increase its production of wine by 10,000 cases and reduce its production of computers by 1 computer.

Table 16.1 shows the *net* effect of this shift in the utilization of resources on *world* output of computers and of wine. World output of computers increases (by 1 computer) and world output of wine increases (by 5,000 cases) as a result of the redeployment of resources in each country. Thus *specialization increases world output*.

Moreover, if world output of each commodity is increased by shifting 1 unit of U.S. resources from wine to computers and shifting 1 unit of French resources from computers to wine, it follows that world output of each commodity will be increased further if each country shifts *more* of its resources in the same direction. This is because the amount of resources required to produce each

▪ **TABLE 16.1**

Case of Absolute Advantage

| | INCREASE OR DECREASE IN OUTPUT OF: | |
	COMPUTERS	WINE (thousands of cases)
Effect of U.S.'s shifting 1 unit of resources from wine to computers	+2	−5
Effect of France's shifting 1 unit of resources from computers to wine	−1	+10
Net Effect	+1	+5

good is assumed to be constant, regardless of how much is produced.

Thus, in this situation, one country—the United States—should specialize in producing computers, and the other country—France—should specialize in producing wine. This will maximize world output of both wine and computers and permit a rise in both countries' standards of living. Complete specialization of this sort is somewhat unrealistic, since countries often produce some of both commodities, but this simple example illustrates the basic principles involved.

TEST YOUR UNDERSTANDING

True or false?

_____ **1** If the United States has relatively bountiful supplies of land relative to Japan, and Japan has relatively bountiful supplies of labor relative to the United States, and if the production of electronic goods requires relatively little land and large amounts of labor, while the production of grain requires relatively little labor and large amounts of land, Japan is likely to export electronic goods and the United States is likely to export grain.

_____ **2** Specialization reduces world output.

_____ **3** Complete specialization of countries in the production of one commodity is realistic.

2 ▪ Comparative Advantage

The case just described is a very special one, since one country (France) has an absolute advantage over another (the United States) in the production of one good (wine), whereas the second country (the United States) has an absolute advantage over the first (France) in the production of another good (computers). What do we mean by the term **absolute advantage?** Country A has an _absolute advantage_ over country B in the production of a good when country A can produce a unit of the good with less resources than can country B. Since the United States can produce a computer with fewer units of resources than France, it has an absolute advantage over France

in the production of computers. Since France requires fewer resources than the United States to produce a given amount of wine, France has an absolute advantage over the United States in the production of wine.

But what if one country is more efficient in producing both goods? If the United States is more efficient in producing both computers and wine, is there still benefit to be derived from specialization and trade? At first glance, you are probably inclined to answer no. But if this is your inclination, you should reconsider—because you are wrong.

A NUMERICAL EXAMPLE

To see why specialization and trade have advantages even when one country is more efficient than another at producing both goods, consider the following example. Suppose the United States can produce 2 computers or 5,000 cases of wine with 1 unit of resources, and France can produce 1 computer or 4,000 cases of wine with 1 unit of resources. In this case, the United States is a more efficient producer of both computers and wine. Nonetheless, world output of both goods will increase if the United States specializes in the production of computers and France specializes in the production of wine.

Table 16.2 demonstrates this conclusion. If 2 units of U.S. resources are shifted from wine to computer production, 4 additional computers and 10,000 fewer cases of wine are produced. If 3 units of French resources are shifted from computer to wine production, 3 fewer computers and 12,000 additional cases of wine are produced. Thus the combined effect of this redeployment of resources in both countries is to increase world output of computers by 1 computer and to increase world output of wine by 2,000 cases. Even though the United States is more efficient than France in the production of both computers and wine, world output of both goods will be maximized if the United States specializes in computers and France specializes in wine.

■ **TABLE 16.2**

Case of Comparative Advantage

| | INCREASE OR DECREASE IN OUTPUT OF: | |
	COMPUTERS	WINE (thousands of cases)
Effect of U.S.'s shifting 2 units of resources from wine to computers	+4	−10
Effect of France's shifting 3 units of resources from computers to wine	−3	+12
Net Effect	+1	+2

Basically, this is so because, although the United States is more efficient than France in the production of both goods, it has a greater advantage in computers than in wine. It is twice as efficient as France in producing computers, but only 25 percent more efficient than France in producing wine. To derive these numbers, recall that 1 unit of resources will produce 2 computers in the United States, but only 1 computer in France. Thus the United States is twice as efficient in computers. On the other hand, 1 unit of resources will produce 5,000 cases of wine in the United States, but only 4,000 cases in France. Thus the United States is 25 percent more efficient in wine.

TRADE DEPENDS ON COMPARATIVE ADVANTAGE

Specialization and trade depend on comparative, not absolute, advantage. A country has a **comparative advantage** in those products where its efficiency relative to other countries is highest. So long as a country has a comparative advantage in the production of some commodities and a comparative disadvantage in the production of others, it can benefit from specialization and trade. A country will specialize in products where it has a comparative advantage, and import those where it has a comparative disadvantage.

Consider the case of France and the United States in Table 16.2. The United States has a comparative advantage in the production of computers and a comparative disadvantage in the production of wine. France has a comparative advantage in the production of wine and a comparative disadvantage in the production of computers. Both countries can benefit if France specializes in wine and the United States specializes in computers.

A GEOMETRIC REPRESENTATION OF COMPARATIVE ADVANTAGE

The principle of comparative advantage, like so many important economic concepts, can be displayed diagrammatically. Again, suppose that in the United States 1 unit of resources will produce 2 computers or 5,000 cases of wine. Consequently, the **production possibilities curve** in the United States—the curve that shows the maximum number of computers that can be produced, given various outputs of wine—is the one in panel A of Figure 16.1. The United States must

give up 1 computer for every additional 2,500 cases of wine that it produces; thus the slope of the U.S. production possibilities curve is −1/2,500.

Also, as in the previous section, we suppose that in France 1 unit of resources will produce 1 computer or 4,000 cases of wine. Thus the production possibilities curve in France is as shown in panel B of Figure 16.1. France must give up 1 computer for every additional 4,000 cases of wine it produces; thus the slope of France's production possibilities curve is −1/4,000.

Now suppose that the United States uses all its resources to produce computers and that France uses all its resources to produce wine. In other words, the United States operates at point A on its production possibilities curve and France operates at point B on its production possibilities curve. Then suppose that the United States trades its computers for France's wine. The line AC in panel A of Figure 16.1 shows the various amounts of computers and wine the United States can end up with if it specializes in computers and trades them for French wine. The line AC is called the **trading possibilities curve** of the United States. The slope of AC is −1 times the ratio of the price of a case of wine to the price of a computer, since this ratio equals the number of computers the United States must give up to get a case of French wine. Similarly, the line BD in panel B of Figure 16.1 shows France's trading possibilities curve. That is, BD represents the various amounts of computers and wine France can wind up with if it specializes in wine and trades it for U.S. computers.

The thing to note about both panels of Figure 16.1 is that each country's trading possibilities curve—AC in panel A, BD in panel B—lies above its production possibilities curve. This means that *both countries can have more of both commodities by specializing and trading than by trying to be self-sufficient*—even though the United States is more efficient than France at producing both commodities. Thus Figure 16.1 shows what was said in the previous section: If countries specialize in products where they have a comparative advantage and trade with one another, each country can improve its standard of living.

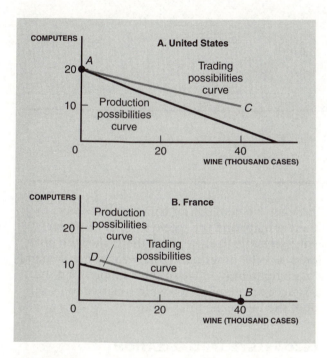

▪ **FIGURE 16.1**

Benefits of Specialization and Trade

The line AC represents the various amounts of computers and wine that the United States can end up with, if it specializes in computers and trades them for French wine. The slope of AC equals −1 times the ratio of the price of a case of wine to the price of a computer, assumed to be 1/3,333. The line BD represents the various amounts of computers and wine that France can wind up with, if it specializes in wine and trades for U.S. computers. The line AC lies above the United States's production possibilities curve and BD lies above France's production possibilities curve. Thus both countries can have more of both commodities by specializing and trading than by attempting to be self-sufficient.

TEST YOUR UNDERSTANDING

True or false?

_____ **1** If Brazil could produce each and every good and service with 80 percent as much of each and every input as Argentina, Brazil would have a comparative advantage over Argentina in all goods and services.

_____ **2** Even though one country may be more efficient than another at producing two commodities, both countries may benefit if each specializes and trades.

_____ **3** Specialization and trade depend on comparative, not absolute, advantage.

Exercise

1 "The principle of comparative advantage doesn't work. The U.S. exports electronic computers to Japan and imports electronic consumer goods like TV sets from Japan." Comment and evaluate.

3 ■ The Terms of Trade

The **terms of trade** are defined as the quantity of imported goods that a country can obtain in exchange for a unit of domestic goods. Thus, in Figure 16.1, the terms of trade are measured by the ratio of the price of a computer to the price of a case of wine—since this ratio shows how many cases of French wine the United States can get in exchange for a computer. In Figure 16.1, assume that this ratio equals 3,333:1. It is important to not that this ratio must be somewhere between 2,500:1 and 4,000:1. By diverting its own resources from computer production to wine production, the United States can exchange a computer for 2,500 cases of wine. Since this is possible, it will not pay the United States to trade a computer for less than 2,500 cases of wine. Similarly, since France can exchange a case of wine for 1/4,000 of a computer by diverting its own resources from wine to computers, it clearly will not be willing to trade a case of wine for less than 1/4,000 of a computer.

But where will the price ratio lie between 2,500:1 and 4,000:1? The answer depends on *world supply and demand for the two products.* The

stronger the demand for computers (relative to their supply) and the weaker the demand for wine (relative to its supply), the higher the price ratio. On the other hand, the weaker the demand for computers (relative to their supply) and the stronger the demand for wine (relative to its supply), the lower the price ratio.

INCOMPLETE SPECIALIZATION

Figure 16.1 shows the United States should specialize completely in computers, and that France should specialize completely in wine. This result stems from the assumption that the cost of producing a computer or a case of wine is constant. If, on the other hand, the cost of producing each good increases with the amount produced, the result is likely to be incomplete specialization. In other words, although the United States will continue to specialize in computers and France will continue to specialize in wine, each country will also produce some of the other good as well. This is a more likely outcome, since specialization generally tends to be less than complete.

TEST YOUR UNDERSTANDING

True or false?

____ **1** The terms of trade are the quantity of imported goods that a country can get in exchange for a unit of domestic goods.

____ **2** The price ratio is independent of world supply and demand.

____ **3** Specialization tends to be less than complete.

Exercises

1 Suppose that the United States can produce 3 computers or 3,000 cases of wine with 1 unit of resources, while France can produce 1 computer or 2,000 cases of wine with 1 unit of resources. Will specialization increase world output?

2 Suppose that the United States has 100 units of resources while France has 50 units. Will the production possibilities curve in each country be the same?

3 Given the information in Exercises 1 and 2, how will firms in France and the United States know whether they should produce wine or computers? Must the government instruct them on this score? Why, or why not?

4 ▪ International Trade and Individual Markets

It has been emphasized that countries can benefit by specializing in the production of goods for which they have a comparative advantage and trading these goods for others where they have a comparative disadvantage. But how do a country's producers know whether they have a comparative advantage or disadvantage in the production of a given commodity? They do not call up the local university and ask the leading professor of economics (although that might not always be such a bad idea). The market for the good provides the required signals for them.

To see how this works, consider a new (and rather whimsical) product—bulletproof suspenders. Suppose that the Mob, having run a scientific survey of professional killers and police officers, finds that most of them wear their suspenders over their bulletproof vests. As a consequence, the Mob's killers are instructed to render a victim immobile by shooting holes in his suspenders (thus making his trousers fall down and trip him). Naturally, the producers of suspenders will soon find it profitable to produce a new bulletproof variety, an innovation which, it is hoped, will make a solid contribution to law and order. The new suspenders are demanded only in the United States and England, since the rest of the world wears belts. The demand curve in the United States is as shown in panel A of Figure 16.2, and the demand curve in England is as shown in panel B. Suppose further that this product can be manufactured in both the United States and England. The supply curve in the United States is as shown in panel A, and the supply curve in England is as shown in panel B.

Take a closer look at Figure 16.2. Note that prices in England are expressed in pounds (£) and prices in the United States are expressed in dollars ($). This is quite realistic. Each country has its own currency, in which prices in that country are expressed. In early 1997, £1 was equal to about $1.60. In other words, you could exchange a

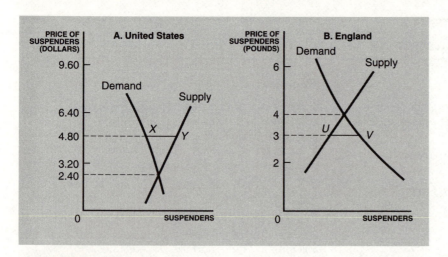

■ **FIGURE 16.2**

Determination of Quantity Imported and Exported under Free Trade

Under free trade, price will equal $4.80 or £3. The United States will export *XY* units, England will import *UV* units, and *XY* = *UV*.

pound note for $1.60—or $1.60 for a £1 note. For this reason, the two panels of Figure 16.2 are lined up so that a price of $3.20 is at the same level as a price of £2, $4.80 is at the same level as £3, and so on.

NO FOREIGN TRADE

To begin with, suppose that bulletproof suspenders cannot be exported or imported, perhaps because of a very high tariff (tax on imports) imposed on them in both the United States and England. (You can readily imagine members of both Congress and Parliament defending such a tariff on the grounds that a capacity to produce plenty of bulletproof suspenders is important for national defense.) If this happens, the price of bulletproof suspenders will be $2.40 in the United States and £4 in England. Why? Because, as shown in Figure 16.2, these are the prices at which each country's demand curve intersects its supply curve.

FOREIGN TRADE PERMITTED

Next, suppose that international trade in this product is permitted, perhaps because both countries eliminate the tariff. Now what will happen? Since the price is lower in the United States than in England, people can make money by sending this product from the United States to England. After all, they can buy a pair of suspenders for $2.40 in this country and sell it for £4 (=$6.40) in England. But they will not be able to do so indefinitely. As more and more suspenders are supplied by the United States for the English market, the price in the United States must go up (to induce producers to produce the additional output) and the price in England must go down (to induce consumers to buy the additional quantity).

When an equilibrium is reached, *the price in the United States must equal the price in England.* If this did not happen, there would be an advantage in increasing U.S. exports (if the price in England were higher) or in decreasing U.S. exports (if the price in the United States were higher). Thus only if the prices are equal can an equilibrium exist.

At what level will this price—which is common in both countries—tend to settle? Obviously, *the price must end up at the level where the amount of the good one country wants to export equals the amount the other country wants to import.* That is, it must settle at $4.80, or £3. Otherwise, the total amount demanded in both countries would not equal the total amount supplied in both countries.

THE SIGNAL OF MARKET FORCES

At this point, you can see how market forces indicate whether a country has a comparative advantage or a comparative disadvantage in the production of a certain commodity. *If a country has a comparative advantage, it turns out—after the price*

of the good in various countries is equalized and total world output of the good equals total world demand for it—that the country exports the good under free trade and competition. In Figure 16.2, it turns out—as you've just seen—that the United States is an exporter of bulletproof suspenders under free trade, because the demand and supply curves in the United States and England take the positions they do. The basic reason the curves take these positions is that the United States has a comparative advantage in the production of this good. Thus, to put things in a nutshell, a country's producers can tell (under free trade) whether they have a comparative advantage in the production of a certain commodity by seeing whether it is profitable for them to export it. If they can make a profit, they have a comparative advantage.

 TEST YOUR UNDERSTANDING

True or false?

_____ **1** The price must end up at the level where the amount of the good one country wants to import equals the amount the other country wants to export.

_____ **2** If a country has a comparative advantage in the production of a good, this country will produce the good under free trade and competition.

Exercises

1 According to Hendrik Houthakker, "Our workers get high real income not because they are protected from foreign competition, but because they are highly productive, at least in certain industries." Do you agree? Why, or why not?

2 According to Richard Cooper, "Technological innovation can undoubtedly strengthen the competitive position of a country in which the innovation takes place, whether it be one which enlarges exports or displaces imports." Has this been true in the U.S. pharmaceutical industry?

---

5 ▪ Tariffs and Quotas

WHAT IS A TARIFF?

Despite its advantages, not everyone benefits from free trade. On the contrary, the well-being of some firms and workers may be threatened by foreign competition; and they may press for

a **tariff,** a tax the government imposes on imports. The purpose of a tariff is to cut down on imports in order to protect domestic industry and workers from foreign competition. A secondary reason for having tariffs is to produce revenue for the government.

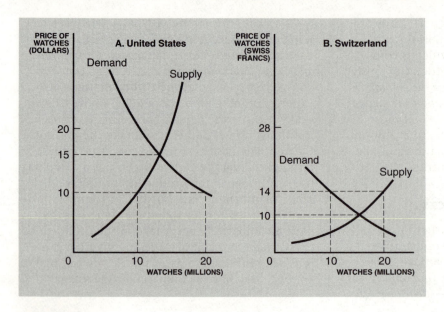

▪ **FIGURE 16.3**

Effect of a Tariff on Swiss Watches

Under free trade, price would equal $10, or 14 Swiss francs. If a tariff of $10 is imposed on each watch imported from Switzerland, there will be a complete cessation of imports. Price in the United States will increase to $15, and price in Switzerland will fall to 10 Swiss francs.

To see how a tariff works, consider the market for wristwatches. Suppose that the demand and supply curves for wristwatches in the United States are as shown in panel A of Figure 16.3, and that the demand and supply curves for wrist-watches in Switzerland are as shown in panel B. Clearly, Switzerland has a comparative advantage in the production of wristwatches, and under free trade the price of a wristwatch would tend toward $10 in the United States and toward 14 Swiss francs in Switzerland. (Note that 1.4 Swiss francs are assumed to equal 1 dollar.) Under free trade, the United States would import 10 million wristwatches from Switzerland.

Now if the United States imposes a tariff of $10 on each wristwatch imported from Switzerland, the imports will completely cease. Any importers who buy watches in Switzerland at the price (when there is no foreign trade) of 10 Swiss francs—which equals about $7—must pay a tariff of $10; this makes their total cost about $17 per

watch. But this is more than the price of a watch in the United States when there is no foreign trade (which is $15). Consequently, there is no money to be made by importing watches—unless Americans can be persuaded to pay more for a Swiss watch than for an identical U.S. watch.

THE SOCIAL COSTS OF TARIFFS

What is the effect of the tariff? The domestic watch industry receives a higher price—$15 rather than $10—than it would without a tariff. And the workers in the domestic watch industry may have more jobs and higher wages than without the tariff. The victim of the tariff is the U.S. consumer, who pays a higher price for wrist-watches. Thus the domestic watch industry benefits at the expense of the rest of the country. But does the general public lose more than the watch industry gains? In general, the answer is yes. The tariff reduces the welfare of the country as a whole.

The tariff in Figure 16.3 is a **prohibitive tariff**—a tariff so high that it stops all imports of the good in question. Not all tariffs are prohibitive. (If they were, the government would receive no revenue at all from tariffs.) In many cases, the tariff is high enough to stop some, but not all, imports; and, as you would expect, the detrimental effect of a nonprohibitive tariff on living standards is less than that of a prohibitive tariff. But this does not mean that nonprohibitive tariffs are harmless. On the contrary, they can do lots of harm to domestic consumption and living standards.

WHAT IS A QUOTA?

Besides tariffs, other barriers to free trade are **quotas,** which many countries impose on the amount of certain commodities that can be im-

ported annually. The United States sets import quotas on sugar and has exerted pressure on foreigners to get them to limit the quantity of steel and textiles that they will export to us. To see how a quota affects trade, production, and prices, return to the market for wristwatches. Suppose the United States places a quota on the import of wristwatches: no more than 6 million wristwatches can be imported per year. Figure 16.4 shows the effect of the quota. Before it was imposed, the price of wristwatches was $10 (or 14 Swiss francs), and the United States imported 10 million wristwatches from Switzerland. The quota forces the United States to reduce its imports to 6 million.

What will be the effect on the U.S. price? The demand curve shows that, if the price is $12, U.S. demand will exceed supply by 6 million watches; in other words, the United States will import 6 million watches. Thus, once the quota is imposed, the price will rise to $12, since *this is the price that will reduce U.S. imports to the amount of the quota.* A

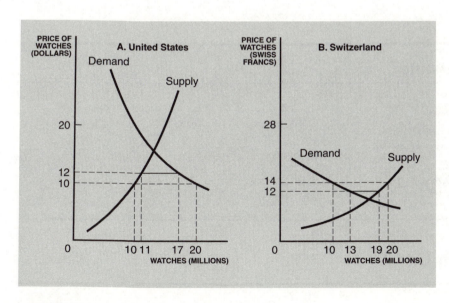

▪ **FIGURE 16.4**

Effects of a Quota on Swiss Watches

Before the quota is imposed, the price is $10, or 14 Swiss francs. After a quota of 6 million watches is imposed, the price in the United States rises to $12, and the price in Switzerland falls to 12 Swiss francs.

quota—like a tariff—increases the price of the good. (Note too that the price in Switzerland will fall to 12 francs. Thus the quota will reduce the price in Switzerland.)

THE SOCIAL COSTS OF QUOTAS

Both a quota and a tariff reduce trade, raise prices, protect domestic industry from foreign competition, and reduce the standard of living of the country as a whole. But most economists tend to regard quotas with even less enthusiasm than they do tariffs. Under many circumstances, a quota insulates local industry from foreign competition even more effectively than a tariff does. Foreigners, if their costs are low enough, can surmount a tariff barrier; but if a quota exists, there is no way they can exceed the quota. Moreover, a (nonprohibitive) tariff provides the government with some revenue, while quotas do not even do that. The windfall price increase from a quota accrues to the importer who is lucky enough or influential enough—or sufficiently generous with favors and bribes—to get an import license. (However, if the government auctions off the import licenses, it can obtain revenue from a quota.)

EXPORT SUBSIDIES AND OTHER NONTARIFF BARRIERS TO FREE TRADE

Finally, **export subsidies,** another means by which governments try to give their domestic industry an advantage in international competition, are also a major impediment to free trade. Such subsidies may take the form of outright cash disbursements, tax exemptions, preferential financing or insurance arrangements, or other preferential treatment for exports. Export subsidies, and other such measures, frequently lead to countermeasures. Thus, to counter foreign export subsidies, the U.S. government has imposed duties against such subsidies on goods sold here.

Other nontariff barriers to free trade include licensing requirements and unreasonable product quality standards. By granting few licenses (which are required in some countries to import goods) and by imposing unrealistically stringent product quality standards, governments discourage imports.

 TEST YOUR UNDERSTANDING

True or false?

_____ **1** The protection of certain industries for the purpose of national defense is the only argument ever given for barriers to free trade.

_____ **2** Under free trade a country's economic welfare is always lower than under a tariff.

_____ **3** Quotas can be even more effective than tariffs in keeping foreign goods out of a country.

Exercise

1 Would you favor a high tariff on imported steel if you were a steel worker?

▪ CHAPTER REVIEW

KEY TERMS

absolute advantage

comparative advantage

production possibilities curve

trading possibilities curve

terms of trade

tariff

prohibitive tariff

quotas

export subsidies

COMPLETION QUESTIONS

1 In the absence of trade, suppose that wheat would sell for $3 per bushel in the United States and for £2 in England and that cloth would sell for $3 per yard in the United States and for £.5 in England. If 1£ = $2.25, the United States will (export, import) _____ wheat because U.S. wheat can be bought for £_____ by the English. England will (export, import) _____ cloth because English cloth can be bought for $_____ by Americans.

2 If the United States exports corn to France, this results in a(n) (increase, decrease) _____ in the price of corn in the United States and a(n) (increase, decrease) _____ in the price of corn in France. If France exports wine to the United States, this results in a(n) (increase, decrease) _____ in the price of wine in the United States and a(n) (increase, decrease) _____ in the price of wine in France.

3 Relative to 100 years ago, the United States exports (fewer, more) _____ manufactured goods and (fewer, more) _____ raw materials.

4 Trade permits specialization, and specialization increases _____.

5 Specialization and trade depend on _____ advantage between countries.

6 The _____ curve shows the maximum amount of one product that can be produced, given various outputs of an alternative product.

7 Assuming for simplicity that only two countries exist, the price of a good tends to settle at the level where the amount of the good that one country exports (equals, is unequal to) _____ the amount that the other country imports.

8 Both _____ and _____ generally increase the price of an imported good. Two ways in which governments try to help protect their domestic industries are by _____ and _____.

9 One country has a(n) _____ advantage over another when it can produce one unit of a good with fewer resources than can the other country.

10 Suppose that one country has a comparative advantage in producing one good and another country has a comparative advantage in producing another good. Then if each country specializes in producing the good in which it (has, has not) _____ the comparative advantage, each (can, can not) _____ benefit from trade.

11 _____ indicate whether a country has a comparative advantage or disadvantage in producing

ANSWERS TO COMPLETION QUESTIONS

export
$1\frac{1}{3}$
export
$1\frac{1}{8}$

increase

decrease

decrease

increase

more
fewer

output

comparative

production possibilities

equals

tariffs, quotas

tariffs, quotas
absolute

has

can

Market forces

a commodity. If there is a comparative advantage, after the price of a good in various countries is equalized and the total world output of the good equals the total world demand for it, a country will (export, import) _____ the good under free trade and competition.

export

12 Specialization can reduce production costs to a lower level than would be possible if each country tried to be _____ .

self-sufficient

NUMERICAL PROBLEMS

1 Suppose that the demand and supply curves for transistor radios in the United States are as follows:

PRICE (dollars)	QUANTITY DEMANDED	QUANTITY SUPPLIED
	(millions)	
5	5	2
10	4	3
15	3	4
20	2	5

Further suppose that the demand and supply curves for transistor radios in Japan are:

PRICE (expressed in dollar equivalent of Japanese price)	QUANTITY DEMANDED	QUANTITY SUPPLIED
	(millions)	
5	2.5	1
10	2.0	3
15	1.5	5
20	1.0	7

a Suppose that there is free trade in transistor radios. What will be the equilibrium price?

b Which country will export transistor radios to the other country?

c How large will be the exports?

d Suppose that the United States imposes a tariff of $10 per transistor radio. What will happen to exports and imports?

2 Suppose that the United States can produce 3 electronic computers or 3,000 cases of wine with 1 unit of

resources, while France can produce 1 electronic computer or 5,000 cases of wine with 1 unit of resources.

a Will specialization increase world output?

b Is this an example of absolute or comparative advantage?

c If the maximum number of computers that can be produced per year in the United States is 1,000, draw the U.S. production possibilities curve on the graph below.

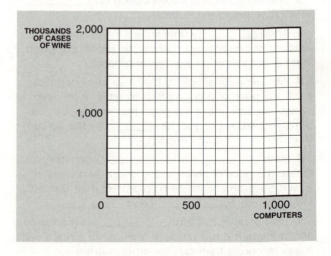

d In the diagram above draw the trading possibilities curve if the United States produces only computers and trades them for French wine (at a price for each computer that is equivalent to 2,000 cases of French wine). Does this curve lie above the production possibilities curve?

e If the maximum number of cases of wine that can be produced per year in France is 2 million, draw the French production possibilities curve on the next page.

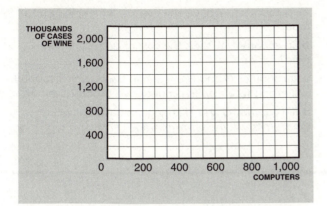

f In the diagram above draw the trading possibilities curve if France produces only wine and trades it for U.S. computers (at a price for each computer that is equivalent to 2,000 cases of French wine). Does this curve lie above the production possibilities curve?

3 Suppose that labor is the only input and that two countries, Argentina and Brazil, can produce the following amounts of two commodities, bananas and nuts, with a day of labor:

	BANANAS (lb)	NUTS (lb)
Argentina	10	3
Brazil	5	4

a In order for both countries to gain from trade, between what limits must the ratio of the prices lie?

b Suppose that there is free trade and the price of bananas increases relative to the price of nuts. Is this change in the terms of trade to the advantage of Argentina or Brazil?

4 Countries A and B are neighbors and produce only food and machines. Both countries' production possibilities curves are straight lines. Country A has 500 units of resources, while country B has 200 units of resources. In country A, 1 unit of resources can produce 22 units of food or 11 units of machinery. In country B 1 unit of resources can produce 15 units of food or 10 units of machinery. Before there was any international trade, output in the two countries was:

	OUTPUT (units)	
	FOOD	MACHINERY
Country A	836	1,320
Country B	2,250	500

a What is the price of a unit of machinery (in terms of food) in each of the countries when they do not trade with each other? Explain why.

b Can the two countries benefit from international trade? If so, explain why.

c Between what limits will the ratio of the price of machinery to the price of food be once international trade begins?

5 In problem 2, suppose that the price of a computer rises from the equivalent of 2,000 cases of wine to the equivalent of 4,000 cases of wine. In other words, 1 computer now exchanges for 4,000 cases of wine, rather than 2,000 cases of wine.

a Do the results indicate that the United States can consume less than before? More than before? Explain.

b Do the results indicate that France can consume less than before? More than before? Explain.

6 Countries D and E have not traded with each other because of political differences. Suddenly, they reconcile their political differences and begin to trade. Cigars are relatively cheap, but beef is relatively expensive in country D. Beef is relatively cheap, but cigars are relatively expensive in country E.

a When these countries begin to trade, will the demand for cigars produced in country D increase or decrease? Will the price of cigars increase or decrease in country D?

b Will the demand for cigars produced in country E increase or decrease? Will the price of cigars increase or decrease in country E?

c Will the demand for beef produced in country D increase or decrease? Will the price of beef increase or decrease in country D?

d Will the demand for beef produced in country E increase or decrease? Will the price of beef increase or decrease in country E?

e Will the demand for resources used in country D to produce cigars increase or decrease? Will the demand for resources used in country E to produce beef increase or decrease?

f Will the demand for resources used in country E to produce cigars increase or decrease? Will the demand for resources used in country D to produce beef increase or decrease?

7 You can construct country G's production possibilities curve from the data on page 228. You can also construct country H's production possibilities curve. The only goods produced in either country are food and clothing.

COUNTRY G			COUNTRY H		
POSSIBILITY	FOOD OUTPUT	CLOTHING OUTPUT	POSSIBILITY	FOOD OUTPUT	CLOTHING OUTPUT
A	0	32	A	0	24
B	5	24	B	4	18
C	10	16	C	8	12
D	15	8	D	12	6
E	20	0	E	16	0

a In country *G* what is the cost of clothing in terms of food?

b In country *H* what is the cost of clothing in terms of food?

c If countries *G* and *H* engage in trade, which country will export food? Which country will export clothing?

d If countries *G* and *H* engage in trade, between what limits will the terms of trade lie?

 ANSWERS TO
TEST YOUR UNDERSTANDING

SECTION 1

TRUE OR FALSE: 1. True 2. False 3. False

SECTION 2

TRUE OR FALSE: 1. False 2. True 3. True

EXERCISE

1. The United States may have a comparative advantage in computers, but not in TV sets.

SECTION 3

TRUE OR FALSE: 1. True 2. False 3. True

EXERCISES

1. Yes, since the domestic opportunity cost of a computer is 1,000 cases of wine in the United States and 2,000 cases in France. The United States has a comparative advantage in computers, and France has one in producing wine. The United States is 3 times as efficient as France in computers, but only 50 percent more efficient in wine production.

2. No.

3. No, forces of supply and demand will set the price of each good in world markets so that U.S. firms will find it profitable to make and export computers, while French firms will find it profitable to make and export wine.

SECTION 4

TRUE OR FALSE: 1. True 2. True

EXERCISES

1. Yes, protection is likely to reduce, not increase, a country's standard of living. On the other hand, a country's standard of living tends to be directly related to its productivity.

2. Yes.

SECTION 5

TRUE OR FALSE: 1. False 2. False 3. True

EXERCISE

1. You might favor it because it would raise the chances of your keeping your job.

■ CHAPTER 17
International Finance

Essentials of **International Finance**

■ The exchange rate is the number of units of one currency that exchanges for a unit of another currency.

■ Under flexible exchange rates, the equilibrium price of a foreign currency (for example, the German mark) is given by the intersection of the demand and supply curves for the foreign currency.

■ From World War II to 1973, most exchange rates were fixed by government action and international agreement.

■ The U.S. balance of payments accounts are an important record of the flow of payments between the United States and other countries. Debit items are items for which Americans must pay foreigners; credit items are items for which Americans are paid by foreigners. The sum of the debit items equals the sum of the credit items.

1 ■ International Transactions and Exchange Rates

Suppose you want to buy a book from a German publisher, and that book costs 20 marks. (The German currency consists of marks, not dollars.) To buy the book, you must somehow get marks to pay the publisher, since this is the currency in which the publisher deals. Or, if the publisher agrees, you might pay in dollars; but the publisher would then have to exchange the dollars for marks, since its bills must be paid in marks. Whatever happens, either you or the publisher must somehow exchange dollars for marks, since international business transactions, unlike transactions within a country, involve two different currencies.

If you decide to exchange dollars for marks to pay the German publisher, how can you make the exchange? The answer is simple. You can buy German marks at a bank, just as you might buy lamb chops at a butcher shop. Just as the lamb chops have a price (expressed in dollars), so the German marks have a price (expressed in dollars). The bank may tell you that each mark you

buy will cost you $.60. This makes the *exchange rate* between dollars and marks .60 to 1, since it takes .60 dollars to purchase 1 mark.

In general, *the exchange rate is simply the number of units of one currency that exchanges for a unit of another currency.* The obvious question is: What determines the exchange rate? Why is the exchange rate between German marks and U.S. dollars what it is? Why doesn't a mark exchange for 25 cents, rather than 60 cents? This basic question will occupy you in the next several sections.

THE FOREIGN EXCHANGE MARKET

Since 1973, the major trading countries of the world have permitted exchange rates to fluctuate relatively freely. There is a market for various types of foreign currency—German marks, British pounds, French francs, and so on—just as there are markets for various types of meat. In the case of the German mark, the demand and supply curves may look like those shown in Figure 17.1.

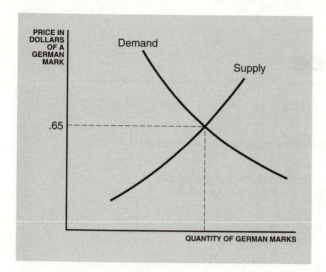

▪ **FIGURE 17.1**

Determination of the Exchange Rate between Dollars and German Marks under Freely Fluctuating Exchange Rates

Under freely fluctuating exchange rates, the equilibrium price of a German mark would be $.65 if the demand and supply curves for marks are as shown here.

The demand curve shows the amount of German marks that people with dollars will demand at various prices of a mark. The supply curve shows the amount of German marks that people with marks will supply at various prices of a mark. Since the amount of German currency supplied must equal the amount demanded in equilibrium, *the equilibrium price (in dollars) of a German mark is given by the intersection of the demand and supply curves.* In Figure 17.1, this intersection is at $.65.

THE DEMAND AND SUPPLY SIDES OF THE MARKET

Look in more detail at the demand and supply sides of this market. On the *demand* side are people who want to import German goods (like the book you want to buy) in the United States, people who want to travel in Germany (where they'll need German money), people who want to build factories in Germany, and others with dollars who want German currency. The people on the *supply*

side are those who want to import U.S. goods into Germany, Germans who want to travel in the United States (where they'll need U.S. money), people with marks who want to build factories in the United States, and others with marks who want U.S. currency.

When Americans demand more German cameras or Rhine wine (causing the demand curve to shift upward and to the right), the price (in dollars) of the German mark will tend to increase. Thus, if the demand curve for marks shifts as shown in Figure 17.2, the result will be an increase in the equilibrium price (in dollars) of a mark from $.65 to $.70. Conversely, *when the Germans demand more U.S. cars or computers (resulting in a shift of the supply curve downward and to the right), the price (in dollars) of the German mark will tend to decrease.*

To see why an increase in German demand for U.S. cars or computers shifts the supply curve downward and to the right, recall that the supply curve shows the amount of marks that will be supplied at each price of a mark. Thus a shift downward and to the right in the supply curve means that more marks will be supplied at a

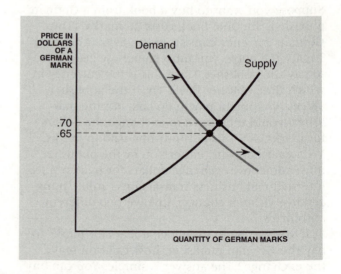

▪ **FIGURE 17.2**

Effect of Shift in Demand Curve for German Marks

Because of the demand curve's shift to the right, the equilibrium price of a German mark increases from $.65 to $.70.

given price (in dollars) of the mark. Given the posited increase in German demand for U.S. goods, such a shift in the supply curve would be expected.

APPRECIATION AND DEPRECIATION OF A CURRENCY

Two terms frequently encountered in discussions of the foreign exchange market are **appreciation** and **depreciation.** When country A's currency becomes more valuable relative to country B's currency, country A's currency is said to appreciate relative to that of country B, and country B's currency is said to depreciate relative to that of country A. In Figure 17.2, the mark appreciated relative to the dollar and the dollar depreciated relative to the mark. This use of terms makes sense. Since the number of dollars commanded by a mark increased, the mark became more valuable relative to the dollar and the dollar became less valuable relative to the mark.

 TEST YOUR UNDERSTANDING

True or false?

_____ **1** The exchange rate is the number of units of one currency that exchange for a unit of another currency.

_____ **2** When Americans demand more German goods, this tends to lower the price (in dollars) of the German mark.

_____ **3** When the dollar becomes more valuable relative to the German mark, the dollar is said to appreciate relative to the mark.

Exercises

1 Suppose that the demand curve for German marks is as follows:

QUANTITY DEMANDED (billions of marks)	PRICE (in dollars) OF A MARK
20	.20
15	.30
10	.40
5	.50

Plot this demand curve on a graph. What sorts of groups, organizations, and individuals are part of the demand side of this market.

2 Suppose that the supply curve for German marks is as shown below. Plot this supply curve on the same graph as the demand curve in Exercise 1.

QUANTITY SUPPLIED (billions of marks)	PRICE (in dollars) OF A MARK
8	.20
9	.30
10	.40
11	.50

3 Based on the information in Exercises 1 and 2, what is the equilibrium value of the exchange rate if it is completely flexible?

---

2 ▪ Determinants of Exchange Rates

We have seen that flexible exchange rates are determined by supply and demand, but what are some of the major factors determining the position of these supply and demand curves? Under flexible exchange rates, the exchange rate between any two currencies will reflect differences in the price levels in the two countries, and differences in economic growth rates and interest rates. Consider the exchange rate between the U.S. dollar and the German mark. If the United States has a higher inflation rate, a higher rate of economic growth, and a lower interest rate than Germany, the dollar will tend to depreciate relative to the mark, for the reasons discussed in the following paragraphs.

RELATIVE PRICE LEVELS

In the long run, the exchange rate between any two currencies may be expected to reflect differences in the price levels in the two countries. (This is the so-called *purchasing-power parity* theory of exchange rate determination.) To see why, suppose that Germany and the United States are the only exporters or importers of automobiles, and that automobiles are the only product they export or import. If an automobile costs $8,000 in the United States and 20,000 marks in Germany, what must be the exchange rate between the dollar and the mark? Clearly, a mark must be worth .40 dollars, because otherwise the two countries' automobiles would not be competitive in the world market. If a mark were set equal to .60 dollars, this would mean that a German automobile would cost $12,000 (that is, 20,000 times $.60), which is far more than what a U.S. automobile would cost. Thus foreign buyers would obtain their automobiles in the United States.

On the basis of this theory, you would expect that, *if the rate of inflation in country A is higher than country B, country A's currency is likely to depreciate relative to country B's.* Suppose that costs double in the United States but increase by only 25 percent in Germany. After this burst of inflation, an automobile costs $16,000 (that is, 2 times $8,000) in the United States and 25,000 marks (that is, 1.25 times 20,000 marks) in Germany. Thus, based on the purchasing-power parity theory, the new value of the mark must be .64 dollars, rather than the old value of .40 dollars. (Why .64 dollars? Because this is the exchange rate that makes the new cost of an automobile in the United States, $16,000, equivalent to the new cost of an automobile in Germany, 25,000 marks.) Because the rate of inflation is higher in the United States

than in Germany, the dollar depreciates relative to the mark.

RELATIVE RATES OF GROWTH

Although relative price levels may play an important role in the long run, other factors tend to exert more influence on exchange rates in the short run. In particular, *if one country's rate of economic growth is higher than the rest of the world, its currency is likely to depreciate.* If a country's economy is booming, this tends to increase its imports. If there is a boom in the United States, Americans will tend to import a great deal from other countries. If a country's imports tend to grow faster than its exports, its demand for foreign currency will tend to grow more rapidly than the amount of foreign currency that is supplied to it. Consequently, its currency is likely to depreciate.

RELATIVE INTEREST-RATE LEVELS

If the rate of interest in Germany is higher than in the United States, banks, multinational corporations, and other investors in the United States will sell dollars and buy marks in order to invest in the high-yielding Germany securities. Also, German investors (and others) will be less likely to find U.S. securities attractive. Thus the mark will tend to appreciate relative to the dollar, since the demand curve for marks will shift to the right and the supply curve for marks will shift to the left. In general, *an increase in a country's interest rates leads to an appreciation of its currency, and a decrease in its interest rates leads to a depreciation of its currency.* In the short run, interest-rate differentials can have a major impact on exchange rates, since there is a huge amount of funds that are moved from country to country in response to differentials in interest rates.

THE ADJUSTMENT MECHANISM UNDER FLEXIBLE EXCHANGE RATES

Under flexible exchange rates, what ensures a balance in the exports and imports between countries? Such a balance is achieved through changes in exchange rates. Suppose that for some reason Britain is importing far more from the United States than the United States is from Britain. This will mean that the British, needing dollars to buy our goods, will be willing to supply pounds more cheaply. In other words, the supply curve for British pounds will shift downward and to the right, as shown in Figure 17.3. This will cause the price of a pound to decline from P_1 dollars to P_2 dollars. Or, from Britain's point of view, the price (in pounds) of a dollar will have been bid up by the swollen demand for imports from the United States.

Because of the increase in the price (in pounds) of a dollar, U.S. goods will become more expensive in Britain. Thus the British will tend to reduce their imports of our goods. At the same time, since the price (in dollars) of a pound has decreased, British goods will become cheaper in the United States, and this will stimulate the United States to import more from Britain. Consequently, as the United States's currency appreciates in terms of theirs—or, to put it another way, as theirs depreciates in terms of the United States's—the British are induced to import less and export more. Thus there is an automatic mechanism to bring trade between countries into balance.

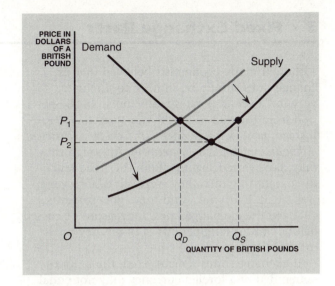

▪ **FIGURE 17.3**

Adjustment Mechanism

If Britain imports more from the United States than the United States does from Britain, the supply curve for British pounds will shift downward and to the right; this results in a decline of the price of the pound from P_1 to P_2 dollars. If Britain tries to maintain the price at P_1 dollars, the British government will have to exchange dollars for $(Q_S - Q_D)$ pounds.

 TEST YOUR UNDERSTANDING

True or false?

_____ **1** If the rate of inflation in Italy is higher than in the United States, the Italian lira is likely to appreciate relative to the U.S. dollar.

_____ **2** An increase in Britain's interest rates promotes the appreciation of its currency.

Exercise

1 In 1981, the annual inflation rate in Argentina pushed above 100 percent for the fourth time in five years. Whereas 40,000 Argentinian pesos were a fortune in 1948, they could not buy a simple restaurant meal with wine in 1981. According to the

United Nations, the behavior of Argentina's price level during the 1970s was as follows:

YEAR	PRICE LEVEL (1970 = 100)
1970	100
1971	135
1973	342
1975	1,202
1977	18,050

During the 1970s, do you think that the Argentinian peso depreciated or appreciated relative to the dollar?

3 ■ Fixed Exchange Rates

Although many economists believed that exchange rates should be allowed to fluctuate, very few exchange rates really did so in the period from the end of World War II up to 1973. Instead, *most exchange rates were fixed by government action and international agreement.* Although they may have varied slightly about the fixed level, the extent to which they were allowed to vary was small. Every now and then, governments changed the exchange rates, for reasons discussed below; but for long periods of time, they remained fixed.

If exchange rates remain fixed, the amount demanded of a foreign currency may not equal the amount supplied. Consider the situation in Figure 17.4. If A is the demand curve for German marks, the equilibrium price of a mark is $.40. But suppose the fixed exchange rate between

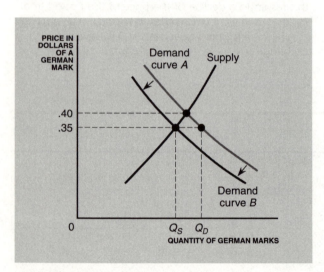

■ **FIGURE 17.4**

Fixed Exchange Rate

The equilibrium price of a German mark is $.40 if A is the demand curve. If $.35 is the fixed exchange rate, the U.S. government may try to shift the demand curve for marks from A to B, and thus bring the equilibrium exchange rate into equality with the fixed exchange rate.

dollars and marks is .35 to 1—that is, each mark exchanges for $.35. Unless the government intervenes, more German marks will be demanded at a price of $.35 per mark than will be offered. Specifically, the difference between the quantity demanded and the quantity supplied will be $Q_D - Q_S$. Unless the government steps in, a black market for German marks may develop, and the real price may increase toward $.40 per mark.

TYPES OF GOVERNMENT INTERVENTION

To maintain exchange rates at their fixed levels, governments can intervene in a variety of ways. For example, they may reduce the demand for foreign currencies by reducing defense expenditures abroad, by limiting the amount that their citizens can travel abroad, and by curbing imports from other countries. Thus, in the case depicted in Figure 17.4, the U.S. government might adopt some or all of these measures to shift the demand curve for German marks downward and to the left. If the demand curve can be pushed from A to B, the equilibrium price of a German mark can be reduced to $.35, the fixed exchange rate. For the time being, there will no longer be any mismatch between the quantity of marks demanded and the quantity supplied.

When exchange rates are fixed, mismatches of this sort cannot be eliminated entirely and permanently. To deal with such temporary mismatches, governments enter the market and buy and sell their currencies in order to maintain fixed exchange rates. Take the case of post-World War II Britain. At times the amount of British pounds supplied exceeded the amount demanded. Then the British government bought up the excess at the fixed exchange rate. At other times, when the quantity demanded exceeded the amount supplied, the British government supplied the pounds desired at the fixed exchange rate. As long as the equilibrium exchange rate was close to (sometimes above and sometimes below) the fixed exchange rate, the amount of its currency the government sold at one time equaled, more or less, the amount it bought at another time.

But in some cases governments have tried to maintain a fixed exchange rate far from the equilibrium exchange rate. The British government tried during the 1960s to maintain the price (in dollars) of the pound at $2.80, even though the equilibrium price was about $2.40. The situation was as shown in Figure 17.5. Since the quantity of British pounds supplied exceeded the quantity demanded at the price of $2.80, the British government had to buy the difference. That is, it had to buy $(Q_S - Q_D)$ pounds with dollars. Moreover, it had to keep on exchanging dollars for pounds in these quantities for as long as the demand and supply curves remained in these positions. Such a situation could not go on indefinitely, since the British government eventually had to run out of dollars. How long it could go on depended on how big Britain's reserves of gold and foreign currency were.

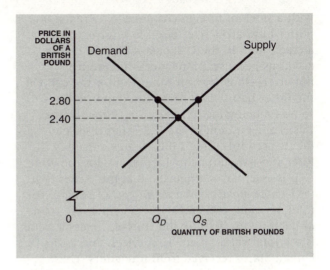

▪ **FIGURE 17.5**

The Market for British Pounds in the 1960s

Because the British pound is overvalued at $2.80, the quantity of pounds demanded (Q_D) is less than the quantity supplied (Q_S).

 TEST YOUR UNDERSTANDING

True or false?

_____ **1** To maintain exchange rates at fixed levels, governments may cut defense expenditures abroad.

_____ **2** Under fixed exchange rates, governments buy and sell their currencies.

_____ **3** From the end of World War II to 1973, most exchange rates were fixed by government action, but this is no longer true.

Exercise

1 Suppose that the exchange rate is fixed, and that the price (in dollars) of a mark is set at $.30. If the quantity of marks demanded is less than the quantity supplied, what sorts of government actions will have to be taken?

---

4 ▪ The Balance-of-Payments Accounts

The U.S. government publishes its **balance-of-payments accounts,** which are an important record of *the flow of payments between the United States and other countries.* There are two types of items in the balance-of-payments accounts: debit items and credit items. **Debit items** are items for which Americans must pay foreigners—items that use up the United States's foreign currency. **Credit items** are items for which Americans are paid by foreigners—items that provide the United States with a stock of foreign currency. If a French importer buys a U.S. car to sell in France, this is a credit item in the U.S. balance-of-payments accounts because a foreigner—the French importer—must pay an American for the car. On the other hand, if an American importer buys some French wine to sell in the United States, this is a debit item in the U.S. balance-of-payments accounts. The United States must pay the foreigner—the French winemaker—for the wine.

It is essential to understand at the outset that *the balance-of-payments accounts always balance.* The total of credit items must always equal the total of debit items, because the sum of the debit items is the total value of goods, services, and assets the United States received from foreigners. These goods, services, and assets must be paid for with credit items, since credit items provide the foreign currency required by foreigners. Since the debit items must be paid for by the credit items, *the sum of the credit items must equal the sum of the debit items.*

Under a system of fixed exchange rates, economists and financial analysts look at whether a country has a balance-of-payments deficit or surplus to see whether its currency is above or below its equilibrium value. What is a **balance-of-payments deficit?** What is a **balance-of-payments surplus?**

BALANCE-OF-PAYMENTS DEFICIT

If a country's currency is *overvalued* (that is, if its fixed price exceeds the equilibrium price), the quantity supplied of its currency will exceed the quantity demanded. Let's return to the case in which the price of the British pound was set at $2.80. Under these circumstances, the quantity supplied of pounds exceeds the quantity demanded by $(Q_S - Q_D)$ pounds, as shown in Figure 17.6. This amount—$(Q_S - Q_D)$ pounds—is Britain's balance-of-payments deficit (see Figure 17.6). It is the number of pounds that Britain's central bank, the Bank of England, must purchase. To pay for these pounds, the Bank of England must give up some of its *reserves* of foreign currencies or gold.

In a situation of this sort, there may be a run on the overvalued currency. Suppose that specu-

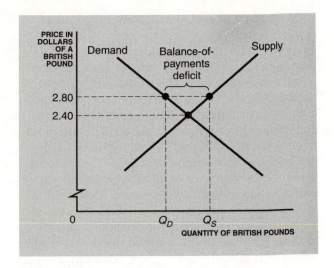

▪ **FIGURE 17.6**

Balance-of-Payments Deficit

Because the British pound is overvalued at $2.80, the quantity of pounds demanded (Q_D) is less than the quantity supplied (Q_S). The shortfall—that is, $(Q_S - Q_D)$ pounds—is the balance-of-payments deficit.

lators become convinced that the country with the balance-of-payments deficit cannot maintain the artificially high price of its currency much longer because its reserves are running low. Because they will suffer losses if they hold on to a currency that is devalued, the speculators are likely to sell the overvalued currency (in Figure 17.6, the British pound) in very large amounts and thus cause an even bigger balance-of-payments deficit for the country with the overvalued currency. Faced with the exhaustion of its reserves, the country is likely to be forced to allow the price of its currency to fall.

BALANCE-OF-PAYMENTS SURPLUS

If a country's currency is *undervalued* (that is, if its price is less than the equilibrium price), the quantity demanded of its currency will exceed the quantity supplied. During the early 1970s, the price of the German mark was set at $.35, even though its equilibrium price was about $.40. As shown in Figure 17.7, the quantity of marks demanded exceeds the quantity supplied by $(Q'_D - Q'_S)$ marks under these circumstances. This amount—$(Q'_D - Q'_S)$ marks—is Germany's balance-of-payments surplus (see Figure 17.7). Germany can keep the price of the mark at $.35 only if it provides these $(Q'_D - Q'_S)$ marks in exchange for foreign currencies and gold. By doing so, it increases its reserves.

Whereas a country with an overvalued currency is likely to be forced by the reduction in its reserves to reduce the price of its currency, a country with an undervalued currency is unlikely to be forced by the increase in its reserves to increase the price of its currency. And a country with an undervalued currency often is reluctant to increase the price of its currency, because of political pressures by its exporters (and their workers), who point out that such a revaluation would make the country's goods more expensive in foreign markets and thus would reduce its exports. Consequently, when exchange rates were fixed, countries with undervalued currencies were less likely to adjust their exchange rates than countries with overvalued currencies.

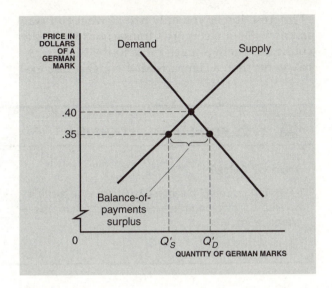

▪ **FIGURE 17.7**

Balance-of-Payments Surplus

Because the German mark is undervalued at $.35, the quantity of marks demanded (Q'_D) is greater than the quantity supplied (Q'_S). The surplus—that is, $(Q'_D) - (Q'_S)$ marks—is the balance-of-payments surplus.

 TEST YOUR UNDERSTANDING

True or false?

____ **1** The balance of payments accounts always balance.

____ **2** When IBM Corporation's British subsidiary sends its profits to the United States, this is a credit item in the United Kingdom's balance-of-payments accounts.

____ **3** When Volkswagen buys a plant in Pennsylvania, this is a credit item in the U.S. balance-of-payments accounts.

____ **4** If a U.S. importer buys a German car and sells it in the United States, this is a credit item in the U.S. balance of payments.

---

5 ▪ The Balance of Trade

The newspapers often mention the balance of trade. The **balance of merchandise trade** refers only to a part of the balance-of-payments accounts. A country is said to have a *favorable* balance of merchandise trade if its exports of merchandise are more than its imports of merchandise, and an *unfavorable* balance of merchandise trade if its exports of merchandise are less than its imports of merchandise.

Although the balance of merchandise trade is

of interest, it tells you only part of what you want to know about a country's transactions with other countries. There is much more to the balance of payments than a comparison of merchandise exports with merchandise imports. Moreover, a "favorable" balance of trade is not necessarily a good thing, since imports, not exports, contribute to a country's standard of living.

 TEST YOUR UNDERSTANDING

True or false?

_____ **1** A country's balance of merchandise trade is favorable if merchandise exports are less than merchandise imports.

Exercise

1 "Under flexible exchange rates, reserves play a much less important role than under fixed exchange rates." What does this mean? Do you agree? Why, or why not?

■ CHAPTER REVIEW

KEY TERMS

exchange rate
appreciation
depreciation

balance-of-payments accounts
debit items
credit items

balance-of-payments deficit
balance-of-payments surplus
balance of merchandise trade

COMPLETION QUESTIONS

1 If the U.S. economy is growing more rapidly than other economies, the United States's (exports, imports) _____ are likely to grow more rapidly than its (exports, imports) _____. Thus, U.S. demand for foreign currency will grow (more, less) _____ rapidly than the amount of foreign currency supplied. Consequently the dollar is likely to _____.

2 If the rate of interest is higher in Japan than in Germany, investors will sell _____ and buy _____ in order to switch from the lower-yielding German securities to the higher-yielding Japanese securities. Consequently the mark will tend to _____ relative to the yen.

3 When exchange rates are allowed to fluctuate freely, they are determined by _____.

4 A country's _____ measures the flow of payments between it and other countries.

ANSWERS TO COMPLETION QUESTIONS

imports
exports
more

depreciate

German marks
Japanese yen

depreciate

supply and demand

balance of payments

5 When country A's currency becomes more valuable relative to country B's currency, country A's currency is said to _____ relative to that of country B, and country B's currency is said to _____ relative to that of country A.

appreciate
depreciate

6 In a country's balance-of-payments accounts, the total of _____ items must always equal the total of _____ items, because the sum of the _____ items is the total value of goods, services, and assets the country receives from foreigners. These goods, services, and assets must be paid for with _____ items, since _____ items provide the foreign currency required by foreigners.

credit
debit
debit

credit
credit

7 Debit items (provide, use up) _____ foreign currency, and credit items (provide, use up) _____ foreign currency. Since the amount of foreign currency _____ must equal the amount _____, the sum of the credit items must equal the sum of the debit items.

use up

provide
used up
required

NUMERICAL PROBLEMS

1 The supply curve for Japanese radios to the U.S. market is shown below for two periods of time.

a One curve is before a depreciation of the dollar relative to the yen; one curve is after it. Which curve is which? Why?

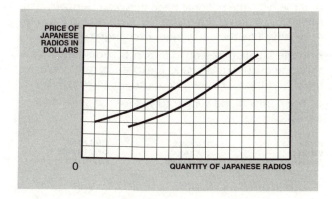

b What will be the effect of the depreciation on the dollar price of Japanese radios?

c What will be the effect on U.S. expenditures (in dollars) for Japanese radios, if the demand for them in the United States is price elastic?

d What will be the effect on U.S. expenditures (in dollars) for Japanese radios, if the demand for them in the United States is price inelastic?

2 Suppose that the demand curve in Japan for U.S. computers is as shown below.

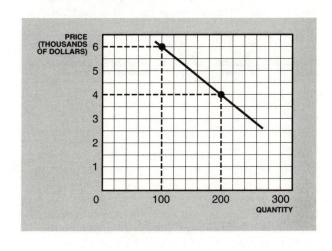

a If the Japanese yen depreciates relative to the U.S. dollar, will the quantity of computers sold in Japan at a dollar price of $4,000 rise or fall?

b Under these circumstances, will the demand curve rise or fall?

c Under these circumstances, will the dollar expenditures on U.S. computers in Japan rise or fall?

3 The following transactions occurred between the land of Oz and the rest of the world:

	(millions of dollars)
Purchases by residents of Oz of securities from foreigners	50
Imports by Oz of goods and services	100
Exports by Oz of goods and services	120
Gifts received from other countries	30
Sales of securities to foreigners	60
Gold imports	60

Show that the sum of the debit items equals the sum of the credit items in the balance-of-payments accounts for Oz.

4 a Suppose that people in Germany want to import a product from the United States. If the product costs $5 in the United States, how much will it cost in Germany if the exchange rate is 3 marks = 1 dollar? If the exchange rate is 4 marks = 1 dollar? If the exchange rate is 2 marks = 1 dollar?

b Suppose that the quantity of the product (in part a) demanded in Germany is related to its price (in marks) in the way indicated below. The table below shows the desired expenditure by Germans on this product at various levels of the exchange rate. Fill in the blanks.

EXCHANGE RATE	U.S. PRICE OF GOOD (dollars)	GERMAN PRICE OF GOOD (marks)	QUANTITY DEMANDED	TOTAL DESIRED EXPENDITURE (dollars)
4 marks = 1 dollar	5	_____	500	_____
3 marks = 1 dollar	5	_____	1,000	_____
2 marks = 1 dollar	5	_____	1,200	_____

c Plot the relationship between the price of a dollar (in marks) and the quantity of dollars demanded by the Germans to buy the product in parts a and b.

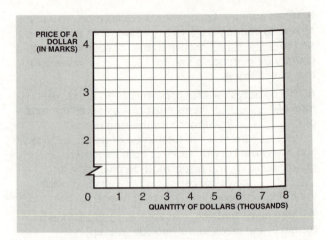

5 a Suppose that people in the United States want to import a product from Germany. The following table relates to the demand for this good in the United States. It shows the desired expenditure on this product by Americans at various levels of the exchange rate. Fill in the blanks.

EXCHANGE RATE	GERMAN PRICE OF GOOD (marks)	U.S. PRICE OF GOOD (dollars)	QUANTITY DEMANDED	TOTAL DESIRED EXPENDITURE (dollars)
4 marks = 1 dollar	12	_____	2,000	_____
3 marks = 1 dollar	12	_____	1,250	_____
2 marks = 1 dollar	12	_____	500	_____

b If the only international trade between Germany and the United States is that described here and in Problem 4, what will be the equilibrium exchange rate?

c In the situation described in part b, would there be a shortage or surplus of marks if exchange rates were fixed, and the exchange rate for the mark was $.30?

6 The demand and supply curves for the Swiss franc are as follows:

PRICE OF FRANC (dollars)	MILLIONS OF FRANCS DEMANDED	MILLIONS OF FRANCS SUPPLIED
.80	300	400
.70	320	370
.60	340	340
.50	360	310
.40	380	280

a What is the equilibrium price (in Swiss francs) for the dollar?

b What is the equilibrium price (in dollars) for the Swiss franc?

c How many dollars will be bought in the market?

d How many Swiss francs will be bought in the market?

7 The demand curve for British pounds is as follows:

PRICE OF BRITISH POUND (dollars)	MILLIONS OF POUNDS DEMANDED
2.00	200
2.10	190
2.20	180
2.30	170
2.40	160
2.50	150

a Suppose that the British government sets the exchange rate at $2.40, and that the quantity of pounds supplied at this exchange rate is 180 million pounds. Will the British government have to buy or sell pounds? If so, how many?

b If the British government has to buy pounds with dollars, where will it get the dollars?

✔ ANSWERS TO TEST YOUR UNDERSTANDING

SECTION 1

TRUE OR FALSE: 1. True   2. False   3. True

EXERCISES

1. and 2. Demanders of marks include buyers of German exports, foreign tourists in Germany, and foreign buyers of German financial assets. Both the demand curve and the supply curve are shown below.

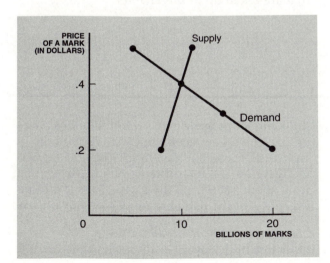

3. $.40 per mark, since at this exchange rate the quantity of marks demanded equals the quantity supplied.

SECTION 2

TRUE OR FALSE: 1. False   2. True

EXERCISE

1. It depreciated relative to the dollar.

SECTION 3

TRUE OR FALSE: 1. True   2. True   3. True

EXERCISE

1. Eventually, the price of a mark may have to be reduced.

SECTION 4

TRUE OR FALSE: 1. True   2. False   3. True   4. False

SECTION 5

TRUE OR FALSE: 1. False

EXERCISE

1. The market, through changing exchange rates, tends to erase payments imbalances within a flexible exchange rate system. Reserves are required to maintain fixed exchange rates in the face of payments imbalances.

■ CHAPTER 18

Should the 1994 Trade Agreement Have Passed?

1 ■ Introduction

In November 1994, one of the big questions in Washington, D.C., was whether Congress would approve a world trade agreement which had taken 12 years to negotiate and which involved 123 countries. President Clinton said, "We must pass [it], and we should do it right away. It is critical for U.S. leadership in the world."[1] But Jesse Helms, incoming chairman of the Senate Foreign Relations Committee, threatened to withhold cooperation with the Clinton administration's foreign policy initiatives unless the vote was delayed until the new Congress convened in January 1995. Vice President Gore responded that "It is abundantly clear that a delay . . . would kill it."[2]

This agreement, the result of the so-called Uruguay Round negotiations, called for the reduction of tariffs on merchandise trade, as well as new international rules concerning agriculture,

textiles, trade in services, investment, and intellectual property rights. According to President Clinton's Council of Economic Advisers, "The Uruguay Round will increase American output because the specialization encouraged by more-open markets will raise productivity."[3]

But not everyone felt the agreement was in their interest. In North Carolina, Senator Helms's home state, many people who worked at textile mills feared that they could be hurt by reduced tariffs. According to Senator Ernest Hollings of South Carolina, "Free Trade is the new Vietnam policy. You destroy your economy to save the world."[4] How far should the United States go toward free trade? Why shouldn't it protect its industries and workers from foreign competition? These are the basic and controversial questions that are taken up in this chapter.

2 ■ The Period Up to 1950

To begin with, look at the United States's past performance in this regard. In its early years, the United States was a very protectionist country. During the nineteenth century and well into the twentieth, the industrial Northeast was particularly strong in its support of tariffs. Furthermore,

the Republican party, which generally held sway in U.S. politics between the Civil War and the New Deal, favored a high tariff. Thus, as shown in Figure 18.1, the tariff remained relatively high from about 1870 until the early 1930s. With the exception of the period around World War I, av-

[1] *New York Times*, November 17, 1994, p. A1.

[2] Ibid., p. A22.

[3] *Economic Report of the President*, 1994, p. 234.

[4] *New York Times*, November 20, 1994, p. 4E.

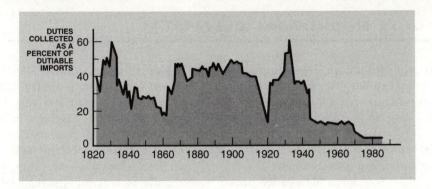

▪ **FIGURE 18.1**

Average U.S. Tariff Rates

The tariff generally remained high from about 1870 to the early 1930s; in recent decades it has decreased substantially.

erage tariff rates were about 40 to 50 percent. With the enactment of the Smoot-Hawley Tariff of 1930, the tariff reached its peak—about 60 percent.

With the Democratic victory in 1932, a movement began toward freer trade. The Trade Agreements Act of 1934 allowed the president to bargain with other countries to reduce barriers to trade. The president was given the power to lower U.S. tariffs by as much as 50 percent. In 1945, the president was given the power to make further tariff reductions. Between 1934 and 1948, tariff rates fell substantially, as shown in Figure 18.1. In 1947, the United States and 22 other countries signed the *General Agreement on Tariffs and Trade (GATT)*, which called for all participating countries to meet periodically to negotiate bilaterally on tariff cuts. Any tariff cut negotiated in this way was to be extended to all participating countries. By 1948, the United States was no longer a high-tariff country; the average tariff rate was only about 10 percent.

3 ▪ The Kennedy Round and the European Community

During the 1950s, there were no further decreases in the tariff—but there were no substantial increases either. The movement toward freer trade was continued by President Kennedy in 1962, and during the 1960s, the Kennedy Round of GATT negotiations took place among about 40 countries in an attempt to reduce tariffs. In 1967, the United States agreed to cut tariffs by about one-third on a great many items.

The negotiations during the 1960s were prompted by the establishment of the *European Economic Community (EEC)*—or *Common Market*. The EEC was composed originally of Belgium, France, West Germany, Holland, Italy, and Luxembourg; and in the late 1970s, Britain, Denmark, and Ireland joined. When the EEC was formed, the member countries agreed to reduce the tariff barriers against one another's goods—but not against the goods of other countries. Exporters in the United States were concerned about this, because the members of the Common Market still maintained their tariff barriers against U.S. goods. While the Kennedy Round negotiations succeeded in reducing some of the tariff barriers between the United States and the Common Market, important tariff barriers remained, particularly for agricultural products.

4 ■ Further GATT Negotiations and NAFTA

In 1973, over 100 countries met in Tokyo to plan a new round of trade negotiations. The aim was to make progress toward the reduction of both tariffs and nontariff barriers to trade. (In recent years, tariffs have been replaced to some extent by nontariff barriers to trade.) After over five years of difficult negotiations, an agreement was approved in April 1979. This agreement called for the industrial countries to reduce tariffs on thousands of goods by an average of about 33 percent during an eight-year period. It also tried to reduce export subsidies, phony technical standards for imports (used to keep out foreign goods), and barriers to international bidding for government contracts.

In the 1980s, a new round of negotiations, called the Uruguay Round, began. An attempt was made to curtail domestic subsidies for farmers, which distort international trade, as well as to reduce nontariff barriers to trade. Also, the industrialized countries like the United States tried to get the developing countries like India and Brazil to protect intellectual property rights (like patents and copyrights) more effectively. The negotiations did not fulfill these objectives. In December 1990, the trade officials participating in the negotiations gave up, and suspended the talks. But international discussions of these issues continued, and eventually agreement was reached on some of these matters in late 1993. On December 1, 1994, after the controversy described at the beginning of this chapter, Congress passed the agreement.

In 1993, Congress also ratified the North American Free Trade Agreement (NAFTA), which created a free-trade area composed of Canada, Mexico, and the United States. Fought by labor unions and environmentalists in particular, this agreement was expected to promote economic growth in these countries. According to the Clinton administration, it "is an epochal agreement, and its passage was a triumph of facts over fear."[5]

5 ■ Strategic Trade Policy

In recent years, an influential band of young economists, led by MIT's Paul Krugman and others, have argued that, in today's world, countries may find it worthwhile to engage in strategic trade policies to secure higher incomes for their residents. Thus, if only two highly profitable firms can exist in a particular industry, it may make sense for countries to use subsidies or tariffs to raise the probability that one of their firms will be one of the fortunate pair. Or if certain high-technology industries result in large technological benefits to the rest of the economy, it may make sense to use subsidies or tariffs to promote and protect these sectors.

Of course, all of this departs from the conventional economic view that nations are best off by promoting free trade. As Krugman indicates,

The new approaches open up the possibility that there may be "strategic" sectors after all. Because of the important roles now being given to economies of scale, advantages of experience, and innovation as explanations of trading patterns, it seems more likely that . . . labor or capital will sometimes earn significantly higher returns in some industries than in others. Because of the increased role of technological competition, it has become more plausible to argue that certain sectors yield important [social benefits], so producers are not in fact paid the full social value of their production.

What all this means is that the extreme pro-free-trade position—that markets work so well that they cannot be improved on—has become untenable. In this sense the new approaches to international trade provide a potential rationale for a turn by the United States toward a more activist trade policy.[6]

[5] *Economic Report of the President*, 1994, p. 230.

[6] Paul Krugman (ed.), *Strategic Trade Policy and the New International Economics* (Cambridge, Mass.: MIT Press, 1986), p. 15.

However, these new approaches raise a great many unanswered questions. How can you identify strategic sectors? It is very difficult to specify the industries where the returns to capital and labor are very high and where public policy could raise GDP by encouraging them to go into the sector. Also, it is very difficult to measure the extent of the social benefits that will result from various kinds of investments. To what extent will these new approaches be used by interest groups to advocate policies that will not benefit the country as a whole? Given the vagueness of the criteria for identifying strategic sectors, many groups could use these ideas to justify protection for themselves and their allies.

Because of such questions, many economists, such as Princeton's Avinash Dixit, are skeptical concerning the usefulness of strategic trade policy. According to Dixit, "The idea that free trade promotes the general interest, and that departures from it are motivated by various special interests, . . . still stands and continues to govern the overwhelming majority of the volume of world trade. . . ."[7] Nonetheless, there can be no doubt that the proponents of strategic trade policy have had a substantial impact on economists and policymakers.

6 ▪ Increased Protectionism

Recent years have seen a marked increase in protectionist feelings in the United States. As Western Europe and Japan have become more formidable competitors abroad and at home, many industries have pressed for quotas and higher tariffs. The automobile, steel, and textile industries have been among the most frequent petitioners for protection. In 1981, the Japanese agreed to limit import of Japanese autos into the United States to 1.68 million per year; by 1988, the quota was increased to 2.3 million per year. The United States stopped asking for the restraints in 1985, but Japan "voluntarily" decided to keep them.

In the mid-1980s, hundreds of petitions were filed by industry and labor, asking the federal government to protect them from imports. In considerable part, this was due to the very strong dollar. The dollar's value relative to other currencies rose markedly during the early 1980s, the result being that foreign goods became much cheaper to U.S. buyers. Also, in some industries like semiconductors, the quality of foreign goods sometimes exceeded that of U.S. suppliers. Faced with very stiff competition from imports, U.S. firms asked the government for protection. In the late 1980s and early 1990s, although the value of the dollar fell substantially, protectionist pressure continued.

[7] Ibid., p. 302.

7 ▪ Applying Economics: The Pros and Cons of Tariffs and Quotas

The following two problems are concerned with the arguments for and against tariffs and quotas.

PROBLEM 18.1 One of the most convincing arguments for tariffs or quotas is the desirability of maintaining a domestic industry for purposes of *national defense*. Thus, even if the Swedes had a comparative advantage in producing airplanes, the United States would not allow free trade to put its domestic producers of aircraft out of business if it felt that a domestic aircraft industry was necessary for national defense.

Although the Swedes are by no means unfriendly, the United States would not want to import its entire supply of such a critical commodity from a foreign country, where the supply might be shut off for reasons of international politics. (Recall the Arab oil embargo of 1973.)

This is a perfectly valid reason for protecting certain domestic industries, and many protective measures are defended on these grounds. To the extent that protective measures are in fact required for national defense, economists go along with them. The restrictions entail social costs, but these costs may well be worth paying for enhanced national security. The trouble is that many barriers to free trade are justified on these grounds when in fact they protect domestic industries only tenuously connected with national defense. Moreover, even if there is a legitimate case on defense grounds for protecting a domestic industry, subsidies are likely to be a more straight- forward and efficient way to do so than tariffs or quotas.

a. Is national defense the only justification for tariffs or quotas? Can they be justified to foster the growth or development of young industries?

b. Are tariffs and quotas often imposed to protect domestic jobs and to reduce unemployment at home? If so, are they the most sensible means of attaining these objectives?

c. Are tariffs or quotas sometimes imposed to prevent a country from being too dependent on only a few industries? For example, consider a Latin American country that is a major producer of bananas. Under free trade, this country might produce bananas and little else, and thus put the entire economy at the mercy of the banana market. If the price of bananas fell, the country's economy might be hurt badly. Under these circumstances, might this country adopt tariffs or quotas? Would the tariffs or quotas be on bananas? If not, what would they be on?

d. Can tariffs sometimes improve a country's terms of trade—that is, the ratio of its export prices to its import prices? If so, how?

PROBLEM 18.2 Many arguments for tariffs or quotas are fallacious. Special-interest groups—particular industries, unions, and regions—have a lot to gain by getting the government to enact protective tariffs and quotas. And Congress and the executive branch of the government are often sensitive to the pressures of these groups, which wield considerable political power. Faced with a choice between helping a few powerful, well-organized groups and helping the general public—which is poorly organized and often ignorant of its own interests—politicians frequently tend to favor the special-interest groups. After all, these groups have a lot to gain and will remember their friends, while the general public—each member of which loses only a relatively small amount—will be largely unaware of its losses anyhow. Having decided to help these groups, representatives or senators may not exert themselves unduly to search out or expose the weakness in some of the arguments the groups use to bolster their position.

a. One frequently encountered fallacy is the following: "If foreigners want to trade with us, they must be benefiting from the trade. Consequently, we must be giving them more than we get—and it must be in our interest to reduce trade." What is wrong with this argument?

b. Another fallacy that often appears in political (and other) debate is as follows: "A tariff or quota is required to protect our workers from low-wage labor in other countries. Since U.S. labor (at $10 per hour) clearly cannot compete with labor in Asia or Latin America (some of which works at extremely low wage levels), we have no choice but to impose tariffs or quotas." What is wrong with this argument?

c. Still another fallacy that makes the rounds (and which Abraham Lincoln is supposed to have subscribed to) is the following: "It is better to buy from other Americans because then we have both the goods that are bought and the money, whereas if we buy from foreigners we have the goods but they have the money." What is wrong with this argument?

8 ■ Applying Economics: The Auto and Shoe Industries

The following two problems deal with the effects of tariffs or quotas in the automobile and shoe industries.

PROBLEM 18.3 When the first Japanese cars arrived on the West Coast in the 1970s, no one saw them as a threat to U.S. jobs. Although they were cheaper and more fuel-efficient than U.S.-made cars, most Americans couldn't be bothered; with gasoline at 30 cents a gallon, the difference in cost between a car that got 30 miles per gallon and one that got 10 was not very great, even for someone who drove a lot.

But all this changed with the Arab oil embargo of 1973. As gas prices climbed, Americans took another look at small foreign cars. With expensive U.S. labor and outmoded facilities on one side, and Japanese efficiency and management techniques on the other, Japan seemed to be winning the war in the showroom.

Although imports may create as many jobs as they consume in the long run, in the short run many smokestack industry workers can be left permanently unemployed or underemployed. Worried U.S. workers wanted protection, and they found a strong advocate in Representative John Dingell, one of the leaders of an emerging protectionist movement in Congress. Dingell spoke with President Reagan and Trade Representative William Brock, and urged that if voluntary restrictions on Japanese auto imports weren't adopted, Congress would impose mandatory ones. Faced with this choice, the Japanese agreed in negotiations to voluntary restrictions.

The restrictions worked. As the number of Japanese auto imports dropped between 1981 and 1982, domestic auto industry employment rose. But the cost of saving hundreds of *thousands* of U.S. jobs was restricted choice and higher prices for hundreds of *millions* of U.S. consumers. Hefty dealer markups were imposed on the scarcer but still-popular imports, and as sticker prices rose on Toyotas and Datsuns, General Motors, Ford, and Chrysler found that they could raise prices too.

a. Who were hurt by the restrictions on Japanese auto imports?

b. Who were benefited by the restrictions on Japanese auto imports?

c. Does free trade benefit everyone? Why or why not?

d. In 1993, Robert Lutz, president of the Chrysler Corporation, said that "the European Community told Japanese automakers that they can have no more than 16 percent of the European auto market through the end of this century. . . . [By] and large, they have, in my opinion, found a much better trade-off than we have between the so-called rights of the consumer and *also*—very—legitimate rights of those very same citizens to be gainfully employed."[8] Do you agree? Why or why not?

e. Robert Crandall of the Brookings Institute estimated that auto import quotas resulted in about a $400 per car increase in the price of U.S. cars and a $1,000 per car increase in the price of Japanese imports, with a total annual cost to U.S. consumers of over $4 billion. According to Crandall, "The cost per job saved, therefore, was nearly $160,000 per year."[9] Does this cost seem excessive? Why or why not?

PROBLEM 18.4 The quantity of shoes demanded in the United States at each price of a pair of shoes is shown in Figure 18.2. In addition, the quantities of shoes supplied by U.S. producers and by foreign producers at each price are shown too.

a. Assuming that the market for shoes is competitive, what is the equilibrium price of a pair of shoes in the United States?

[8] R. Lutz, "Managed Trade," in E. Mansfield (ed.), *Leading Economic Controversies of 1997* (New York: Norton, 1997).

[9] R. Crandall, "Import Quotas and the Automobile Industry", *Brookings Review,* Summer 1984, p. 16.

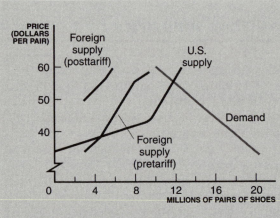

▪ **FIGURE 18.2**

b. What proportion of the U.S. market goes to foreign producers of shoes?

c. Suppose that the United States imposes a tariff of $15 per pair of shoes. How many pairs of shoes will foreign producers now supply if the price is (1) $50, (2) $55, (3) $60? (Note that a $50 price together with a $15 tariff means that the price to the foreign producer is $50 − $15, or $35.)

d. After the imposition of the tariff, what is the equilibrium price?

e. After the imposition of the tariff, what proportion of the U.S. market goes to foreign producers of shoes?

f. How much revenue does the U.S. government get from this tariff?

9 ▪ Applying Economics: The U.S. Chronic Trade Deficit

The following two problems are concerned with the persistent deficit in the U.S. balance of trade.

PROBLEM 18.5 You probably know that the United States has been importing more than it has been exporting in recent years; in other words, it has been experiencing a trade deficit. What is less well known is that this trade deficit was not very large until the early 1980s. The deterioration of the U.S. trade balance was not confined to certain sectors. Between 1982 and 1986, the U.S. merchandise trade balance worsened in nine of ten major product classifications. Also, our bilateral trade balances with practically all of our major trading partners, such as Japan, worsened during this period. During the late 1980s, our trade deficit seemed to decline, but remained large, as shown in Figure 18.3.

a. Should the United States be concerned about a large trade deficit of this sort? Why or why not?

b. Isn't it obvious that the United States should impose tariffs and quotas to reduce its imports? Isn't this the way to bring its imports into line with exports? Why or why not?

c. Paul Volcker, former chairman of the Federal Reserve, said in 1984, "Over the past year, our needs have been increasingly met by savings from abroad in the form of a new capital inflow. . . . We simply can't have it both ways—on the one hand, look abroad for increasing help in financing the credits related to our budget deficit, our housing, and our investment, and on the other hand, expect to narrow the growing gap in our trade accounts. At the end of the day, the counterpart of a net capital inflow is a net deficit on our current account—trade and services—with other countries." Does this mean that there is little the United States can do about its trade deficit? Why or why not?

PROBLEM 18.6 Some observers believe that the U.S. trade deficit is due to barriers erected by foreign countries against the importation of our goods and services. Others say it is because U.S. industry cannot compete with foreign producers. In 1993, Robert Parry, president of the Federal Reserve Bank of San Francisco, said: "I think we can find the sources of the trade deficit in certain macroeconomic fundamentals—namely our own government budget deficit and our investment and saving patterns."[10] Recall from Chapter 1 that

$$GDP = C + I + G + (X - M_I), \quad (18.1)$$

where C is consumption expenditure, I is investment expenditure, G is government expenditure, and $(X - M_I)$ is net exports. Since GDP can only be consumed, saved, or taxed, it is also true that

$$GDP = C + S + T, \quad (18.2)$$

where S is saving and T is taxes.

a. On the basis of Equations (18.1) and (18.2), show in an equation how $(X - M_I)$ depends on $(S - I)$ and $(G - T)$.

b. If $(S - I)$ is held constant, will increases in the government budget deficit cause increases in the trade deficit? Why or why not?

c. If the government budget deficit is held constant, will reductions in $(S - I)$ cause increases in the trade deficit? Why or why not?

d. Do you agree that the United States's trade deficit may be due to the government budget deficit and its investment and saving patterns?

[10] R. Parry, "U.S. Trade Deficits and International Competitiveness," in Mansfield, *Leading Economic Controversies of 1997.*

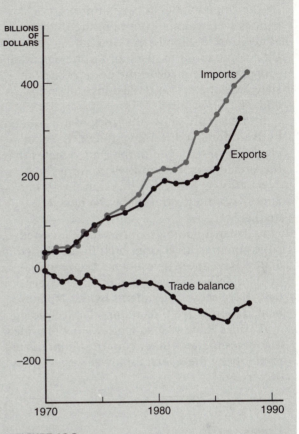

▪ **FIGURE 18.3**

U.S. Imports, Exports, and Trade Balance, 1970–1989

10 ▪ Applying Economics: Are Foreigners Buying Up the United States? Is NAFTA a Mistake?

The final two problems deal with investment by foreigners in the United States and with the North American Free Trade Agreement.

PROBLEM 18.7 Besides being concerned about their country's chronic trade deficit, many

Americans have been uneasy about the sale of U.S. facilities to foreigners. When the Sony Corporation bought Columbia Pictures and when the Mitsubishi Estate bought Rockefeller Center, there was considerable controversy. Fear was expressed that foreigners were buying up the United States at bargain prices, that foreigners were gaining control of the United States, and that foreigners were taking over U.S. corporations to steal our technology. Many proposals were made in the Congress and in state legislatures that foreign investment be curbed.

a. Table 18.1 shows the stock of inward and outward foreign direct investment. Have foreigners invested more in the United States than the United States has in their countries?

b. Why do foreigners invest in the United States? Are they attracted by the huge U.S. market?

c. Japanese auto producers have invested large amounts in factories built in the United States. Have these investments been motivated by their desire to steal U.S. automotive technology? Have these investments by the Japanese helped to improve U.S. automotive technology?

d. Does Table 18.1 support the popular idea that investment in other countries is motivated primarily by the search for lower wages? Why or why not?

■ **TABLE 18.1**

Stock of Inward and Outward Foreign Direct Investment, 1992

COUNTRY	(billions of dollars)
Investment by foreign firms in the United States (Inward)	
Japan	97
United Kingdom	95
Netherlands	61
Canada	39
Germany	29
All countries	420
Investment by U.S. firms abroad (Outward)	
United Kingdom	78
Canada	68
Germany	35
Switzerland	29
Japan	26
All countries	487

SOURCE: *Economic Report of the President*, 1994.

e. Some people object to the movement of U.S. factories outside the United States on the grounds that jobs are being exported. Is it true that, if a U.S. firm builds a plant in Europe or Asia, the effect will be to reduce its employment in the United States? Why or why not?

f. In November 1994, Sony Corporation reported that it had incurred losses of over $3 billion on its investment in Columbia Pictures and Tristar Pictures, and Mitsubishi Estate disclosed that it might have to default on the mortgage on Rockefeller Center.[11] Does it appear that Japanese investors threaten to take over U.S. industry?

PROBLEM 18.8   The reduction of trade barriers between Mexico and the United States caused great controversy. For example, Lane Kirkland, former president of the AFL-CIO, the leading labor organization in the United States, was vehemently opposed to NAFTA. In 1993, he said that: "What Mexico brings . . . is essentially this—a plentiful and growing supply of very badly paid labor, under a government that intends to keep it that way. . . . [D]ownhill is where American wages, standards and jobs would go. . . ."[12]

a. Isn't it obvious that U.S. jobs will be transferred to Mexico, given that wages are relatively low there? Why or why not?

b. Isn't it obvious that U.S. firms will invest more in Mexico and less in the United States, and that this will be detrimental to the United States? Why or why not?

c. The Clinton administration argued that NAFTA would help to raise the rate of economic growth in Mexico. According to President Clinton's Council of Economic Advisers, "A stable and prosperous Mexico is important to the United States for both economic and geopolitical reasons."[13] Do you agree? Why or why not?

[11] *New York Times*, November 18, 1994.
[12] L. Kirkland, "Labor Unions and Change," ibid.
[13] *Economic Report of the President*.

11 ▪ Conclusion

Regardless of whether you are a laborer or a manager, a Californian or a New Yorker, a Democrat or a Republican, you are bound to be affected, often very substantially, by the policies of the United States and other countries regarding international economics. As you've seen, the prices of products (ranging from autos to shoes), the nature and availability of jobs, and the location of industries are influenced by international trade and international finance. To understand developments in these areas, and how they affect you, it is essential that you understand the material in Chapters 16 and 17.

APPENDIX
Markets and Prices

Capitalist economies use the price system to perform the basic tasks any economic system must carry out. However, the U.S. economy is a mixed capitalist system, not a pure one. Both government and private decisions are important. This does not mean that the price system is unimportant. On the contrary, the price system plays a vital role in the U.S. economy, and to obtain even a minimal grasp of the workings of our economic system, you should understand how the price system operates. This appendix takes up the nature and functions of the price system, as well as some applications of our theoretical results to real-life problems.

1 ▪ Consumers and Firms

Take consumers and firms, the basic building blocks that make up the private, or nongovernmental, sector of the economy. What is a consumer? Sometimes—for example, when a person buys a beer on a warm day—the consumer is an individual. In other cases—for example, when a family buys a new car—the consumer may be an entire household. **Consumers** purchase the goods and services that are the end products of the economic system.

There are over 10 million firms in the United States. About nine-tenths of the goods and services produced in this country are produced by firms. (The rest are provided by government and not-for-profit institutions like universities and hospitals.) A **firm** is an organization that produces a good or service for sale. In contrast to not-for-profit organizations, firms attempt to make a profit. It is obvious that our economy is centered around the activities of firms.

Like consumers, firms are extremely varied in size, age, power, and purpose. Consider two examples, Peter Amacher's drugstore on Chicago's South Side and the General Motors Corporation. The Amacher drugstore, started in 1922 by Mr. Amacher's father-in-law, is known in the retail drug trade as an independent, because it has no affiliation with a chain-store organization. Mr. Amacher and two other pharmacists keep the store open for business 13 hours a day, except on Sundays. The store sells about $150,000 worth of merchandise per year.

In contrast, General Motors is one of the giants of U.S. industry. It is the largest manufacturer of automobiles in the United States. Besides cars, it makes trucks, locomotives, aircraft engines, household appliances, and other products. It has long been a leading symbol of industrial might, but during the 1980s and early 1990s it encountered formidable competition, particularly from Japanese cars.

2 ■ Markets

Consumers and firms come together in a market. The concept of a market is not quite as straightforward as it may seem, since most markets are not well defined geographically or physically. For example, the New York Stock Exchange is an atypical market because it is located principally in a particular building. For present purposes, *a market can be defined as a group of firms and individuals that are in touch with each other in order to buy or sell some good.* Of course, not every person in a market has to be in contact with every other person in the market. Persons or firms are part of a market even if they are in contact with only a subset of the other persons or firms in the market.

Markets vary enormously in their size and procedures. For some goods, like toothpaste, most people (assuming they have their own teeth and are interested in keeping them) are members of the same market; for other goods, like Picasso paintings, only a few connoisseurs (dealers, collectors, and museums in certain parts of the world) may be members of the market. And for still other goods, like lemonade sold by neighborhood children for a quarter a glass at a sidewalk stand, only people who walk by—and are brave enough to try the stuff—are members of the market. Basically, however, all markets consist primarily of buyers and sellers, although third parties like brokers and agents may be present as well.

Markets also vary in the extent to which they are dominated by a few large buyers or sellers. For example, in the United States, there was for many years only one producer of aluminum. This firm, the Aluminum Company of America, had great power in the market for aluminum. In contrast, the number of buyers and sellers in some other markets is so large that no single buyer or seller has any power over the price of the product. This is true in various agricultural markets, for example. When a market for a product contains so many buyers and sellers that none of them can influence the price, economists call the market **perfectly competitive.** For simplicity's sake, make the assumption in this appendix that markets are perfectly competitive.

3 ■ The Demand Side of a Market

Every market has a demand side and a supply side. *The **demand** side can be represented by a **market demand curve,** which shows the amount of the commodity buyers would like to purchase at various prices.* Consider Figure A1, which shows the demand curve for wheat in the U.S. market during the mid-1990s.[1] The figure shows that about 2.3 billion bushels of wheat will be demanded annually if the farm price is $3.50 per bushel, about 2.4 billion bushels will be demanded annually if the farm price is $3.10 per bushel, and about 2.5 billion bushels will be demanded annually if the farm price is $2.70 per bushel. The total demand for wheat is of several types: to produce bread and other food products for domestic use, for feed use, for export purposes, and for industrial uses. The demand curve in Figure A1 shows the total demand—including all these components—at each price.

Take a good look at the demand curve for wheat in Figure A1. This simple, innocent-looking curve influences a great many people's lives. After all, wheat is the principal grain used for direct human consumption in the United States. To states like Kansas, North Dakota, Oklahoma, Montana, Washington, Nebraska, Texas, Illinois,

---

[1] Officials of the U.S. Department of Agriculture provided this information. Of course, these estimates are only approximations, but they are good enough for present purposes.

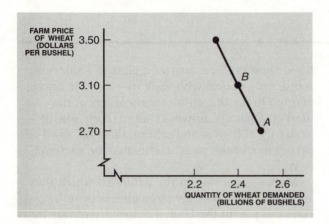

■ **FIGURE A1**

Market Demand Curve for Wheat, Mid-1990s

The curve shows the amount of wheat buyers would demand at various prices. At $2.70 per bushel, about 9 percent more wheat can be sold than at $3.50 per bushel.

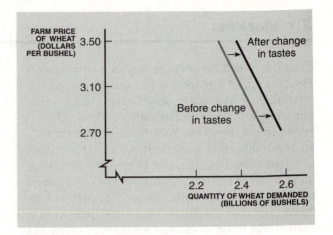

■ **FIGURE A2**

Effect of Increased Preference for Wheat on Market Demand Curve

An increased preference for wheat would shift the demand curve to the right.

Indiana, and Ohio, wheat is a very important cash crop. Note that the demand curve for wheat slopes downward to the right. In other words, the quantity of wheat demanded increases as the price falls. This is true of the demand curve for most commodities: they almost always slope downward to the right. This makes sense; you would expect increases in a good's price to result in a smaller quantity demanded.

Any demand curve is based on the assumption that the tastes, incomes, and number of consumers, as well as the prices of other commodities, are held constant. Changes in any of these factors are likely to shift the position of a commodity's demand curve, as indicated below.

CONSUMER TASTES If consumers show an increasing preference for a product, the demand curve will shift to the right; that is, at each price, consumers will desire to buy more than previously. On the other hand, if consumers show a decreasing preference for a product, the demand curve will shift to the left, since at each price, consumers will desire to buy less than previously. Take wheat: If consumers become convinced that foods containing wheat prolong life and promote happi-

ness, the demand curve may shift, as shown in Figure A2. The greater the shift in preferences, the larger the shift in the demand curve.

INCOME LEVEL OF CONSUMERS For some types of products, the demand curve shifts to the right if per capita income increases; for other types of commodities, the demand curve shifts to the left if per capita income rises. Economists can explain why some goods fall into one category and other goods fall into the other, but at present this need not concern you. All that is important here is that changes in per capita income affect the demand curve; the size and direction of this effect vary from product to product. In the case of wheat, a 10 percent increase in per capita income would probably have a relatively small effect on the demand curve, as shown in Figure A3.

NUMBER OF CONSUMERS IN THE MARKET Compare Austria's demand for wheat with that of the United States. Austria is a small country with a population of less than 8 million; the United States is a huge country with a population of over 200 million. Clearly, at a given price of wheat, the quantity demanded by U.S. consumers will

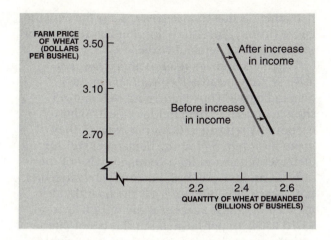

▪ **FIGURE A3**

Effect of Increase in Income on Market Demand Curve for Wheat

An increase in income would shift the demand curve for wheat to the right, but only slightly.

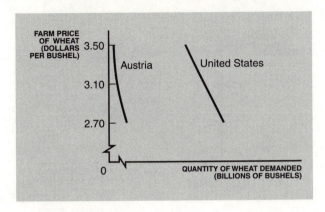

▪ **FIGURE A4**

Market Demand Curve for Wheat, Austria and the United States

Since the United States has far more consumers than Austria, the demand curve in the United States is far to the right of Austria's.

greatly exceed the quantity demanded by Austrian consumers, as shown in Figure A4. Even if consumer tastes, income, and other factors were held constant, this would still be true simply because the United States has so many more consumers in the relevant market.[2]

LEVEL OF OTHER PRICES   A commodity's demand curve can be shifted by a change in the price of other commodities. Whether an increase in the price of good B will shift the demand curve for good A to the right or the left depends on the relationship between the two goods. If they are substitutes, such an increase will shift the demand curve for good A to the right. Consider the case of corn and wheat. If the price of corn goes up, more wheat will be demanded since it will be profitable to substitute wheat for corn. If the price of corn drops, less wheat will be demanded since it will be profitable to substitute

corn for wheat. Thus, as shown in Figure A5, increases in the price of corn will shift the demand curve for wheat to the right, and decreases in the price of corn will shift it to the left.[3]

THE DISTINCTION BETWEEN CHANGES IN DEMAND AND CHANGES IN THE QUANTITY DEMANDED

It is essential to understand the difference between a *shift in a commodity's demand curve* and a change in the *quantity demanded of the commodity*. A shift in a commodity's demand curve is a change in the *relationship* between price and quantity demanded. Figures A2, A3, and A5 show cases where such a change occurs. A change in the quantity demanded of a commodity may occur even if *no* shift occurs in the commodity's

---

[2] Note that no figures are given along the horizontal axis in Figure A4. This is because we do not have reasonably precise estimates of the demand curve in Austria. Nonetheless, the hypothetical demand curves in Figure A4 are close enough to the mark for present purposes.

[3] If goods A and B are complements, an increase in the price of good B will shift the demand curve for good A to the left. Thus an increase in the price of chips is likely to shift the demand curve for salsa to the left. Why? Because chips and salsa tend to be used together. The increase in the price of chips will reduce the quantity of chips demanded; this in turn will reduce the amount of salsa that will be demanded at each price of salsa.

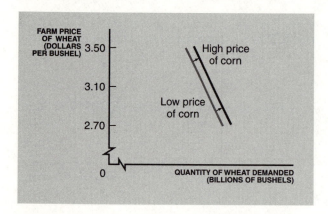

▪ **FIGURE A5**

Effect of Price of Corn on Market Demand Curve for Wheat

Price increases for corn will shift the demand curve for wheat to the right.

demand curve. For example, in Figure A1, if the price of wheat increases from $2.70 to $3.10 per bushel, the quantity demanded falls from 2.5 to 2.4 billion bushels. This change in the quantity demanded is due to a *movement along* the demand curve (from point *A* to point *B* in Figure A1), not to a *shift* in the demand curve.

When economists refer to an *increase in demand*, they mean a *rightward shift* in the demand curve. Thus Figures A2, A3, and A5 show increases in demand for wheat. When economists refer to a *decrease in demand*, they mean a *leftward shift* in the demand curve. An increase in demand for a commodity is not the same as an increase in the quantity demanded of the commodity. In Figure A1, the quantity demanded of wheat *increases* if the price falls from $3.10 to $2.70 per bushel, but this is not due to an increase in demand, since there is no rightward shift of the demand curve. Similarly, a decrease in demand for a commodity is not the same as a decrease in the quantity demanded of a commodity. In Figure A1, the quantity demanded of wheat *decreases* if the price rises from $2.70 to $3.10 per bushel, but this is not due to a decrease in demand, since there is no leftward shift of the demand curve.

4 ▪ The Supply Side of a Market

So much for your first look at demand. What about the other side of the market: supply? *The* **supply** *side of a market can be represented by a* **market supply curve** *that shows the amount of the commodity sellers would offer at various prices.* Continuing with the case of wheat, Figure A6 shows the supply curve for wheat in the United States in the mid-1990s, based on estimates made informally by government experts.[4] According to the figure, about 2.2 billion bushels of wheat would be supplied if the farm price were $2.70 per bushel, about 2.4 billion bushels if the farm price were $3.10 per bushel, and about 2.6 billion bushels if the farm price were $3.50 per bushel.

[4] Officials of the U.S. Department of Agriculture provided these estimates. Although rough approximations, they are good enough for present purposes.

Look carefully at the supply curve shown in Figure A6. Although it looks innocuous enough, it summarizes the potential behavior of thousands of U.S. wheat farmers, and their behavior plays an important role in determining the prosperity of many states and communities. Note that the supply curve for wheat slopes upward to the right. In other words, the quantity of wheat supplied increases as the price increases. This seems plausible, since increases in price give a greater incentive for farms to produce wheat and offer it for sale. Empirical studies indicate that the supply curves for a great many commodities share this characteristic of sloping upward to the right.

Any supply curve is based on the assumption that technology and input prices are held constant. Changes in these factors are likely to shift the position of a commodity's supply curve.

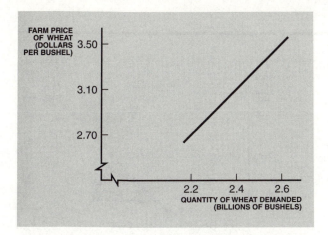

▪ **FIGURE A6**

Market Supply Curve for Wheat, Mid-1990s

The curve shows the amount that sellers would supply at various prices. At $3.50 per bushel, about 18 percent more wheat would be supplied than at $2.70 per bushel.

TECHNOLOGY Technology can be defined as society's pool of knowledge concerning the industrial arts. As technology progresses, it becomes possible to produce commodities more cheaply, so firms often are willing to supply a given amount at a lower price than formerly. Thus technological change often causes the supply curve to shift to the right. This certainly has occurred in the case of wheat, as shown in Figure A7. There have been many important technological changes in wheat production, ranging from advances in tractors to the development of improved varieties, like semidwarf wheats.

INPUT PRICES The supply curve for a commodity is affected by the prices of the resources (labor, capital, and land) used to produce it. Decreases in the price of these inputs make it possible to produce commodities more cheaply, so that firms may be willing to supply a given amount at a lower price than they formerly would. Thus decreases in the price of inputs may cause the supply curve to shift to the right. On the other hand, increases in the price of inputs may cause it to shift to the left. For example, if the wage rates of farm labor increase, the supply curve for wheat may shift to the left, as shown in Figure A8.

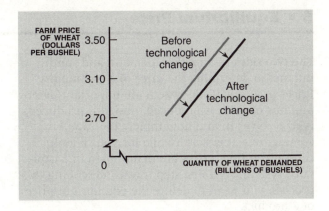

▪ **FIGURE A7**

Effect of Technological Change on Market Supply Curve for Wheat

Improvements in technology often shift the supply curve to the right.

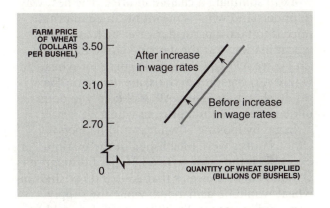

▪ **FIGURE A8**

Effect of Increase in Farm Wage Rates on Market Supply Curve for Wheat

An increase in the wage rate might shift the supply curve to the left.

An *increase in supply* is defined to be a *rightward shift* in the supply curve; a *decrease in supply* is defined to be a *leftward shift* in the supply curve. A change in supply should be distinguished from a change in the quantity supplied. In Figure A6, the quantity supplied of wheat will increase from 2.2 to 2.4 billion bushels if the price increases from $2.70 to $3.10 per bushel, but this is not due to an increase in supply, since there is no rightward shift of the supply curve in Figure A6.

5 ▪ Equilibrium Price

The two sides of a market, demand and supply, interact to determine the price of a commodity. Prices in a capitalistic system are important determinants of what is produced, how it is produced, who receives it, and how rapidly per capita income grows. It is worthwhile for you to look carefully at how prices are determined in a capitalist system. As a first step toward describing this process, you need to define the equilibrium price of a product.

Put briefly, *an equilibrium is a situation where there is no tendency for change;* in other words, it is a situation that can persist. Thus an **equilibrium price** *is a price that can be maintained.* Any price that is not an equilibrium price cannot be maintained for long, since there are basic forces at work to stimulate a change in price. The best way to understand what is meant by an equilibrium price is to take a particular case, such as the wheat market. Put the demand curve for wheat (in Figure A1) and the supply curve for wheat (in Figure A6) together in the same diagram. The result, shown in Figure A9, will help you determine the equilibrium price of wheat.

Begin by looking at what would happen if various prices were established in the market. For example, if the price were $3.50 per bushel, the demand curve indicates that 2.3 billion bushels of wheat would be demanded, while the supply curve indicates that 2.6 billion bushels would be supplied. Thus if the price were $3.50 a bushel, there would be a mismatch between the quantity supplied and the quantity demanded per year, since the rate at which wheat is supplied would be greater than the rate at which it is demanded. Specifically, as shown in Figure A9, there would be an **excess supply** of 300 million bushels. Under these circumstances, some of the wheat supplied by farmers could not be sold, and as inventories of wheat built up, suppliers would tend to cut their prices in order to get rid of unwanted inventories. Thus a price of $3.50 per bushel would not be maintained for long, and for this reason $3.50 per bushel is not an equilibrium price.

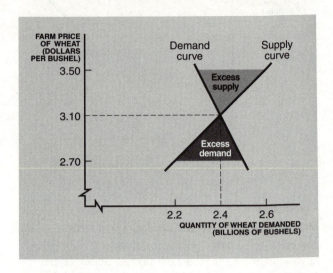

▪ **FIGURE A9**

Determination of the Equilibrium Price of Wheat, Mid-1990s

The equilibrium price is $3.10 per bushel, and the equilibrium quantity is 2.4 billion bushels. At a price of $3.50 per bushel, there would be an excess supply of 300 million bushels. At a price of $2.70 per bushel, there would be an excess demand of 300 million bushels.

If the price were $2.70 per bushel, on the other hand, the demand curve indicates that 2.5 billion bushels would be demanded, while the supply curve indicates that 2.2 billion bushels would be supplied. Again you find a mismatch between the quantity supplied and the quantity demanded per year, since the rate at which wheat is supplied would be less than the rate at which it is demanded. Specifically, as shown in Figure A9, there would be an **excess demand** of 300 million bushels. Under these circumstances, some of the consumers who want wheat at this price would have to be turned away empty-handed. There would be a shortage. And given this shortage, suppliers would find it profitable to increase the price and competition among buyers would bid the price up. Thus a price of $2.70 per bushel could not be maintained for long, so $2.70 per bushel is not an equilibrium price.

Under these circumstances, the equilibrium price must be the price at which the quantity demanded equals the quantity supplied. Obviously, this is the only price at which there is no mismatch between the quantity demanded and the quantity supplied, and consequently it is the only price that can be maintained for long. In Figure A9, the price at which the quantity supplied equals the quantity demanded is $3.10 per bushel, the price where the demand curve intersects the supply curve. Thus $3.10 per bushel is the equilibrium price of wheat under the circumstances visualized in Figure A9, and 2.4 billion bushels is the equilibrium quantity.

6 ▪ Actual Price

The price that counts in the real world, however, is the **actual price,** not the equilibrium price, and it is the actual price that you are seeking to identify. In general, economists simply assume that the actual price will approximate the equilibrium price; this seems reasonable enough, since the basic forces at work tend to push the actual price toward the equilibrium price. Thus if conditions remain fairly stable for a time, the actual price should move toward the equilibrium price.

So long as the actual price exceeds the equilibrium price, there will be downward pressure on price. Similarly, so long as the actual price is less than the equilibrium price, there will be upward pressure on price. Thus there is always a tendency for the actual price to move toward the equilibrium price. But you should not assume that this movement is always rapid. Sometimes it takes a long time for the actual price to get close to the equilibrium price. Sometimes the actual price never gets to the equilibrium price because by the time it gets close, the equilibrium price changes (because of shifts in either the demand curve or the supply curve or both). All that safely can be said is that the actual price will move toward the equilibrium price. But of course this information is of great value, both theoretically and practically. For many purposes, all that is needed is a correct prediction of the direction in which the price will move.

7 ▪ The Price System and the Determination of What Is Produced

Having learned how prices are determined in free markets, you can now explore somewhat more fully how the price system goes about performing the four tasks that face any economic system. Specifically, what determines (1) how the level and composition of society's output is established, (2) how each good and service is produced, (3) how the goods and services that are produced are distributed among the members of society, and (4) how the rate of growth of per capita output is determined?

Begin by considering the determination of what society will produce: How does the price system carry out this task?

A product's demand curve is an important determinant of how much firms will produce of the product, since it indicates the amount of the product that will be demanded at each price. From the point of view of the producers, the demand curve indicates the amount they can sell at each price. In a capitalist economy, firms are in business to make money. Thus the manufacturers of any product will turn it out only if the amount of money they receive from consumers exceeds the cost of putting it on the market. Acting in accord with the profit motive, firms are led to produce what the consumers desire. You saw in a previous section that if consumers' tastes shift in favor of foods containing wheat, the demand curve for wheat will shift to the right; this will increase the price of wheat. Given the shift in the demand curve, it is profitable for firms to raise output. Acting in their own self-interest, they are led to make production decisions geared to the wants of the consumers.

Thus the price system uses the self-interest of the producers to get them to produce what consumers want. Consumers register what they want in the marketplace by their purchasing decisions, which can be represented by their demand curves. Producers can make more money by

responding to consumers' wants than by ignoring them. Consequently, they are led to produce what consumers are willing to pay for. (In addition, as you have seen above, the level of production costs as well as demand determines what will be produced.) Note that producers are not forced by anyone to do anything. They can produce air conditioners for Eskimos if they like, and if they are prepared to absorb the losses. The price system uses prices to communicate the relevant signals to producers, and metes out penalties and rewards in the form of losses or profits.

8 ▪ The Price System and the Determination of How Goods Are Produced

Next, consider how society determines how each good and service is produced. How does the price system carry out this task? The price of each resource gives producers an indication of how scarce this resource is and how valuable it is in other uses. Clearly, firms should produce goods and services at minimum cost. Suppose that there are two ways of producing tables: technique A and technique B. Technique A requires four hours of labor and $10 worth of wood per table, whereas technique B requires five hours of labor and $8 worth of wood. If the price of an hour of labor is $4, technique A should be used since a table costs $26 with this technique, as opposed to $28 with technique B.[5] In other words, technique A uses fewer resources per table.

The price system nudges producers to opt for technique A rather than technique B through profits and losses. If each table commands a price of $35, then by using technique A producers make a profit of $35 − $26 = $9 per table. If they use technique B, they make a profit of

$35 − $28 = $7 per table. Thus producers, if they maximize profit, will be led to adopt technique A. Their desire for profit leads them to adopt the techniques that will enable society to get the most out of its resources. No one commands firms to use particular techniques. Washington officials do not order steel plants to substitute the basic oxygen process for open hearths, or petroleum refineries to substitute catalytic cracking for thermal cracking. It is all done through the impersonal marketplace.

You should not, however, get the idea that the price system operates with kid gloves. Suppose all firms producing tables used technique B until this past year, when technique A was developed: in other words, technique A is based on a new technology. Given this technological change, the supply curve for tables will shift to the right, and the price of a table will fall. Suppose it drops to $27. If some firm insists on sticking with technique B, it will lose money at the rate of $1 a table; and as these losses mount, the firm's owners will become increasingly uncomfortable. The firm will either switch to technique A or go bankrupt. The price system leans awfully hard on producers who try to ignore its signals.

[5] To obtain these figures, note that the cost with technique A is four labor-hours times $4 plus $10, or $26, while the cost with technique B is five labor-hours times $4 plus $8, or $28.

9 ▪ The Price System and the Determination of Who Gets What

Take a look now at how society's output will be distributed among the people. How does the price system carry out this task? The amount of goods and services people receive depends on their money income, which in turn is determined under the price system by the amount of various resources that they own and by the price of each resource. Thus, under the price system, each person's income is determined in the marketplace: people come to the marketplace with certain resources to sell, and their income depends on how much they can get for these resources.

The question of who gets what is solved at two levels by the price system. Consider an individual product: for example, the tables discussed in the previous section. For the individual product, the question of who gets what is solved by the equality of quantity demanded and quantity supplied. If the price of these tables is at its equilibrium level, the quantity demanded will equal the quantity supplied. Consumers who are willing and able to pay the equilibrium price (or more) get the tables, while those who are unwilling or unable to pay it do not get them. It is just as sim-

ple—and as impersonal—as that. It doesn't matter whether you are a nice guy or a scoundrel, or whether you are a connoisseur of tables or someone who doesn't know good workmanship from poor. All that matters is whether you are able and willing to pay the equilibrium price.

Next, consider the question of who gets what at a somewhat more fundamental level. After all, whether consumers are able and willing to pay the equilibrium price for a good depends on their money income. As you have already seen, consumers' money income depends on the amount of resources of various kinds that they own and the price that they can get for them. Some people have lots of resources: they are endowed with skill and intelligence and industry, or they have lots of capital or land. Other people have little in the way of resources. Moreover, some people have resources that command a high price, whereas others have resources that are of little monetary value. The result is that under the price system, some consumers get a lot more of society's output than others.

10 ▪ The Price System and Economic Growth

Now look at the task of determining a society's rate of growth of per capita income. How does the price system do this? A country's rate of increase of per capita income depends on the rate of growth of its resources and the rate of increase of the efficiency with which they are used. First, consider the rate of growth of society's resources. The price system controls the amount of new capital goods produced much as it controls the amount of consumer goods produced. Similarly, the price system influences the amount society invests in educating, training, and upgrading its labor resources. To a considerable extent, the amount invested in such resource-augmenting

activities is determined by the profitability of such investments, which is determined in turn by the pattern of prices.

Next, consider the rate of increase of the efficiency with which a society's resources are used. Clearly, this factor depends heavily on the rate of technological change. If technology is advancing at a rapid rate, it should be possible to get more and more out of a society's resources. But if technology is advancing rather slowly, it is likely to be difficult to get much more out of them. The price system affects the rate of technological change in a variety of ways: it influences the profitability of investing in research and development, the profitability of introducing new processes and products into commercial practice, and the profitability of accepting technological change—as well as the losses involved in spurning it.

The price system establishes strong incentives for firms to introduce new technology. Any firm that can find a cheaper way to produce an existing product, or a way to produce a better product, will have a profitable jump on its competitors.

Until its competitors can do the same thing, this firm can reap higher profits than it otherwise could. Of course, these higher profits will eventually be competed away, as other firms begin to imitate this firm's innovation. But lots of money can be made in the period during which this firm has a lead over its competitors. These profits are an important incentive for the introduction of new technology.

11 ▪ The Circular Flows of Money and Products

So far you have been concerned largely with the workings of a single market. But how do all of the various markets fit together? This is a very important question. Perhaps the best way to begin answering it is to distinguish between product markets and resource markets. As their names indicate, **product markets** are markets in which products are bought and sold and **resource markets** are markets in which resources are bought and sold. First consider product markets. As shown in Figure A10, firms provide products to consumers in product markets and receive money in return. The money the firms receive is their receipts; to consumers, on the other hand, it represents their expenditures.

Next, consider resource markets. Figure A10 shows that consumers provide resources—including labor—to firms in resource markets, and they receive money in return. The money the consumers receive is their income; to firms, on the other hand, it is part of their costs. Note that the flow of resources and products in Figure A10 is counterclockwise: *consumers provide resources to firms which in turn provide goods and services to consumers.* On the other hand, the flow of money in Figure A10 is clockwise: *firms pay money for resources to consumers who in turn use the money to buy goods and services from the firms.* Both flows—that of resources and products and that of money—go on simultaneously and repeatedly.

So long as consumers spend all their income, the flow of money income from firms to consumers is exactly equal to the flow of expenditure

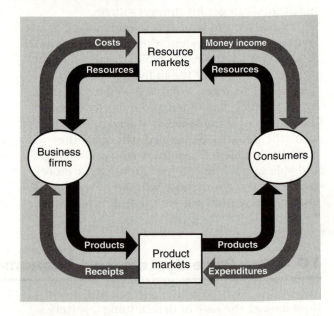

▪ **FIGURE A10**

The Circular Flows of Money and Products

In product markets, consumers exchange money for products and firms exchange products for money. In resource markets, consumers exchange resources for money and firms exchange money for resources.

from consumers to firms. Thus these circular flows keep rolling along. As a first approximation, this is a perfectly good model. But capitalist economies have experienced periods of widespread unemployment and severe inflation that this model cannot explain. Also, note that the simple economy in Figure A10 has no government sector. In Chapters 6 to 8 and 12, we bring the government into the picture. Under pure capitalism, the government would play a limited role in the economic system, but in the mixed capitalistic system we have in the United States, the government plays an important role indeed.

12 ▪ Limitations of the Price System

Despite its many advantages, the price system suffers from limitations. Because these limitations are both significant and well known, no one believes that the price system, left to its own devices, can be trusted to solve all society's basic economic problems. To a considerable extent, the government's role in the economy has developed in response to the limitations of the price system, which are described below.

DISTRIBUTION OF INCOME

There is no reason to believe that the distribution of income generated by the price system is *fair* or, in some sense, *best*. Most people feel that the distribution of income generated by the price system should be altered to suit humanitarian needs—in particular, that help should be given to the poor. Both liberals and conservatives tend to agree on this score, although there are arguments over the extent to which the poor should be helped and the conditions under which they should be eligible for help. But the general principle that the government should step in to redistribute income in favor of the poor is generally accepted in the United States today.[6]

PUBLIC GOODS

Some goods and services *cannot be provided through the price system because there is no way to exclude citizens from consuming the goods whether they pay for them or not.* For example, there is no way to prevent citizens from benefiting from national expenditures on defense, whether they pay money toward defense or not. Consequently, the price system cannot be used to provide such goods; no one will pay for them since all will receive them whether they pay or not. Further, some goods, like the quality of the environment and national defense (and others cited below), *can be enjoyed by one person without depriving others of the same enjoyment.* Goods with the above characteristics are called **public goods.** The government provides many public goods. Such goods are consumed collectively or jointly, and it is inefficient to try to price them in a market. They tend to be indivisible; that is, they cannot easily be split into pieces and be bought and sold in a market.

EXTERNAL ECONOMIES AND DISECONOMIES

In cases in which *the production or consumption of a good by one firm or consumer has adverse or beneficial uncompensated effects on other firms or consumers, the price system will not operate effectively.* An **external economy** is said to occur when consumption or production by one person or firm results in uncompensated benefits to another person or firm. A good example of an external economy exists where fundamental research carried out by one firm is used by another firm. (To cite one such case, there were external economies from the Bell Telephone Laboratories' invention of the transistor. Many electronics firms, such as Texas Instruments and Fairchild, benefited considerably from Bell's research.) Where external economies exist, it is generally agreed that the price system will produce too little of the good in question and that the government should supplement the

---

[6] Also, because the wealthy have more money to spend than the poor, the sorts of goods and services that society produces will reflect this fact. Thus luxuries for the rich may be produced in larger amounts, and necessities for the poor may be produced in smaller amounts than some critics regard as sensible and equitable. This is another frequently encountered criticism of the price system.

amount produced by private enterprise. This is the rationale for much of the government's huge investment in basic science. An **external diseconomy** is said to occur when consumption or production by one person or firm results in uncompensated costs to another person or firm. A good example of an external diseconomy occurs when a firm dumps pollutants into a stream and makes the water unfit for use by firms and people downstream. Where activities result in external diseconomies, it is generally agreed that the price system will tolerate too much of the activities and that the government should curb them.

NUMERICAL PROBLEMS

1 Assume that the market for electric toasters is competitive and that the quantity supplied per year depends on the price of a toaster as follows:

PRICE OF A TOASTER (dollars)	NUMBER OF TOASTERS SUPPLIED (millions)
12	4.0
14	5.0
16	5.5
18	6.0
20	6.3

Plot the supply curve for toasters. Is this a direct or inverse relationship? Are supply curves generally direct or inverse relationships?

2 Suppose that the quantity of toasters demanded per year depends on the price of a toaster as follows:

PRICE OF A TOASTER (dollars)	NUMBER OF TOASTERS DEMANDED (millions)
12	7.0
14	6.5
16	6.2
18	6.0
20	5.8

Plot the demand curve for toasters. If the price is $14, will there be an excess demand for toasters? If the price is $20, will there be an excess demand? What is the equilibrium price of a toaster? What is the equilibrium quantity? (Use the data in Problem 1.)

3 Suppose that the government imposes a price ceiling on toasters. In particular, suppose that it decrees that a toaster cannot sell for more than $14. Will the quantity supplied equal the quantity demanded? What sorts of devices may come into being to allocate the available supply of toasters to consumers? What problems will the government encounter in keeping the price at $14? What social purposes, if any, might such a price ceiling serve? (Use the data in Problems 1 and 2.)

4 Suppose that the government imposes a price floor on toasters. In particular, suppose that it decrees that a toaster cannot sell for less than $20. Will the quantity supplied equal the quantity demanded? How will the resulting supply of toasters be taken off the market? What problems will the government encounter in keeping the price at $20? What social purposes, if any, might such a price floor serve? (Use the data in Problems 1 and 2.)

APPENDIX
Answers to Odd-Numbered Numerical Problems

CHAPTER 1

1. a. Gross domestic product in current dollars in 1997 equals 1.10 × 1.03 × gross domestic product in current dollars in 1995. The price level in 1997 is 10 percent higher than in 1995. Thus, in terms of 1995 dollars, GDP in 1997 is $\frac{1.10 \times 1.03}{1.10}$ × GDP in 1995. In other words, it is 3 percent higher than in 1995.

   b. $1.8 million

   c. $800 million

3. a. Profit for tomato producer: $40,000
      Profit for catsup producer: $60,000

   b. $500,000

   c. $200,000

   d. $300,000

   e. **Gross Domestic Product, Hanover**
(thousands of dollars)

Wages	250
Rent	65
Interest	50
Profits	100
Indirect business taxes	15
Depreciation	20
Total	500

5. a. Yes, if the country consumes more than it produces.

   b. Yes, if inventories are reduced enough to cause gross private domestic investment to be negative.

7. This would mean that a negative amount of plant and equipment wore out, which clearly is unrealistic.

CHAPTER 2

1.

	1996	1997
Percent employed	93.0	94.0
Total employment	90.6 million	94.4 million
Total unemployment	6.8 million	6.0 million

3. No, even though some people may have protected themselves, many others were hurt by the resulting redistribution of income. Also, an inflation of this sort is likely to affect the efficiency of the economy.

CHAPTER 3

1. a.

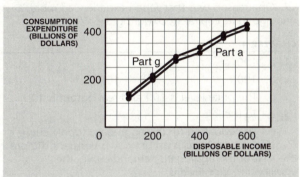

   b. 0.8, 0.6, 0.4.

   c. A shift in the consumption function, because consumption expenditure is higher at each level of disposable income.

   d.

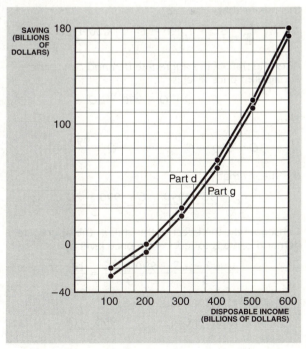

e. 0.2, 0.4, 0.6.

f. One in each case.

g. See answers to parts a and d.

3. Consumption expenditure falls by 10 cents and saving increases by 10 cents.

5. a. Yes.

b. No.

c. Yes.

d. Yes.

e. No.

7. One reason was that Japan experienced more damage to its capital stock during the War.

CHAPTER 4

1. a. 100.

b. 100.

c. The price level is 100 and real output is 140.

3. a. To the left.

b. The equation for the aggregate supply curve is $P = C + Q$, where C is an unknown constant. Before the shift of the aggregate demand curve, the equilibrium price level is

$$P = C + Q = 1,000 - 2Q.$$

Thus,

$$3Q = 1,000 - C, \quad \text{or} \quad Q = \frac{1,000 - C}{3};$$

this means that

$$P = \frac{3C + 1,000 - C}{3} = \frac{1,000 + 2C}{3}.$$

After the shift of the aggregate demand curve, the equilibrium price level is

$$P = C + Q = 990 - 2Q.$$

Thus,

$$3Q = 990 - C, \quad \text{or} \quad Q = \frac{990 - C}{3};$$

this means that

$$P = \frac{3C + 990 - C}{3} = \frac{990 + 2C}{3}.$$

Consequently, the effect of this shift in the aggregate demand curve is to reduce the price level by

$$\frac{1,000 + 2C}{3} - \frac{990 + 2C}{3} = \frac{10}{3}.$$

c. Q decreases from

$$\frac{1,000 - C}{3} \quad \text{to} \quad \frac{990 - C}{3}.$$

In other words, Q decreases by 10/3 billions of dollars.

CHAPTER 5

1. a. Yes.

b. Yes.

c. No. It is a coincident series.

d. No. These indicators have turned down on a number of occasions in recent years when the economy did not turn down subsequently.

e. No.

3. a. Yes.

b. Yes.

c. Yes.

d. To a considerable extent, yes.

e. To some extent, but inflation declined faster than he forecasted it would.

5. a. Yes.

b. Yes. Yes.

c. Yes.

d. No.

7. a. Yes.

b. Yes.

c. It will shift to the right.

d. Point C.

e. Because there will probably be high unemployment, with its attendant social costs.

CHAPTER 6

1. a. No.

b. Yes.

c. Yes. The aggregate demand curve is likely to be shifted to the right.

3. a. $1,100 million.

b. Equilibrium GDP will increase by $20 million.

c.

GDP (millions of dollars)
1,080
1,200
1,320
1,440
1,560

d. $1,200 million.

e. Government expenditure is $350 million, and taxes are $200 million, so the government is running a deficit of $150 million.

f.

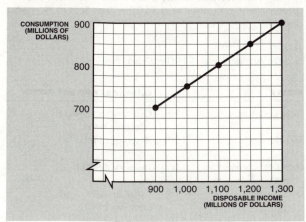

g.

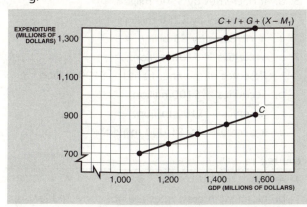

h. The $C + I + G + (X − M_1)$ line is shown above. $1,200 million. This is the equilibrium value of GDP.

i. There is an inflationary gap.

j. Yes. You should use an analysis that does not assume the price level to be constant.

CHAPTER 7

1. a. The government is running a deficit of $.2 billion. Since it would run a surplus at full employment of $.2 billion, the budget does not seem too expansionary.

b. There will be a deficit of $.3 billion.

3. a. $10,000.

b. No.

c. The interest cost would be $400, and the principal would be $10,000.

CHAPTER 8

1. a. Not necessarily. If the actual GDP is well below the potential GDP, this may not be true.

b. Yes if they result in excessive unemployment.

c. Because these programs are economically important in particular states, politicians from these states fight to prevent the cancellation of these programs.

d. This is one interpretation of Figure 8.1, but not the only one.

e. It may do so, because it increases the demand for loanable funds. Yes.

f. It would be very difficult, if not impossible, to use fiscal policy for this purpose.

3. a. Some, but not all, economists believe that discretionary fiscal policy can be detrimental to good economic performance. This is an area where economists disagree.

b. Because it was a period of prosperity. No.

c. The Council believed that: "Government should credibly commit to follow such policies consistently."

d. If government spending is increased during periods of substantial unemployment, but not reduced substantially during periods of prosperity, this can occur.

5. a. Yes.

b. Let DI equal disposable income, G equal government expenditure, T equal taxes, and GDP equal gross domestic product. In billions of dollars, the consumption function is $50 + .75\ DI$; $G = 40$; and $T = 40$. If planned investment equals 10 (and both exports and imports equal 0), desired spending on final goods and services equals

$$50 + .75\ (GDP − 40) + 40 + 10.$$

Thus,

$$GDP = 100 + .75\ (GDP − 40) = 70 + .75\ GDP$$

$$.25GDP = 70$$

$$GDP = 280$$

Since GDP will be less than 300 (the full-employment level), there will be a recessionary gap.

c. Yes. G must equal 45. The government must run a deficit of $5 billion.

d. Yes, T must fall by $6\frac{2}{3}$. Thus, the government must run a deficit of $6\frac{2}{3}$ billion.

e. Often, it is not realistic.

f. Yes.

7. a. No.

b. No.

c. It seems reasonable, but not certain.

d. Los Angeles, Washington, and Norfolk head the list. Probably.

e. Because many defense expenditures are for aircraft and communications equipment. Because more spending might be for housing.

CHAPTER 9

1. a. The aggregate demand curve will shift to the right.

   b. The aggregate demand curve will shift to the left.

3. a. The demand curve for money.

   b. 10 percent.

   c. No. It will shift upward and to the right.

5. 10 percent.

7. Velocity based on M1 and M2 was as follows:

YEAR	BASED ON M1	BASED ON M2
1967	4.36	2.33
1969	4.61	2.46
1971	4.71	2.34
1973	5.02	2.38
1975	5.41	2.40
1977	5.88	2.46

Velocity was more stable when M2 is used than when M1 is used. Velocity was not the same during 1990 as in 1967 to 1977.

9. a. Yes.

   b. Yes. The slope changes from −0.04 to −0.08.

   c. No, because if this equation holds, M is negative if i is greater than 15.

CHAPTER 10

1. a.

ASSETS		LIABILITIES AND NET WORTH	
(dollars)			
Reserves	400,000	Demand deposits	2,400,000
Loans and securities	3,000,000	Net worth	1,000,000

   b. No. It can refuse to renew loans or sell securities.

3. a. Yes. $125,000.

   b. Yes. $125,000.

5. a. $260 billion.

   b. $256 billion.

   c. $207 billion.

CHAPTER 11

1. a.

FEDERAL RESERVE

ASSETS		LIABILITIES	
(millions of dollars)			
Government securities	−100	Member bank reserves	−100

COMMERCIAL BANKS

ASSETS		LIABILITIES	
(millions of dollars)			
Reserves	−100	Demand deposits	−100

   b. Yes. The public has $100 million more in U.S. government securities and $100 million less in demand deposits.

   c. No. Yes.

   d. An increase. $100 million. No.

3.

ASSETS		LIABILITIES AND NET WORTH	
Gold certificates	10	Outstanding Federal Reserve notes	90
Securities	100	Reserves of member banks	30
Loans to commercial banks	10	Treasury deposits	5
Other assets	10	Other liabilities and net worth	5
	130		130

5. a. It decreases by $500 million.

   b. It increases by $250 million.

   c. It increases by $5 billion.

7. a. Securities − $100 million.

   Reserves of member banks − $100 million.

   b. Securities + $100 million.

   Reserves − $100 million.

   c. It decreases by $1,000 million.

CHAPTER 13

1. a. Yes.

   b. Nominal interest rates are not corrected for inflation; real interest rates are. Real interest rates influence investors' decisions.

   c. No.

   d. Yes.

   e. No.

3. a. To reduce the rate of growth of the money supply.

   b. To discourage spending.

   c. To reduce spending.

   d. Yes.

5. a. Yes. The interest rate has increased.

   b. Yes. The growth rate of the quantity of money has increased.

   c. No. The Fed will be criticized by one group or the other.

7. a. Yes.

   b. Yes.

   c. Yes.

   d. Yes.

CHAPTER 14

1. a. Beyond 3 million hours of labor, the marginal product falls. The average product of labor increases up to 3 million hours of labor, then falls.

b. 2 tons of steel per hour of labor. 3 tons of steel per hour of labor.

c. It doubled; that is, there was a 100 percent increase.

d.

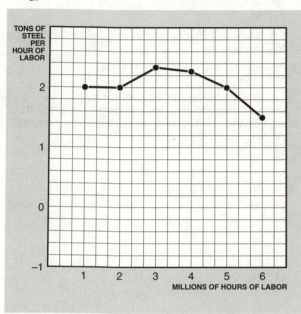

3. a. It will increase full-employment GDP by 3\frac{1}{3}$ million.

b. 1$\frac{2}{3}$ percent per year.

c. The growth rate will be 3$\frac{1}{3}$ percent per year.

d. Minus 2$\frac{1}{3}$ percent per year. Minus $\frac{2}{3}$ percent per year.

5.

AVERAGE PRODUCT OF CAPITAL	MARGINAL PRODUCT OF CAPITAL
N.A.	100
100	110
105	100
103$\frac{1}{3}$	90
100	80
96	60
90	

CHAPTER 15

1. a. No. It is important because it restricts the rate of growth of output.

b. Students of this period believe so.

c. Yes.

d. Yes.

e. Yes.

f. Yes.

3. a. Not necessarily. Firms or others might fund it.

b. Not necessarily. Firms or others might fund it.

c. Not necessarily. A not-for-profit institution might fund it.

d. If no other group would support this work, it was justified.

e. Same as part d.

5. a. .25 (13 − 11) = .5 million dollars.

b. The tax credit reduces the cost of R and D.

c. The loss of tax revenue seemed comparatively high.

d. R and D can be defined to include many activities that have little to do with major industrial technology. If the expenditures for which the credit is claimed are not R and D, the credit is unlikely to achieve its purposes.

CHAPTER 16

1. a. $10.

b. and c. Japan will export 1 million transistor radios to the United States.

d. Exports and imports will drop.

3. a. The price of a pound of bananas must be between 3/10 and 8/10 of the price of a pound of nuts.

b. Argentina

5. a. More.

b. Less.

7. a. An extra unit of clothing costs 5/8 of a unit of food.

b. An extra unit of clothing costs 2/3 of a unit of food.

c. Country *H.* Country *G.*

d. The price of a unit of clothing will lie between 5/8 and 2/3 of the price of a unit of food.

CHAPTER 17

1. a. The higher curve is the one following the depreciation. Because of the depreciation, it takes more dollars to elicit the same supply as before.

b. It will increase the price.

c. It will reduce expenditures.

d. It will increase expenditures.

3.

ITEM	DEBIT	CREDIT
	(millions of dollars)	
Imports	100	
Exports		120
Purchase of securities	50	
Sale of securities		60
Gifts		30
Gold imports	60	
Total	210	210

5. a.

U.S. PRICE OF GOOD	TOTAL DESIRED EXPENDITURE
$3	$6,000
$4	$5,000
$6	$3,000

b. 3 marks = 1 dollar.

c. More marks would be demanded than supplied. There would be a shortage of marks.

7. a. Buy, 20 million pounds.

b. From its reserves.

CHAPTER 18

1. a. No. Yes.

b. Yes. Many economists do not think so.

c. Yes. Yes. No. They would be on whatever good the country decided to produce to reduce its dependence on bananas.

d. Yes. If the United States imposes a tariff on bananas, and thus cuts down the demand for them, the reduction in its demand is likely to reduce the price of bananas abroad.

3. a. U.S. consumers.

b. U.S. auto producers.

c. No.

d. Most economists tend to emphasize the benefits of free trade.

e. Many people considered it excessive.

5. a. As Paul Volcker put it, we "can't afford to become addicted to drawing on increasing amounts of foreign savings to help finance our internal economy."

b. No. No.

c. No.

7. a. No.

b. Yes.

c. No. Yes.

d. No.

e. No.

f. No.

GLOSSARY OF TERMS

Absolute advantage the ability of one country to produce a good or service more cheaply than another country.

Adaptive expectations situation where people change their forecasts of the variable in question to conform to its current level.

Aggregate demand curve a curve, sloping downward to the right, that shows the level of real national output that will be demanded at various economywide price levels.

Aggregate production function the relationship between the amount used of each of the inputs available in the economy and the resulting amount of potential output, that is, the most output that existing technology permits the economy to produce from various quantities of all available inputs.

Alternative cost the value of what certain resources could have produced had they been used in the best alternative way; also called **opportunity cost.**

Antitrust laws legislation (such as the Sherman Act, the Clayton Act, and the Federal Trade Commission Act) intended to promote competition and control monopoly.

Appreciation of currency an increase in the value of one currency relative to another.

Asymmetric information situation where all participants in a market do not have the same information (for example, sellers may know more about the quality of a product than do potential buyers).

Automatic stabilizers structural features of the economy that tend by themselves to stabilize national output, without the help of new legislation or government policy measures.

Average product of an input total output divided by the amount of input used to produce this amount of output.

Average product of labor total output per unit of labor.

Average propensity to consume the fraction of total disposable income that is spent on consumption; equal to personal consumption expenditure divided by disposable income.

Balance-of-payments deficit the difference between the quantity supplied and the quantity demanded of a currency when the currency is overvalued (that is, priced above its equilibrium price).

Balance-of-payments surplus the difference between the quantity demanded and the quantity supplied of a currency when the currency is undervalued (that is, priced below its equilibrium price).

Balance sheet an accounting statement showing the nature of a firm's assets, the claims by creditors on those assets, and the value of the firm's ownership at a certain point in time.

Balanced budget a budget in which tax revenues cover government expenditures.

Base year a year chosen as a reference point for comparison with some later or earlier year.

Bond a debt (generally long term) of a firm or government.

Budget a statement of the government's anticipated expenditures and tax revenues for a fiscal year.

Budget deficit a budget in which tax revenues fall short of government expenditures.

Budget surplus a budget in which tax revenues exceed government expenditures.

$C + I + G + (X - M_I)$ line a curve showing total intended spending (the sum of consumption expenditure, investment expenditure, government expenditure, and net exports) at various levels of gross domestic product.

$C + I + G$ line a curve showing total intended spending (the sum of intended consumption expenditure, investment expenditure, and government expenditure) at various levels of gross domestic product, in the simple case where net exports are zero.

Capital resources (such as factory buildings, equipment, raw materials, and inventories) that are created within the economic system for the purpose of producing other goods.

Capital consumption allowance the value of the capital (that is, the plant, equipment, and structures) that is worn out in a year; also called **depreciation.**

Capital formation investment in plant and equipment.

Capital goods output consisting of plant and equipment that are used to make other goods.

Capital-output ratio the ratio of the total capital stock to annual national output.

Capitalism an economic system characterized by private ownership of the tools of production, freedom of choice and of enterprise whereby consumers and firms can pursue their own self-interest, competition for sales among producers and resource owners, and reliance on the free market.

Central bank a government-established agency that controls the supply of money and supervises the country's commercial banks; the central bank of the United States is the Federal Reserve.

Commercial banks financial institutions that hold demand and other checkable deposits and permit checks to be written on them, and lend money to firms and individuals.

Comparative advantage the law that states that a country should produce and export goods for which its efficiency *relative to other countries* is highest; specialization and trade depend on comparative, not absolute advantage.

Compensation of employees the wages and salaries paid by employers to the suppliers of labor, including supplementary payments for employee benefits (such as payments into public and private pension and welfare funds).

Complements commodities that tend to be consumed together, that is, commodities with a negative cross elasticity of demand such that a decrease in the price of one will result in an increase in the quantity demanded of the other.

Constant dollar amounts amounts measured in base-year dollars (that is, according to the purchasing power of the dollar in some earlier year), in order to express value in a way that corrects for changes in the price level.

Consumer an individual or household that purchases the goods and services produced by the economic system.

Consumer goods output consisting of items that consumers purchase, such as clothing, food, and drink.

Consumer Price Index a measure of U.S. inflation, calculated by the Bureau of Labor Statistics, originally

intended to measure changes in the prices of goods and services purchased by urban wage earners and clerical workers and in 1978 expanded to cover all urban consumers.

Consumption function the relationship between consumption spending and disposable income, that is, the amount of consumption expenditure that will occur at various levels of disposable income.

Corporate profits the net income of corporations (that is, corporate profits before income taxes), including dividends received by the stockholders, retained earnings, and the amount paid by corporations as income taxes.

Corporation a fictitious legal person separate and distinct from the stockholders who own it, governed by a board of directors elected by the stockholders.

Council of Economic Advisers a group established by the Employment Act of 1946, whose function is to help the president formulate and assess the economic policies of the government.

Creeping inflation an increase in the general price level of a few percent per year that gradually erodes the value of money.

Crowding-out effect the tendency for an increase in public sector expenditure to result in a cut in private sector expenditure.

Crude quantity theory of money and prices the theory that if the velocity of circulation of money remains constant and real gross domestic product remains fixed at its full-employment level, it follows from the equation of exchange that the price level will be proportional to the money supply.

Cyclical unemployment joblessness that occurs because of business fluctuations.

Cyclically adjusted budget balance the difference between tax revenues and government expenditures that would result if gross domestic product were at its potential, not its actual, level.

Deflating the conversion of values expressed in current dollars into values expressed in constant dollars, in order to correct for changes in the price level.

Demand curve for loanable funds a curve showing the quantity of loanable funds that will be demanded at each interest rate.

Demand curve for money a curve representing the quantity of money that will be demanded at various interest rates (holding real gross domestic product and the price level constant).

Demand deposits checking accounts; bank deposits subject to payment on demand.

Demand-side inflation an increase in the general price level that is triggered by rightward shifts of the aggregate demand curve (too much aggregate spending, too much money chasing too few goods).

Depreciation the value of the capital (that is, plant, equipment, and structures) that is worn out in a year, also called a **capital consumption allowance.**

Depreciation of currency a decrease in the value of one currency relative to another.

Depression a period when national output is well below its potential (that is, full-employment) level; a severe recession.

Diffusion process the process by which the use of an innovation spreads from firm to firm and from use to use.

Direct regulation government issue of enforceable rules concerning the conduct of firms.

Discount rate the interest rate the Federal Reserve charges for loans to commercial banks.

Discretionary policy policy that is formulated at the discretion of the policymakers (in contrast to rigid policy rules or feedback policy rules).

Disposable income the total amount of income people receive after personal taxes.

Easy monetary policy a monetary policy that increases the money supply substantially and reduces interest rates.

Economic resources resources that are scarce and thus command a nonzero price.

Economics the study of how resources are allocated among alternative uses to satisfy human wants.

Effluent fee a fee that a polluter must pay to the government for discharging waste.

Equation of exchange a way of restating the definition of the velocity of circulation of money, such that the amount received for the final goods and services during a period equals the amount spent on those final goods and services during the same period (that is, $MV = PQ$).

Equilibrium a situation in which there is no tendency for change.

Equilibrium level of gross domestic product the value of gross domestic product at which the flow of income generated by this level of output results in a level of spending precisely sufficient to buy this level of output.

Equilibrium price a price that shows no tendency to change, because it is the price at which the quantity demanded equals the quantity supplied; the price toward which the actual price of a good tends to move.

Exchange rate the number of units of one currency that can purchase a unit of another currency.

Excise tax a tax imposed on each unit sold of a particular product, such as cigarettes or liquor.

Expansion the phase in the business cycle after the trough during which national output rises.

Exports the goods and services that a country sells to other countries.

External diseconomy an uncompensated cost to one person or firm resulting from the consumption or output of another person or firm.

External economy an uncompensated benefit to one person or firm resulting from the consumption or output of another person or firm.

Federal Open Market Committee (FOMC) a group, composed of the seven members of the Federal Reserve Board plus five presidents of Federal Reserve Banks, which makes decisions concerning the purchase and sale of government securities, in order to control bank reserves and the money supply.

Federal Reserve Board the Board of Governors of the Federal Reserve System, composed of seven members appointed by the president for 14-year terms, whose function is to promote the country's economic welfare by supervising the operations of the U.S. money and banking system.

Federal Reserve System a system established by Congress in 1913 that includes the commercial banks, the 12 Federal Reserve Banks, and the 7-member Board of Governors of the Federal Reserve System.

Feedback policy rule a rule allowing the behavior of the variable governed by the policy rule to change, depending on future circumstances.

Final goods and services goods and services that are destined for the ultimate user (such as food purchased for family consumption).

Firm an organization that produces a good or service for sale in an attempt to make a profit.

Fiscal policy the policy of the government regarding taxes and government expenditures, the object being to stabilize the economy.

45-degree line a line that contains all points where the amount on the horizontal axis equals the amount on the vertical axis.

Fractional-reserve banking the practice whereby banks hold less cash than the amount they owe their depositors.

Free resources resources (such as air) that are so abundant that they can be obtained without charge.

Frictional unemployment temporary joblessness, such as that occurring among people who have quit jobs, people looking for their first job, and seasonal workers.

Full employment the minimum level of joblessness that the economy could achieve without undesirably high inflation, recognizing that there will always be some frictional and structural unemployment.

Gold exchange standard an exchange rate system developed after World War II, under which the dollar was directly convertible into gold at a fixed price, and other currencies, since they could be converted into dollars at fixed exchange rates, were thus indirectly convertible into gold at a fixed price.

Gold standard a method of exchange rate determination prevailing until the 1930s, under which currencies were convertible into a certain amount of gold.

Government purchases federal, state, and local government spending on final goods and services, excluding transfer payments.

gross domestic product (GDP) the value of the total amount of final goods and services produced by the economy during a period of time; this value can be measured either by the expenditure on the final goods and services, or by the income generated by the output.

Gross private domestic investment all additions to the country's stock of private investment goods, that is, all investment spending, including purchases of tools, equipment, and machinery, all construction expenditures, and the change in total inventories.

Hysteresis situation where the natural rate of unemployment depends on the actual rate of unemployment.

Implicit contracts agreements between workers and firms that are not found in any formal, written contracts.

Imports the goods and services that a country buys from other countries.

Income tax a federal, state, or local tax imposed on personal income and corporate profits.

Incomes policy a policy to control inflation that sets some targets for wages and prices in the economy as a whole, gives particular firms and industries detailed guides for making wage and price decisions, and provides some inducements for firms and unions to follow these guidelines.

Indirect business taxes taxes (such as general sales taxes, excise taxes, and customs duties) that are imposed not directly on the business itself but on its products or services, and hence are treated by firms as costs of production.

Inflation an increase in the general level of prices economywide.

Innovation the first commercial application of a new technology.

Innovator a firm that is first to apply a new technology.

Input any resource used in the production process.

Interest the payment of money by borrowers to suppliers of money capital.

Interest rate the annual amount that a borrower must pay for the use of a dollar for a year.

Intermediate good a good that is not sold to the ultimate user, but is used as an input in producing final goods and services (such as flour to be used in manufacturing bread).

IS **curve** a curve showing, for each level of the interest rate, the level of GDP that will satisfy the equilibrium condition that intended spending on output must equal GDP.

Keynesians economists who share many of the beliefs of John Maynard Keynes. His principal tenet was that a capitalist system does not automatically tend toward a full-employment equilibrium (due in part to the rigidity of wages). Keynesians tend to believe that a free-enterprise economy has weak self-regulating mechanisms that should be supplemented by activist fiscal (and other) policies.

Labor human effort, both physical and mental, used to produce goods and services.

Labor force the number of people employed plus the number of those unemployed (that is, actively looking for work and willing to take a job if one were offered).

Labor productivity the average amount of output that can be obtained for every unit of labor.

Laffer curve a curve representing the relationship between the amount of income tax revenue collected by the government and the marginal tax rate, that is, how much revenue will be collected at various marginal tax rates.

Land natural resources, including minerals as well as plots of ground, used to produce goods and services.

Law of diminishing marginal returns the principle that if equal increments of a given input are added (the quantities of other inputs being held constant), the resulting increments of product obtained from the extra unit of input (that is, the marginal product) will begin to decrease beyond some point.

Law of increasing cost the principle that as more and more of a good is produced, the production of each additional unit of the good is likely to entail a larger and larger opportunity cost.

Legal reserve requirements regulations, imposed by the Federal Reserve System in order to control the money supply, requiring banks (and other institutions) to hold a certain fraction of deposits as reserves.

Liabilities the debts of a firm.

LM **curve** a curve showing, for each level of the interest rate, the level of GDP that will satisfy the equilibrium condition that the public be satisfied to hold the existing quantity of money.

Loanable funds funds (including those supplied by households and firms that find the rate of interest high enough to get them to save) that are available for borrowing by consumers, businesses, and government.

Long-run aggregate supply curve a vertical line showing the level of real national output at various economywide price levels when input prices are flexible.

Lucas aggregate supply curve according to Robert Lucas, only unexpected changes in the price level will result in changes in aggregate supply (holding the expected price level constant, the level of real GDP is directly related to the actual price level, according to the Lucas aggregate supply curve).

M1 narrowly defined money supply, which includes coins, currency, demand deposits, and other checkable deposits.

M2 broadly defined money supply, which includes savings deposits, small time deposits, money market mutual fund balances, and money market deposit accounts, as well as the components of the narrowly defined money supply, M1 (coins, currency, demand deposits, and other checkable deposits).

Marginal cost the addition to total cost resulting from the addition of the last unit of output.

Marginal product of an input the addition to total output that results from the addition of an extra unit of input (the quantities of all other inputs being held constant).

Marginal product of labor the additional output resulting from the addition of an extra unit of labor.

Marginal propensity to consume the fraction of an extra dollar of disposable income that is spent on consumption.

Marginal propensity to save the fraction of an extra dollar of disposable income that is saved.

Marginal tax rate the proportion of an extra dollar of income that must be paid in taxes.

Market a group of firms and individuals that are in touch with each other in order to buy or sell some good or service.

Market demand curve a curve, usually sloping downward to the right, showing the relationship between a product's price and the quantity demanded of the product.

Market supply curve a curve, usually sloping upward to the right, showing the relationship between a product's price and the quantity supplied of the product.

Medicaid a federal program that pays for the health care of the poor.

Medicare a compulsory hospitalization program plus a voluntary insurance plan for doctors' fees for people over 65, included under the Social Security program.

Model a theory composed of assumptions that simplify and abstract from reality, from which conclusions or predictions about the real world are deduced.

Monetarists economists generally sharing the belief that business fluctuations are due largely to changes in the money supply. Many monetarists think that a free-enterprise economy has effective self-regulating mechanisms that activist fiscal and monetary policies tend to disrupt. Some monetarists, like Milton Friedman, advocate a rule for stable growth in the money supply of 3 to 5 percent per year.

Monetary base the reserves of commercial banks plus currency outside banks.

Monetary policy the exercise of the central bank's control over the quantity of money and the level of interest rates in order to promote the objectives of national economic policy.

Money anything that serves as a medium of exchange and a standard and store of value; the unit in which the prices of goods and services are measured.

Money income income measured in current dollars (that is, actual money amounts).

Moral suasion the Federal Reserve's practice of exhorting banks to go along with its wishes, in the absence of any actual power to force the banks' compliance.

Multinational firm a firm that makes direct investments in other countries, and produces and markets its products abroad.

National debt the amount owed by the government. To cover the difference between its expenditures and its tax revenues, the government sells bonds, notes, and other forms of IOUs.

National income the total amount of wages, interest, rents, and profits paid out (or owed) by employers.

Natural rate of unemployment the unemployment rate when the economy is at full employment.

Near-money assets (such as government bonds) that can be converted into cash, though not quite as easily as time and savings accounts.

Net exports the amount spent by foreigners on a country's goods and services (exports) minus the amount a country spends on foreign goods and services (imports).

New classical macroeconomists a group, led by Robert Lucas, that believes that the government cannot use monetary and fiscal policies to close recessionary and inflationary gaps because, if firms and individuals formulate their expectations rationally, they will tend to frustrate the government's attempts to use activist stabilization policies.

New Keynesians a group that believes, like Keynesians, that prices and wages tend to be rigid in the short run, but in contrast to the Keynesians, this group has developed theories to explain why such wage and price stickiness can be expected.

Nominal expressed in current dollars (that is, actual money amounts).

Normative economics economic propositions about what ought to be, or about what a person, organization, or country ought to do.

Open market operations the purchase and sale of U.S. government securities on the open market by the Federal Reserve in order to control the quantity of bank reserves.

Opportunity cost the value of what certain resources could have produced had they been used in the best alternative way; also called **alternative cost.**

Overvaluation of currency the setting of a currency's price above the equilibrium price.

Peak the point in the business cycle where national output is highest relative to its potential (that is, full-employment) level.

Perfect competition a market structure in which there are many sellers of identical products, where no one seller or buyer has control over the price, where entry is easy, and where resources can switch readily from one use to another. Many agricultural markets have many of the characteristics of perfect competition.

Personal consumption expenditures the spending by households on durable goods, nondurable goods, and services.

Phillips curve a curve representing the relationship between the rate of increase of the price level and the level of unemployment.

Positive economics descriptive statements, propositions, and predictions about the economic world that are generally testable by an appeal to the facts.

Potential gross domestic product the total amount of goods and services that could have been produced had the economy been operating at full capacity or full employment.

Precautionary demand for money the demand for money because of uncertainty about the timing and size of future disbursements and receipts.

Price index the ratio of the value of a set of goods and services in current dollars to the value of the same set of goods and services in constant dollars.

Price system a system under which every good and service has a price, and which in a purely capitalistic economy carries out the basic functions of an economic system (determining what goods and services will be produced, how the output will be produced, how much of it each person will receive, and what the country's growth of per capita income will be).

Primary inputs resources (such as labor and land) that are produced outside of the economic system.

Product market a market where products are bought and sold.

Production function the relationship between the quantities of various inputs used per period of time and the maximum quantity of output that can be produced per period of time, that is, the most output that existing technology permits the firm to produce from various quantities of inputs.

Production possibilities curve a curve showing the combinations of amounts of various goods that a society can produce with given (fixed) amounts of resources.

Profit the difference between a firm's revenue and its costs.

Progressive tax a tax whereby the rich pay a larger proportion of their income for the tax than do the poor.

Prohibitive tariff a tariff so high that it prevents imports of a good.

Property tax a tax imposed on real estate and/or other property.

Proprietors' income the net income of unincorporated businesses (that is, proprietorships and partnerships).

Prosperity a period when national output is close to its potential (that is, full-employment) level.

Public goods goods and services that can be consumed by one person without diminishing the amount of them that others can consume. Also, there is no way to prevent citizens from consuming public goods whether they pay for them or not.

Public sector the governmental sector of the economy.

Pure rate of interest the interest rate on a riskless loan.

Quota a limit imposed on the amount of a commodity that can be imported annually.

Rate of return the annual profit per dollar invested that business can obtain by building new structures, adding new equipment, or increasing their inventories; the interest rate earned on the investment in a particular asset.

Rational expectations expectations that are correct on the average (that is, forecasting errors are random); the forecaster makes the best possible use of whatever information is available.

Real expressed in constant dollars.

Real business cycle models theories asserting that business fluctuations are due largely to shifts in the aggregate supply curve resulting from new technology, good or bad weather, and so on.

Real income income measured in constant dollars (that is, the amount of goods and services that can be bought with the income).

Recession the phase in the business cycle after the peak during which national output falls.

Regressive tax a tax whereby the rich pay a smaller proportion of their income for the tax than do the poor.

Resource market a market where resources are bought and sold.

Resources inputs used to produce goods and services.

Retained earnings the total amount of profit that the stockholders of a corporation have reinvested in the business, rather than withdrawing as dividends.

Rigid policy rule a rule specifying completely the behavior of the variable governed by the policy rule (for example, Milton Friedman's suggestion that the money supply be set so that it grows at a fixed, agreed-on rate).

Runaway inflation a very rapid increase in the general price level that wipes out practically all the value of money.

Sales tax a tax imposed on the goods consumers buy (with the exception, in some states, of food and medical care).

Saving the process by which people give up a claim on present consumption goods in order to receive consumption goods in the future.

Saving function the relationship between total saving and disposable income, that is, the total amount of saving that will occur at various levels of disposable income.

Say's Law the principle that the production of a certain amount of goods and services results in the generation of an amount of income precisely sufficient to buy that output.

Short-run aggregate supply curve a curve, sloping upward to the right, that shows the level of real national output that will be supplied at various economy-wide price levels when input prices are fixed.

Social Security a program that imposes taxes on wage earners and employers, and provides old-age, survivors, disability, and medical benefits to workers covered under the Social Security Act.

Stagflation a simultaneous combination of high unemployment and high inflation.

Structural unemployment joblessness that occurs when new goods or new technologies call for new skills, and workers with older skills cannot find jobs.

Substitutes commodities with a positive cross elasticity of demand (that is, a decrease in the price of one commodity will result in a decrease in the quantity demanded of the other commodity).

Supply curve for loanable funds a curve showing the relationship between the quantity of loanable funds supplied and the interest rate.

Supply-side economics a set of propositions concerned with influencing the aggregate supply curve through the use of financial incentives such as tax cuts.

Supply-side inflation inflation resulting from leftward shifts of the aggregate supply curve.

Tariff a tax imposed by the government on imported goods (designed to cut down on imports and thus protect domestic industry and workers from foreign competition.)

Tax avoidance legal steps taken by taxpayers to reduce their tax bill.

Tax evasion misreporting of income or other illegal steps taken by taxpayers to reduce their tax bill.

Technological change new methods of producing existing products, new designs that make it possible to produce new products, and new techniques of organization, marketing, and management.

Technology society's pool of knowledge concerning how goods and services can be produced from a given amount of resources.

Terms of trade the ratio of an index of export prices to an index of import prices.

Tight monetary policy a monetary policy that restrains or reduces the money supply and raises interest rates.

Trading possibilities curve a curve showing the various combinations of products that a country can get if it specializes in one product and trades that specialty for foreign goods.

Transactions demand for money the holding of money in cash or in checking accounts in order to pay for final goods and services; the higher the level of real GDP and the price level, the greater the quantity of money demanded for transactions purposes.

Transfer payments payments made by the government or private business to individuals who do not contribute to the production of goods and services in exchange for them.

Trough the point in the business cycle where national output is lowest relative to its potential (that is, full-employment) level.

Undervaluation of currency the setting of a currency's price below the equilibrium price.

Unemployment according to the definition of the Bureau of Labor Statistics, joblessness among people who are actively looking for work and would take a job if one were offered.

Unemployment rate the number of people who are unemployed divided by the number of people in the labor force.

Value-added the amount of value added by a firm or industry to the total worth of a product.

Velocity of circulation of money the rate at which the money supply is used to make transactions for final goods and services, that is, the average number of times per year that a dollar is used to buy the final goods and services produced by the economy. It equals GDP divided by the money supply.

Wage and price controls limits imposed by the government on the amount by which wages and prices can increase in order to reduce the inflation rate at a given unemployment rate.

Wage rate the price of labor.

INDEX

Page numbers in **bold type** indicate definitions.